Men to Boys

Men to Boys

The Making of Modern Immaturity

Gary Cross

Columbia University Press   *New York*

Columbia University Press
Publishers Since 1893
New York   Chichester, West Sussex

Copyright © 2008 Gary Cross
All rights reserved

Library of Congress Cataloging-in-Publication Data
Cross, Gary S.
    Men to boys : the making of modern immaturity / Gary Cross.
        p. cm.
    Includes bibliographical references and index.
    ISBN 978-0-231-14430-8 (cloth : alk. paper) —
    ISBN 978-0-231-51311-1 (e-book)
    1. Men—United States. 2. Men in popular culture—United States.
    3. Masculinity—United States. I. Title.

HQ1090.3.C76   2008
305.310973'0904—dc22   2008005693

∞
Columbia University Press books are printed on permanent and durable acid-free
paper.
This book is printed on paper with recycled content.
Printed in the United States of America
c 10 9 8 7 6 5 4 3 2

Contents

Men to Boys

Introduction

WHERE Have ALL the MEN Gone?

Everywhere I turn today I see men who refuse to grow up—husbands of thirty-five who enjoy playing the same video games that obsess twelve-year olds; boyfriends who will not commit to marriage or family; and fathers who fight with umpires or coaches at their son's little league games. We all know men in their thirties or forties who would rather tinker with their cars than interact with their families, fathers who want to share in their children's fads, and even bosses and political leaders who act like impulsive teenagers. Many are frustrated and confused about what maturity is and whether they can or want to achieve it. I call them boy-men. I've noticed how men deep in their twenties or even thirties, when their parents and grandparents had themselves been parents and homeowners, have not yet settled down. Some haven't even left home. The singles culture celebrated in situation comedies like *Friends* is a world apart from the experience of young adults in previous generations. A common query (really a complaint) today, especially from women, is, where have all the men gone? What they seem to imply is that perfectly normal men who in previous generations would have been expected to be grown-ups continue to act, look, and think like teenagers.

But, of course, the problem goes much deeper—from the failure of millions of husbands and fathers to commit to the financial and personal duties of marriage and family to a culture that seems increasingly ignorant of the past and unwilling to assume fiscal or environmental responsibilities for the future. Boy-men are the cause of much of the cynicism in the culture and the coarsening of conversation and social rituals. Although there are many manifestations of this phenomenon in social relations, economic life, and even politics, it is most often expressed in the culture of men, in the films and TV they watch and the activities of their leisure hours.

The issue of modern immaturity goes beyond the jeremiads of the left or the right. It goes to our embrace of a commercial culture that feeds on stunted human growth and to our society, which is fixed narrowly on living for today. Such behavior is undeniably part of a larger cultural trend. Boy-men across the country have their own stories, and many factors produce this resistance to "growing up," such as economic constraints and anxieties about the mating mistakes of parents. But any way you look at it, the boy-man has become a central character in our culture and, even if men do find ways of meeting their economic and even social obligations, the culture of immaturity has become the norm rather than the exception.

As a sixty-year old father of two sons (and a daughter), I find myself thinking a very uncool yet all so predictable thought: Whatever is this generation coming to? Inevitably the subject of boy-men comes up in conversations with other fathers in the same situation. One, whose twenty-six-year old son recently returned home to finish college, calls them "basement boys." These young men find not only free lodging, meals, and security at home but also the freedom to come and go at will and, in the privacy of their converted subterranean lairs where no one will tell them to make their beds, to play endlessly on their Playstation consoles. As a history professor from a typical state university, I have seen the same thing in thirty-five-year-old professionals who fill their great rooms with the latest and most expensive video game hardware and who would have a pool table in the dining room if their wives would let them. I see male college students who play, alone or with pals, the latest version of Grand Theft Auto on Friday night rather than going out on dates.

"Honestly, I associate maturity with not having any fun. People use maturity like you're not going out and partying on a Saturday night," explains Steve from New Jersey, who, at twenty-nine, still lives with his mother. "I'm gonna be thirty years old. When I'm thirty-one or thirty-two, I'll have children. And in the meantime so, maybe, I got to have a little bit of fun in my twenties." Steve, who has an MBA, still loves to play video games. His favorite in 2006: TrueCrime New York City, "I could play up to six hours a day." He admits to enjoying the cyber-play of "beating up hookers and shooting cops in the head."[1]

It would be easy to dismiss the basement boys as slackers, a characterization given these Generation X males when the term was first invented in the late 1980s. But I think that it is more complex than that. Obviously, they are settling down later. Young men, once considered ineffectual or of "doubtful" sexuality if they were unmarried at twenty-five, now go deep into their twenties and thirties single and remain unattached longer between marriages. Once the key marker of maturity, marriage has declined sharply in the United States, dropping from 70 percent of households in 1970 to just 53 percent in 2000. There are many reasons for adults being unmarried (from widowhood, poverty, and women's reduced dependency on men, to a commitment to the playboy life). Yet of the growing percentage of single-person householders, a quarter in 2000 were under thirty-five. While in 1980 only 6 percent of men reached their early forties without marrying (compared to 5 percent of women), by 2004, that percentage had increased to 16.5 for men (and 12.5 for women). Living outside marriage, either alone or in cohabitation, has increased enormously, from 38 million American adults in 1970 to 82 million in 2000. Cohabiting couples now number 5.5 million (up from 3.1 million in 1990), or 9 percent of all couples living together. Perhaps the most telling statistics are these: in a recent study, 55 percent of American men aged eighteen to twenty-four were found to be living at home with their parents, and 13 percent between twenty-five and thirty-four years of age still live at home, compared to only 8 percent of women. Today, men spend less of their lives in the self-denying settings of family and marriage. And this is hardly unique to Americans. Up to half of Italian men between the ages of twenty-five and thirty-five still live with their parents.[2]

As singles, ensconced within male or youth peer cultures, men today have plenty of time and opportunity to live the life of the boy-man. No longer marrying at twenty-two or twenty-three as did many of their boomer fathers, but often not until their thirties (twenty-seven on average), they have a long time to nurture the boy-man's life and to develop habits of thought and practice that few "good women" can break even when it becomes time to "settle down."[3] Sitcoms like *Seinfeld* or *Friends* may not accurately reflect the reality of the single's life (and certain *Sex and the City* does not), but they do mirror the dreams of many singles, especially men.

In some ways this rejection of maturity is quite irrational, for immaturity is often anything but life-enhancing. If being unmarried is a measure of "adultescence," single American men are seven times more likely to go to prison than married men, four times more likely to be victims of violent crime, and twice as likely to be in an accident than the married. Bachelors are much less likely to hold a full time job (62 vs. 75 percent). It is also true that single American men tend to be less well off than married ones (only 21 percent earning more than $50,000, compared with 49 percent of their married counterparts). Bachelors' lower income may be one of the reasons why they are bachelors, but the single life may leave men without the emotional stability and ambition to earn more. And, despite legend, single American men seem to have less sex: only 26 percent claim to have it twice a week compared to 43 percent of married men. Yet despite all this, more and more men are avoiding the benefits of the "responsible life."[4]

How do we understand the decision of men to delay or avoid marriage? A biological explanation is certainly tempting. As scientists tell us, the longing of young adult men for competitive gang life is shared with other primates as they wait for the opportunity to mate. This may explain the violence sometimes associated with single men in same-sex groups. By nature, it seems that men want to both spread their seed and protect their offspring, and this makes them uncertain and confused providers. Moreover, the fact that women today are often delaying marriage and child rearing to establish careers makes the choice of seed spreading outside the "pair bond" more common. In sum, men remain longer in the gang, that is, the irresponsible life. They are allowed, almost obliged, to cling to their teenage mindsets. Some cynics (or evolutionary anthropologists) might just say that men have always been boys—oversexed, irresponsible, self-indulgent, and prone to violent competitiveness. This ignores, however, centuries of culture, especially the civilizing efforts of our Victorian predecessors that created models of maturity in men. And, while these efforts were not always successful and often were tainted with hypocrisy, they did produce many men who were not boys. Something has changed.[5]

If you ask a single man of thirty or older why he is still unattached, he will probably say that he simply cannot do as his father or grandfather did: provide for a wife and family at his age.[6] "A lot of men my age feel pretty off stride because economically many of us are not in a position to be a sole provider," said Martin, a forty-six-year-old journalist, who has never been married and has no children. This abiding sense of failure is sometimes exacerbated by persistent resentment of the rise of women's economic and social equality. "I got slapped in

1980," continues Martin, "when I was in college because I opened a door for a woman. . . . Women within 5 year range of my age either way will carry on that they want men to be sensitive and go to baby showers and all that crap, but they also feel kind of short changed when the guy kind of doesn't take total control. The mutual expectations are very distorted."[7]

Still, when I hear these complaints, I cannot help but think, are times that bad for men starting out? Weren't economic conditions worse in the 1970s when I was their age? And, the women's movement has been as good for many men as it has for women, economically and socially. I wonder if something else was at work. Maybe for many, not settling down was a choice, and that decision may reflect a profound cultural change.

Today, in some circles there is a veritable rejection of maturity in all of its meanings. Living for today, disdainful of pretense and formality, ever open to new thrills and experiences, but also mocking convention in celebrations of amoral violent fantasy, crude vulgarity, and unrestrained appetite, the boy-man makes a fetish of the "cool." He turns maturity into a joke, a pitiful loss to be avoided at almost all costs. Men spend billions to retain the bodies and hair of their youth, going well beyond the rationale of "good health," ordinary vanity, or even the practical requirements of being competitive in the sex market. Narcissism, traditionally seen as a feminine trait, is now associated with perpetuating male youth.

The culture of the boy-men today is less a life stage than a lifestyle, less a transition from childhood to adulthood than a choice to live like a teen "forever." What sort of youth may they be trying to perpetuate? Certainly not the goody-two-shoes lad anxious to please or the youth hell-bent on making his mark on the world. Rather, basement boys long to be the fun-loving chap, "naughty" but nice enough to be indulged by women, and free, at least in fantasy or leisure, from the responsibilities of career and family. And they obsess about adventure. Of course, this quest for excitement has been true of youth from time immemorial. But recently the male quest for adventure has tended to lose its "civilized trappings"—with goals of service and sacrifice to a greater good—and become instead the pursuit of the pleasure of the adrenaline flow. Even more obviously, adventure no longer is about initiation into manhood. It is play and it never ends. Modern male adventure embraces the purity of excitement in action-figure movies, video games, and fantasy weekends of paint-ball warfare. This unalloyed pursuit of sensual intensity has transformed old mostly male pleasures. Who hasn't noticed the blinking lights, ubiquitous video screens, and fireworks that ring the modern baseball stadium, making them look more like game arcades than the ball-parks of the past?

These themes dominate popular commercial culture today, oc-cupying hours of night-time television, worming their way into the scripts of movies and the lyrics of popular songs, and becoming the hooks of more and more sales pitches. No generation has been more shaped by that culture than young men today. Trapped on a seemingly endless treadmill, the boy-man finds quick satisfaction in a string of relationships, fads, and other thrills, easily exploited by advertisers and merchandisers. Anyone who has seen a beer commercial on *Monday Night Football* or recalls the antics of sitcom character Al Bundy (the shoe salesman whose lifetime highlight was making four touchdowns in one high school football game) knows the meaning of the phrase "men will be boys!" Some of us may snicker at an eighty-year-old Hugh Hefner surrounded by twenty-year-old blonds at his Playboy Man-sion, but many men secretly (and openly) admire his "achievement." Probably more people are appalled by shock jock Howard Stern. His popularity rose to the point that Sirius Satellite Radio paid him about $220 million in stock to move to their stations from regular radio in 2006. He decided to make the change after repeated fines from the government's watchdog agency, the FCC, for his lewd comments on his daily radio and TV shows. So Stern is now free to organize such programs off their radar as "The Crack Whore View," where real-life prostitutes discuss their lifestyles. Earlier, Stern's TV show consisted mostly of his leering at and taunting women to reveal blurred breasts and buttocks to him and his cronies in the indulgent company of female sidekick Robin Quivers, who somehow made their boorish behavior OK. Though in his forties, Sterns seems like the high school student who loudly jokes about girls' bra sizes as they pass in the halls. Stern himself went further, admitting that "I am perpetually a nine-year-old child" and "that is probably why I am still successful."[8]

But the causes and consequences of men trying and often suc-ceeding in perpetuating adolescent boyhood go way beyond the ab-surdities of Hefner or Stern. Boy-men are the tastemakers who cause profit-seeking Hollywood executives to stuff the multiplexes with endlessly repetitive action films and amazingly dumb comedies full of potty humor.

Just recall the endlessly sophomoric antics of the frenetic, wildly self-indulgent, but extremely popular comics whose excesses on the screen reflected their real lives. Remember John Belushi and Chris Farley? Both were part of an old tradition of the fat man jester, perpetuated in film (and TV) figures like Fatty Arbuckle, Oliver Hardy, and Jackie Gleason, who give us permission to laugh at their physical awkwardness and indulgences. But Belushi and Farley went further than their processors. In films like *Animal House* and *The Blues Brothers*, Belushi exuded a boyish rebellion. He was, as his friend Dan Aykroyd sadly said in 1982 at the time of Belushi's death from a drug overdose, "a good man, but a bad boy," someone who needed "an additional illicit thrill to make it all worthwhile." Farley in his string of B-movies appealed to teen and college males with his total lack of restraint. He played the childlike loser in the body of a self-indulgent man. Like his idol, John Belushi, and to no one's surprise, he, too, died at the age of thirty-three in 1997, in Farley's case of a heart attack caused by excesses in food, drink, and drugs. It seems that he was unable in reality, as in his movie roles, to live a balanced, adult life.[9]

These tragedies make brief morality tales in the news and may seem far from the lives of regular people. The fact, however, that such movies and similar TV shows draw millions of adults with endless comedic celebrations of the taste of fourteen-year-old boys suggests that there is more than fantasy and fun at work here. We find boy-men appealing.

A few years ago, such immature characters served mostly as comic relief, checked by the seriousness of a sidekick. Boy-man Jimmy Kimmel played opposite the brainy and much older Ben Stein in a quiz show, *Win Ben Stein's Money* (1997). Adam Carolla was the with-it jokester, making the serious advice of addiction physician Dr. Drew Pinski palatable on *Loveline* (1997), an MTV call-in show about sex for youth. By 1999, that pairing of maturity and immaturity was no longer necessary. Kimmel and Carolla teamed up to host the Comedy Channel's *Man Show*, built on the right of all boy-men, no matter their age, size (the show featured a midget), race, or class, to leer at women jumping on trampolines. The *Man Show* made into reality the laughable make-believe NO MAM club of sitcom loser Al Bundy in *Married with Children*, which ran on the Fox TV network from 1987 to 1997. At that club, members endlessly whined about their wives in Al's garage and got endless joy out of gawking at the "babes" working at the "Nudie Bar."

All of this, you might say, is just fantasy, fun, and, for a very few like Hefner, a lucrative game that has little to do with the way American men really live today. Some of my examples may seem extreme, such as Chris Farley, and it is possible that those who enjoy Howard Stern simply can't get dates. But these media characters reflect everyday life in the early twenty-first century. And they give men permission to linger in the world of teenagers.

How do we explain the media's celebration of the puerile and its apparent embrace by many adult men? Part of the answer may lie in the fact that the number of teenagers has surged since 1990 (expected to rise from 24.6 to 30 million by 2010). Merchandisers always target such growth groups, especially if they spend as young single men have long done. New technology may also play a role. While as Michiko Kakutani of the *New York Times* noted (in 1997), the Internet "was once touted as a resource for scholars [it] is rapidly becoming a playground for sophomoric nerds, a place to exchange dirty pictures, sick jokes and narcissistic pleas for attention"—and this was written before the Internet really took off.[10] Male teens and youths dominate this and other new technologies in this "information age," coloring the whole culture.

Similarly, the behavior and dress of contemporary black sports celebrities such as Dennis Rodman and the lyrics of rap and hip-hop music show a new rebellion against paternal authority and a quest for preserving the intensities of youth. Rodman's notorious "look" on the basketball court, with his tattoos and dyed hair, as well as his display of flamboyant clothing and "bling" jewelry off the court, is an almost cartoonish rejection of the old expectation of the respectable and respectful black athletic. Rodman is making very clear that he is no Joe Lewis, the famous boxer of the 1930s who "knew his place" and tried not to antagonize his white fans or his elders. Even while African American hip-hop entrepreneurs were in person hardly boy-men, often their songs appealed to a "live fast, die young" mentality. Songs like Sean Combs's 1997 hit "It's All About the Benjamins" (i.e., hundred-dollar bills) and "Bad Boy for Life" celebrate a get-yours-while-you-can philosophy. In ways, this is a black version of James Dean, as hip-hop artists reject the father in their critique of the civil rights movement and its leaders as irrelevant today. It is as if there were no past and no certain future, just the here and now. The boy-man may be especially evident in the culture of middle-class white men, but it extends across race and class.[11]

As a baby boomer (in fact, a member of its "senior class"), I have to admit that my first impulse was to think what "elders" from time immemorial have thought: "The young today have lost their bearings, succumbed to the easy life, and lack sufficient appreciation of the accomplishments of those who came before." Well, maybe the lament would be a bit more sophisticated than that. After all, I am a historian by trade and know better. But I have to admit that I have joined those dinner party conversations of aging boomers who complain that young men have too much "screen time" with all of today's electronic gadgets. We go on to proclaim self-righteously that the young today lack the experience of a challenging and ennobling historical crisis (like Vietnam and the civil rights movement, not to mention World War II) to steel them for goals beyond the cheap thrill and go-with-the-flow culture that surround them. Maybe someone at the dinner party would add in the spirit of generosity that we haven't always provided models of maturity. Then there would be laughter and a change of subject.

Not so fast! Let's consider two other members of that senior class of boomers, our last two presidents.

"I am struck by the immaturity of this administration, whatever the ages of the officials involved," writes Bob Herbert in the *New York Times* (2004), in reference to President George W. Bush.

> It's as if the children have taken over and sent the adults packing. The counsel of wiser heads, like George H. W. Bush, or Brent Scowcroft, or Colin Powell, is not needed and not wanted. Some of the world's most important decisions—often decisions of life and death—have been left to those who are less competent and less experienced, to men and women who are deficient in such qualities as risk perception and comprehension of future consequences, who are reckless and dangerously susceptible to magical thinking and the ideological pressure of their peers.

Of course, this could be written off as the rant of a Democrat. But it is interesting that the author notes the indifference of Bush the younger to the views of the experience of Bush the elder. Is this ideological or generational? Probably both, but Herbert believed the Bush II administration deliberately rejected "wisdom" because it was the voice of elders. A perhaps telling remark suggesting the depth of Bush the Younger's boyish rebellion was captured by journalist Bob Woodward. When he asked George W. Bush if he had consulted his father before invading Iraq, the son replied, "He is the wrong father to appeal to in terms of strength. There is a higher father that I appeal to."[12]

A different sort of immaturity was evident in the behavior of Bush's predecessor. President Bill Clinton once even admitted about himself and his wife: "I was born at sixteen and I'll always feel I'm sixteen. And Hillary was born at age forty." This reflects his early responsibilities as a child, but also the fact that he never overcame those adolescent traits. According to Rich Lowry of the *National Review*, Clinton, as president, revealed a "death-driven addictive personality with a strong streak of immaturity, an eagerness to please, and a tendency to live in his own, private world." This, too, may be merely a partisan right-wing attack. But many with no ideological axe to grind have said the same thing, like British journalist E. Jane Dickson, who claims that Clinton was the "Ur-adultescent, the naughty boy repressed and excited by controlling women." Of course, not all of our leaders are boy-men, but we seem to elect more than a few of them. That may be because they, more than we fellow boomers would readily admit, represent their generation.[13]

Looking back on my youth, I certainly would not have predicted this for the opening decade of the twenty-first century. Yes, we were rebels in the 1960s, but we thought we were going to build a better world. Along with the grown-up Billy Gray, who as a child played "Bud," the son of Jim Anderson in the 1950s sitcom *Father Knows Best*, we mocked the phoniness of the perfect family presumably portrayed in such programs. Still, we thought that we would build more honest families, where men related to and didn't merely lecture at their children and recognized equality between husbands and wives. Without necessarily using these terms, we thought we would improve on the maturity of our fathers, become "new men," a damn sight better than the stick-figure cowboys that played at manhood in silly showdowns on the streets of Tombstone on 1950s TV. We had potluck banquets on Thanksgiving where everyone, men and women, brought dishes, and we reveled in the superiority of our events to the strained family gatherings we knew as children, where women cooked and washed up and men carved (maybe) and watched football. We took to heart Bob Dylan's words: "Come mothers and fathers / Throughout the land / And don't criticize / What you can't understand / Your sons and your daughters / Are beyond your command / Your old road is rapidly agin'. / Please get out of the new one / If you can't lend your hand / For the times they are a-changin'." This was hardly an anthem of permanent adolescence, but a confident (indeed arrogant) call for a new model of growing up and leadership.

But as we have been lamenting for decades now, it did not happen quite as we had expected. Not only did we become "the man" rather than "new men" and sell out (a fact that is hardly surprising), but, contrary to the oft-stated comment of the cynic, we did not become our fathers. Instead, we reveled in our status as youth long after it was gone. We remained in many ways the teenage sons of our fathers, and some of us never gave up rebelling against our elders. Our joy in rejecting our fathers trumped our vision for a new future.

In April of 1970, when I was an antiwar activist at Washington State University, I wrote a leaflet "warning" students about a band of "troublemakers" who were going to be stationed outside the student union, where Senator Henry (Scoop) Jackson was going to speak on the first Earth Day. Of course, those ruffians were we, a small group opposed to Jackson's support for the defoliation of Vietnam in the raging war of that time. We had cleared the local grocery stores of their marshmallow stocks and made them available to the crowd of students as they entered the hall. Looking back, I can't imagine why we weren't arrested. I would never approve of such an act of disrespect for free speech today. At the time, we thought this was a clever protest of the hypocrisy of our state's senator, but I still recall being surprised by one thing—the enthusiasm with which the students pelted Jackson. Looking back now, I think what we really were doing was throwing marshmallows at our fathers. And, Jackson acted like the father too, bravely taking the "punishment" and telling us we weren't so clever because others had tried the same trick before. I think he threw some back at us.

I don't want to reduce 1960s radicalism to an oedipal crisis (it certainly was much more about political and social change). Still, my generation gained more pleasure from rejecting elders and reveling in our youth than in creating a better meaning of maturity. Is it any surprise that Madison Avenue and Hollywood picked up on our joy, selling back our quest for timeless youth as the Pepsi Generation and offering us (and some of our parents who secretly admired our freedom) "Youngmobiles" (a clever ad name for the stogy Oldsmobile)? We made nostalgia for our youth a standard of fun and freedom. We were still glorying in it in 2006 when the sixty-something Rolling Stones sang their anthem song "Satisfaction" at the fortieth Superbowl halftime show. As the group's leader, Mick Jagger, noted, the song was older than the Superbowl itself. But my boomer friends and I didn't care. It reminded us that our youth was still alive (and Jagger proved it in his amazingly spry performance).

Looking back, the problem has been that my generation, despite its fairly normal economic successes, has not produced many paragons of maturity. "I do not see any particularly viable model (of the modern man) being forged to accommodate the expectations of females. Or expectations males have for themselves," said Martin, the forty-six-year-old journalist quoted earlier. "There is not a clear path towards the kind of indisputable maturity that my fathers' generation could feel."[14]

Is it any surprise that when we rejected the models of our fathers we left our sons with few images of what it meant to be a grown, mature man? While we baby boomers discarded the traditional markers of maturity and tried to recover our boyhood in our leisure hours, our sons' generation made youth a permanent way of life, at least in their leisure. In the 1960s, youth felt like liberation, but today it is often a burden.

It is not that we are unaware of the problem. Recent films like *Sideways* portray middle-aged men who haven't grown up and don't know how. And contemporary sitcoms built around the peer culture of basement boys (like *Two and a Half Men*) are as much humorous put-downs of that culture as they are cynical celebrations of it. Since the 1970s, there has been a steady stream of books like *The Peter Pan Syndrome* lamenting the emotional straitjacketing of men fixated on puerile dreams of male heroism and toughness, frightened of their own feelings, or incapable of rising above a teenager's narcissism to find lasting relationships. Baby boomer men in their youth may have hoped to improve on their fathers, becoming more engaged parents and partners. Some may have done so, but the dream of a more sensitive manhood has longed turned sour, and today few offspring of baby boomers share that idealism. Instead, today's young have often embraced the boomers' rejection of their elders without much vision of the future. The cultures of peers, media, and consumption all conspire to keep men prisoners of their own immaturity no matter the insights and efforts of loved ones, mental health professionals, social reformers, or church leaders. Beyond the narrow and often stultifying environs of "life-transforming" cults (like the Promise Keepers or Iron Man retreats), today's culture has not provided a compelling image of the "grown-up." My generation has indeed failed to provide models of maturity even for the young to rebel against.

This led me to think that I needed to revisit the generation of my father, the people whose maturity made us reject maturity. The ironic fact is that, even though in 1970 we threw marshmallows at the father (at least metaphorically), many of us eventually came around to see him as part of Tom Brokaw's "Greatest Generation." We admired his adventurous initiation into manhood—World War II—as many of us came to see that experience. We recognized his sacrifice and envied the power and prestige that this seemed to give him after the war—parades for the heroic return of veterans, the GI Bill, and the opportunity to build businesses, careers, and families. We admired especially the seriousness of his life—seen in everything from his growing up during the depression and war to his assuming responsibility for his family (often large) afterward. He was the model of male maturity. When we were children, we saw him in Hopalong Cassidy, Gene Autry, Sky King, and Matt Dillon in the westerns. We saw him also in leading men like Cary Grant, Humphrey Bogart, and Spencer Tracy, middle-aged men in our childhoods who seemed to accept graciously their graying hair, widening girths, and adult roles even after exciting youths playing physical, sexy parts. We cannot help but notice the difference between Hugh and Cary Grant.

But there were more subtle "fathers," such as Don Herbert, the science teacher whose *Watch Mr. Wizard* on Saturday afternoons in the 1950s featured Herbert leading bright teen boys (seldom girls) through experiments, gently correcting their misjudgments while showing them the mysteries of light or explosives. Conductor Leonard Bernstein, whose *Young People's Concerts* combined symphonies and lessons in music history and form, was also a model of maturity. And the audience of kids showed respect by all appearing in their Sunday best.

"I looked at my dad and he was my model for being a man and as I got older I wasn't becoming that person," said Jorge, a fifty-seven-year-old professor in Pennsylvania. "I carried forward into adulthood interests I had developed in childhood like my interest in World War II history and in model airplanes but those weren't things my dad did. So I had a hard time convincing myself I was an adult. I saw elements of childhood in myself as an adult, so it seemed to me I wasn't a fully formed adult."[15]

Many of my generation would heartily agree. The so-called Greatest Generation is tacitly the model of manhood that boomer men clearly cannot live up to and their sons scarcely know. And that sense of "inadequacy" is surely part of the problem of the boy-man today.

But thinking more about my father's generation made me quite naturally recall my father. He hardly fit the image of the Cary Grant of the movies. Few did. Even Cary Grant once said that he wished he could be "Cary Grant." Although my father (born in 1922) was drafted in the army during the war, as a twenty-one-year old he worked in the typing pool at Fort George Wright in Spokane and saw no combat. There he met my seventeen-year-old mother at a roller-skating rink. As a couple, they won trophies for their dancing, but their glory times were short-lived. Marriage came early and so did four children while my father (and mother) studied at the local teacher's college, where my father eventually got a job as a biology instructor. When the youngest child was barely five, my father "ran off" with his lab assistant. In many ways, he was the rebel that Barbara Ehrenreich writes about in *Hearts of Men*, who engaged in a "flight from commitment." He went on to teach biology at a California community college and ten years later "ran away" with a second lab assistant. He abandoned a middle-class, middle-age life to go back to graduate school as a forty-three-year-old. But soon he grew restless and, caught up in the counterculture of the late 1960s, he quit his Ph.D. program. He moved into a commune of "geodesic domes" north of San Francisco only to have his third companion move out, leaving him proprietor of a natural-food store. Bored with a life of waiting for people to come to him, in 1975 he threw all of his meager savings into hiring an exclusive matchmaker to get him (as he told me) a "rich and beautiful woman" when he was about fifty-three years old. He succeeded in still another adventure—linking up with a rich (and lovely) woman. The last time I saw him was in 1979 when he was preparing for a round-the-world boat tour. Well, it didn't happen (I'm not quite sure why), and he abandoned his benefactor, moving on again. In 1988, he died more or less alone at the age of sixty-six at a "residence hotel" in San Francisco. Nothing so Greatest Generation about this life. He was no war hero, avoided responsibility, and in a lot of ways refused to grow up. Of course, it was more complicated: He was dutiful about child support, very supportive of me, and his "rich and beautiful" companion met me to spread his ashes. Though he was a rolling stone, in his few personal effects, he included a card in his wallet showing that he was a docent at the San Francisco zoo.

An unusual story, but, as a historian, I know that his restlessness was hardly unique. My father was one of the rebels and outcasts of his generation. There were different kinds: the Jack Kerouacs on the road and the Allen Ginsbergs howling in San Francisco rejected the provider's role in the suburban world of houses shaped like "little [cracker] boxes." (I lived in one before my father left). Hugh Hefner is the most obvious example still around. While Hefner has long relished his role as an icon of carefree sexuality, his real achievement is remaining a boy all his life. "Hef" lives on his own playground, complete with flamingos, monkeys, peacocks, and the famous "grotto," a cave with a Jacuzzi and places for sex play. This bacchanalian scene is many a boy's dream of easy sex and careless delight, devoid of the traditional adult realities of family and monogamy. In fact, Hefner and his three live-in ladies of the moment, starred in the E! Network reality hit *The Girls Next Door* in 2007. In this show, the girls spend their time playing slip'n'slide, modeling bunny costumes, and attending parties, while Hef shuffles around in his P.J.'s with a grin on his face.

This more or less has been Hefner's life since founding *Playboy* back in 1953. He built a publishing empire based on the lifestyle of unrealistic and childish male wish fulfillment. Despite his magazine's long interest in avant-garde arts and literature, Hefner freely admits that his tastes haven't changed since he was a teenager—beginning with the peanut butter sandwiches and cold chicken that stuff his handy refrigerators. He has never lost his attraction for the blonds, who look eerily like the showgirls in the Busby Berkeley movies of the late 1930s, when Hefner was an impressible boy. He never had to give up those carefree years of chasing girls for maturity in marriage, instead insisting on remaining throughout most of his life the model of the boy-man.

Yes, Hefner did take a brief respite from perpetual adolescence when in July 1989 he married again, at the age of sixty-three, a twenty-six-year-old former Playmate, Kimberley Conrad. But in 1998 they separated, and Hefner returned to his beloved playboy life, moving Kimberly to a house "next door" with their sons. Why couldn't he give it up? "Maybe experience in life is not what is appealing to me," Hefner confessed in a 2003 interview; "maybe it's the unsophisticated enthusiasm that comes with youth" that worked for him. He dated the very young, because, although "chronologically, I'm 77, but in reality I'm a very young man." At the mansion, "Life here is a grownup adolescent dream." In fact, Hefner prided himself on his never having to grow up. He refused to take on the role of the elder, reflecting back on both his accomplishments and mistakes, and instead insisted on remaining throughout his entire life the model of the boy-man.[16]

Hefner was not the only icon of boy-man-hood. Less well known was Ed (Big Daddy) Roth. When other men were settling down raising families, this proud boy-man won local fame in southern California as a maker of flamboyant hot rods. In the early 1960s, he designed a popular line of in-your-face T-shirts featuring Rat Fink, a scruffy and cynical reverse of the cute and loveable Mickey Mouse. Disdainful of authority and responsibility for most of his life, Roth represented those men coming out of World War II who could not settle down and, even if they did not always live hard and die young, certainty did not grow up as they grew old.[17]

I see in my father's generation not only tough models to live up to but harbingers of the rebellion of my generation and the refusal of my sons' generation to embrace maturity. In truth, of course, this dissidence goes back even further. But it is important to stress that the ideal grown-up of the 1950s and 1960s was hard for even men of that era to live up to. Not only were they supposed to be heroes in war and in work, but experts exhorted them to be modern fathers (and husbands). By the 1940s, the father had very little role in raising or training children, yet he was expected to be "more" than a provider. He was to be a pal to his children as well as a model of responsibility to family and society. Looking back on shows like *Father Knows Best*, I see not the Olympian patriarch "fixing" the problems of his ordinary family but a weekly course in the fine points of progressive parenting. The father, Jim Anderson, played by Robert Young, let the kids learn from their own mistakes, knew just when to be strong, and could tell the difference between the big and little things even if the kids (and wife) did not. This was a tough and bewildering act to follow for men of that era. And, beginning in the 1950s, some men consciously refused to play the part. Some slipped out the back, Jack. Others found solace in being one of the "boys" at the bar or on the hunting trip. Still others found pleasure in the retreat to the basement workshop. They became the first basement boys.

But the rebels of the Greatest Generation did more than take flight. They took pleasure in the romantic quest for intense and varied experience as well as in a cynical disdain for genteel sensibilities. They were the first generation to be "cool," fascinated with the transgressive and exciting culture of the street and played the role of rebels against bourgeois competition and providership. The "cool," emerging first in the teenage and youth years of my father with comic books, swing and jazz bands, and film noir, responded to longings and feelings that the censors like Hollywood's Hays Office had long smothered. More subtly, my father's generation was the first to react openly and massively to the emotional and sexual repression of genteel American society. They were also the first generation to reject as teens the "cute" culture of modern American childhood with its focus on the youngster's innocent delight and the appreciative if sometimes bemused adult. This nexus, so familiar in the modern rites of family holidays (like the Christmas-morning unwrapping ritual or the obligatory Disneyland trip), was at the heart of the 1950s sitcom and survived in many ways up to *The Cosby Show* of the late 1980s. But the rebels of my father's generation saw all this as phony, hypocritical, and sappy. Their rebellion became a lifelong cause. Ed Roth and Hugh Hefner never grew up, and they were proud of it. We see their legacy everywhere in today's popular culture, from the over-the-top smart-ass cynicism of *The Family Guy* to the twenty-something self-absorption of *Friends*.

The making of modern immaturity spans across my, my sons', and my father's generations. In different ways, each age group contributed to this shift of men to boys. Yet beyond these variations were three trends that encompassed all three generations (and beyond):

1. Our age has systematically rejected the Victorian patriarch without finding an adequate alternative. The decline of deference, the rise of feminism, and the growth of technological innovation has meant that there is much less of a "payoff" for male maturity in families and on the job. Much of this is for the good, but in the process some men have abandoned the traditional ideals of paternal responsibility to family, community, and culture without replacing them with new models of "grown-up" behavior.

2. Over time, being a kid has become much more satisfying than it was in the past when the young submitted to their elders and did without while the aged had distinct privileges. Of course, youth has and continues to have its traumas: work and school, subordination to elders, and the uncertainties of the future that may be even greater today than in the past—and I don't mean to discount their importance. But these anxieties and frustrations in a context of greater freedom of cultural and consumer expression—in ever expanding venues of youth-oriented movies, TV shows, video games, and amusement parks, for example—produced a longing for and the possibility of experiencing the rich but escapist culture of the boy-man. Even after

men assume adult roles, they increasingly become nostalgic for the play of their childhood and youth as they age. And, today men are able to extend the pleasures of the cool teen deep into their twenties and beyond because they spend less of their lives in the self-denying settings of family and marriage.

3. Makers of modern consumer and media culture have gradually learned to feed on this rejection of past models of maturity and the desire to return to or retain childhood. In turn, they have figured out how to sell back to men this longed-for image of perpetual youth. Over time, this makes youth, once a life stage, into a permanent and highly desirable lifestyle. The result is that men and boys play with the same toys and are attracted to the same novelties and celebrities in a culture of intensity.

Of course, all this can be overstated. Not everyone experienced this change or realized it the same way. Racial minorities and working class and rural men often did not fit easily into the story that I have sketched here. And I must admit that I am emphasizing the experience of the white middle-class American male, even though I will refer to differences (as well as similarities) with other men. Sometimes it is hard to tell the difference between fun-loving men and boy-men. Extending youth, its freedoms, and its delay of life-defining choices can be an opportunity, a beneficial by-product of modern affluence. Certainly I am not advocating a return to Victorian patriarchy. The rejection of traditional markers of maturity has freed men from the obligation to become stuffy or overly serious as they grow older. It has made possible the choice to be open to change and new experiences for a lifetime. Why should men be expected to embrace the traditional markers of maturity and become self-consciously serious? Why not wear a baseball cap and jeans at fifty and drive a Jeep instead of a Buick sedan at sixty? I wear such caps, even if I don't drive a Jeep. Maturity has always been a burden on the chronologically advanced, and not just in physical terms. It has limited what oldsters can say, do, and be. Typical images of maturity can be painful stereotypes. No one wants to be an "old fogy." The admonition to "act your age" has killed a lot of life. The modern bias toward youth has encouraged an openness to change and embrace new experiences. It helped eliminate Victorian standards of emotional and intellectual rigidity. Most of all, the "young at heart" can connect easily with the truly young because of a willingness to discard the authoritarian ways of the past.

As disturbing and foolish as many boy-men may appear, most American males grow up to be productive citizens and more or less caring husbands and responsible fathers. In a lot of ways, the boy-man is merely playing—indulging himself in a game, donning a costume and mask, acting a role. And this play reveals the frustrations and stultifications of enforced responsibility. The games of the boy-man let the adult man protest (usually gently) the rules of family and work without disrupting either. All this playing around may mean nothing more. The boy-man may be, when it really counts, a real man.

But is it all play? If so, a lot of it isn't making people very happy. For years, magazine articles and books have reminded us of the frustration experienced by women in pursuit of these Hugh Grant want-to-bes, skilled at romance but unwilling to commit and incapable of love. Typical is Barbara Dafoe Whitehead's *Why There Are No Good Men Left: The Romantic Plight of the New Single Woman* (2003). The title says it all. The oft-repeated dilemma is that men can have "the benefits of a wife without shouldering the reciprocal obligations of a husband," as Whitehead explains. Why should single men accept the responsibilities of their fathers when the costs of avoiding marriage are so low and the benefits are so high, especially when there is often no penalty for breaking up with a girlfriend? They can get sex without commitment, perhaps avoid an early divorce and its costs, and face few pressures to get married. The costs of such relationships, however, are obvious to women, children, . . . and boy-men.[18]

In their closely protected hours of leisure and fantasy free from work and family cares, male culture has often become a strangely unreal quest for perpetuating boyhood, of endlessly repeating the novelty of youth. The ideal of the boy-man denies the virtues of age and often the responsibilities of the older to the younger generation. It has obscured the possibility of being a grown-up who keeps growing up, in other words, becoming mature.

I emphatically am not making an essentialist argument about "maturity." I am not saying that there are some basic criteria that define "true" maturity and that the last half century has been about a decline of those characteristics. I am arguing instead that the standards of maturity that were so strongly expressed in the postwar popular culture have declined. Moreover, these markers were always ambiguous and riddled with contradiction and confusion, and many from the World War II generation could not or would not adopt them. I claim that those criteria (ranging from family providership and an ideal of maturing taste and refinement to formality in dress and manner) have diminished over the course of the last half century in the popular culture. In some degree, this decline was an expression of historical adaptation to new times and the abandonment of characteristics that restrained the expressiveness of men. But I also argue that these markers of maturity have not been replaced by new ones more appropriate for our times and that this has led to the phenomenon of the "boy-man" and its correlative culture of cynicism and thrill seeking. I am not blaming this on the current generation of young men, but instead I am arguing that that the "boy-man" is a part of a much longer process with roots in both the boomer and World War II generations and in the historical change in the roles of men. At the same time, I insist that the modern culture of the "boy-man" has created serious but not insuperable problems than need to be addressed by all.

In this book, I address these and related issues by exploring the emergence of today's boy-man. I will show the comedy and tragedy as well as the confusions and struggles of boy-men and how and why they emerged in recent years. I will do so by taking the reader back across the experience of three generations of American men's culture. This will be a personal as well as a historian's take on the phenomenon of the boy-man. As such, at points I will emphasize my experience—my part of the boomer generation, my recollections of and revised opinions about the past, and my views of the present. This will inevitably tell the story from the angle of white middle-class society (though I came from an odd corner of it). Even so, this will not be an autobiography. I am not vain enough to think that would hold readers. Rather it will be a personal reflection as informed in detail by the historical record.

Without being overly formulaic, I root my argument in the relationship between cultural change (as expressed in a wide range of popular and commercial forms) and the emergence of three commonly identified generational cohorts. These consist of men like my father who came to maturity during or close to World War II, boomer males like me who entered adulthood in the mid-1960s, and men like my sons who grew up in the 1980s and 1990s. Demographic characteristics, parent's styles of childrearing, and formative political, social, and economic experiences identify these cohorts in successive chapters. I will focus, however, on how popular culture both shaped and reflected the childhood, youth, and adult lives of each cohort. I also identify changes in that popular culture across the experiences of the three generations. I am not claiming any direct relationship between real behavior and popular cultural change but rather that culture in its subtle change can reveal what social data and even psychological observation may not. For example, I show how the change in the situation comedy from the late 1950s to the late 1960s and finally to the late 1980s and 1990s reflects very different notions of growing up and being mature for each of the three age groups. As a second example, I show how the popular cultures of men and boys have gradually become similar. I do this by contrasting the gap between children's and adult westerns in the 1950s with the closer links in content and style between kids' action-adventure cartoons and R-rated action-adventure films in the 1980s and 1990s. As a third example, I show how the Disney-style amusement park introduced to boomers and their World War II–era parents in the 1950s became complexes of roller coaster thrills in the 1980s and 1990s, reflecting the new aesthetic of Generation X youth. This approach allows me to go beyond the common sociological arguments about the so-called Greatest Generation, the baby boomers, and Generation X (and Y) to explore how these age groups were linked to broad changes in the popular culture. Inevitably, there will be some "slippage" in these categories given the imperfect way that generation and culture line up, but I'll try to align them. Two chapters will be devoted to each of the three generations.

Major themes of this book are taken from the experience of white American men, and I certainly do not claim that this experience can be attributed to all male Americans. At the same time, I will draw also upon the distinct elements of the culture of minority men. For example, I will consider the rebellion of boomer African American males in the late 1960s against the nonviolent ethos of the early civil rights generation as well as the emergence of a thrill culture in blaxploitation movies in the 1970s and later rap music.

In the course of the book, I will draw on a wide variety of sources—from collections of movies and TV shows and advertisements to popular magazine articles about fatherhood and male hobbies—all in pursuit of changing images of male maturity and immaturity. Although the book will focus on popular culture (both shaping and reflecting changes in the markers of male maturity), I will also draw upon the sociological literature to identify changing characteristics of my three generations. This is definitely a work of humanistic reflection, rather than social science or media studies. In the broad tradition of history, this book finds significance and trends in relating diverse evidence across time.

Obviously, a book that will cover such a vast array of themes and culture will have to be selective, perhaps even at points idiosyncratic. Others might treat in more detail popular music, sports, or men's fiction, for example, and I hope that some do in future studies, but I try to cover this enormous topic with sufficient focus to make for clarity, even if that requires compromise.

So why is this an age of boy-men? What happened to maturity and its markers—the look, the behavior, the social and cultural recognition of grown-ups? Why and how did men come to perpetuate boyhood, at least in their "real" lives of leisure? What does all of this say about our culture? This book will attempt to answer these questions.

chapter 1.

When FATHERS Knew BEST
(or Did They?)

I begin this story with a search for "grown-up" men in the past. Looking back I found them in some of the classic images of maturity as I
remember them from 1950s TV and especially old movies that I saw
at ten years old in the cool of our basement on hot summer afternoons and on the late show on weekends. Of course, I'm thinking
of leading men like Cary Grant, Spencer Tracy, Gary Cooper, and
Clark Gable. I admired the decisiveness, seriousness, and dignity that
they projected. They even looked older and more serious than their
successors today. The postwar grown-up was more than a style or
look. He was a man who came back from the war and adapted to
civilian life. And, no one thought that this was to be easy. *The Best
Years of Our Lives* (the most popular film of 1946 and indeed of the
late 1940s) tells this story in the experience of three vets meeting on
a B-17 bomber that carries them back to their typical hometown of
Boonville and their trials of coping with civilian life and family again.
The eldest, an army sergeant, has to reacquaint himself with his now
teenage son, his wife of twenty years, and his grown-up daughter as
well as with a desk job in a bank. The highest ranked (air force captain) has to face a war-bride wife who turns out to be unfaithful and a
bleak future going back to his old job as a "soda jerk." The youngest, a
sailor, fears that his family and girlfriend will reject him or feel sorry
for him, having lost both hands in the war. In the end, all make honorable, if uncertain decisions. The sergeant adapts despite a drinking
problem; the sailor marries his girl and learns to accept his disability;
the captain gets into the salvage business after his wife leaves him and

makes himself acceptable for marrying the sergeant's daughter. We are left with a happy ending but also with a feeling that all three have their work cut out for them. *The Best Years* is about real people who have to make serious choices and will have to make adjustments.

When I saw these movies for the first time, I may have missed their maturity. There were certainly many men to look up to on rainy and cold Saturdays in front the set: Hopalong Cassidy, Gene Autry, Roy Rogers, and Sky King from the westerns each offered something a little different. Don Herbert, a science teacher, on *Watch Mr. Wizard* actually taught someone very much like us the mysteries of electricity and vacuums. And it was popular enough (or TV executives were supportive enough) to stay on the air from 1951 to 1965. Conductor Leonard Bernstein taught boomers music history and composition on his equally long running *Young People's Concerts* from 1958 to 1972. Both shows presented models of maturity. They were there for us kids, and early TV programmers were eager for our parents to know that the new gadget offered us models to aspire to.

I also watched adult clowns—from reruns of the Three Stooges with their very physical humor to the childlike incompetence of the pudgy Lou Costello, who was always manipulated by his sidekick Bud Abbott, and Jerry Lewis, whose high-pitched voice and awkward angularity seemed to disguise his real age. On TV, there was Pinky Lee, a frenetic fool dressed in a silly pink-striped suit, whose looks and manner Pee Wee Herman copied in the 1980s. Even the host on *The Howdy Doody Show*, Buffalo Bob Smith, though separate from the kids in the "Peanut Gallery" and the marionette "stars" of the show, was more like a member of the gang than a father figure. That was surely true of Jimmy and Roy on the Mickey Mouse Club. They were really just part of the revue of the kids singing and dancing, likewise festooned with those ridiculous mouse-ears caps, rather than paternal leaders. The grandfatherly Roy gave no advice that I recall; instead, he gently displayed his amateur skill in drawing cartoons. But these comic or childlike figures had a different role than did Hoppy and Mr. Wizard. They were there to make us kids comfortable in our childhood because they were as, and often more childish than we were. This was an appeal that was passed down through the years (today in the childish enthusiasm of the cartoon figure SpongeBob SquarePants and his sidekick, the innocent Patrick, who so much remind me of Howdy Doody characters). The difference was that in my 1950s youth there were lots of father figures on the screen as well.

Gunslingers for Kids

The most common grown-up man on the little screen, however, was generally not a father but the solitary figure of the cowboy. Still, the western had the biggest impact on both my and my father's generations' idea of the grown-up man. I have long regretted all the hours that I spent in front of the set watching the shootouts and galloping horses without being able now to recall a single plot, but I could have hardly avoided them at the time. By 1959, there were twenty-seven westerns on prime-time TV, not to mention the kiddy westerns on the weekends and after school.[1] Looking back as a historian, I find this very strange. Why would an increasingly suburbanized American male, who spent five days a week in an office, often went to church on Sunday, and took the kids to Little League games and dancing classes on Saturdays, want to spend two or three hours every night watching men his own age largely without family responsibilities engage in shootouts on dusty streets? Why would boys brought up surrounded by the glories of new cars, the space program, and the promise of the "push-button" age spend endless hours practicing their "draw" with their Roy Rogers six-shooter and playing with their Fort Apache playsets?

To make a bit of sense of this, we need to recall that the western had long defined masculinity in America for men as well as boys. In the 1900s and through the 1920s, the western became popular across the generations, elevating it far above its early popularity in the cheap dime novel. It captured the imaginations of Americans of all ages through Buffalo Bill Cody's Wild West shows and the serials of the silent movies. Western writers like Zane Grey even published in such middle-class magazines as *Colliers* and *Harpers' Monthly*. Between 1930 and 1955, Hollywood produced 2,772 western movies, often filmed at company-owned ranches and featuring the best-known stars and directors.[2] Westerns reached adult male audiences across social classes. Such men were attracted to a nostalgic "return" to the simplicity, excitement, and virtue of an age before cities, factories, and offices. The genre reflected and reinforced myths about rugged and unadorned Americans in heroic struggle with evil (far from the tawdry commercialism of the twentieth century) and destined to conquer a continent from wild men and unruly nature. The western hero was independent and daring. He challenged the greed of the empire builders on the frontier, but he also stood for law and order. "Though he lives intensely, he has a calm self-assurance, a knowledge that he can handle anything," noted historian David Davis.[3] A century ago, adult men whose real lives were increasingly regimented by factory or office work and who labored under the heel of the time-motion boss or fickle customer could identify with the rough, tough figures portrayed in the silent movies by William Hart. His Broadway role in *The Squaw Man* (1905) led to a twenty-year career playing unglamorous, hard-fighting, hard-drinking, and even melancholic cowboys in silent movies. These westerns showed a man's world where women were childlike and mostly dependent, upholders of religious values, shunned or used as heroic props by death-obsessed gunslingers.[4]

But there were also more playful cowboy characters who were more suitable models for kids. Tom Mix, who came from the Wild West shows and the circus, appealed to boys with his roping and shooting skills and offered far less somber images of the western hero's life. In the 1910s, parents associated the western with their own youth (having been raised on western dime novels and stories in pulp magazines), and they nostalgically passed this genre onto their own children in the form of cowboy suits and toy "six-shooters." By the 1930s, westerns had become in large part a boy's genre. These included afternoon radio programs like *Tom Mix and His Ralston Straight Shooters* as well as western serials shown during children's Saturday matinees. Republic Studios made a hero of Gene Autry in 1935 and, when he demanded too high a salary in 1939, added Roy Rogers to their roster. Gene and Roy (along with Tex Ritter) sang love songs to girls but also crooned to the wide open spaces as they rode into town to rescue hard-working farmers and wimpy storekeepers, as well as, of course, their pretty daughters from the torments of greedy land grabbers or gangs of killers.[5]

The singing and rhinestone cowboy had an appeal across age and sex. But there was not much doubt as to who admired Hopalong Cassidy. Played by William Boyd, an aging leading man from the silent era, Hopalong of the Bar 20 Ranch clearly reached a juvenile audience with his clean-cut heroism in a series of sixty-six movies. Boyd's "Hoppy" had little in common with the grizzled, hard-drinking character (with a namesake limp) from Clarence Mulford's novel. On the screen, Boyd turned Hoppy into a black-and-white image (he in black and his horse Topper in white) who bristled with moral certainty. Made from 1935 and 1948, the movie series offered a formulaic appeal, complete with a young sidekick (with whom kids could identify) and "old" comical sidekicks like Gabby Hayes (who sometimes worked without his false teeth to appear older than he was and who seemed to be afraid of women). Stirring orchestral music enlivened the frequent chases on galloping horses when Hoppy vanquished sundry bad guys. Boyd was lean and powerful (unlike the grizzled sidekicks), but he didn't hide his silver hair and grown-up bearing. Boyd prudently bought the movie series and transferred it to TV in 1949, cutting down the feature-length films for a weekly series that aired until 1955 with additional made-for-TV episodes. Boyd naturally cashed in on his appeal to early baby boomer lads, peddling his name and image on lunchboxes and gun and holster sets and playing before sellout crowds on national tours. But he also founded "Hoppy's Troopers," kids clubs with a code of conduct demanding that members be kind to the weak, be loyal to nation and friends, and work hard. Each TV episode ended with a little homily. I remember watching him in about 1954, not long after our family got its first TV set, admonishing us eight-year-olds to respect policemen and never to call them "coppers."[6]

Hoppy's success on TV paralleled others. In fact, early TV westerns were usually copies of the (mostly juvenile) cowboy B movies from the 1930s and 1940s. Roy and Gene both had TV shows in the early 1950s, and others such as *The Lone Ranger* (1949–1957) and *The Cisco Kid* came "over" from radio.[7] Each offered a child-friendly version of the Old West. One interesting exception was *Sky King* (1951–62), set in modern Arizona and replacing the horse with Song Bird, a small airplane. It featured Sky, a pilot and owner of the Flying Crown Ranch, his niece, Penny, and for a time his nephew, Clipper, both in their teens. The adventures revolved around the plane, which came in handy when Sky rescued the kids after they were captured by smugglers or enemy agents who took them to remote cabins. In addition to the excitement, there was almost always a gentle moral: the possibility, for example, for a bad boy who had escaped from reform school to be redeemed through the understanding and strength of Sky and his "family" at the Flying Crown and his learning to make the "right choice" in turning on his "evil family" of crooks. Sky taught Penny and Clipper that the "law of cooperation" between the Kings prevailed over the "law of the jungle" of selfish gang members. One episode that featured Penny even made the point that the woman's place is not necessarily in the home (as the chauvinist Clipper believed) but "where she is needed."[8] All of these characters and their stories were fun and often thrilling, but they also told us much about how our elders expected us to grow up.

Cowboy Loners and Suburban Dads

While these westerns presumably taught us kids to be responsible and courageous (as well as to be quick on the draw), there were other westerns, especially prominent after the war, that were more for adults, especially men. Though they were more realistic, they, too, had their moral lessons about being a grown-up man. While the B western migrated from the Saturday matinee to Saturday TV, the serious western saw something of a revival at the movie house after World War II. Carrying on the old tradition of William Hart was *The Gunfighter* (1950), where an aging hero faces the futility of his life of killing. John Wayne's formula westerns in the 1930s became serious psychological tales, as, for example, in *The Searchers* of 1956 and even more in his westerns of the 1960s and 1970s, such as *True Grit* and *The Shootist*. These westerns were not about good guys rescuing the helpless; nor were they mere confrontations between good and evil. Not the freedom of the frontier but its bareness and limitations dominated these films. Not daring choice but the pressures of obligation appealed to adult men who had long outgrown the romance of singing cowboys and the thrill of Tom Mix's rope tricks.[9]

More mature westerns came to the tube, moving the genre from the child's Saturday morning to the adult's prime time. Among the first was *Death Valley Days* (1952–1975), an anthology series of stories and fables of prospectors, gamblers, and other characters of the Old West that made this the third longest running TV program ever, with 452 episodes. Ronald Reagan served as host for several years before launching his political career as California governor. The longest running TV program was *Gunsmoke* (with an astonishing 633 episodes) seen for twenty years after its premier in 1955. It was the most popular program between 1957 and 1961 and near the top for years thereafter.[10]

Watching these westerns after decades of disparaging them made me see them in a new light and understand why adult men might have watched them a half century ago. If Hoppy and Roy gave boys heroes and adventure, *Gunsmoke*'s Marshal Matt Dillon of Dodge City gave our fathers something, too. Dillon was more than the stolid six-foot, seven-inch figure played by James Arness gunning down the weekly villain in the ritual duel on the dusty street in front of Miss Kitty's saloon. This show didn't last for twenty years on such a childish principle. Rather than being about male bravado and the thrill of the final confrontation, *Gunsmoke* usually featured complex characters and plots. Dillon himself was flawed but only because the sin of pride sometimes distorted his virtue of courage and responsibility. In the first episode, he refused help from others in his multiround match with Dan the quick-drawing gunman, but he finally found Dan's weakness (he was a quick draw but a bad aimer), giving Matt the decisive advantage when he refused Dan's demand that they duel at close range. But Matt's prevailing strength was not mere steadfastness but moral maturity. He was able to see the difference between the law and justice when he protected a reformed man and community leader accused of being a former member of a murderous gang. *Gunsmoke* was as often about redemption as retribution. Although the show included unheroic characters (who contrasted with Matt), especially "Doc" and the deputy (the lame Chester followed by the hillbilly Festus), even this old gimmick (in the tradition of Gabby Hayes) was subtler than I had recalled it. Doc, even without a gun, could be courageous, as in his efforts to find a home for newborn triplet sons of a murderer. Despite fears of the townspeople that these boys had "bad blood," Doc refused to give in to the demand that they be sent to an orphanage. With Matt, he knew that "nobody is a born criminal." While the ending was certainly maudlin (a couple with ten children took in the triplets), the story elevates the "unmasculine" Doc, making him a hero by defending the infants in front of a judge who would have otherwise (and quite correctly) sent them to an institution. One of the most subtle episodes aired in 1973. In "Matt's Love Story," a gambler wanted for murder ambushes the marshal, leaving him for dead. Though stricken with amnesia, Matt is nursed back to health by a very tough and independent widow rancher. This could have been a conventional story of Matt's recovery of strength and memory ending with the gambler's death and Matt's dutiful return to Dodge City (which, of course, happens). Still, the "love affair" with the tough widow, "Mike," and the eventual confrontation with the gambler is amazingly subtle (not to mention its dialogue, saturated in similes and metaphors). The gambler, being taken back to be tried for murder, helps Matt confront truly bad guys (a gang who tried to seize Mike's land) and, when shot, the gambler dies in a philosophical exchange that a Shakespeare want-to-be would have been proud of. This is a far sight better than the old time shoot-outs. More that this, *Gunsmoke* was about responsible decision making in complex, even ambiguous situations. It was hard for Matt to go back to Dodge City, and the gambler made a choice that belied his past sociopathic behavior. But these weren't cynical tales of moral relativism; the moral lesson was seldom far from view. In another episode, the rational and mature Doc prevailed over the impetuous Festus, who wanted to call an inexperienced posse to chase down a gang that had shot Matt. Later Matt teaches a young man, who was quick on the draw but unwilling to kill even in defense, the need to protect the weak with deadly force. In both cases, age and wisdom won out. Doc knew that many would be killed in a poorly planned attack on the gang, and Matt offered the lad the hard but experienced truth: "thinking the worst is a good way to stay alive."[11]

Dillon was always the grown-up, killing reluctantly and with a sense of responsibility. He was there for the nurturing if practical and seasoned Miss Kitty, but he always had his priorities straight, never giving in to lust, ever mindful of his duty. Of course, this was all romanticized and pretty unrealistic. Are we really to believe Matt and Kitty never had an affair? Are we to suppose that Kitty didn't have whores upstairs in the saloon? Today, all this would have been part of the story, but the *Gunsmoke* of 1955 to 1975 did not need any of that and still it was "adult."

Other adult westerns were less mature as understood at the time (and did not last so long). *The Life and Legend of Wyatt Earp* (1955–1961) opened with a ballad celebrating the savior sheriff of Wichita, Kansas, and later Tombstone, Arizona, who reluctantly gave up a "normal" life as a settler to be "brave, courageous, and bold" in pursuit of justice. We are told in the theme song: "He cleaned up the country, the old Wild West country / and made law and order prevail / and none can deny it, the legend of Wyatt / forever will live on the trail." In the premier episode, he fights a corrupt judge and avenges the death of the old sheriff as he is "forced" to take on the duties of the law. In another episode, he reforms a corrupt sheriff and rebuffs an attractive woman and her appeal to follow her to San Francisco and take a soft, lucrative job. Instead, he goes back to the thankless task of protecting the dusty town of Tombstone. Pretty classic western stuff, but even *Earp* had its subtlety, as in the story of China Mary, whose "wet-nosed son" rebels against her accommodation to white society and tragically has to die. *Have Gun Will Travel* (1957–1963) featured the preposterous theme of Paladin, a hired gun who was willing to travel all over the west in defense of the little guy. His clients were somehow able to pay Paladin's fee of $1,000 allowing him to live in style in an elegant hotel in San Francisco when not working. Still, the traditional format—outside hero saving the besieged western town or ranch from local predators—took greater sophistication from Richard Boone's plain looks (hardly the fresh-faced cowboy) combined with his elegant allusions to Aristotle and Shakespeare and his witty, often sarcastic speech. Paladin was no hick cowboy, but a West Point graduate (a fact that I admit was lost on me when I saw *Have Gun Will Travel* as a twelve-year-old but probably not on grown-ups), naming himself after a legendary officer in Charlemagne's court, a western knight-errant. And the adult western did not even have to be about gunslingers and lawmen. *Cheyenne* (1955–1962) featured the adventures of a former army scout who wandered across the west after the Civil War. In a typically complex story involving issues of trust and courage, Cheyenne Bodie wounds a gold prospector who, thinking Bodie wanted to steal his gold, had tried to shoot him. Cheyenne goes on to help the man's wife nurse him back to health, confronts a gang of real robbers, and faces Indians who, seeking to prevent a white invasion of their land, set out to wipe out the prospectors and evidence of the discovery of gold.[12]

Rawhide, remembered today mostly for the amusing rendition of its theme song in the film *The Blues Brothers*, was one of the most grown-up of the adult westerns. It opened with a documentary-style voice-over explaining the cattleman's work and life (the travails of driving herds 1,000 miles north to market from the grazing land in southern Texas or the origins of the feuds between cowboys and farmers, e.g.). The hero, trail boss Gil Favor, is anything but a gunman. In one episode, he recognizes the limits of his men "half of them green, half of them rusty," but, even though he must control them (banning their drinking in towns), he insists that they are "all good men to start with." He is the model of the modern leader, and, as such, he has to assume responsibility. He talks his men into returning to the herd after they were seduced by gold fever and gives himself up to a lynching party of angry farmers seeking a scapegoat for the accidental death caused by his cattle men. And, the fight between the cowboys and the plowboys is treated as a tragedy rather than an opportunity for exciting gunplay, as Favor makes tough choices to avoid bloodshed and the farmers see the personal bitterness of the wife of the dead man and reject her demand that Favor be killed. These are stories moral dilemmas and choices. In fact, their moral vision is surprisingly liberal for the time (as Favor saves a Hispanic worker from attack by Anglo farmers, for example).[13]

Wagon Train (1957–1965) and *The Virginian* (1962–1971) shared the same quality: grown men being responsible. Of course, with the western so ubiquitous in the 1950s, a spoof was inevitable. It came in *Maverick* (1957–1960), James Garner's breakthrough role as a cowardly gambler who uses deceit and charm to get out of scrapes. While he didn't always escape gunplay and fistfights, he surely tried to avoid them. But once again, this show avoided the temptation to make this character into a rogue or the evil ones into silly simpletons. But good inevitably prevails, as when Maverick, in the first episode, tricks a greedy mine owner into raising his miners' wages and helping the small operators.[14]

Most prime-time westerns met adult tastes (even while kids watched most of them). They seldom included children in the regular cast and rarely took the perspective of youth. *The Rifleman* (1958–1963) was a curious exception. Many my age will recall mostly the opening sequence, when the steely eyed, square-jawed Lucas McCain, played by Chuck Connors, a six-foot-five former baseball player, with rolled up sleeves showing his muscular arms, fires his modified lever-action Winchester in rapid succession at an inadequately armed six-gun-shooting bad guy. But looking back, *The Rifleman* was as much about the growing up of his subteen son, Mark (played by former *Mickey Mouse Club* star Johnny Crawford), and his learning the hard life of a rancher in New Mexico as this gimmicky variation on the usual shoot-out show. In one episode, Mark learns that he is too young to fall in love with the new girl in town and to buy his dad's surplus land in order to marry her. Lucas treats his son's childish delusion with respect and Mark discovers in the process how to treat a lady when the girl goes for a self-centered older guy. In other episodes, Mark learns about telling the truth and the difference between "Old World" and modern American ways of treating women. More familiar today through reruns is the family western *Bonanza* (1959–1973), built around a patriarchal widowed rancher and his three sons, Adam, Hoss, and Little Joe. Despite lots of family scrapes, the Cartwrights bond to protect their property from thieving outsiders in Virginia City, Nevada, during the Civil War period. The political undertone is certainly conservative, but *Bonanza* is also about the moral ambiguities of character and relationships.[15]

These "adult westerns" were about escape from the humdrum and feminized world of the 1950s, a fantasy of rugged individualism, courage, and grit in an emerging world of station wagons full of kids. But they were also about idealizing the man who squarely faced responsibility and served as a model for growing up and being a grown-up in the 1950s. They were told at a right angle to reality, as in the conversations of boys in sandboxes and men at bars, never face to face. But men and boys probably got the point.

Westerns dominated the imagination of postwar men, but there were also the doctor shows, *Dr. Kildare* (1961–1966), *Ben Casey* (1961–1966), and *Marcus Welby, MD* (1969–1976). Like so much television programming of this era, this genre drew from the movies of the 1930s, especially the melodrama of the *Dr. Kildare* series (with Lew Ayres in the title lead and Lionel Barrymore as the elder Dr. Gillespie). Emergency-room histrionics and tear-jerking exchanges between caring doctors and dying patients dominated these weekly series. Because I found these shows sappy as a boy, I never saw what they were also about—the contrast between the experience, caution, and wisdom of the old doctor and the impetuous but energetic devotion of the young doctor. Ben Casey, a young, muscular resident surgeon with especially hairy arms and chest, brooked no incompetence from nurses, less-devoted doctors, or meddling relatives of patients in his drive to save lives. He didn't even have much time for female doctors who he believed were too emotional. Naturally, all this got him into trouble with his superiors. Regularly Casey had to be bailed out by his mentor Dr. Zorba—but not before Zorba gave him a lot of fatherly advice about the need for patience, understanding the other guy's point of view, and rational forethought. As Zorba said in the premiere, Casey was a "fresh boy." School had "taught him all about medicine, but nothing about life." Dr. James Kildare was a less muscular personality, but in his opening show, his father figure and mentor, Dr. Leonard Gillespie, had to tell him how to let a sick patient be herself as she died from a rare disease.[16]

While the elder doctors were often cautious and even had lost some of the vital idealism of the young Kildare and Casey, the main lesson of these shows was the wisdom of the mature and the need for the growing up of the young. In these medical shows, as in the

westerns, I saw daily models of manhood and of the lessons of learning from experience and one's elders. So did the men of my father's
generation. They were repeatedly admonished to follow these ideals
when they served as soldiers in World War II and Korea, learning,
perhaps from the sergeant, to become a band of brothers. They became providers to large families when they returned and served as
responsible members of their communities throughout their lives in
civil organizations.

The Things of the Grown-up

The movies and TV told men and boys how to act. They also told them
how to look. The scene of Cary Grant dressed in a natty suit while in
the middle of farmland and being attacked by a villainous crop-dust-
ing plane in *North by Northwest* (1959) sticks in my mind as a lesson
in how a gentleman should be well dressed no matter the occasion.
Reading an obscure but probably representative *Men's Clothing Survey* conducted by the *Chicago Tribune* in 1958 brought home to me
just how men of my father's generation took this to heart. The survey
found that men (especially from the middle class) were entirely predictable. They were ignorant (even disdainful) of technical details of
fabric, cut, and fashion and wanted clothes that offered physical comfort and made a man feel "unconcern about his clothing," meaning
that his garb neither made him feel conspicuously faddish nor stodgy.
Although men wanted to feel "like somebody" in their clothes, they
were wary of novelty, especially radical style changes. Instead, they
would gradually adapt to sartorial evolution. While the 1958 survey
found a trend toward the acceptance of casual clothing for leisure,
63 percent still believed that men should wear ties to go out to most
places.[17] Anything less would have been immature. Little had changed
for decades, in fact, since the early nineteenth century invention of
the sober bourgeois suit. An ad for Hart, Schaffner and Marx suits
in 1912 would have appealed to the man of 1958 as well: "you fellows
who know and like the smart distinction of style" also want a "style
that stays stylish." Others chimed in offering "nothing extreme" and
"impressive individuality without sacrifice of dignity." Another ad for
suits bragged: "they will give you the spell of power that a strong personality always casts."[18] The suit promised a dash of individuality on a
solid foundation of social acceptability.

This was true even in the slightly racy *Esquire*. A 1949 issue, for example, featured "tasteful" cheesecake pictures of young women and cartoons warning of the perils of too many children and of gold diggers. Still, *Esquire* upheld the traditional standard of male sartorial dignity in features and ads displaying coordinated ties, shirts, and suits topped off with appropriate accessories like Kaywoodie pipes. Even ads for summer casual clothing offered only slight deviations— "feather-light ventilators" in otherwise strictly formal shirts, some with French cuffs. Men smiled even with the top button buttoned in the heat of the day. *Esquire's* idea of cute informality was a dad and his young son dressed in matching suits with fedoras. The persistence of the hat strikes us today as the most curious marker of maturity, especially the "banded" fedora that clearly marked the man from the boy (and, which is to say almost the same thing, the middle-class man from the cap-wearing workman).[19]

In the 1950s and early 1960s, of course, we do see some concessions to informality, but they were subtle, even hidden: Bermuda shorts, claimed *Look Magazine* in 1949, were being worn by "all" men in the trendy winter resorts. The Stetsen "Falcon" hat of 1963 featured a "pinch front that will appeal to the wide awake" and Jockey offered patterned boxers. But, for the most part, being mature meant being formal and adapting very slowly to fashion change. Even for the young man, the ideal was to deviate only slightly from his elders. An ad scene (1956) featuring a middle-aged executive shaking hands with a fresh college graduate showed a modest contrast: the elder wore a black and the younger a grey suit. As late as 1965, *Esquire's* Spring Term collection featured college men in yellow, blue, and checked blazers, even striped sport shirts, but they were still in suits even if the fedora had finally disappeared. Until the late 1960s, even rockers (like the Beatles on the *Ed Sullivan Show* in 1964) still wore suits and ties on stage.[20]

Of course, for men, appearance was always supposed to be secondary. In the 1950s (as earlier), the real mark of maturity in men was competence, often technical. Since the beginning, car makers sold mostly to men, and their ads flattered male egos with amazingly detailed lists of technological innovation with very little explanation. Their buyers in 1950 would know (or pretend to know) the importance of new weight distributions, cam design, an improved turning gear, and super-fitted pistons, as well as sound-conditioned roof, doors, and body panels. Naturally, the 1953 Oldsmobile Rocket featured a higher compression engine with 165 horsepower. TV ads for vehicles sometimes played up to male fantasies of cowboy ruggedness, independence, and adventure. A commercial for the 1957 Ford Ranchero called this half-ton car-truck a "pack horse," and a cowboy on a horse lassoed the Ford Fairlane because he wanted a "long lean car with lots of punch." Still, appeals to male car buyers mostly concerned grown-up technical issues about power, stability, and even safety—not fantasy, thrills, or even power for its own sake. In the early 1950s, Fibber McGee of radio comedy fame pitched AC oil filters to men but also gently advised them that they could be real men and still let their dealers replace their oil filters. Many men, even professionals, resisted this, insisting on their "rights" as the sex of technical competence. In the late 1960s, when I got my first car, my male peers shamed me into changing my own oil (despite the lack of a "mechanical" father in the house to teach me how), and I nearly destroyed my engine for my trouble when I didn't put the drain plug back on correctly.[21]

That voice of male technical authority prevailed also in ads for women's domestic and cleaning goods. On TV, men, often in laboratory dress, introduced women to automatic washing machines and dishwashers. As silly as they look today, 1950s ads showed an image of a knight selling Ajax cleanser with the promise of being "stronger than dirty" and the genielike image of Mr. Clean magically and powerfully whisking bathtubs into sparkling cleanliness (at a time, of course, when few men ever took a sponge to a bathroom).[22] Curious, really, but no one saw the contradiction at the time. The presumption was that men, real men, brought the tools *into* the house, even if they did not always use them.

Of course, images of men and their goods sometimes stressed status and success. TV ads for Cadillacs displayed men in tuxedos (with their befurred wives) climbing into their luxury cars in front of the country club with "admiring eyes" following. Lincoln ads bragged about their fine leather interiors, and even the sporty 1956 Ford Thunderbird was backset with "classic" Greek columns. Cars, even more than clothes, were about achievement, but not about mere showing off. Even the ads for the cars with the wild fins, exotic chromed grills, and playful two-tone paint jobs (famously on the 1957 Edsel) claimed that their styling was in fact conservative and that it was bound to stay. Cars separated the men from the boys (or, to say the same thing, from men who remained boys in their lack of success and who drove last year's car). That was the point of the upward incline of automobile brands best illustrated by General Motors's full line of cars, rising from the Chevrolet for the plebs up the long slope beginning with the Pontiac, on to the Oldsmobile, Buick, and finally the pinnacle, the Caddy. The car that men owned marked success, but also maturity.[23]

Maturity and economic success or power had long been linked. This is why subordinate males, no matter their age, and, most pointedly, black slaves (and black men in the South until the civil rights revolution) had been called "boys." But there was also a culture of masculine maturity that sometimes muted class and privilege. Most obviously we see this in beer and liquor ads. Sometimes these sale scenes were set in bars, but in the 1950s these ads also reveled in the fraternity of men gathering for beers before Thanksgiving dinner or in a garage conclave of neighborhood men celebrating an afternoon of raking leaves or woodworking. The drink, of course, separated the men from the kids, but it also suggested "beverages of moderation," as a *Collier's* ad in 1948 called beer drunk in and around the home. It wasn't the "kick" of the alcohol or the ecstasy of the drinking crowd that was supposed to be the appeal. Rather, it was the "gusto" of fellow feeling that the glass of Schlitz offered or even the comforting thought that by drinking a Blatz one was enjoying a "flavor [that] runs deep" in American history, dating back to the western frontier days when men were men. Included in this, of course, was an idea of masculinity that rejected refinement or finery. Ads assured men that Aqua Velva aftershave wasn't perfume in fancy bottles that made men smell like women but a product that simply left men feeling "cool and refreshed." Contrast this with an ad for Body Shot, an aerosol fragrance offered in 2006 that young men were told to shoot on themselves when feeling the need to attract women. In the 1950s, that would have been what women did, not men. As with clothing, most male goods were sold by reassuring men of their difference from women. And being a grown-up didn't change that.[24]

Still, there was a lot more to men in the 1950s than "dignity," competence, and gender difference. Trolling through magazine ads and TV commercials that appeared in the 1950s while looking for clues about the stuff of grown-up men, I was struck that a lot of what these messages sold to men wasn't for them but for their families. In so many ways, this provider's role defined male maturity. Men learned this in the 1940s, when the theme was hammered into them (and women) while they were at war, far from being able to "provide."

Wartime ads offered soldiers (and the families they left behind) the tantalizing dream of a "Ford . . . in your Future" and the promise of a happy world of both traditional white picket fences and brand-new white enameled refrigerators that soldiers could offer their adoring wives and children when they returned.[25] For celebrating the first Christmas back with the family, a Coca Cola ad pictured a soldier laid out on his coach, throwing his baby in the air with his wife and Coke beside him. Another ad for Christmas in 1945 showed a dad pointing out to his wife and kids a sign he had put on his garage: "Reserved for our new Plymouth." Yes, dad was back, and he was going to provide, even if the family would have to wait for postwar production to gear up before he could provide the family a new car.[26]

If the lesson was not learned during and right after the war, it was continuously taught in ads and in the themes of TV sitcoms for a generation thereafter. A sales pitch made by Ozzie and Harriet Nelson on their sitcom in the mid-1950s was common: buy a Hotpoint dishwasher for the harried wife for Valentine's Day. Another ad from 1959 showed perhaps a plausible scene. A dad out for a drive with his family, seeing that the car door won't close, drops in at a Chevy showroom and dazzles the wife and kids as he cavalierly buys a new car on the spot and they happily drive off. For decades men had been told: prove your responsibility and provider's role with life insurance to make sure (even if you aren't there) that your kids can "go far" in life. A new twist from Farmer's Insurance came in 1965: quit smoking so that you'll live longer and see that boy you're playing football with today grow up. In many subtle and obvious ways, men were told their role in the new consumer economy was quite simply to provide and to enjoy it.[27] Few would miss the Federal Housing Administration's appeal in 1959 to the male's duty to buy a home: "As President Dwight Eisenhower said recently, except for a wedding ring there is no more valuable purchase that any man can make than a home. . . . You have taken on new responsibilities and obligations. As a property owner you have a new standing in the community."[28]

Remembering Andy Hardy

In ways the ads on the TV sets of World War II vets were truer to life that the programs. The bachelor Marshal Dillon certainly didn't have much to say about the real workaday world of the 1950s family man and had nothing to do with the provider's role seen in the ads that often paid for his show. Of course, for men of the 1950s Dillon's persona may have been wish fulfillment or nostalgia for those "carefree days" before they were tied down. Even this most domesticated of generations still looked for their heroes beyond the family. But no one was deluded. They knew that the grown-up man, as Barbara Ehrenreich showed in *Hearts of Men*, was supposed to be a provider, and that meant being a dad, not a heroic loner.[29]

So of course there were a lot of stories about men in fatherlike roles that I saw as a child, even though many of these were old movies from the 1930s seen on TV. I was touched by watching Spencer Tracy in *Captains Courageous* (1937) on the tube, playing Manuel the fisherman, who makes a spoiled brat into a caring person. Tracy also assumed the role of Father Flanagan in *Boys Town* (1938), transforming the street-tough boy with the right blend of love and expectation. I was particularly struck by the famous "Andy Hardy" movies. There were fourteen in the series from 1938 to 1946, winning a special Oscar for "representing the American Way of Life" in 1943.

I don't know how many "Andy Hardys" I saw on TV. They were all about the same, really, anticipating the sitcoms of the 1950s. I recall especially those extraordinary exchanges between Mickey Rooney, who plays the exuberant if often naïve teenager Andy, and Lewis Stone in the role of his father, a white-haired local judge. In the picket-fenced small town of Carvel, Andy's success in puppy love and occasional triumphs as a "big man on campus" at the prom is dwarfed by his laughable if loveable antics. Shorter than both his father and even his on-again-off-again girl friend Polly Benedict, Rooney looks the boy perpetually trying to be a man. Over and over, his bluster is betrayed by his awkwardness, naïveté, and inexperience. In the end, he is obliged to seek his father's gentle but wizened counsel.[30]

In *Love Finds Andy Hardy*, he pines for an "older woman" he met as a freshman at college, who instead of responding to his infatuation gets engaged to a successful thirty-six-year-old man. Andy decides not to go back to college and instead wants to "make good" in a business venture to prove his mettle to the girl. As happened in virtually every film in the series, his father (often at the request of his mother) has a man-to-man talk with Andy. The Judge recalls how he wanted to run away to South America when he was young but realized, "There is no short cut for success." In *Andy Meets the Debutante*, a seventeen-year-old Andy falls for magazine celebrity Daphne Fowler and goes to New York City to meet her. His father admits that he "understands" Andy's interest in "Cleopatra" but warns him that she brought disaster to "Mark Anthony." In another version of the trip to New York (*Life Begins for Andy Hardy*), Andy decides to defer going to college and try his luck at getting a job. He tells his dad that he doesn't want to spend ten years studying so he can follow his dad into law and instead "wants to be retired by middle age." His understanding, if worried parents let him test the waters and watch him as he drives off for the big city, yelling, "I'm never going to make any more mistakes." Of course, he has trouble finding a job and lands in the clutches of a manipulative older woman at the office where he finally gets work as an office boy. Inevitably, the Judge offers still another lecture—this time about the need to stay away from premarital affairs and the "habits" that they bring. Still, he lets Andy carry on, but when the "older woman" calls his dad "holier than thou," Andy defends the old man and discovers that she is a gold digger. Of course, in the end, Andy returns to Carvel, ready for still another lesson in growing up.

Watching these corny old movies again made me think about whether there are modern equivalents of these father and son roles. There were few obvious candidates. The recent trend has been the portrayal of men who fear growing up to be "judges." Recall Hugh Grant's portrayal in *Nine Months* (1995) of the self-centered boyfriend who is so fearful of losing his freedom and youth in fatherhood that he breaks up with his pregnant live-in girlfriend. Only when he discovers that the baby will give him his fading youth back does he change his mind, give up his Porsche, buy a family car, and marry the mother of his child. Another theme is fathers who are obsessed with pleasing their offspring (*Jingle All the Way* of 1996 and *Mrs. Doubtfire* of 1994, for example). Still other films feature fathers who are "brought up" by their children. In *Jack the Bear* (1993), Danny DeVito, the single dad who plays the host on a horror movie program on local TV competes with his nine-year-old son Jack for the attention of the neighborhood kids. When they come over to Jack's house they ask, "Can your dad come out and play?" Only when a real horror show invades his home in the form of a deranged neighbor intent on killing his son does the dad begin to grow up. Even more extreme is *Big Daddy* (2000). Adam Sandler plays the thirty-two-year-old Sonny Koufax, a lawyer who lives off a $200,000 lawsuit and works one day a week at a New York tunnel tollbooth. Only after his dissolute life is shattered when his live-in girlfriend moves out does Sonny make the slightest gesture at growing up. He tries to win her back by "adopting" a five-year-old boy (the son of a friend who unexpectedly arrives on the scene). Even though the film has the expected ending when Sonny accepts responsibility and raises his own family, the story hangs on the comedy of Sonny's outrageous "fathering." This includes teaching the child to throw branches in the path of in-line skaters in Central Park and the two relieving themselves on a building wall. In the end, as Sonny realizes that the boy needs more than a boy-man to play with, he grows up through the child. Still, the schmaltzy resolution hardly overcomes the adolescent humor (a Sandler trademark) based on the proposition that a man can relate to a boy only by accentuating his own immaturity.

Of course, all of these modern stories of fatherhood are comedies, hardly to be taken as models of behavior. But we are supposed to be as sympathetic toward the leading characters as we were toward Andy. We are to root for them and feel empathy for their predicaments, even as we enjoy their dilemmas. We see them in ourselves. The critical difference today is that the joke is on the father and not the son. Today, the father has the unsettled role.

Another difference that struck me is that in the Hardy series the Judge looks and acts, well, like a judge, wizened, often kindly, but firm. He even looks old. Yet Lewis Stone was only fifty-eight when he opened the series in 1937; Steve Martin was already sixty when he played the father of twelve kids in the remake of *Cheaper by the Dozen* in 2005. Though both are grey, Martin plays an energetic football coach and had none of the Judge's bemused sobriety. In the "Hardy years," Americans were comfortable with (and even demanded) maturity; today they are (and do) not.

Both the old and new stories are ultimately about growing up. In this similarity lies the key difference. Whereas the Andy Hardy series is about the foibles and missteps of a teenage son hell-bent on becoming a man, our modern heroes are not sons of guiding fathers but much older, without dads, and much less certain about the virtues of maturity. In fact, they want to avoid it at almost all costs. Andy Hardy's future is certain; he may not marry Polly (that's OK, because that "love" is just child's play), but he will follow in his father's footsteps and become a lawyer and maybe even a judge. In Andy Hardy, the knowing smile of the Judge lets the viewers in on just how far his son has to go to see the world through a man's eyes. With the Judge's gentle advice, Andy learns that lesson, eventually admits his errors of youth, and so continues his march to maturity.

The guiding hand of the father is absent in our latter-day heroes, and so is the clarity about the ultimate triumph of the hero in responsible manhood. Instead, the dilemma (and humor) lies in the fact that these modern heroes are so poorly prepared for fatherhood. Alternatively, they resist the transition to adult responsibility, seek to win their children's love through obsessive gift-giving, or simply find it difficult to play the role of the grown-up in caring for the child. No Judge Hardys here, not even in the making!

Looking today at the Hardy movies, we are amused by their apparent naïveté or even dishonesty. We see immediately that Andy is an invention of adults, absurd in his innocence and obedience, even in the setting of late-1930s small-town America and the movie theater audiences of that era. Andy certainly reassured parents who saw their own offspring drift into a world of bobby socks and swing music and even gain freedom in the uncharted world of cheap old jalopies and high school dances. Andy's antics in his own innocent and charming world of cars and proms told fretful adults that their kids would turn out all right. Today, most parents would find that concern naïve or quaint and, even more, the portrayal of Andy's adventures as idealized and improbable. Since the 1950s, Americans (or at least Hollywood producers) have demanded greater "realism" in how the movies portray family life. Perhaps, the teens in *Rebel Without a Cause* (1955) were really more true to life. Probably fewer parents today really expect their offspring to be Andys, and I doubt that any teenage boy today would find Andy to be anything but ridiculous and utterly uncool. The old models of father and son have gone.

As "phony" as the Hardy series was, audiences in the 1930s saw the Judge as an ideal modern father. Even if exaggerated in his stature and steadiness, the Judge was not an old-fashioned patriarch, distant or self-centered. Rather, he was a "modern" reassuring presence, a father who knew the difference between little and big things. As important, Andy was the ideal son on his way to manhood. Despite Andy's bluster, he was not a rebel or smart-ass. Although he was more up-to-date than his dad in his know-how of cars and ham radios, he was still a boy fumbling his way into responsibility, a mature perspective, and a true and certain future. Today we have rebelled against *both* of these *idealized* roles without replacing them with new ideals, and this says a lot about why we have boy-men today.

To make sense of the appeal (and ultimate rejection) of the model of growing up in Andy and maturity in the Judge, we need to delve a bit deeper into their respective parts. Behind the assured but gentle façade, Judge Hardy was actually a role full of ambiguity and contradiction. The Judge certainly reflected the traditional authority of fathers, especially successful middle-class fathers, who took advantage of their accumulated wealth, a legacy of deference to male family heads, and access to law and public resources to make major decisions affecting their wives and children. But for over a century that authority had been in decline even while the financial power of fathers over the family may have increased. In the nineteenth century, many men abandoned the home-based family farm, store, or craft shop for salaried jobs in factories and offices, making the father's role primarily that of the breadwinner. As he left each morning, not to return for ten or more hours, wives and mothers became the effective heads of households in their nurturing and physical caring roles. Gone was hands-on fathering in everything from early child care and discipline to character building and job training of (especially) male offspring. Whatever parental roles were not assumed by women were taken over by public education, impersonal forms of child labor, and eventually youth organizations like the scouts. The historian Stephen Frank argues that fatherhood in the nineteenth century shifted from direct and daily male authority to a more institutional patriarchy, built on the father's near monopoly of household earnings. His need to play a formal, distant role was reinforced by the demands of the man's world of career-ladder climbing, hard-working self-control, and dark-suit-wearing sobriety (at least in the middle class). Sons learned how to become men less from the father in the home than by separating from parent and home in schools and sports, anticipating the public roles that they would play as adults. Men found comradeship, escape, and a confirmation of male superiority in a separate world of clubs, taverns, and, especially, fraternal organizations. This conformed, of course, with what the westerns taught both men and boys. A man's world was a world largely without women and families.[31]

To be sure, some middle-class Victorian fathers replaced their old day-to-day authority in the home with a new, more playful role as "daddy." When free from work at home, especially on rare holidays, these fathers enjoyed frolicking with their young children. This is an image that is romanticized in Dickens's image of Bob Cratchit and his family in *A Christmas Carol*. By cultivating a sentimental view of parenting, middle-class fathers could separate themselves from the working-class men who continued to send their offspring off to work at a tender age. Still, fathers inevitably became more distant from their families in the century before Judge Hardy.

In the years after World War II, Americans mostly treated this loss as natural, and even with bemusement. The longest running (nonmusical) Broadway play up to its time, *Life with Father*, was based on a memoir about a boy growing up in the New York City household of Clarence Day in the 1880s. It was made into a hit movie in 1947 with William Powell in the lead. The story celebrates a lost world of Victorian patriarchy, even as it recognizes signs of its inevitable decline. Audiences took delight in the elder Day's dated self-assurance. When the author/son of the memoir said he wanted to grow up to be a cowboy, his father simply said: "No I didn't. He said I might as well be a tramp." His provider's role gave him privileges (a well-cooked steak and the ability to force his boys to learn musical instruments while he was away, for example). Still, the mother and kids got around the father's wishes, and, despite a committed disdain for religion, he ultimately submits to being baptized on the demand of his wife.[32]

This was an appealing image of the patriarch in 1947, even if everyone knew Day's Victorian values were no more. They knew, too, that the provider's role had a tragic face. Willy Loman's failure in the play *Death of a Salesman* (1949) is the most obvious example of this. For years before, Americans had realized that the provider father was not an easy part to play, and everyone knew that the personal and direct authority of fathers had eroded. By the 1920s the role of the father was so undermined that sociologists and moralists (at this time often the same people) called for a renewal of the fatherly role. Ernest Mowrer, Ernest Burgess, and, after World War II, O. S. English led this charge. Few had hopes of "returning" to the preindustrial father (long hours away from home made this impossible). Still, these authorities admonished men to pay attention to their offspring. "Modern" men were to become male role models for sons to protect them from feminization by excessive mothering at home. As Freudian thought spread, psychologists insisted also that fathers serve as "love" objects to their daughters (to give them an ideal to look forward to in future marriage choices). According to these experts, modern fathers were to be pals to their children, at least, in the hope of understanding them and gaining their confidence. In playful settings, fathers could also pass down virtues that no longer were learned in milking cows or shoeing horses. "What better way," noted historian Robert Griswold, for children "to learn patience, control, courage, and humility than at the end of a fishing pole?"[33]

Samuel Drury, writing in 1930 to the "man who wants to be a better father," recognized that women, not men, are "the heaviest investor in the family concern." The dad had been relegated to the role of "chancellor of the exchequer, curator of grounds and buildings, or . . . big policeman." Yet, for Drury and his generation, the father still had to resemble figures like Judge Hardy. In a book devoted to bridging the gap between fathers and sons, he insisted that "the natural barriers that divide the generations will stand. They should, for they produce respect for middle life and the veneration for old age. A father is not getting close to his son by disregarding the facts of age or the prestige of parenthood." But, because the father no longer worked with or trained his son, he had a special need to get to know his boy's interests and aspirations in and through the child's own world of play and sport. The goal was not for the father to regress into a sharing of the joys of boyhood with his son, but to "use" play to teach "sportsmanship." The key for Drury was to understand that the child is important "not for what it is, or does, or thinks, but for what it may be, and achieve and decide tomorrow." And the father was to get the boy there.[34]

These ideals hardly changed the fact that fathers remained primarily providers, without the time or presence to shape their sons in the way that Drury advocated. And as families became increasingly dependent on the market for food and wedded to an escalating culture of consumption, with its cars, fashions, and plug-in appliances, the father had little choice but to spend long hours away from the home earning the money that made the consuming family possible. Thus, fathers, according to Griswold, became curious figures, "combination playmates and bankers" to the kids. Given the fact that they often had more time and even talent at serving the role of provider than the pal, it should be unsurprising that nine-year-old children favored mothers over fathers by 72 percent to 12 percent in a 1936 survey.[35] It seems that the Judge was admired, respected, but not loved in the way that Mrs. Hardy was.

All this puts Judge Hardy in a special light. What made him an attractive character was that he was a model, doing what was so difficult to do in real life. He portrayed a modern father who guided rather than dictated, who wondered at but still accepted the new. Most of all, his ability to understand his son's longings, balanced by a perspective from the past, gave him the tools to gently lead the impetuous Andy toward a responsible future.

At the same time as most Americans (especially the middle class) glorified the father in all his modern ambiguity, respectable society disdained the self-centered playboy bachelor. Even more, it mocked the incompetent and weak working-class father who could neither lead nor provide for his family. American popular culture has long ridiculed the bumbling father (contrasted with the savvy mother and children). Through comedy, the buffoon dad reaffirmed the moral superiority of the middle class and its familial ideal. George McManus's 1904 comic strip *The Newlyweds* paired a doting but incompetent father with an all-knowing and ever-tolerant mother who tried to raise a willful and somehow "wise" Baby Snookums. This was but the first in a long parade of bumbling dads featured in such comic strips as *Bringing up Father, The Nebbs, The Gumps*, and *Blondie*. They were followed on radio and TV with *Fibber McGee and Molly, The Life of Riley, The Flintstones*, and, more recently, *The Simpsons*. Often the dads are working-class or insecure ethnic strivers. A lot of these comic situations revolved around the blustering would-be patriarch who thinks he knows how to make a fortune (or diaper a baby) but makes a fool of himself instead. Tellingly, the father is inept in both the modern worlds of work and family and has yet to learn how to adapt to change. This is no surprise because middle-class culture has long identified the failure to be either a good provider or to adapt to modernity (including new family roles) with the working classes and their presumed inferiority. Even more, the bumbling dad breaks from the "norm" because he is really a child with the emotional, narcissistic, unrestrained characteristics of a boy. This means his family has to assume the responsibility of "bringing up Father." The so-called natural (i.e., middle-class) pattern was the opposite, fathers bringing up children in all of the ambiguity of that task. These exceptions emphatically prove the rule.[36]

If the Judge represented the mature male and father in the 1930s, Andy was part of a long tradition of plucky lads and sons on their way to responsible manhood. For decades before, American boys had read stories of youngsters rising from rags (or at least from jobs as office boys) to riches (beginning with Horatio Alger's *Ragged Dick* of 1867). By 1906, Edward Stratemeyer, Alger's protégé, mass-produced boys' books, offering tales of character-forming challenges to the ultimate goal of growing up. Stratemeyer's writers churned out the adventures of the Rover Boys (first appearing in 1899), the Bobbsey Twins (1903), Tom Swift (1910), the Hardy Boys (1927), and finally, almost as an afterthought, for girls the Nancy Drew mysteries (1930). His Tom Swift was a typical character in the genre: this unflappable teenager was the son of an inventor from upstate New York who followed his elder's path by exploring the modern world of technology and travel. Tom entranced his young readers with his detailed accounts of building and using motorcycles, motor boats, airships, televisions, and other new devices. He offered them the fantasy of freedom from the constraints and boredom of small-town family life and school. At the same time, his extraordinary adventures never led him too far or too long from home, parents, and preparation for future success. In fact, he grew up to be like his parents: Tom Swift married the girl next door and had a son, Tom Swift Jr., who continued the series into the 1960s.[37] Just as we would expect of Andy.

In the first half of the twentieth century, this goody-two-shoes ideal was reaffirmed in boy's magazines like the *Youth's Companion* and *St. Nicholas*. They featured stories about the world and the men, be they inventors, explorers, sports heroes, businessmen, or statesmen, who were changing and conquering the world.[38] George Bailey, the hero of *It's a Wonderful Life*, the perennial favorite Christmas film first released in 1947, would certainly have read these stories and magazines. He longed to escape Bedford Falls and become an engineer but instead agreed to take over his father's "broken down" building and loan company. He was a perfect Tom Swift.

Hero worship, adventure, and fascination with technology were part of the quest for manhood early in the twentieth century. The toy maker Albert C. Gilbert (1884–1961), inventor of the Erector Set in 1913, sold a heroic dream along with his playsets of metal strips bolted together to form miniature railroad and industrial equipment. Through his promotions of the erector and science sets, he offered boys a model of manly achievement as well as boyish adventure in stories about his own life. A Tom Swift in the flesh, Gilbert was both a descendant of a governor of the New Haven Colony and a child of the frontier (born in Oregon with part of his youth spent in Idaho). Gilbert was educated at Yale but he also was a champion pole-vaulter and an Olympian in 1908. While he earned a medical degree, instead of becoming a physician he manufactured magical tricks for boys. By 1913, he empowered boys with the promise of growing up while playing with his construction toys, chemistry sets, and electric trains.[39] Gilbert's "Books for Real Boys" were juvenile versions of the "how-to" articles that filled the pages of *Popular Science* and *Popular Mechanics*, which attracted adult males.[40] Again, this was George Bailey's boyhood dream of adventure and building bridges far away from Bedford Falls.

So powerful were these images that they could be the model even for the boyhood of disadvantage. In the same year as *Andy Hardy Finds Love*, Mickey Rooney appeared in *Boys Town* (1938) as Whitey Marsh, a fatherless teen street tough saved from a life of crime and prison by a substitute Judge Hardy, Father Flanagan. And if the stories of gang boys (the Dead End Kids and the Bowery Boys, e.g.) did not always have a savior father, these street urchins still found redemption when they had a "chance" to show their worth. Typical was the Dead End Kids title *Angels with Dirty Faces*. Redemption in maturity could come to all.

Fathers Knowing Best in 1950s–1960s TV

The amusing stories of the Judge's assuring counsel and Andy's clumsy efforts to be the big man on campus prefigured the "cuteness" of the 1950s TV situation comedy. Of course, sitcoms were not all about such themes, quite the opposite, especially in the early years of TV. In fact, the genre was first developed for radio in the comedy of errors *Amos and Andy* (1928). This popular program featured black men (played by whites) struggling to make a living with their rickety Fresh Air Taxi cabs and the often self-imposed predicaments of Amos, Andy, and their scheming friend, Kingfish. I saw the TV version (with black actors that lasted only briefly in the early 1950s) in reruns in the early 1960s. Although long noted for its racist stereotypes, the program's emphasis upon the bumbling male, marred by a childish lack of emotional self-control and an overwhelming self-centeredness, would shape other sitcoms featuring ethnic or working-class characters.[41] *The Life of Riley* (also a migrant from radio to TV) focused on Chester A. Riley, originally from Flatbush but after the war a well-paid assembly-line worker at an airplane factory near Los Angeles. He was the classic working-class guy, now a comfortable new suburbanite but limited by education and culture in coping with the modern demands of family. Each week Chester showed another way to screw up. He jumps to the false conclusion that his wife was having a nervous breakdown, meddles in his adult daughter's plans to buy a house, gets mixed up with crooks who offer him cheap gifts for friends back home while he is on vacation, and interferes with his son's goals by trying to get him on the high school football team. Regularly Chester is reduced to blurting out his trademark lament, "What a revoltin' development this is!" Chester succumbs over and over to his emotional immaturity and to the schemes of his coworker Gillis and neighbor Dudley. His wife, Peg, and his two children, Babs and Junior, are his long-suffering victims. Junior in high school is studious, athletic, cool, and collected and has plenty of opportunity to say "Oh, brother" when Chester messes up or makes a big deal out of nothing. Chester Riley and his son are mirror opposites of the Judge and Andy. In fact, that is the comedic point. The role reversal of the incompetent/immature father and capable/emotionally stable child is a not-too-subtle put-down of the working-class or ethnic man who proves, in both his parental inadequacies and his professional failures to be the inferior of the middle-class male WASP.[42]

Even the early middle-class sitcom *Trouble with Father*, which featured Stu Erwin as the principal of Hamilton High, usually revolved around the trouble Erwin gets himself and his family into (like his effort to make his own dishwasher to save money or his attempt to spice up the high school newspaper by ghostwriting a gossip column).[43] As in the well-known sitcom *The Honeymooners*, adult men were the butt of the joke. Of course, there was the popular *I Love Lucy* (1951–1957) as well as the nearly forgotten *Life with Elizabeth* (1952–1955) and the *George Burns and Gracie Allen Show* (1950–1958) that featured women in the fool's role. Gracie Allen's harebrained antics drove the Burns and Allen duo as George Burns stood aside from the action and gave bemused knowing comments. Neither theme contributed much to the "respect" of fathers or mothers, as many lamented at the time. But comedy in America mostly came from the antiauthoritarian traditions of the comic strip and vaudeville. Among the more popular stars of early TV shows was Milton Berle (on TV from 1948 to 1956), whose bawdy humor included cross-dressing. Similar, though somewhat less brash, were Sid Caesar, Jack Benny, and Jackie Gleason.[44]

Soon, however, a more family- and middle-class-friendly comedy would begin to push the bumbling father and ditsy wife (as well as bar-room humor) aside. A new kind of domestic sitcom emerged by the mid-1950s, shifting the joke from the adult to the child, cute if continually confused and in need of the bemused and gentle guidance of parents, especially the dad. We see the arrival of wholesome, middle-class scenes—white picket fences, column-framed front doors, small-town neighbors, and ideal families—in *The Adventures of Ozzie and Harriet, Father Knows Best, The Donna Reed Show,* and *Leave It to Beaver,* all appearing between 1952 and 1966. Ethnic humor, even in the loveable *Goldbergs,* which played on radio and TV between 1929 and 1956, became passé. In the 1950s, network executives believed that Americans wanted to see happy, wholesome suburbanites, what many took as their future, not their pasts. Even the urbane and sophisticated *New York Times* praised *Father Knows Best* in 1955 for "restoring parental prestige on TV."[45]

While the whole thing was a bit alien to me (being a part of the still unusual world of the single-parent family), I certainly watched these shows and found them not only entertaining but models of family life, especially of the good dad. Maybe they were escapist and unrealistic, showing fathers who never seemed to work or at least had more time to get involved with the family than most fathers actually had. Perhaps journalist David Halberstam's portrayal of *Ozzie and Harriet* as "living in a wonderfully antiseptic world of idealized homes in an idealized unflawed America" is fair. It is obvious that this show tried to ease anxious parents into accepting their teenagers' new world of rock, wild dancing, and longer hair. As their impish younger son Rick (referred to in the early 1950s as the "irrepressible" Ricky) gradually deepened his voice and grew tall and good-looking and interested in girls, he became suave and cool and yet always the respectful gentleman. He was certainly a good model for the grey suit or even the colorful blazer in the collegiate clothing ads in *Esquire.* In perhaps the best known episode of the program, aired in 1957, Rick's rock career is launched when he is allowed to sit in with the swing band at his parent's country club dance. After he sings his rock song, he happily joins his parents (who in real life had met in Ozzie's dance band in the early 1930s) in harmonizing on "My Gal Sal." In this brilliant piece of generational reconciliation, the mixed-aged TV audience learned that there was nothing to fear in the teens despite news of the racially and sexually charged singing of Elvis and Little Richard.[46]

But looking back, I wonder if these shows didn't offer more than escape and comfort to anxious Americans of the 1950s. First, listening to the early radio versions of *Father Knows Best* (aired from 1949 to

1953) and then watching the TV version (shown from 1954 to 1963), I was surprised by the differences. While the only actor that appeared in both versions, Robert Young, played the father, the fictional characters were the same: parents Jim and Margaret Anderson and the children, Betty, an older teen; Bud, about fifteen; and Kathy, the baby of about nine or ten. But the stories changed. In the earlier radio version, episodes certainly were built around some cute "dilemma" of one of the kids (Bud quitting school or clumsily attempting to date a girl or Betty's demanding to be treated as an adult or her infatuation with an over-aged crooner). Still, the radio version of Jim was often anything but the father who knew best. He tried some "clever" parenting tricks (like letting Bud "quit" school and work for him around the house or letting Betty dress as she pleased), but all these backfired. Frequently, he blustered about how when he was a child "we were told to respect our elders." Comedic scenes were made of his incompetence at fixing a clock.[47]

Yet, when the show went to TV, things changed. The stories were still built around the foibles and immaturity of the kids: Betty's overbearing confidence and snobbery, Bud's lack of direction and his wisecracks, and Kathy's anxieties about being the baby of the family, for example. But father really came to know best (most of the time). When Bud wants to buy an outboard boat motor instead of apply himself at school, Jim warns that by getting low grades "you're throwing away your future." He even teaches Bud why his sisters and mother want to reenact the wedding vows of Bud's parents. But his most common advice was for the kids to be themselves and that he and his wife should trust them. When Betty starts dating a "fast" boy, Jim says to a worried Margaret, "we can't keep her in a glass case." Even when the parents drag Betty to "State" to show her where they went (and presumably Betty should go) to college, Jim eventually sees that "something is very wrong." He lets his daughter make up her own mind about college when an old professor reads back to him an essay he wrote there twenty years earlier: "education should lead students down new paths." If father knew best, he seems to have learned it from progressive childrearing experts like Benjamin Spock, who insisted parents should trust their children and give them support and, where necessary, structure. Over and over, the kids solve their own problems: Betty learns not to project her needs on her baby sister when she is Kathy's summer camp counselor. And both Betty and Bud realize that they don't have to conform to the make-out culture even if they found it in romantic novels. Most of all, Jim doesn't have to lord over them, because the children were brought up with wonderful models in the mature love of their parents. As Jim watches Bud wait for the return of his lost homing pigeon, he and Margaret fret about Betty moving into an apartment before she is ready to leave home. While Jim reassures a worried Bud, he also tells Margaret that they must "gamble on [Betty's] common sense," "trust her," and wait for the return of both the pigeon and Betty. While issues of growing up and mutual understanding prevail, some episodes went beyond the home to acts of charity for those not blessed with the Anderson household. The family takes in a boy who, it turns out, is homeless and shows respect for an old, broken-down teacher by holding a "banquet" for him. Corny, yes, but doubtless also reassuring and even educational to the millions of families who watched it.[48] Jim Anderson was not the all-knowing patriarch. Instead, he was the model of a confident but also permissive parent whose maturity rather than childish insecurity or indifference allowed him to "trust" his kids.

The theme of the nurturing, permissive dad ran through the sitcoms of the late 1950s. On the *Donna Reed Show*, the husband Alex Stone was a pediatrician who worked out of the home. He had a very gentle touch (helping his daughter cope with her crush on rock star Buzz Berry or gently encouraging Donna to moderate her permissiveness with the kids after she gave a dogmatic speech to the PTA about trusting the child).[49] Ozzie Nelson made a career out of playing the role of the easy-going dad in the long-running *Adventures of Ozzie and Harriet*. He occasionally slips into nostalgia for the good old days or complains about the loss of patriarchal authority in the home but soon shrugs this off. As historian James Gilbert notes, Ozzie offered the World War II generation a model for coping with the new world of child-focused families and assertive wives (at least in the home). Ozzie is helped in this task by a relaxed and indulgent wife and amazingly "normal" sons, David and Rick. When Ozzie thinks that David is going to elope with a girl, he backs down and says, "It will probably all turn out for the best," as it, of course, does when the parents find out that it was all a misunderstanding. It is amazing that this show lasted on TV from 1952 to 1966. It was slow paced, uneventful, and predictable. But the secret of its success was its seeming banality. When kids were young, they were cute; as they grew up, their problems were not so bad; and most of all, parents, especially dads, did best when they adjusted to their loss of authority and importance in the whole process.[50]

A slight variation was *My Three Sons*, built around the mild-mannered engineer and widower Steve Douglas, played by the aging movie star Fred MacMurray. His three sons (ranging from cute kid, Chip, to the middle child, Robbie, and the cool teen, Mike) were cared for by a mother substitute, a grandfatherly cook. He was brash, traditional, and hostile, for example, to sex education, but oddly maternal and protective, especially when a woman entered the house and threatened his domestic authority. The first cook, Bud, played by William Frawley (1960–1964), and then the former sailor Charlie, played by William Demarest (1965–1972), with their gruff ways and emotional responses to crises, are oddly reminiscent of the western sidekicks like Gabby Hayes. Their function was comic relief, of course, but they also served as a foil to the calm father figure. Steve Douglas intervened only to gently serve as the conscience of the boys, reminding Mike, for example, "you just gave your word" to sing for Charlie in one episode, or to mediate conflicts between the boys, with the observation that life is an "endless series of slight adjustments."[51] As with the other sitcom dads, Steve was the model of the calm, tolerant, but self-assured grown-up.

Not all fathers in fantasy or fact coped so well. Certainly Riley didn't, but he was invented before this became popular or required. Another exception was Danny Thomas on *Make Room for Daddy* (1953–1965) who played a Lebanese nightclub performer living in a New York apartment with his wife and three kids (Terry, Rusty, and Linda). This scenario certainly didn't fit the suburban/small-town mold of the Andersons, but Danny's family problems were similar. Still, Danny wasn't a permissive dad, and that was half the comedy of the show. He lost control, and that got him into trouble. In one episode, Danny gets rid of a boy interested in his teenage daughter Terry only to "drive" her into an infatuation with his colleague, the obviously much older Dean Martin. Yet behind his gruffness and traditionalism was commonsense parenting. He yells at Terry when she begins to hang out with an urbane friend, "a Junior League Vampire," as he called her, and when Terry starts wearing tight dresses and going to restaurants with her friend. Yet, despite the fact that Danny wants to keep his daughter like a "kangaroo in the pouch," it turns out that the worldly girl with the permissive jet-setting parents really longs for the protection and love of a family like Danny's. In the end,

Danny's way was the right way. In another episode, after Danny tries to give up his yelling and controlling ways (on advice from his doctor), his family wants the old Danny back because that is who he is and how he loves them. Perhaps life with "Daddy" would be simpler and easier if Danny was a modern father, but he is caring in his own way, and that is all that matters.[52]

Of course, not all the sitcoms of the 1950s were about families and the perils and promises of parenting. *The Bob Cummings Show*, featuring a bachelor photographer in his thirties, was about the "wolf," who used his job to chase pretty women. Although there is a lot of sexual innuendo with talk of "built" girls and "it's what's up front that counts," compared to the grossness of contemporary sitcoms like *Two and a Half Men*, *Bob Cummings* was pretty mild. Most interesting, the joke was frequently Bob's frustration at getting the girl rather than a mockery of the family man. And Bob shows care for the upbringing of his teenage nephew, with whom he shares a house, along with his widowed sister, who is always trying to get Bob to "settle down." Of course, while Bob loves his home life with his sister (and opposes selling the house in one episode), he just can't give up his freedom even when that freedom is often his worst enemy. As in a lot of comedy, Cummings was the exception that proved the rule. He represents the decadence of the Los Angeles playboy that confirms the virtue of the middle-American father.[53]

The key to good fathering, however, was not just being a calm and supportive presence but recognizing the needs and "stages" of the child's growing up. That theme ran through all the family sitcoms: from Kathy's childish preoccupations and Betty's obsessions with status and boys in *Father Knows Best* to Rusty's resistance to playing with his little sister and anxiety about becoming the quarterback on the football team in *Make Room for Daddy*, the joke often took the form of a bemused tolerance for immaturity, recognizing it for what it was. These shows were "cute," and, while this appealed especially to women, there was also a link between the cute child and the model father.

Certainly the best example of this was *Dennis the Menace* (first appearing in 1951 as a comic strip). Dennis was the culmination of decades of evolution in the image of the impish boy as the naughty, even malicious child, becomes progressively the innocent but curious "cutie." The *Katzenjammer Kids* (appearing at the beginning of comic strips in 1897) featured two boys who tormented adults (Mama, the Captain, and the school Inspector) with pranks. Although the adults sometimes got even and often thrashed the boys, the Kids never learned any lesson, and the war between the generations just went on week by week. While part of an antiauthoritarian, even anarchic tradition of popular comedy, this was still a pretty rough way of seeing kids and, to accommodate more middle-class tastes, successful cartoonists gradually toned it down. In *Buster Brown*, a hit comic strip figure in 1902, a mischievous lad tormented his dog and played tricks on his mother and others, which usually led to a spanking. But unlike the Katzenjammer Kids, Buster ended most strips with a little speech usually admitting the errors of his ways. For the early twentieth century, he was the very image of the "cute" boy. Others followed, such as *Skippy*, a popular comic strip by Percy Crosby that appeared between 1926 and 1945. Although he used his slingshot on other boys in the library, Skippy lacked the Katzenjammer Kids' nastiness and tried to be good, even though like all real boys he failed much of the time. And he isn't punished. H. A. Rey's storybook figure, *Curious George* (1940) completes the transition. George, a monkey, is really a boy, and the Man in the Yellow Hat is really his father, as every four-year-old for more than a half century instinctively knew when read Curious George stories before bedtime. There is not a hint of malice in the erring George. He is merely "curious" when he gets into trouble by releasing animals at the circus, for example. All this makes him "cute." And, as important, the "father" is no longer judgmental.[54]

Hank Ketcham's *Dennis the Menace* of a decade later is merely the culmination of this trend. Dennis is never punished because he really isn't at fault. All the trouble he gets into results from his natural curiosity, imagination, and, especially, unconscious honesty. Often it is only the adult's fussiness (as in the encounters with the neighbor, the overwrought Mr. Wilson) that gets him into trouble. In the TV version (1959–1963), Dennis is forever upsetting domestic tranquility as, for example, when he "helps" Mr. Wilson wash his dog and accidentally squirts him with a garden hose. Dennis, of course, is entirely innocent. He is only being a "boy" when he refuses to play with Margaret because he knows that she "can't play catch" and complains that "before you know it, we're playing house." Dennis doesn't understand the often absurd and fussy ways of adulthood and innocently wreaks havoc when he gives the neighborhood spinster a valentine that she thinks came from a confirmed bachelor, setting off a predictable comedy of errors. Moreover, because of his naïveté, he can speak the truth that adults cannot say. While his dad shares his son's dislike for liver, Dennis will speak his mind when his dad can't. There is a curious bonding between dad and Dennis in sharing boyish likes and dislikes that adds to the cuteness of the series.[55] The war between generations is reduced to the adults' bemused tolerance of the spunky child, fumbling through growing up, but also sometimes wise or at least honest in his naïveté.

Surely the crown jewel of the family sitcom is *Leave It to Beaver* (1959–1963). The father, Ward Cleaver, is the epitome of the modern dad: he is understanding and wary of following in the harsh and un-feeling footsteps of his own father, forever calling to mind the stresses (and pleasures) of his own youth and willing to see the world from his sons' viewpoint. Naturally, Ward and his wife June are frequently be-mused by the antics and anxieties of their boys, Wally and the young Beaver. The joke is forever on the child, learning by trial and error the ways of growing up. Despite his sometimes stern "man to man" talks with Beaver in his book-lined study because of some transgression, the only real sin is when Beaver doesn't tell the truth. Far from being traditional and patriarchal, these fathers who "knew best" were really permissive and progressive, tolerant bemused guides of children who would doubtless find their way.[56]

1950s Fathers in Confusion

My generation later rejected and mocked these stories, but I see now that often behind the all-too-perfect families and sometimes corny moralisms were attempts to grapple with some of the real issues of the era. These 1950s stories tell us that what Americans expected from the "perfect" dad and the well-raised child had changed between the Hardys and Dennis the Menace. The Judge was certainly quicker with advice and Andy was faster to take it than was true even with the "pa-triarchal" Jim Anderson and the good boy Bud. Probably Dennis's dad in the 1960s would have been more permissive than the Judge in cop-ing with a teenage Dennis (who doubtless would have been more cool than goody-two-shoes). More important, however, even if in the 1950s fathers still knew best and sons recognized this fact (at least on TV), there was already confusion, and that showed up in the sitcoms. The World War II generation of young men faced a new dilemma. They had to cope with both the continued erosion of patriarchal authority and the new expectation that they become playmates to their children. This was reflected in the family sitcom. Its images of manhood and good fathering were not merely models of behavior but, through their comedy and pathos, provided solace and therapy to men who faced the difficulties of living up to these confusing standards.

Both fathers and sons had become problematic. The "problem" of the father was certainly not new to the postwar years, but it became much more prominent because of the father's absence during the war. Again and again, popular magazines and childrearing experts asked how children would adapt to the disappearance of the father's discipline and role modeling. Of even more concern was how children (and mothers) would react to his return. Fathers were warned to expect young children to be distant at first. A children's picture book addressed this problem by encouraging the youngster to prepare elaborately for dad's return. And fathers were told to expect a long adjustment to living again with the stresses of family life. As Benjamin Spock observed, "the poor father is the complete outsider . . . feeling useless and miserable" in the festival of baby birthing after the war.[57]

The postwar years seemed to pose special problems for fathers. Observers expected a boom of births as couples renewed their affections and made up for lost time in filling long-empty or half-filled nests. Indeed, in 1946, 2.2 million couples married, a record for thirty-three years, and 3.4 million babies were born, a fifth more than in 1945, the last year of the war. Psychologists and educators hoped that a renewal of family life that had been long neglected during the war and the Depression would launch a modern and presumably better society in which fathers (as well as mothers) learned how to be better parents, rearing better "adjusted" children. Still others looked to "restore" the authority of the male provider after the traumas of the previous twenty years. The underlying question shared by many was, what roles would men play in this new and expanded world of parenting? All this heightened an abiding anxiety that fathers had been edged out of the childrearing enterprise. Since at least the 1920s, manuals and magazines devoted to child rearing had become holy Scripture to many American mothers. The physicians and psychologists who wrote them quite consciously encouraged mothers to become their agents in the home, sometimes driving a wedge between husband and wife in the process. Not surprisingly, as the popular press noted, some men felt that the smothering mother left the father with "no effective emotional authority" in the home, and this led to "child centered anarchy" which allowed the young to "grow up in an envelope of mush."[58]

The overprotective mother was a threat to the well-being of the child (a theory reinforced with the popularity of the Freudian oedipal complex at the time). The only solution was to get the dad back into the game of child rearing. But how? He was seldom at home, and when he was, what relevance did he have? All of his traditional roles had been taken away, or so it seemed. The only thing left was something relatively new: play and spending. Father-child leisure activities substituted for the bonding and educational function of work and job training, while consumption gave fathers status and affection as providers of wonder and happiness to children. As Robert Griswold notes, postwar fathers also adapted to a more playful form of child rearing (especially with the very young) to "fill the void" of dull and frustrating jobs and marriages. Fatherhood increasingly became a form of recreation rather than work. It isn't surprising then that in a 1957 survey, 63 percent of fathers were positive about parenting as compared to only 54 percent of often overworked mothers.[59]

Still, the leap from the "serious" role of fathers on the job to their "unimportant" role in a home of children troubled many, and not only the traditionalists. Frank Gilbreth Jr.'s remembrance of his 1920s upbringing by his father, a famous efficiency manager (recalled in the 1948 book and later film *Cheaper by the Dozen*), was an attempt to bridge the gap. This self-confident father of twelve brought home his expertise in industrial efficiency: "it was just about impossible to tell where his scientific management company ended and his family life began." Indeed, he viewed his home and family as a laboratory to try out new ideas, keeping his children on their toes, forcing them to learn Esperanto and Morse code during vacations, and using meals to teach manners. Still, he shared "recreation" with his children, enjoyed their skits (even when they poked fun at him), and willingly accepted the democracy of family councils. Although enchanting and amusing to many, the Gilbreth approach was, to say the least, an improbable model. It was hardly adaptable to the postwar family. Gilbreth was too much the authoritarian, and he would have had nothing but scorn for those "expressive values"—advanced by the new child psychologists—that were supposed to make children autonomous and creative. His idea of transferring the engineer's values to the home

was entirely out of tune with the nurturing, playful domestic environment that postwar Americans expected.[60]

This curious nostalgia for an earlier mode of fathering pointed
to a much larger problem—the ambiguity and confusion about what
fathers were to do in the postwar home and, even more, about what
it meant to grow up male. The common but confusing alternative to
Gilbreth's eccentric tradition was permissive parenting, inviting the
father to play the pal. *Parents' Magazine* in 1945 told fathers to make
themselves "acceptable" to their offspring. To win their hearts, you
must "keep yourself huggable" and be kind and gentle if you expect
your children to be also. "Be the one to think up the nice things to do."
Don't yell at your son in front of "his gang"; instead, treat him with
the "respect" bestowed on a "business associate" to foster "comradeship." *Hygeia* asked fathers not to toughen up their boys and instead
let them set the agenda for play and warned that love and respect for
the modern father came not from his asserting authority but from his
"pleasurable contacts with his children."[61]

In an article published in 1950 called "Pals Forever," *Parents'
Magazine* recalls how a father made his six-year-old son into a "good
friend and companion" by joining the YMCA's Father and Son Indian
Guides (started in 1925), which organized dads and boys into "Indian" tribes. The father was Black Hawk and the son Grey Hawk (like
the father and son suits). Decisions to take hikes or go to ball games
were made by equal vote of parents and kids. Fathers, the article con-
cludes, should not wait until their boys were adults to relate to them.
Instead, fathers had to get down to their level to establish a relationship early or not expect one at all. All this could be seen as instru-
mental, as it often was—an alternative way of establishing parental
authority through playful father-child bonding. Yet, Marion Faegre's
manual *Children Are Our Teachers* of 1953 insisted that we should understand our children as "a source of enrichment and knowledge,"
not, as claimed by Samuel Drury in 1930, merely potential adults.[62]

Making dad into a "pal" was part of a broader progressive agenda
based on parental "teamwork." No longer were mothers to turn fathers into bogeymen who could be used to threaten the kids with
punishment ("wait until your father comes home"), but both were
to adapt similar disciplinary styles. The family was to be a "cooperative democracy" where both parents would share physical care,
discipline, the planning of recreation and education, and management of the household budget. Faegre's childrearing manual offered

advice, perspective, and workshop activities to help prepare parents for their modern roles. Employing the latest trends in psychology, Faegre stressed that couples needed to be aware of their own values and expectations from their family backgrounds (advice Ward Cleaver surely took). They should discard dysfunctional behaviors, be conscious of and adapt to their children's personalities and play patterns, and find ways to reduce family stresses with skillful planning and assigning all family members appropriate responsibilities. These were thoughtful but time-consuming techniques, and they obviously required both parents.[63]

This is one reason women's magazines admonished husbands and fathers to abandon the old attitude that men and domesticity did not mix. No longer were men expected to slip away as did Jiggs in the comic strip *Bringing Up Father* to drink and play cards with his old pals nor to think of household chores as "beneath them." Rather, in the mid-1950s, a *McCall's* article insisted that the modern man "putters around the house" fixing and improving furnishings and even reads to, bathes, and dresses the kids.[64]

Certainly, much of this was wishful thinking. Still, there was a subtle change in how men were to be mature and act as fathers. An older view of maturity as rational, self-controlled, and ever willing to sacrifice for the group gave way in the 1950s to the notion of being "independent and liking it" and of being flexible and able to compromise and recognizing the uniqueness of others. This meant not a rigid list of mature character traits but, according to a 1962 *McCall's* article, a certain willingness to accept one's own and others' frailties and to embrace the child within from time to time. The goal was no longer to be a hero but a "man of all seasons."[65]

Of course, not everyone embraced this image of the easy-going dad or this model of maturity. Given the context of the conservative 1950s, that image is surprisingly progressive. Inevitably, a backlash came even as the permissive revolution was being launched. As early as 1950, the childrearing authority O. Spurgeon English complained that "permissive methods" of childrearing "have encouraged many parents to allow their children to get out of hand and become nuisances in the home, as well as outside of it." He went so far as to say that it was better occasionally to spank the young child rather than to lecture or engage in a long battle of wills. Another writer worried that "if we give them a get-something-for-nothing philosophy by granting their every wish, we may end up with boys and girls who won't grow up." Another fretted that fathers who appeared weak and indulgent would reap rebellion and crime in their boys. According to the popular belief of the time, these dads "made" homosexual sons.[66]

More important, in 1954, scarcely eight years after his first "permissive" edition of *Baby and Child Care* appeared, Benjamin Spock was already suggesting a reversal of the "over permissiveness trend." He warned against the "tyrannical character" of eight-month-old babies who never sleep and affirmed the right of parents to expect "politeness and cooperation" from their older children. In 1959, the often-cited anthropologist Margaret Mead observed that postwar parents may have rebelled against their own authoritarian upbringing and even "secretly encouraged naughtiness," but that was a brief phase and now parents were looking for a more sensible happy medium.[67] Cultural conservatives like the Catholic Hilda Graef complained in 1960 that "fathers no longer dared to forbid their sons anything for fear they would develop Oedipus complexes." The role of the parent and especially the father, she claimed, was not to encourage independence, flexibility, and tolerance in children but to engage them in a "constant struggle against self desires" and to resist "commercial entertainment that plays on the instincts." Growing up was about controlling the passions, and that meant fathers needed to exercise "firm, but kind, insistence on what is good for" the child.[68]

These contradictory exchanges among the experts (that straddled both the left and right) surely must have confused parents, especially fathers. What were they to think when they read in the *New York Times Magazine* (1955) that the "democratic father" often became angry at his disorderly children, but, instead of enforcing discipline, he withdrew from child rearing and turned it over to the smothering mother, producing the "neurotic child from a happy (permissive) home." So was he to "lower the boom" after he had been told to be a pal for years? How was he to respond to the experts who chided fathers for taking the pal role too seriously by invading their children's space? A 1959 article in *Life* insisted that dads "act their age" in play and generally not take over their children's play and fantasy worlds. The pal dad was a complex, deeply confusing role.[69]

The pal dad was an answer to the reduced role of the father in modern life, but did even the experts believe in it? After all, across the childrearing bookshelves they all offered quite traditional advice. From English and Sidonie Gruenberg in the early 1950s to Bruno Bettelheim (1956), T. Berry Brazelton (1971) and Spock (1974), they insisted that fathers be models for their children but also that this did not take a lot of time or emotional involvement. Bettelheim claimed that fathers should not be measured by their skills as bottle feeders and diaper changers. Their main role was to "represent the world" to children and to embody "responsibility" and the male's contribution to society. He went so far as to say, "Fulfillment of manhood is not achieved through fatherhood," but in becoming a father, the man represents his role as a contributor to the next generation by exuding a "quiet confidence." Not exactly the pal dad. Spock may not be so old-fashioned in tone, but he, too, claimed that simply being there was enough, that the "boy does 9/10 of the work" in his natural tendency to imitate his father.[70] A *Good Housekeeping* piece stressed that the dad should be mostly a "Fix-it Man." Over and over, quality time and simply being there was stressed so that children would not become "one-sided."[71]

In the face of all of this contradictory advice, what was a father to think? The real situation of men, especially as fathers, was ambiguous and confusing enough. And the demands of work and career certainly cut into their playing new roles as fathers. Despite all the strong images of the mature man in the movies, on TV, and in the messages of advertising, they were, after all, merely ideals, models that were hard to live up to. No wonder men fled to the westerns. These fantasies offered freedom from the "mush" of fathering, and they gave men something to share with their boys (if not necessarily their daughters). No surprise that the sitcoms were also popular. These TV shows not only reflected the ideology of the pal dad but helped him to cope with its ambiguities with humor. Still, no matter how appealing the image of the grown-up, no matter the prestige of the provider in the postwar economic boom that made even goofballs like Chester A. Riley tolerable to his family, fathers clearly did not know best. And at least some men understood this and rebelled.

chapter 2.

Living FAST,
(Sometimes) DYING Young

Despite all the images of men that I saw while growing up, many of my father's generation could not measure up. They could not cope with the ambiguities of modern maturity and fatherhood or simply rejected their virtues. My father's story of multiple marriages and adventure was certainly rare in my world. Ours was the only mother-led family on our middle-class block in the "provincial" town of Spokane, Washington. We were the bohemians (helped by the fact that my mother was an art teacher and painted abstract pictures), and the neighbors felt sorry for us. We had two fellow art teachers over for holiday dinners. They were the Two Kens to us kids though later I learned that they were gay partners. It was natural for our neighbors to find our family odd. Divorce rates actually dropped in the 1950s from 3.5 per thousand marriages in 1945 to 2.1 in 1958 (though they were higher than in the 1930s or ever before). Men married young, as early as a median age of 22.5 years in 1956. It seemed that almost every man bought into the provider's role—few sought to prolong their independence or the playful self-indulgence of the teenager. Yet there were rebels lurking in the shadows of suburbia.

We see glimpses of that rebellion on the screen. Alongside all those movies with happy-family endings, such as *The Best Years of Our Lives, Father of the Bride*, or *Mr. Blandings Builds His Dream House*, were some very different productions. Film noir movies (including *Detour, Dead on Arrival, Dark Passage*, and *Double Indemnity*) offered images of men with dark, uncertain passions facing unpredictable or hostile worlds. Set not in America's Pleasantvilles but in the tough neighborhoods of cities or along lonely highways were stories about grifters, con men, or just nobodies on the road, and few were redeemed in the course of the story. Film noir, with sources in the hard-boiled detective novels and magazines of the 1920s and 1930s, offered a cynical view of human nature. Not only neurotic gangsters (like James Cagney's mother-obsessed psychopathic character in *White Heat* of 1949) but also morally muddled cops (as in *The Asphalt Jungle*) took center stage. Here was the underworld of urban crime, violence, madness, but also a place of middle-class deception (like the murderous duo of an insurance salesman and a businessman's wife in *Double Indemnity*). Drawing on stories of hard-boiled detectives by Dashiell Hammett, Raymond Chandler, James Cain, and Cornell Woolrich, film noir rejected the whodunit tradition of the cool and rational Sherlock Holmes and Charlie Chan so common in 1930s movies.[1]

In *The Maltese Falcon* (based on Hammett's book), Sam Spade, according to writer John Leland, "was his own invention, . . . unmarried, childless and motherless. He cowed neither to women nor to work."[2] Another theme was returning vets who did not adjust psychologically to life back home (victims of amnesia and homelessness, for example) or even who refused to return to their roots, preferring army buddies or even drifting from town to town (*Crossfire*). Many were stories of men who even when they wanted to come home found their families destroyed or themselves unwanted (*The Big Heat* or *The Blue Dahlia*). In the film noir, the war was not the backdrop to a glorious return to domesticity and responsibility but a haunting memory of a violent past that would not go away, reappearing in the psyches or on the mean streets of American cities. Unlike *The Best Years of Our Lives*, film noir men did not return to the embrace of a loving woman but to a castrating wife or to a loneliness that made the hero susceptible to sexual manipulation by the femme fatal (as in *The Woman in the Window*, *The Postman Always Rings Twice*, or *Scarlet Street*).[3]

Film noir was the relatively respectable face of the dark side of postwar American culture (slipping by the censors at the motion-picture industry's Hays Office). Other forms of it were not on the marquees of Main Street but in pulp magazines sold from obscure corners of city newsstands or in plain-paper-wrapped parcels. Crime writers like Jim Thompson and Charles Willeford churned out violent tough-guy thrillers. Scandal rags like *Confidential* spilled the dirt on celebrities, outing Liberace in 1957, for example. "Nudie-cutie" magazines featured Mamie Van Doren and Jayne Mansfield. The now cult figure of Bettie Page, with her trademark girl-next-door pout, shapely body, and black bangs made a brief career (1950 through 1957) out of posing in varying states of undress for "camera clubs" and appearing in whimsical sado-masochistic photospreads that caught the eye and ire of congressional investigators in 1955. While anyone who really wanted this stuff could find it, it was in the shadows just as gambling was confined to Nevada and the dark corners of American cities, not on the Internet and in suburban shopping malls as it is today.[4]

Of course, no one should be surprised that the America that flocked to see Spencer Tracy play the upper-middle-class *Father of the Bride* would also be a market for sleaze and cynicism. How many returning veterans could afford to fuss about an expensive wedding and, more to the point, how many identified with bourgeois respectability rather than the out-of-place loner? Nor should we be shocked that the dark side would appeal only to a minority. In fact, postwar Americans (presumably of all classes) preferred musical biopics about the vaudeville star Al Jolson, biblical epics (*Samson and Delilah*), and sentimental or comedic musicals (*The Bells of St Mary's* and *Road to Utopia*). These films were among the twenty most popular in the years 1946 through 1950. Others included historical melodramas (*Forever Amber* and *Unconquered*), along with profamily stories (*The Egg and Me, Life with Father*, and, leading them all, *The Best Years of our Lives*). *The Postman Always Rings Twice* earned barely one-third as much as *Best Years* (3.9 to 11.5 million dollars).[5] Americans certainly wanted to "return" to those days where endings were happy and where paths to maturity were clear and fathers ruled with bemused benevolence.

So then is there any reason to take seriously these signs of rebellion? More to the point, was there really a crisis of masculinity or a rejection of conventional maturity? The historian James Gilbert had a point when he argued that this undercurrent of violent, even misogynist culture was marginal and that despite men's anxieties about change—from a loss of virile self-mastery in "other-directed corporate America" to their "displacement" in the family—much of this macho stuff was merely fantasy. Gilbert shows that there were many styles and attitudes of mature masculinity from which to chose in the 1950s: from Billy Graham's emotionally intense, born-again Christianity to the sophisticated hedonism of Hugh Heffner's culture maven

Auguste Spectorsky, and even Ozzie Nelson's quizzical adjustment to the new domesticity. All of these were, as Gilbert notes, "men in the middle," neither fathers who knew best nor cynical dropouts.[6]

Still, undercurrents of rebellion kept welling up in postwar America, shaping a counterculture that continues to have an impact today. Returning veterans, though publicly feted, were still seen as a source of disruption. *Time* magazine warned of a coming crime wave, and psychologists and others feared that soldiers still in their teens had established a child-mother relationship with their officers and would find it difficult to adjust to roles as fathers and husbands in civilian life.[7]

If, to some, returning soldiers were barbarian boys, the larger question was how they would adjust to a home life dominated by women. Here we see one of the most extraordinary themes of postwar male rebellion, expressed forcefully and absurdly by Philip Wylie's attack on "Momism," published first in 1942. At a time when men by the millions were away from and longed to return to their wives, girlfriends, and mothers, Wylie issued a blistering attack on women, especially the alluring beauty that became the domineering wife and mother. "The pretty girl . . . blindfolded her man so he would not see that she was turning from a butterfly into a caterpillar. She told him, too, that although caterpillars ate every demanded leaf in sight, they were moms, hence sacred . . . thus the women of America raped the men, not sexually, unfortunately, but morally, since neuters come hard by morals." Like in the cartoons in *Esquire* and even the *Saturday Evening Post*, Wylie mocked the mom "for the money she spends on perms and bon bons and the time she wastes at PTA meetings." Wylie's venom had no limits: "She is the bride at every funeral and the corpse at every wedding." Yet so strong a hold does she have over her sons that "men live for her and die for her, dote upon her and whisper her name as they pass away." The result is the permanent infantilization of men: "Her 'boy,' having been 'protected' by her love, and carefully, even shudderingly, shielded from his logical development through his . . . childhood . . . is cushioned against any major step in his progress toward maturity." She sees that the boy wins the oedipal struggle: thus "the sixteen-year-old who tells his indignant dad that he, not dad, is going to have the car that night and takes it—while mom looks on, dewy-eyed and anxious—has sold his soul to mom and made himself into a lifelong sucking-egg." He tops all of this off with this amazingly bitter remark: "men weren't fighting for freedom in the war, but for security. They had fought, not to save liberty, but for hot dogs, the corner drugstore, . . . and the girl next door, mom briefly disguised as Cinderella."[8]

Wylie's rant was certainly meant to provoke, but it was echoed in many corners, some unexpected. Wylie and his ideas were featured in *Playboy* in 1956 and 1958, but similar views appeared in *Look*, *Life*, and *Cosmopolitan*, warning that Momism was raising divorce rates and making men culturally and even physically impotent.[9] A cartoon appearing in the July 1959 issue of *Cosmopolitan* (then still a general mass-circulation magazine) showed mom pushing dad like a plow with the son on top with a whip and the daughter holding the money bag. The absurdity of this joke reveals real fear and resentment of male readers. No wonder some of them were hesitant to embrace the duties of marriage, family, job, and self-repression in providership and became rebels instead.

Rebels Seen from Afar

Rebels are usually outsiders, mocked or feared by the status quo. Ours were no different, but they shared much with insiders and won secret and sometimes open admiration from men who played by the rules. By the 1950s there were such well known rebels as Jack Kerouac and Allen Ginsberg, who, despite their radical rejection of middle-class male maturity with its virtue of "settling down," still won at least a voyeur audience in the middle-class popular press with their Beat writings. Just as familiar is Hugh Hefner, who showed that "real men" could remain unmarried in maturity and yet be heterosexual and, even more, hedonistic, and not providers (if it were done with "style"). Less well known are another group of rebels, the hot-rodders, who as young veterans returned home to the male comradeship and thrills through building and racing souped-up castaway cars. What is especially interesting is that many of these young men continued to live the hot-rod culture, at least in their leisure, long after they "should have" given up this youthful "fling." Ed Big Daddy Roth and his life in the hot-rod culture of southern California will illustrate this story, though it was the Beats who provided a more public rebellion.

The Beat Generation began with the 1944 meeting of Allen Ginsberg, Jack Kerouac, and William Burroughs at Columbia University and was inspired by the unrestrained and sometimes criminal lives of their friends Neal Cassady and Herbert Huncke. The leading trio had different backgrounds and temperaments: Ginsberg, of a leftist New Jersey Jewish family whose mother suffered from mental illness, became an itinerant showman of philosophical bent. Kerouac, a working-class Catholic from Lowell, Massachusetts, was a writer of increasingly sober autobiography. And Burroughs, a scion of faded wealth and power, who introduced the others to the edgy life of gay and criminal Times Square, wrote opaquely, based on his often drug-drenched life. All, however, rejected conventional manhood, making youthful self-discovery a permanent way of life.[10]

In many ways, the Beats and their fellow travelers in jazz and art were Peter Pans, perpetually running off to Neverland. Kerouac found his on the road through the seedy sides of Chicago and Detroit or the villages of Mexico, while Burroughs played Pan throughout his peripatetic life as he wandered in a drug-hazed whirl through rural Texas, Mexico City, Tangiers, and Paris. All lived fast, and many died young to borrow James Dean's rumored expression shortly before his death at twenty-four: jazz performer Charles Parker dead at thirty-four; painter Jackson Pollock at forty-four; Neal Cassady at forty-one, from exposure beside a railroad track in Mexico; and Kerouac at forty-seven, nearly alone and drinking himself to oblivion in the bars of Lowell after having denounced his erstwhile Beat friends. Though Burroughs and Ginsberg somehow survived until 1997 despite their bouts with drugs and alcohol poisoning, dying at eighty-three and seventy-one, none of the rebels had successful marriages or long-time relationships (some were gay or bisexual).[11] But even more to the point, as Ginsberg wrote in his journal (1954), "the social organization which is most true of itself to the artist is the boy gang." They carried out a "quintessential male fantasy" of self-reinvention, of "birth without a womb" in the words of Leland.[12] If the beats were Peter Pans, or perhaps better the Lost Boys, they were so by choice.

Still, even if they were essentially following the twisting river of Mark Twain's Huck Finn and thought of themselves as descendants of the ruggedly independent mountain men, the Beats were really modern Americans with serious critiques of everyday life, especially of the bureaucratic, other-directed America of the 1950s.[13] They were not merely escaping from the fate of their peers: the demanding wife, whiny kids, and driving boss; they were on a mission. The trio of Burroughs, Ginsberg, and Kerouac embraced the French-inspired "New Vision" of Lucien Carr (another undergraduate at Columbia), the notion that raw self-expression is creativity and can be found only by avoiding conventionality and seeking the "derangement of the senses."[14]

Naturally, this quest for marginal experience led them to bouts in mental hospitals (Ginsberg), addiction (Burroughs), and even encounters with crime and violence. They reveled in the free and chaotic lives of petty criminals. In 1944, Burroughs was fascinated with Herbert Huncke, a hobo adventurer who taught him how to supplement his $200 monthly subsidy from family by rolling drunks in the subway to help him sustain his drug habit. Neal Cassady, who claimed to have stolen 500 cars when he was between fourteen and twenty-one years of age and was forever in search of kicks, inspired Kerouac to write *On the Road*. With his conservative French Canadian, working-class Catholic background, Kerouac found fascinating this utterly untethered "sideburned hero of the snowy West." Cassady inspired Kerouac into a frenzied typing of *On the Road* in a single paragraph on a 120-foot roll of teletype paper in 1951 (it was published in 1957). But more than that, Cassady was the book's hero, Dean Moriarty, whose story was drawn from their romp across the country, meeting whores in Chicago, driving fast through Iowa, bumming it on skid rows, and encountering village life in Mexico.[15] Similarly, Ginsberg drew inspiration for his most famous work, the poem *Howl* (1956), from a friend's experience in a mental asylum and that led him to conclude that the insanity of "normal" America was worse: "Boys sobbing in armies! Old men weeping in the parks!" Enlightenment was to be found on the edge, even in pain.[16]

There was no point in cultivation or refinement because the Beats lived in the present and rejected "improvement" as a loss of spontaneity and creativity.[17] As Paul Goodman noted at the time in his famous *Growing up Absurd*, the Beats saw salvation in heightened experience, which they contrasted with the hell of the domesticated bourgeois. But "since the cool behavior of these usually gentle middle-class boys looks like adolescent embarrassment and awkwardness rather younger than their years, one wonders whether ordinary growth in experience would not be more profitable enterprise and ultimately get them much further out." Gently, Goodman was suggesting that it takes perspective and experience to know what is "transcendent," but the Beats were "boys" who made a project of not growing up.[18]

Of course, public response to the Beats was, for the most part, far less sophisticated. It was mostly a curious mix of hysteria and derision as the authorities confiscated copies of *Howl* and Burroughs's *Naked Lunch* as obscene, while popular magazines like *Life* ran a feature, "Squaresville USA vs. Beatsville" (September 1959), based on hysterical reaction of residents of Hutchinson, Kansas, to the rumor that beatniks were about to invade their quiet little town. Even a B movie called *The Beat Generation* featured scenes of reefer-smoking, bongo-playing, and poetry-chanting "Beats" in black berets, jeans, and turtlenecks as backdrops to a story of a sociopathic rapist.[19]

Even more common were belittling distortions of the Beats, as when Herb Caen of the *San Francisco Chronicle* mocked them with the label "beatniks" (as "far out" as the recently launched *Sputnik*), a term that tarred the beats with a "red" or Russian sounding name. The popular press foisted upon this self-consciously serious group an image of conformist anticonformists in black turtlenecks with a studied aversion to work, expressed best perhaps by Maynard G. Krebs in the sitcom *The Many Loves of Dobie Gillis*. And it was easy to turn the Beat movement into a commodity. Even *Playboy* advertised: "Join the beat generation! Buy a beat generation tieclasp! A beat generation sweatshirt! A beat generation ring!" *On the Road* was tamed in *Route 66*, a TV serial that appeared in the early 1960s. Even Ginsberg and his buddies in 1959 became a traveling circus, giving poetry readings and interviews to the delight of the press, who unvaryingly made them the fools by presenting them as naïve and slovenly.[20]

Still, behind the attacks and derision, Americans were intrigued. The Beats were published by major presses (Harcourt and Ace), and *On the Road* was on the best-seller list for five weeks, peaking at number eleven. Warner offered to make *On the Road* into a movie, and Kerouac published bits of his writings in *Playboy* in 1959. Young women, who thought he was the glamorous bad boy Dean, threw themselves at him. [21] There was certainly a lot of voyeurism in the appeal of the Beats. I recall my father's fascination with the San Francisco's beat scene from his vantage as a community-college biology teacher in Yuba City, California. On a visit there in 1964, he took me to visit the famous City Lights bookstore. It was a kind of pilgrimage from the hinterland. What appealed to him and so many others "trapped" in humdrum lives was the daring and the nonconformity of the Beats and their escape from the treadmill of the rat race and the status seeker's unending climb. Reinforcing all this was the popular sociology of David Riesman's *The Lonely Crowd*, Robert Linder's *Must You Conform?*, William Whyte's *Organization Man*, and Vance

Packard's popular books about suburban status seeking and manipulation in advertising. Even *Look* and other mainstream magazines
lamented the man's descent into domestic servitude at the hands of
wives, bosses, and commercial conformity.[22]

Paul Goodman's *Growing up Absurd* echoed the Beats when he
set out to show "how it is disparately hard . . . for an average child to
grow up to be a man" in "our present organized system of society"
that "does not want men" because "they are not safe. They do not
suit." Norman Mailer's "The White Negro" despaired of "slow death
by conformity" and insisted that "security is boredom and therefore
sickness." He celebrated the Beat Generation's life "in the present, in
that enormous present which is without past or future, memory or
planned intention."[23]

Most men certainly did not follow Kerouac's road except to watch
Route 66 on TV in the early 1960s. But the fact that these rebels were
part of the fantasy life of American family men suggests that they
were more than bugaboos reassuring the men of Pleasantville of the
wisdom of their choices. The disappointments of being a responsible
adult were reflected in the bohemian dream life of thirty-five-year-
old men even as they sat comfortably in their Lazy Boys, TV tray at
hand in control of prime-time "family" TV.

Surely a bigger part of the imagination of the average Joe was the
boy of boys, *Playboy's* Hugh Hefner (born in 1926). At a time (1948
through 1958) when 85 percent of new homes were built in the suburbs, when anyone still a bachelor at thirty was advised to go to a psy-
chotherapist, and when family togetherness was displayed on *Saturday Evening Post* covers that showed dad in his apron presiding over
weekend barbecues, Hefner made a fortune preaching the virtues and
pleasures of urban living and the right of adult men to enjoy with the
woman of the moment the fruits of their own work.[24]

While married conventionally when he was twenty-three in Chicago, Hefner was never the family man. Although he was hard working and always attentive to the financial needs of his wife and the
daughter who soon arrived, Hefner was enamored by sex for sex's
sake. He reacted negatively to the religious scruples of his Method-
ist mother and was enchanted by the findings of the Kinsey report
of 1948 that showed presumably just how sex-crazed most American
men really were. He devoured the girlie magazines of the era (*Wink,
Flirt, Cutie, Giggles*, etc.) but also admired the sophisticated male hedonism of *Esquire* and even briefly worked at that magazine before

it moved from Chicago to New York. Though college educated (on the GI Bill) and briefly a graduate student in sociology at Northwestern University, his real interest was entertainment journalism. As a sixth grader, he drew sci-fi and horror comics, imitating a genre that was just appearing on the scene in the late 1930s. While subsisting on a string of jobs in advertising and publishing after the war, Hefner dreamed of starting his own magazine, a combination of *Esquire* and the nudie magazines. He succeeded in late 1953 when he first published *Playboy*. Hefner's life as well as his work became the very opposite of the idealized mature man. He kept a bed at the office, and, while he remained married until 1959, much earlier he led a life that mirrored the image of the playboy in his magazine, largely ignoring his daughter until she was an adult.[25]

While others worked eight to five, Hefner played through the night, and, after he moved into his Playboy Mansion in central Chicago in 1960, he went to work at five p.m., taking the mile trip in a limo with TV, bar, and phone. Gradually, in the 1960s, he did all of his work from the mansion, where his every need was attended to as if he were an oriental potentate in his seraglio. None of this was ever hidden from the press (who loved to report on "Hef's" outrageous lifestyle); in fact, it was trumpeted in *Playboy*. Readers lived Hef's life vicariously through the magazine, and, by becoming "key holders" to Hefner's string of Playboy Clubs (starting in 1960), they could actually enter a fantasy bachelor pad and be served drinks by Playboy Bunnies (but, of course, like the women in the magazine, they were to be only seen and not touched).[26]

Hefner was a rebel, but no Beat. In his *Playboy* philosophy columns that went on for 250,000 words and were published in twenty-five issues of the magazine beginning in 1962, Hefner insisted instead that he was part of the "upbeat generation," a rebel with a cause, an optimist who celebrated individuality, achievement, entrepreneurship, and especially sensual freedom. In this long series of rambling essays, Hefner boasted that he was helping to create a new, more healthy and honest morality based on accepting "God's handiwork of sexuality." Appearing on the scene toward the end of the McCarthy era and with the emergence of a new affluence, Hefner saw himself as part of that rising generation of young men who had thrown off the shackles of the 1930s "common man." He and his readers had time and money to cultivate their uninhibited tastes for fine wine, women, and song, as documented by Auguste Spectorsky in *The Exurbanites*.

Indeed, Hefner hired this sophisticated Paris-born taste maker to edit the cultural features that were the bread of the Playboy sandwich, between which was the nude centerfold.[27]

From his first issue (October 1953), Hefner made clear that *Playboy* was not for the "man's man" who hunted or fished. "We like our apartment" and "inviting in a female for a quiet discussion on Picasso, Nietzsche, jazz, sex." Later in *Playboy Philosophy* he elaborates, explaining that his magazine "is edited for a select audience of young, literate, urban men, who share with us a particular point of view" and who see life as "a happy time." The playboy who works hard has the right also to play hard: "He must be an alert man, an aware man, a man of taste, a man sensitive to pleasure, a man who—without acquiring the stigma of the voluptuary or dilettante—can live life to the hilt." His often-published photo spread under the title "What Sort of Man Reads Playboy?" was directed to advertisers touting the fact that readers were affluent and would spend, especially for new products. *Playboy* heralded the "philosophy" that pleasure was a duty.[28]

His magazine suggested that readers actually had the time and money to afford, for example, to live in the gadget-filled "Playboy's Penthouse" whose floor plan appeared in September 1956. In order to maintain this image, Hefner rejected ads that might suggest *Playboy* readers were "losers" (hair restorers, trusses, self-improvement books, or weight-loss treatments). In fact, the magazine actually appealed to young and aspiring playboys who had not yet acquired Hef's sophistication. Though Hefner was slow to adapt to the youth culture of rock (preferring the grown-up music of jazz), about a third of his readers were college students in a 1955 survey. Features assumed that readers bought cufflinks but maybe needed advice to "avoid coronation-size jewelry—it tends to be vulgar." He assumed that some readers wanted more than articles on male fashion and home furnishings, the "Playboy Adviser" (a feature that seemed to reveal readers' obsession with penis size), and the nudie shots and rakish cartoons. For these would-be sophisticates, Spectorsky introduced stories and interviews by literary and cultural luminaries of the day—from Vladimir Nabokov, John Steinbeck, Igmar Berman, and Stanley Kubrick to Jean-Paul Sartre, Martin Luther King Jr., and even Fidel Castro.[29]

All this stress on art, culture, and especially tasteful spending could have tarred *Playboy* with the brush of the foppish dilettante or even the homosexual—newsstand poison in the 1950s and 1960s—but the centerfold knocked out that problem. The "Playmate of the

Month" was not only a draw in its own right, but it shouted loudly to any and all that *Playboy* was a heterosexual man's magazine. The centerfold nude made it legitimate for "real men" to intrude on women's (and gays') turf by reading about and even spending on tasteful things for themselves.[30]

Playboy worked not just because it delivered something new but because it conformed to a widespread image of the liberated man. There were many *Playboy*-style icons in the 1950s: Sammy Davis Jr., Dean Martin, and especially Frank Sinatra were the men of the moment in their "Rat Pack," playing both on stage and on the strip in Las Vegas in the early 1960s. Then there was the hedonistic, heterosexual bachelorhood acted out, if not lived in reality, by Rock Hudson (*Pillow Talk* [1959], e.g.). Even the very middle-aged Bob Hope kept up the image of the "wise-cracking Lothario." In the 1960s, the James Bond movies, their American equivalent in Derek Flint (*Our Man Flint* [1965]), and the TV crime show *77 Sunset Strip* (with Efrem Zimbalist Jr. and Roger Smith) all featured playboy adventurers.[31]

This formula worked well for Hefner and for an amazingly long time despite the ups and downs of his business. Sales of *Playboy* peaked at 4.5 million per month in 1969. Hefner had made efforts to update the magazine, making it more appealing to a youth and countercultural taste by promoting the psychedelic "revolution" and even opposing the war in Vietnam, but this was not enough. In 1969, a new competitor, *Penthouse*, began to out-goggle *Playboy*'s centerfolds with more revealing poses, forcing Hefner into "going pubic" by 1972. Nevertheless, the magazine and Hefner's club and hotel holdings slid until Hugh's daughter took over the business and retrenched in 1982. Nevertheless, Hefner persevered.[32]

Hefner transformed consumption (and hedonism) from a woman's realm (or vice) into a man's prerogative (and obsession) and turned the act of checking out chicks into a presumed fine art. For more than a half century, he has been proud of these achievements. Still, behind all this seeming sophistication is the perspective of the boy-man. This has been never clearer than it is today, when Hefner, in his eighties, grins and cavorts on TV at his California mansion with three blond-haired women young enough to be his granddaughters. He still has the look and manner of the twelve-year-old boy who goggles at his first sight of the centerfold found in his father's sock drawer. Disguising his arrested development is an air of emotional "coolness" and cultural sophistication that has been his stock in trade for over half a century. His Chicago mansion was striking for its huge baronial hall with inlaid frescoes in the ceiling, oak-paneled walls, marble floors, and the inevitable suits of armor on the first floor. When looking for a suitable West Coast lodging in 1971, Hefner selected a pseudo–English Gothic castle on five secluded acres in Holmby Hills, near Hollywood. The aristocratic décor (updated with a daring collection of abstract modern paintings) fits the presumption of the nouveau-riche bourgeois, but in Hefner's case there is more. All this is the "classy" cover for a man with really very unsophisticated boyish tastes. Upstairs in the Chicago mansion was Hefner's famous rotating round bed with a TV camera pointed at the center and lots of switches for creating that "special" effect in light and sound to enhance amorous delight. His refrigerators were full of peanut butter sandwiches (made for a long time with Wonderbread), fried chicken, and Pepsi. In high school, a sometime friend of mine (with skills in electric gadgets) took pride in showing me his *Playboy*-like setup—a "special switch" near his bed to illuminate his sexy strobe light for those special encounters (that he probably only fantasized about). In the 1970s when Hefner commuted between Chicago and Los Angeles, he had his own black DC-9 jet complete with a dance floor, elliptical bed, and sunken Roman bath (before settling permanently in California). For years he alternated playing Monopoly with watching movies most weeknights, and, when video games came out in the late 1970s and 1980s, Hugh played and mastered them with the enthusiasm of a twelve-year-old. A recent "girlfriend," Izabella St. James, wrote: "Hef is a Peter Pan, the boy who never grew up. He built a playground and everyone came to play with him."[33]

His affair in 1969 with Barbi Benton in Los Angeles is particularly revealing. Trolling the environs of UCLA while making a TV show, he spotted a doe-eyed, snub-nosed eighteen-year-old freshman. Later he explained his attraction to the "affair that's the first serious relationship in a girl's life; it permits you to recapture your own early responses. It's a way of holding on to your youth and the enthusiasm you first felt about love and life." He bubbled over with glee when reporting to staff that he had finally "conquered" Barbi. Though he reluctantly met his sweetie's demand for travel (preferring his luxurious tree house instead), he insisted on bringing his buddies with them. By 1976, when it became obvious that Hefner was not interested in marriage and family, they broke up. Still, Barbi could appear in January 2007 on the "E" network's *The Girls Next Door* as the other (older) woman at a dinner with Hef's "current" girl friends. Cavorting with Hef to the seeming irritation of the current girls, Barbi recalled when she met Hef. At that time, she said she couldn't go out with him because she had never dated anyone older than twenty-four, to which Hefner replied that he had never dated anyone over twenty-four either. Barbi indulgently added that this seemed still to be true. One of the current girls, with a look of mock jealousy, reassured herself that she had nothing to fear because Barbi (in her mid-fifties) was too old for Hef at eighty. The journalist Russell Miller summed it up in 1984. Hefner is a man "who refuses to grow up, who lives in a house full of toys, who devotes much of his energy to playing kids' games, who falls in and out of love like a teenager, who enjoys pajama parties and is cross when his gravy is lumpy." Over twenty years later, little if anything had changed.[34]

Still, as with the Beats, Hefner would be merely an oddity if he did not strike a chord in the real world of men trying to be boys and boys trying to be men. His message and magazine worked both ways, as men tied down to family and responsibility admired Hugh's success in attracting women half, even a third of his age. And Hefner's magazine, despite all of its putative refinement, was really for boys wanting to learn about the manly adventure of women's bodies. Often noted is how Hefner's Playmates were posed in the "seduction is immanent" scene. Complementing this image was the "girl-next-door" look to fuel the fantasy that, as Hefner wrote, there are "actually potential Playmates are all around you." To prove it, Hefner persuaded a subscription manager in his own office to pose nude in the early years.[35]

From the 1950s onward, for millions of boys the sight of the centerfold nude was the "flashbulb" moment in the emergence of their active heterosexuality. This event liberated them from the innocence of childhood and introduced them to the fantasy, if not the reality, of adolescent male sexuality. Decades after first seeing the sensuous delights of the centerfold, men remember in vivid detail how they discovered a stack of *Playboys* hidden by their dads in the attic or sheepishly bought on a dare and how they shared this forbidden fruit furtively with friends. Those images, burned in the psyches of boys, long set a standard of beauty and sexuality for them. Hefner still offers a flashbulb experience every month to the young (although there are far more diverse opportunities today than in the 1960s or 1970s). As important, Hefner himself, ever the boy, never has transcended this rite, as it is reported that he still, half a century after the first centerfold, takes personal interest in the monthly centerfold shoot.[36] Neither Hefner nor his readers acquiesced to the dimming of the bulb in middle and old age.

World War II vets, their younger brothers, and eventually their sons may have lived vicariously as boy rebels through Hefner or even Kerouac, but some could do it for real. Men, often starting as teens, found freedom from maturity's burdens under their hot rods and out on the drag strip. While the automobile had long been associated with the responsible male provider, early it became so ubiquitous in America that it could become part of a rebellion against that culture. This happened as early as the mid-1920s in southern California, when young men began to customize hand-me-down cars. They gathered on the dried lakes that stretched across the Mojave Desert from Los Angeles to Muroc to race cheap and outdated Model Ts, made sleeker and more "modern" by dropping the front axle. In 1937, the growing craze led clubs of racers to organize the Southern California Timing Association to set formal rules. By the early 1940s, these old cars (now often Model A Fords, produced from 1927 to 1932) were souped up with overhead-cam cylinder heads, multiple carburetors, and combinations of big and little tires, making for a "raked" look. The SCTA organized competitive "drag" races (originally a timed quarter-mile dash from a standing position). Owners drove their prized rods to the racing strip and then stripped them of hoods (for more air intake), replaced tires with treadless slicks, and rid them of mufflers, all to increase performance and to add to the noisy macho of the race. Another goal was to modify cheap and plentiful old family cars to give them a distinctly defiant look with a chopped-down top, open wheels, and loud exhausts.[37]

In 1941, the racing clubs broke up as men were sent to war. But sixteen-year-olds remained, and they didn't bother with going to the dry lakes: "Wild eyed kids in hopped-up jalopies" roared "up and down the streets . . . at dizzy breakneck speeds," as *Colliers* reported. Cops only added to the problem when they chased the kids fleeing in their cars. Throughout the war, these teens met at drive-ins and conspired to find alternatives to rationed gas, using alcohol and cleaning solvent to fuel their cars and their need to race. In 1947, this had become a regular ritual: "By 10 pm, 100 hopped-up jalopies and denuded low slung hot rods had gathered at a mile and a half stretch of straight highway between suburban Torrance and Redondo Beach," with lookouts posted and flashlights ready to warn of police. "They ripped along two abreast, made oncoming motorists scurry to the side of the road." Soon six police cars arrived and "the speedsters roared away in all directions, careering through side streets and bumping across empty fields with crashing gears and wild open throttles. As usual, police caught only a handful." This scene, reported in magazines and newspapers in the late 1940s, inspired the action in films like *Rebel Without a Cause* (1955), *Hot Rod Rumble* (1957), and *Dragstrip Riot* (1958).[38] Most criminality related to hot rods was caused by teens, but not all. A motorcycle gang called the Boozefighters terrorized the small California town of Hollister in 1947, an event fictionalized in the movie *The Wild One*. These predecessors of the Hell's Angels consisted of disgruntled veterans (led by Arvid Olsen, a member of the acclaimed World War II Fighting Tigers).[39]

Still, the association of the hot-rodder with delinquency was certainly exaggerated. As many have pointed out, dangerous street racing (or games like "chicken") were forcefully combated not only by police but by the reconstituted hot-rod clubs when men returned from the war. The SCTA organized an official Hot Rod Exposition in 1947 for the display of rods rather than reckless racing. This event led to the birth of Robert Peterson's *Hot Rod Magazine* the next year, which regularly denounced street racing, promoted safety and cooperation with police, and featured shows displaying the art and craft of hot-rod customizers. Quickly dragsters abandoned the dry lakes for special-purpose drag strips. *Hot Rod Magazine* gradually became commercialized, spotlighting expensive "aftermarket" accessories and, through advertising, the companies that made them. Other magazines and organizations entered the fray, promoting an increasingly more diverse hobby that had nothing to do with foolhardy kids playing chicken in their illegal cars.[40]

Hot Rod, like many other magazines and clubs, nevertheless retained an aura of rebellion, mocking the flash and expense of standard production cars of the 1950s and glorifying the hard work and skill of customizers. Though parts got increasingly expensive, rodding was still for the average Joe, the "all-American" male who, whenever he could, retreated to the garage or the strip and saw the wife and kids as "getting in the way." Women were to be tolerant, and maybe provide drinks or a clean shirt now and then. This was a world of boys whose play was their "real work" and who played whenever they could.[41]

Tom Wolfe's 1963 essay for *Esquire*, later published in *The Kandy-Kolored Tangerine-Flake Streamline Baby*, introduced many outsiders to the world of men who had succeeded in perpetuating their boyhood of late-1940s dragsters. One of these was Ed "Big Daddy" Roth (1932–2001), whom Wolfe called the "most colorful, the most intellectual and the most capricious" of the car customizers. "He's the Salvador Dali of the movement—a surrealist in his designs, a show-man by temperament, a prankster."[42] Born in Los Angeles, Ed Roth was early in life drawn both to art and car customizing, beginning with his first car at fourteen years of age (a 1933 Ford Coupe). Though educated in automobile engineering at a local technical college for two years, Roth was largely self-taught. Like many who read *Hot Rod Magazine*, he dreamed of making his hobby his life and succeeded in earning a living painting racing stripes on customized cars and, by the late 1950s, constructing his own often bizarre vehicles. These included the Outlaw, the bubble-topped Beatnik Bandit, and the sci-fi inspired Mysterion, made out of junk parts and fiberglass. These were designed to be "cool" and to defy the logic of Detroit and even common comfort (the Bandit could barely accommodate a midget, much less Roth's six-foot, four-inch frame). Roth also earned money to feed his customizing habit by selling T-shirts with authority-defy-ing messages like "Mother Is Wrong" and "Born to Lose" at car shows and drag races. Dressed in outlandish costumes topped off with a rakish top hat and cruising the shows in his 1960 Cadillac hearse with "Chapel of Memories" painted on the side, Roth became a celebrity in dragsterland. Always a huckster in his unconventional way, Roth created a "trademark" icon, Rat Fink, in the late 1950s. With a crazed expression, complete with bulging, bloodshot eyes, oversized jagged teeth, slobbering at the mouth, and a pot belly, Rat Fink was the mad-house mirror image of Mickey Mouse's cuteness. Rat Fink appealed to men who thrilled at defying the corporate commercial world of GM and Disney, but it also attracted a younger crowd, as Roth discov-ered when Revell approached him in 1962. This company, founded right after World War II to manufacture novelty model figures and aircraft for kids, licensed Roth's Rat Fink character to drive minia-tures of his weirdo cars to sell to six- to eight-year-old boys. Soon the ever resourceful Roth was designing a whole line of monster and car toys, even accommodating Revell by designing Battle Rats for combat play. "The kids idolize me because I look like someone their parents wouldn't like," he said in 1964. "I gotta admit, the first monsters I'd designed had a lotta shock-value appeal for kids who wanted to freak out their parents," Roth later observed. His success was that both kids and want-to-be kids found his designs humorous, appealing to the boy-man. Roth blamed the decline of his beloved Finks by the mid-1960s on glue sniffing (the toys were models requiring assembly with glue and thus raised the ire of parents) and, oddly, the Beatles craze, making his dragster culture passé. In fact, Revell dropped his contract in 1967 because of Roth's very public association with the criminal Hell's Angels motorcycle club. By the early 1970s, Roth was forced to sell fifteen of his prized custom cars and had the almost predictable religious conversion (to Mormonism) in 1974. Abandoning his dragster life, he became a sign painter and eventually moved to Utah but never quite gave up his self-admitted addiction to his boyhood life of customizing, drawing bizarre cartoon characters, or going to and writing about car shows. Meanwhile, the Rat Fink image was adapted by surf musicians, punk bands, and other music groups, including the Voodoo Glow Skulls, the Cramps, and White Zombie.[43]

In a rambling autobiography that featured many of his designs, Roth admits to "being a 'bad boy' most of my life. . . . I was kinda like one of my monsters myself. And by the way I have this other problem. I'm the kind of guy that you love to hate. I mean, I can be downright nasty to people, especially when they get near my custom cars." He was like the possessive child, obsessed by his stuff and his own playworld. Even after his religious conversion and abandonment of his crazed life, he still admitted: "My garage is my world. My path to sanity. A place where my tools are an extension of my brains." His life was built on an unwillingness to give up the perspective of the boy's delight at "freaking out" the parent. He claimed Rat Fink "represented the real world to me—not the real world my parents and teachers told me about, but the real real world filled with oodles of different people with a variety of 'attitudes.'" For him, that meant gross-out images of, for example, a "Road Kill Sandwich" and the puerile misogyny of his T-shirt slogan: "The more I learn about women, the more I like my car." His autobiography is full of nostalgia for childhood: "I can still remember the sounds of my youth. Ya know, like, how kids play soldiers. The BRAAAK of the guns goin' off and the RATATATATAT of the toy guns. As we get older we replace these playful sounds with more grown up noises and words like 'I almost have the rent—I know, I know, it's two weeks late.'" While he says nothing about his own five grown-up sons, he is fascinated by his grandson and the boy's "creepy treehouse" where he and his gang "spend most of their time carving knives and other weapons outta tree limbs so they can attack each other in whatever time they have left over!"[44] Roth remained always, defiantly if playfully, the bad boy.

Rebels at Home

Most men of my father's generation did not become Beats, playboys, or hot-rodders, but many found wish fulfillment in reading *On the Road*, the "Playboy Advisor," or *Hot Rod Magazine*. This was part of a silent revolt from providership. Modern fatherhood was confusing by its very nature, and, as we have seen, the helping professions didn't always help men resolve those difficulties. The status of providership often kept the father at work and away from the family and made him a slave to a job he could hate. Finally, consumer culture did not often create bonds between the paternal giver and child receiver. Not only did men sometimes feel like "meal tickets" to their underapprecia-tive dependents, but the very nature of modern consumption divided families by creating peer groups of the young (listening, for example, to forty-five-rpm rock hits in 1950s suburban basement "rec rooms"). The father as pal and a paycheck had its downside, and inevitably some men at least saw this, even if fewer acted on it.[45]

The rebellion was not just from the role as "meal ticket." It was also a retreat from maturity into a playful world of nostalgia for boy-hood, and many more took this route than Route 66. Often under "cover" of being the pal dad, men slipped into the role of the boy-man at home.[46] This did not usually result in the rupture of family life. Af-ter all, men saw the home as the place of play, and their relations with children were often based on play. Still, this retreat did nothing to reduce the ambiguity of the father. Was he to be an authority, a model of adulthood, or was he a child's playmate or even just another kid in the family, playing by himself?

This world of play was one that fathers shared with sons, without necessarily exchanging feelings or fathers imparting "moral values" to them. Though dating from the 1910s, ads in popular magazines encouraged fathers to get to know their sons by purchasing a Lio-nel train set for their boys at Christmas: "Is he growing away from you?" an ad asks fathers in a *National Geographic* of November 1950. "Come down out of the clouds and get down on the floor with your boy and Lionel Trains this Christmas. It will make him happier and you a lot younger." Still there was something deceptive about ads showing father and son happily playing together with Lionel electric trains or making model airplanes or even working together in home workshops. These ads offered the image of bonding across generations and of males sharing a culture of crafts that extended deep into human history. And, to a great extent, that was what was going on. But there was also another message. Hobbies offered men a chance to share in a boy-man world of escape from expectations of maturity, even in neglecting child rearing. While childcare experts called for fathers to be manipulative pals training boys to be men, often these fathers were men just trying to be boys.[47] The trick was the very shift from the good pal dad to the rebellious boy-man that, although it was sometimes outrageous and roundly condemned, at other times was subtle, hardly noticed, and even accepted by wives and others.

As we have seen, this role of the father as a play pal has a long history and has changed over time. In fact, from early in the twentieth century, advice literature demanded less obedience and respect from children and insisted more on affection and adaptation from fathers. In the 1920s, Frank Cheley authored, *Dad, Whose Boy Is Yours?* (a compact manual to be read on the train by busy professional fathers). It promoted playful fathering, demanding that men share nature and good times with their sons, even join the boy's "gang," and thereby recover their youthful vigor. Still, Cheley was always clear that these comradely moments should be opportunities to shape, guide, and otherwise make boys into men. He was confident that after a father had established in play a trusting relationship with his son, the boy would then ask questions that the dad could answer to help guide the child to make the "right" choices and become in time a leader of men and his family. Implicit was confidence that fathers knew best about what the right choices were and how to make boys into manly leaders. Men understood clearly that they were not to "lower" themselves to the mentality of the child or youth, not be boy-men.[48]

This sort of didactic use of the pal role was repeated over and over in the rituals of father-son bonding. It was especially inscribed in the Boy Scouts and Little League. According to a 1945 manual, the scouts were to be led by "men who represent the best manhood of the entire community," to shape the boy's "ideals of citizenship, his attitudes, ambitions, his choice of career, his relationships to his fellow man, his loyalty to American ideals and institutions." This was a tall order for a group of campers and nature enthusiasts. But it makes the point that the collective "best" men of the community could use cross-generational play to perpetuate themselves—and it assumed that boys would accept this presumably subtle molding. Of course, the scouts were not trying to usurp the father-son relationship. They also published a *Book of Hobbies for Fathers and Sons* (1942) to channel the boy's energies and to appeal to his "intense desire to be a boy and act like a man" in activities with dad. "Here is where the father may function with a word of praise to mold the wax of the boy's ego" while canoeing, bird watching, or doing magic tricks. As we all know, scout masters and fathers sometimes did not uphold these vaunted ideals. Not always the "best men" got involved, and many crossed the fine line between using play to "mold" the child and gratifying their personal needs, especially to return to their own childhoods. Still, the scouting movement set the standard of how fathers could make boys into men through childish play.[49]

Little League is another example. Organized first in 1938 for boys six to eighteen years old, it was based on an insightful if patronizing principle. When boys gathered to play baseball in vacant lots, larger boys, often bullies, dominated the game, usually excluding the smaller and less skilled. Little League, run by trained parents, formed age-graded teams with age-appropriate equipment, assuring that boys of the same age (and thus roughly the same skills) competed with one another. The idea was to build "character" by combining competition with sportsmanship. Rules limited the number of players that could try out for any team and required players to live in a specific neighborhood to prevent strong teams from overwhelming the others. Little League spread quickly, federating 1,000 teams and conducting its own World Series in 1948. By the early 1990s, there were leagues in sixty-three countries and about 180,000 teams. Local business groups covered costs of uniforms and equipment.[50]

However, the tendency of coaches to relive their childhoods through Little League or to play at being "big leaguers" through the kids was evident from the beginning. The founder, Carl Stotz of Williamsport, Pennsylvania, a clerk at a local lumberyard, admitted that he was "the little boy who never grew up." He started the first Little League team shortly after watching his nephews play sandlot ball and experiencing a "flashback" to the days when he played baseball. There was a downside to this nostalgia, as dads (and occasionally moms) lived through their sons, leading to much unsportsmanlike behavior. Stotz noted parents' booing umpire calls from the beginning.[51]

Throughout its history, Little League has been as much an opportunity for men to relive their childhoods (and improve on their childhood dreams of playing) as to make boys into men. Some of this was and is harmless, even touching, as when Garret Mathews admitted that he coaches Little League because he wants to be "part of their laughter. To say or do something they might remember after they've hit their final weak roller to second base." Seeing these kids every spring convinced him "that elementary school isn't nearly long enough." But Little League sometimes meets adult needs to the detriment of the kids. In 1992, Jeff Burroughs, a player for the Texas Rangers in the early 1970s, confessed that "my lifelong dream had finally come true. It took me 40 years, but I finally got to be on that most hallowed of all baseball fields, the one in Williamsport, Pennsylvania," when he coached a team that made it to the Little League World Series. It was bigger for him than the kids. Coaches sometimes used "scouts" to hunt up best prospects even though a draft system usually gave the weakest team the first picks. Some even traded players like the professional leagues. One guidebook for coaches admitted that parents often pressured their kids into playing beyond skills or age and that the league sent a letter to parents warning that they would be ejected or their kids would forfeit the game if they didn't control their hostility to umpires. Coaches advised parents to "praise the players in public and only to criticize them in private." The fact that this needed to be said indicates that it often was violated. Over and over, coaches (and interfering dads) lived out in players (and their sons) the "glory" that they missed in their own childhoods or their adult lives. One study in 1979 found that coaches played to the limit of the rules, encouraging the boys to be aggressive and to model themselves after big league players.[52]

In recent years this has often gotten out of hand when fathers regress into the boys that they are supposed to make into men. Because of parents' second guessing coach's decisions (especially with regard to playing their sons), it has sometimes been difficult to recruit volunteer coaches. Frequently the pressure placed on kids is so great that they quit. In 2000, the National Association of Sports Officials began to offer assault insurance against injury to its 19,000 umpires and referees. This was in response to cases such as a father from Davie, Florida, who, while serving as a Little League first-base coach, protested an umpire's call by breaking his jaw. In 2000, Fred Engh, president of the National Alliance for Youth Sports in West Palm Beach, claimed that violence among parents had risen threefold in the past five years. In 1998, Little League officials in a Boston suburb had a plywood fence built behind the backstop to keep emotional parents out of the way. In Georgia, a coach shot a player's father in the arm after the dad complained that his son wasn't pitching enough. An Oklahoma tee-ball coach (played by five- and six-year-olds) was convicted of choking a fifteen-year-old umpire during a game. Elsewhere, parents were obliged to sign a form promising to adhere to an ethics code on the field before their children could play baseball (even though only a handful of parents have been ejected each season). Extreme, of course, but these examples are suggestive of how play organized by men to mold boys' characters can slip into the most obvious form of boy-man behavior. And, though this may be a growing trend, it has been with Little League since the beginning.[53]

Another setting for the pal dad is the modern sport of hunting. As much for urbane northeasterners as for rural southerners and westerners, by 1900 hunting became a seasonal ritual, identified with fathers and forefathers. It often brought together a curious blend of emotions—nostalgia for the disappearing frontier but also emulation of genteel England. The hunter had to prove his independence and resourcefulness but also his knowledge, skill, and virtue by adhering to a code of sportsmanship. Mostly, hunting was a refuge for masculinity during a time when churches and even businesses were becoming feminized. Unlike other manly retreats (gambling and boxing, for example), it could be made genteel or respectable, especially when popularized by the likes of Teddy Roosevelt. Only in the 1970s do we see a marked decline in hunting due to urbanization and alternative sports.[54]

Hunting became a perfect setting for the acting out of Cheley's didactic pal dad after World War II. A typical article in *Parents' Magazine* told the dad to "Take Your Boy Hunting" before "the plastic stuff of character has jelled" to teach a skill and an appreciation of nature. You "will make the boy better adjusted to the world of mature affairs if today you make him acquainted with the out-of-doors." Yet, there was certainly a deeper, less functional agenda, as revealed, for example, by writers in *Field and Stream*. Consider its long-time contributor William Tapply and his memoir about his experience learning to hunt with his father in the 1940s and early 1950s. Tapply believed hunting to be a natural urge that fathers only nurtured when they welcomed sons to their hunting bands, as Tapply's dad did when he was a young boy. Riding in the back of the truck with the dogs, Tapply tagged along for two years before his father allowed him to shoot, thus absorbing love for nature and the art of hunting without any "modern" formal training. Running through this sentimental literature, we see men bonding across age gaps around a presumed primordial need that the modern world has subverted by separating men by profession and age and by domesticating them in a realm of women and modern conveniences. But this was still more than a form of collective male regression. A key to the ritual of hunting was the rite of passage, a moment of maturation when the boy won the right to shoot. Stories of fathers properly, if subtly, preparing sons for this moment, abound. They insist that the man should give the boy a nonfunctioning gun at eight to learn the proper way to care for and carry a weapon. Let him have a twenty-two at ten years of age to shoot rabbits. Insist that he hunt with the father until at least fourteen. Cautionary tales of boys who broke the rules and hunted before they were ready are common. All of this points to more than a concern about safety and shows a longing for a marker of the passing of a tradition from one generation to another. Significantly, a key moment in Tapply's memoir is the time that his father decided to shoot no more. For Tapply, the "circle was closed" as his aged father decided to leave the band of male hunters. Even if the hunter at home and at work was no longer a master of his and his dependents' fates, manly men could form a circle excluding women and males too young (or old) to fire weapons. This was all about being and becoming a grown-up, but in a distinctly artificial, symbolic setting. The hunter admits that these roles cannot be played out in the everyday world of working, commuting, and providing. As a man whose father never got beyond teaching me once to shoot a twenty-two, and who was never admitted to the "circle" of hunters, I still can't help but ask: Can anyone honestly believe that learning to stalk and shoot a deer has anything to do with being a grown-up man today? But it does for many men even if it also is a way sometimes of avoiding the ambiguities of modern maturity.[55]

Other forms of the pal dad went much further, rebelling against not just the modern male provider's job but, more subtly against the childrearing role itself. In comparing the fatherhood manuals from the 1920s with those in the 1950s, I noticed something striking—the decline of appeals to character building. Part of this is because people from different specialties wrote the manuals in the 1920s as compared to the 1950s. Physicians and child-development experts had taken over this role by the 1950s. They abandoned the Victorian ideals of the inner-directed individualist so evident in moralists like Cheley from the 1920s and replaced them with more "democratic" ideas of the pal dad (as seen in chapter 1). The old bourgeois confidence that dads had a legacy and experience to pass on to children had certainly declined, despite vestiges of it still appearing in Scout Master and Little League manuals in the 1950s. But, even more telling, these changes suggest an adaptation to new attitudes for men. As the home and the child became more clearly associated with an escape from work and responsibility, men rejected "growing up," at least in the home. The father's play with the child was no longer a means to the end of "character building" but the man's reward for his sacrifice in work and duty outside the home. His free time became associated with nostalgia for childhood and activities that denied generational divisions in a timeless fantasy of ageless play, where men and boys could join. Organized sport and hunting fit this bill to a degree, but even more so did hobbies.

Of course, the advice literature touted hobbies as vehicles for redeeming family togetherness. "No family is really safe or happy without hobbies," noted one manual written in 1948. Hobbies were surefire ways of directing children's energies into future vocations as business leaders or scientists. At the least, they were positive alternatives to the allures of illicit pleasures that could ruin a boy's future, especially in his teens. But, again, the pal dad enters the picture: the hobby world, according to the advice literature, was to be shared by fathers and sons, free of wives and mothers, so that males could preserve ancient craft traditions or engage in forward-looking technologies. Agnes Benedict's progressive manual *A Happy Home* (with a foreword by Benjamin Spock), largely ignores fathers, even though the book is about family activities to build family bonds. It is only in a chapter on "carpentry" that we read the phrase "especially for fathers" and a promise that woodworking could bring fathers and sons together. The reason that carpentry promised this bonding was simple but revealing: "fathers do not have to make any effort to 'come down' to the children—they are already there and they usually glory in the fact. . . . Insensibly, and without their quite knowing the reason, the gaps between parent and child begin to lessen and invisible barriers break down" as man and boy hammer and saw in this presumably natural male activity. Benedict suggests that men inevitably become boys in crafts and thus can bond with their sons. This Cheley would have embraced. Still, what is missing is the expectation that men offer fatherly advice or serve as models of bourgeois achievement and responsibility. The natural bonding in the fun of re-creating a traditional boy-man activity was now sufficient.[56]

The hobby took the man (and boy) into a world of playful rebellion from the markers of middle-class male maturity. It took place in settings that were ceded (sometimes grudgingly) by wives and mothers—the garage, attic, or basement workshop. The hobbyist world eliminated gaps between the old and young. Adult hobbyists continually evoked memories of childhood longings (dreams of being a boat captain or a train engineer, for example). They sometimes admitted that they were perpetuating a boy's obsession into an adult hobby (such as in agate or stamp collecting). The spark of enthusiasm often seemed to come from that memory of the first childhood encounter with the thrill of the hobby. All this made hobbies a perfect expression of nostalgia and an escape from adult responsibility.

Of course, hobbyists always insisted that they were not engaging in child's play. Craft and collecting magazines stressed how model airplanes, boats, and trains, for example, were not toys but realistic replicas. They were valuable because of the time and skill required to make or collect them, buttressed by the hobbyist's arcane knowledge about the history and technical detail of the activity. Hobbyists always emphasized that they had become more sophisticated and accomplished with years of experience. Common was the exclamation, "look how far I've come since my uncle," for example, "gave me my first stamp when I was nine years old." Most important, the hobbyist rationalized his enthusiasm with the fact that the replicas were based on the real practical world outside the home. All this made the play of grown men more "serious" because there was a progression, even though in the main it really was about regression. At the same time, hobbies gave boys a sense that they were not children playing with toys but were sharing with men in the competence and excitement of the real world of power and innovation. Books on model railroads described the actual worlds of specific freight and passenger rolling stock that model railroaders miniaturized. Enthusiasts for remote-control model airplanes learned about the latest advances in the arms race in their magazines. Men's nostalgia for the past joined the boy's quest for a sense of participation in the "real world." Crafts and collecting put men and boys in an in-between place and time where there was neither adult responsibility nor childish dependency—the realm of the boy-man.[57]

Hobbies also addressed another stressful point to modern men—the distance between the home (a somewhat awkward place where females dominated and males were "obliged" to rest and find leisure) and the outside world of work and mostly male achievement. Men had an emotional interest in narrowing that gap, making themselves in that female/leisure sphere of the home feel part of the world of male achievement. The hobby literature and magazines such as *Popular Science* continually evoked the message that even in the basement workshop the man was in touch with the innovative world of new technology. The hobbyist who made his own bike speedometer would also want to know about the latest uses of the "electric eye" in garage door openers. The model makers Monograph and Revell kept up with the latest innovations in the U.S. Air Force and replicated them in their miniatures. This gave the basement or garage hobbyist the feeling of being part of a wider world of adventure, technological wonder, and power even if they were confined to the unfinished corner of a garage or backyard shed. In effect, this was a way of escaping in fantasy from the wife and mother's domestic space, a playful refuge shared by males both old and young.[58]

The male hobbyists' realm was also a subtle protest against the modern world of female domestic consumption. For example, *Popular Science* featured ads and articles about the latest cars. Instead of stressing the fashion or functionality of the new lines as did family magazines and TV ads, these male magazines emphasized cars' engines, frames, and power trains. Men's magazines frequently offered ideas for "aftermarket" improvements in electronic equipment or cars that appealed to male interest in personalizing, enhancing, and controlling their consumer goods. When *Workbench*, for example, offered plans to make old wheelbarrows into planters and discarded doors into coffee tables, it was appealing to a male quest for mastery and independence through craft skills using simple at-hand materials that mocked the modern division of labor and mass production of consumer goods. Men didn't need to buy everything at stores as women seemed to expect. They could make some things themselves. This craft ethic recalled men's memories of their self-reliance as boys, when the world was less modern, less consumerist, and more masculine.[59]

These appeals worked across generations, offering a world in which fathers and sons could share activities and values, but this didn't necessarily mean that dads introduced sons to the world of the grown-up. After all, hobbies were in part about a retreat from the ambiguities of modern male *adult* roles of work and providing. Hobbies let men and boys share in a boy-man world of escape from the expectations of maturity in the modern world. Despite ads showing father and son happily playing together with Lionel electric trains, making model airplanes, or even working together in home workshops, hobbies didn't necessarily promote cross-generational togetherness. I am not condemning this world; it has given men and boys a lot of usually harmless pleasure. All that I am saying is that it emerged out of the confusions and ambiguities of modern manhood. Childcare experts called men to be pals in play with their sons while training their offspring to be "men." However, in reality men often escaped from this "responsible" and confusing world of fatherhood into a fantasy world of the boy-man, shared with sons, perhaps, but not necessarily devoted to the goal of "growing up."

Whence These Rebels?

So now I come to the point of trying to make sense of all this whirlwind of rebellion even in the midst of the Greatest Generation of grown-ups. Though neither would probably admit it, Allen Ginsberg's reading *Howl* in coffee houses has a lot in common with the accountant's building a model railway in his basement. They both rejected older meanings of manhood and embraced some form of what I have been calling the boy-man. They abandoned Judge Hardy's genteel respectability and responsibility, and sometimes even providership, as well as Andy Hardy's goody-two-shoe striving for self-mastery and maturity. Now is the time to ask: What has happened to the Judge Hardys and their sons, and, more to the point, why isn't this myth still central to our culture?

For both better and worse, two generations ago men began to abandon both the Victorian patriarch and the boyhood striving toward manhood, complete with its comedies (and tragedies). Decades-long rebellion against the Hardys' world has led to the boy-man today, where men enter their twenties and thirties without father figures and with uncertainty about fatherhood. All this points to how modern culture has systematically abandoned the Victorian ideals of patriarchy and boyhood. Here I will return to the Judge and Andy

Hardy to show how and why these early dissidents rejected these models. Of course, we need to acknowledge that rebellion against the middle-class patriarch has deep roots in American society that long predates Ginsberg, Hefner, and Roth. But this rebellion certainly has accelerated since 1945.

So why? Men had different reasons to rebel against adulthood. I have already mentioned in my discussion of Wylie one of the most common theories: men's perceived dependence on "mom" and failure to resolve the early childhood dilemma of the Freudian Oedipus complex. This complex is rooted in the boy's supposed infantile desire for or identity with the actual mom (in competition with the father) and conflicting need to break with that desire and accept his father's leadership in order to develop a mature masculinity. But according to Wylie (and many who followed), if the "mom" dominates her son, the boy will not surmount the oedipal complex and will remain infantile. At the same time, this fear of "Momism" resulted in male rebellion against female-controlled domesticity and its corollary, male providing (as seen in the embrace of Wylie's tirade against Momism). This led to a second path to boy-manhood in hypermasculinity. The Oedipus complex has been used by generations of psychoanalysts to explain the ambiguities of male behavior toward women. But does it explain why there has been a surge of male anxiety about "mom" in the mid-twentieth century?

To find an answer, we must recognize that the "mom complex" is not just or even primarily psychological. It is social and historical, rooted in a nineteenth-century compromise that left men with nearly exclusive power over wage earning while women controlled the "details" of home life, including, critically, the shaping of the identity of young boys. It was this new world in which Freud formulated his theory of the oedipal complex. Accordingly, anxiety about female domestic dominance is rooted in a modern male childhood experience that shapes his response to "moms" long after he has grown up.

Recently Stephen Ducat's *The Wimp Factor: Gender Gaps, Holy Wars, and the Politics of Anxious Masculinity* has resurrected this thesis to explain one of the consequences of "Momism"—the prevalence of hypermasculinity in America. The little boy learns that his early identification with his mother is "shameful" (especially if he has a cold and driven father) and thus often reacts by becoming hard on the outside. Alternatively, boys develop "womb envy," jealous of the reproductive capacity of women, leading to the same result. This escape from the "soft" mother results in a lifelong quest for virility, disdain for nurturing roles and women (as well as "sissy" politics like the welfare state or diplomacy, as opposed to war), and an obsessive need to be "on the road." Ducat put the problem clearly: "masculinity is a hard-won, yet precarious and brittle psychological achievement that must be constantly proven and defended." For some men, that defense means behaving as if they are eternally being challenged by the playground bully or forever wanting to reexperience that first sexual encounter that freed them from their mothers. When such boys grow up, they in turn fail to nurture, producing in their sons the same response and thus "a generational cycle of defensive hypermasculinity." Thus both the macho man perpetually fighting on the playground and the playboy forever seeking that "flashbulb" moment of sexual conquest are fixated on an infantile crisis that never is transcended. Such men never grow up.[60]

I admit that I have never quite bought the Oedipus complex. To me, it always was too simplistic to explain something so complex. Hypermasculinity does seem to be a defensive, regressive behavior that ultimately leads to arrested development. Still, I think that we need a wider explanation for it. We need to go beyond Freud and his Victorian society and consider the social and economic changes that undermined Victorian ideals of male maturity and created the crisis of which the *modern, post-Victorian* Oedipus complex is an expression. That nineteenth-century model was based on male self-restraint, thrift, rational calculation at work, and measured deference to female culture at home. It was "designed" to maximize economic progress in the public sphere (controlled by men). That model also assured stability and nurture in childhood in the home under the hegemony of women. This was a "solution" to the modern problem of dividing public competitive life from private intimate life, and, at many levels, it worked fairly well over a century. However, it posed many problems (most famously isolating and minimizing the role of women in relation to the achievement society outside the home). Even for men, the payoff was never certain (especially in the working class). It also required the absence of dads in boys' lives, which led to moms' playing bigger roles in their growing up and men's fears that their sons would become "sissies." The decline of men's independence with industrialization and the rise of the corporation also eroded the rewards of male self-denial. These trends led men to seek ways of compensating for the perceived decline of masculine power in a male peer culture free from women. We see this in the rise of everything from organized sport and body building to male fraternal organizations and even the male embrace of the "manliness" of war in the late nineteenth century (which led to some of the macho excesses of World War I). Men found ways of thwarting female "overcivilization" by separating boys from women in new organizations like the scouts, school sports, and, eventually, groups like the Little League, led by surrogate dads.[61]

As important, in order to check the "feminization" of boys, men encouraged their "barbarian" instincts. This radically challenged the older goal of male self-restraint suitable for success in business and refined bourgeois domesticity. A reversal of male cultural goals was not easy to justify, but such advocates of a barbarian boyhood as the early-twentieth-century psychologist G. Stanley Hall saw virility and self-controlled domestic manhood as compatible, not as opposites (as did many women quite naturally). Hall argued that barbarian boys would become naturally self-disciplined gentlemen when they grew up. Demanding that young boys learn self-restraint had only made them obsessive or incapable of dealing with stress. Instead, Hall argued around 1900, that by letting boys be "primitives" in aggressive play and sport, they would develop and give expression to their "nerve force," thus avoiding wimpishness. At the same time, this would set the stage for later self-control (as in sportsmanship) and make them vital but rational leaders of men. For Hall and others, the barbarian stage would not make boys into permanent primitives but would act like a smallpox inoculation, laying the groundwork for the ideal gentleman—self-controlled but also courageous and capable of manly action. The boys would grow up to be muscular Judge Hardys.[62]

This cultivation of the female-free male barbarian was certainly a defensive reaction against "Momism" and , in effect, promised to transcend the oedipal stage to full-blooded masculine maturity. The only way that this could work was if boyish hypermasculinity was checked by a code of behavior rooted not in the home (or the increasingly female-dominated church) but in male culture itself. This might mean the elaborate ritual of the Masons or Elks, the amateur and sporting codes of modern games, or the genteel values of the middle-class man in suit and fedora.

The problem was, as we have seen in the case of the Little League, that this second civilizing stage sometimes didn't occur and boys might never transcend their "barbarian stage." Though Hall and others rationalized the extension of a playful boyhood, nothing guaranteed that men would not become "lost boys" in a male Neverland, locked in a culture of aggression, emotional intensity, and thrill seeking, a culture of the cool. There was no guarantee that boys would become Judge Hardys, muscular or otherwise.

Still, is it fair to reduce this rejection of masculine maturity to oedipal crises or even the failure of this revision of Victorian paths to manhood? A Ginsberg or Roth would surely deny that their rebellion against the path to "normal" sexual or social maturity had anything to do with their mothers or the ambiguities of modern child rearing. They would insist that they had moral or philosophical reasons for being alienated from ideals of male maturity. In fact, the principled disenchantment of young men from what society offered them is a major theme of postwar social commentary.

J. D. Salinger's *Catcher in the Rye* may serve to illustrate this philosophical claim and another explanation of male rebellion. This 1947 novel about the teenage Holden Caulfield and his adventures on his way to his New York City home after being expelled from private school has engaged American youths for decades. Salinger takes the voice of a youth who sees his world as phony and unworthy of commitment. What's more, Salinger offers no happy ending of self-discovery and return to the normal route to manhood. There is no solution to his youthful alienation. Caulfield is hardly a product of a bad home. In fact, he has no reason to complain really. His parents are nice enough (though "touchy as hell"). He is hardly a "psycho." Despite being troubled by the early death of a brother, he is very affectionate toward his sister. He admires his older brother even though he thinks he has become a "prostitute" by working as a writer in the movies. Pretty "normal" for a teenager. But he sees his high-class boarding school's claim to "mold" youth into ideal men to be a lie. In fact, he quit a different school because "I was surrounded by phonies. That's all." Later he observes that in school "all you do is study so that you can learn enough to be smart enough to be able to buy a goddam Cadillac some day." While a history teacher and mentor tells him that "life is a game that one plays according to the rules," Holden won't play. With no concern for his future, he wanders back to New York City and to a string of aimless adventures in bars, with a prostitute in a hotel, on a date with a girl he really doesn't like, and back briefly to visit his sister at home. In despair he wishes he was a deaf-mute and would not have to talk or explain himself again. While his sister ·

eventually persuades him to come back home, he won't promise his therapist that he will do better at school next term. He can't predict what he will do.[63]

Of course, Caulfield's alienation could be explained as a psychological disorder, but that is not how many young people read it (I certainly didn't when I read it as a sixteen-year-old). Youth saw Caulfield as true to their own lives, alienated from the "phoniness" of school and the hypocrisy of adulthood. That theme was even sharper in James Dean's roles in the films *Rebel Without a Cause* and *East of Eden* where the angry youth can't make their clueless fathers understand them. Of course, these fathers were weak (Jim Bachus, playing the father in *Rebel*, walks around in an apron and kowtows to his domineering wife). Dean's death shortly before the opening of the film helped create a rebel cult. Among the enthusiasts was a young teenager, Bob Zimmerman (later Bob Dylan), who copied the smirk and jeans of his hero. As popular was the rebel look of Marlon Brando in his role in *The Wild One* as a motorcycle-gang leader who terrorizes a small town in California. According to writer Susan Bordo, Brando inspired the teenaged Bobby Seale, later a leader of the Black Panthers in the 1960s.[64]

But the alienation evoked by these films is not only the "fault" of the selfish or cowardly elder; it became a heroic stance against an unworthy society. This is perhaps best explained by the Yale psychologist Kenneth Keniston in a reference to youth in 1965, almost twenty years after the first appearance of *The Catcher in the Rye*: "Alienation, once seen as imposed *on* men by an unjust economic system, is increasingly chosen *by* men as their basic stance toward society." Like Kerouac or the fictional Holden Caulfield, alienated youth, beginning in the late 1940s, rejected affluent society as boring and "endeavor" as pointless and saw the "emptiness of love," preferring "the role of the detached observer and commentator."[65] These young men rejected the father and the path to fatherhood on principle, a heroic if ultimately empty "no." It would be powerfully echoed in my own generation's great negation and the cynical disengagement that boomers find in their children today.

But, if that was the message of the Beats and James Dean, it was not the tone of Hugh Hefner or of the boyish nostalgia of the hobbyist, nor even the playful in-your-face smart-assery of Big Daddy. These men not only rejected markers of maturity, but embraced the right to a permanent state of "boyhood"—and they didn't see this as an act of despair or escape, either. This brings me to still another explanation of rebellion: some dissidents of the veterans' generation self-consciously rejected the second step in Hall's formula—self-restraint and gentility. They didn't think that they were boys lost in barbarism and instead found themselves playboys in pleasure. This was sometimes refined but almost always commercial, a comforting joy in living in "their youth" and its time and the culture of the cool. Similarly, men did not simply reject providership; they embraced the right to enjoy themselves. While Andy Hardy might have found some of what these rebels did "fun," he would have been appalled by their making that fun a permanent way of life.

Of course, none of this was entirely new to the mid-twentieth century. As early as 1909 the young Randolph Bourne called his generation to rebel against the hollowness of the lives of their parents and to be free from the past.[66] By the late nineteenth century, male consumption—youthful and anything but domestic—was centered in such pleasure zones as Times Square and the West End of old Coney Island. There, men (the wealthy "swells" as well as the stable boys) came to drink, gamble, and meet ladies of the night. This was largely a bachelor culture mostly abandoned upon responsible marriage and was marginal, on the edge of respectability.[67] In other ways, men longed to return to or retain youth. We see it in the cultivation of the look and manner of the perpetual youth in ads and popular culture early in the twentieth century. That was the point of the new clean-cut, beardless faces of young men around 1900. We find it also in Hollywood's love affair with the roles of the debonair men-about-town played by the likes of William Powell and Fred Astaire in the 1930s, who could be "real men" without being responsible providers or fathers. Still, this image was hardly mainstream.

However, gradually the play-loving boy became a model of American masculinity. At the beginning of the twentieth century, the old ideal of manhood as self-determined and self-restraining prevailed in the public view in the new mass-circulation magazines like *Saturday Evening Post, McClure's, American,* and even *Voice of the Negro.* Still, by the 1920s, there were already magazines that equated the manly with style and personal satisfaction (*Sporting Life* and *Vanity Fair,* especially). They appealed to men who had already arrived (or fantasized that they had) and who rejected the ethic of providership and its twin, thrift and self-denial. Instead, they embraced a boyish hedonism. The most successful and emblematic of this new appeal was *Esquire*. From its daring first issue at the depth of the Depression in 1933, it touted not business success or genteel self improvement but the self-assured enjoyment of assumed success in male fashion; self-improvement in body and personality; and the cultivated pleasures of drink, dining, and beautiful women. And, like *Playboy* a generation later, *Esquire* inoculated itself from the taint of foppishness by running aggressively male articles by that man's man Ernest Hemingway and by publishing sexually alluring cartoons ("roguish, yet refined") and the drawings of "perfectly shaped" women by George Petty and Alberto Varga. Age and success meant, for *Esquire* readers, not abandoning a playful youth but enjoying its pleasures with a degree of refinement and more money.[68]

During World War II, other men's magazines began to make similar appeals to the more downmarket crowd. *True* and *Argosy* had long offered gritty adventure, crime, and war stories appealing to the man's man who disdained the "soft" culture of refined pleasures and consumption that attracted *Esquire* readers. But by the 1940s magazines earned their profits less from the sale of their stories than from the sale of advertising. Thus these working-class men's magazines also began to offer hobby and fashion features in the hope of stimulating interest in new forms of male leisure and consumption and to sell ads for these new products. In an article designed to win the traditional thrifty male reader over to the "new" ideal of spending for his own pleasure, *True* appealed to men's "outrage" at the "myth" that "woman is the boss in the home" and that she says what is to be bought. This call for male assertion of his right to buy for himself was a direct challenge to the idea that the grown-up male "provides" for his family and disdains shopping (leaving it to the "little woman"). Despite male readers' resistance to this new stress on sports equipment and fashion, *True* and similar magazines sold men on their right to spend to meet their "needs."[69]

By mid-century, spending and pleasure were associated not only with the "liberated male" but also with youth. The bachelor culture of the early-twentieth-century city cultivated the ideal of youth as a time for spending on oneself. At the same time, the peer groups of teens and youth, fostered by the emergence of mass attendance of high school and even college, provided venues for selling fashion and fads. *Esquire* in the 1930s, followed by *Playboy* in the 1950s, appealed to the collegiate set with fall fashion spreads.[70] These trends culminated in the 1950s, when, as Bill Osgerby in *Playboys in Paradise* shows, this identification of youth with consumption expanded as the number of teens increased from 10 to 15 million. Advertisers recognized a growing market for youth leisure goods, led by cheap forty-five-rpm records and the revolutionary transformation of popular music by rock and roll in 1954, hyped by youth-oriented radio and TV. Similarly, there was a shift in movies to cheap, teen-oriented themes (car racing, the beach, and horror, especially).[71] Although commentators fussed over the commercial manipulation of youth, the larger point was that youth had become a time of fun and spending, no longer simply a period of waiting and subordination to the whims of adults.[72] No wonder men increasingly identified youth as a time of freedom and fun and adulthood as a loss. No wonder that Greatest Generation rebels wanted to extend the pleasure years of youth into adulthood and tried to make it a way rather than a stage of life. And in this sentiment, readers of Kerouac and Hefner shared much with the readers of hobbyist magazines.

Some men of my father's generation rejected as adults the sobriety and maturity of Judge Hardy and his descendents, but they were also repulsed as boys by Andy Hardy's goody-two-shoes model of growing up. They replaced it with the cool. Rooted in a new commercial culture of the comic book, Saturday-matinee crime and science-fiction movies, and the hot music and dance scene, the cool emerged when my father was a child and teenager, almost twenty years before rock and roll. That culture rebuffed the ideals and manners of generations of boys' fictional heroes such as Tom Swift and the Hardy Boys, who knew that they wanted to become men like their fathers. In all of its manifestations, the stories of the cool never included the advising father or the aspiring boy. The cool was mostly a culture where youth were fully formed and static because they didn't have anything to learn. Decades-long rebellion against the Hardys' world idealized fatherless masculinity and glorified the boy-man.

That rebellion from the goody-two-shoes dates back to the high Victorian era of patriarchs, when men began to be nostalgic for a carefree boyhood, and it culminated more recently in challenges to the need for the father and the virtues of following his path. One good early example is Thomas Aldrich's recollection of his childhood summers in New England in *The Story of a Bad Boy* (1869). He learned from other boys that childhood was a special carefree time of fun, innocent enthusiasms, and affections. Aldrich gleefully celebrated his "amiable, impulsive disobedience" to adults. All this got him into trouble, yet he "naturally" learned from his experience and became a successful and decent adult without having to endure many lectures from father in the study or visits to the woodshed. Of course, these stories of boyhood misadventures were merely distant recollections (often distorted by nostalgia). For many men, they may have become, as historian David Leverenz notes, a "way of saying, *Let the past be past*," and of accepting the adult responsibility.[73] But these stories also introduced a subterranean culture that glorified boyhood and, at least implicitly, saw maturity as dull, rigid, and joyless.

Mark Twain's *Tom Sawyer* (1876) and *Huckleberry Finn* (1884) certainly fit this description. Free from the guidance of a father, nothing could confine or define Tom—not the church, home, or school or even his Aunt Polly. This was part of a cultural trend of using youth as the weapon against adult hypocrisy and authority, but Tom and Huck were also part of romantic celebration of the natural decency of the youth who needed no guidance from the elder generation.[74] Even more, Tom and Huck were about an emerging adult nostalgia for childhood freedom or even, as literary critic David Kirby notes, the embrace of Twain's dark humor expressing the "boy's bitter struggle against manhood."[75] This trend culminated in J. M. Barrie's *Peter Pan* (1904). While today seen through the lens of Disney's feature of 1940 as a child's fantasy, *Peter Pan* began as an adult novel, and the play was popular with grown-ups through the 1920s. For grown-ups, Peter Pan was a playful escape from growing up to be insurance salesmen and clerks.[76]

Flight from the pressures of boyhood achievement and fatherly dependability attracted both teens and adults at the beginning of the twentieth century to amusement parks. At Coney Island and its many imitators, amusement park rides were not primarily for children but for young men (and women). As Edward Tilyou (owner of the oldest amusement park at Coney Island) explained in 1922, most men "look back on childhood as the happiest period of their lives . . . [and] this is the mental attitude they like to adopt" at Coney Island. By the 1920s, childhood had become a time of indulgence and, quite naturally, grown-ups sought to "return" to an indulged childhood. While riding a roller coaster, men were expressing not only carefree abandon but their right to pleasure denied them as adults.[77]

At the heart of this rebellion was a challenge to Andy Hardy's path to maturity. Although the sharp edge of teenage alienation in James Dean's *Rebel Without a Cause* would have to wait until the

1950s, already in the decade of the Depression there were signs of the disappearance of the aspiring child. The 1930s brought something few have noticed: the birth of a new children's culture that was experienced by many future vets. There was a subtle shift from the middle-class didacticism of Edward Stratemeyer's boys fiction to a new literary world derived from the working-class adventure of the pulp magazines and movie serials. With this came an abandonment of the parent-pleasing themes of boys' learning and growing up. New stories included fewer fathers and sons and more young heroes. The "cliff-hanger" serials, with their themes of the west, crime, and science fiction had dominated working-class movie houses since 1911. Beginning in the early 1920s and especially by 1930, they had become children's fare on Saturday movie matinees with their exciting scenes of blazing guns and exotic outer-space scenes, accentuated by rhythmic pulsations of music.[78] Another venue of the new boys culture appeared shortly after the coming of network radio in 1926 when the hours between four and six p.m. were devoted to a string of fifteen-minute-long serial broadcasts. Stories featured cowboy Tom Mix, spaceship captain Buck Rogers, and many others beating seemingly impossible odds to win the day.[79] This set the stage for a model of boys fantasy imitated many times—Flash Gordon in the 1930s and 1940s, Captain Video in the 1950s, and, of course, action-hero movies since the late 1970s.[80]

All this may sound like a mere shift in venue from the usual boyish heroics of the Hardy Boys or Tom Swift. But there was another subtle transformation: the father had disappeared. Buck Rogers was not an adventurous boy, and there was no longer a father in the background as in the old Stratemeyer stories. That formula, essential for goody-two-shoes fiction, was gone. Rogers was not a youth on his journey to manhood as was Tom Swift. In the 1930s, boys looked up to the fatherless Buck without being reminded of their own immaturity and the work of growing up (and sometimes of their own fathers' unemployment during the Depression). With origins in pulp fiction, Buck Rogers was a child's version of working-class escapism. Buck was the beginning of the decline of the old link between boyhood aspiration and the guidance of bourgeois fatherhood that had so long been part of boy's stories.

Another challenge to Andy Hardy's version of growing up was the *Superman* comic book. Dreamed up by two teenagers, Joe Shuster and Jerry Siegel in 1932, in time Superman became the very symbol of manly uprightness and Americanism. However, Superman, like his imitator Batman, appeared first as a dark figure, in the image of the hard-boiled crime fighter of working-class pulp fiction. Even more to the point, these superheroes were young adults, not teens still under the tutelage of adults. The older characters were villains or humorous and kindly scientists, never father figures. Young readers no longer identified with a boy on his way to a mature manhood but with a "cool" hero who was neither a father nor a son.[81]

If the new kids culture rejected the old didactic tale, it embraced a new culture of the thrill. The change is subtle. The goody-two-shoes theme survived in the patriotism of the action stories of Captain America (and Superman) during World War II. Still, the growing-up themes of the Stratemeyer and *St. Nicholas* eras gave way to an action-drenched fantasy world. The new kids culture borrowed its stories from the escapist and often violent world of male working-class fiction. By the 1940s, especially, the violence and sexuality of the pulp magazines had seeped into jungle and horror comic books.[82] This happened because children kept reading comics as they entered young adulthood (similar to what happened with video games decades later). Millions of soldiers during World War II read them.[83] In response, publishers shifted story lines to appeal to young adults. The "jungle comics" of the 1930s that had featured the child-pleasing Clyde Beatty, a famous animal trainer, and Tarzan with his pet chimpanzee, Cheta, gave way in the late 1940s to themes of muscular men rescuing buxom women from the jaws of wild animals. By the early 1950s, horror comics like William Gaines's *Vault of Horror* and *Shock SuspenStories* offered tales of husbands decapitating unfaithful wives and men using the body parts of murdered men as bases in a baseball game.[84]

This change involved the merging both of children's and working-class fantasy and also the boy and male young-adult audiences. Judge Hardy would not have approved, and neither did middle-class parents, who, by 1954, caused such uproar that the comic-book industry accepted a "code" that eliminated the most extreme forms of this appeal to the gruesome and sensual. Nevertheless, for all of their efforts, the wall between the child and the young adult had been forever breached, and the era of the goody-two-shoes and Andy Hardy was over.

In their place emerged the image of the "cool" youth, not in the sense of the "cool and collected" confidence of the Tom Swift but, as cultural critic Daniel Harris describes it, the "aesthetic of the street."

The cool offered middle-class boys an alternative to A. C. Gilbert's promise of achievement. It was a thumb in the eyes of parents and their genteel values.[85] Today, we may recognize all this in the grungy look of ten-year-olds, teens' tattoos and pierced body parts, and in the continuing popularity among ten- or twelve-year-olds of horror videos and violent video games.

This rejection of the Judge and Andy was invented by and for the heroes of the Greatest Generation. Many resisted, but others were tempted by the rebellious and dark vision of film noir. Some were drawn to those few artists who rejected the roles of provider and company man, took to the road, and found perpetual youth in sensuality and indulgence—in alienation, hedonism, or both. Others relived or improved upon their boyhoods, even as they claimed to be leading boys in sports or scouting. Still others simply refused to give up their boys toys—whether hot rods, stamp collections, or model airplanes. Many as children rejected the cute and the improving image of the boy, embracing the fatherless world of the cool and the thrilling instead. Behind all those models of male maturity were men failing to cope with the ambiguities of modern manhood, struggling against growing up, longing to return to their private Neverlands, or simply coolly defying the well-trod paths to maturity. Many fathers of the 1950s may have wanted to know best, but, secretly or openly, many men of those years didn't even try. It is no surprise that the sons of these men, my generation, while vaguely dreaming of building a better manhood, built instead a more defiant boyhood.

chapter 3.

TALKING About My GENERATION

Leaving home for college in the fall of 1964, I shared in the extraordinary optimism of a generation. There were 76 million baby boomers and I was at the opening edge. At seventeen years old, a member of the largest age group in the country that year, I joined the half of high school graduates who would attend college in 1964 (up from the 16 percent of my father's generation who did so in 1940).[1] Of course, there was frustration as the Vietnam War heated up and seemed never to end and fears and anger from having to submit to a seemingly supreme (grand) father figure, Louis Hershey, the World War II–era chief of the Selective Service. Still, I recall an amazing confidence so clearly expressed in Dylan's "The Times They Are a-Changin'" and other anthems of the new youth culture. Social scientists and journalists told us that we were on the cusp of a new world, and it didn't take much of this talk to persuade us.

Some of the more "dreamy" of us spoke of a "New Man" in the process of being born. Although that term was used generically to refer to both men and women and disappeared by the early 1970s, it certainly suggested that men as males were about to change as well. This thought was inextricably bound up with a wide-ranging change in attitudes about the world and men's roles in it. And with the emergence of feminism, there was an ever-sharper break with the past—regarding everything from dating and marriage to child rearing and male domestic roles, as well as women's access to jobs, education, and legal rights. In 1967, when I was a college junior, I was on the fringe of all this, but by 1969 I became part of the "movement" and remained attached to it into the 1970s.

Being part of a very brief period of upheaval made us movement youth feel special (even superior), a characteristic that made us insufferable to our elders and to those just a few years younger. A friend who was born toward the end of the baby boom (1959) mockingly refers to those of us at the front end of the boom as the "BGers"—the "Blessed Generation" (at least in our own eyes). As annoying as we were, that confidence also made us creative and daring. And although it was based on our status as youth coming of age at a special time with fresh eyes and unencumbered lives, we rejected the notion that we were merely youth in rebellion from adults or escaping adulthood. For a time, we believed we were creating a new way of being men—a vision worth remembering even if it didn't last.

A lot of this confidence came from the political left. Of course, the radicals of the 1960s were a small minority of the college-aged boomers. Between 1965 and 1968, no more than 3 percent of college students considered themselves activists, and only 20 percent joined even one demonstration. This number grew by 1969. Still, even the May 1970 National Guard shootings of Kent State University students who had occupied the campus in revolt over the American invasion of Cambodia ignited only about two million students in protest, just one-quarter of the 7.9 million students in college at the time.[2] And the Vietnam War directly affected only a minority of young men: between 1964 and 1973, about 27 million American men passed through draft age. But only 8.6 million served in the military, and "merely" 2.15 million went to Vietnam (only 8 percent of American male youth, mostly working class, rural, and minority).[3]

But things heated up for us early boomers when President Johnson on June 30, 1967, issued an order that placed nineteen-year-olds at the top of the draft list and removed graduate school exemptions from the draft. I read about this on July 3 as I was waiting for a bus to go home for the Fourth. It absolutely stunned me. Entering my senior year of college in two months, I had planned to go to graduate school to study medieval history the next year. On the ninety-minute trip home, I could think of nothing but how to "beat" the draft—should I go to Canada, get a medical excuse, whatever. It turned out that the average age of soldiers in Vietnam was about twenty-two (some sources say nineteen) compared to the twenty-six in World War II.[4] Our age group saw the draft and the war as a threat directed to us as youth. After all, America had not been attacked. In our eyes, the North Vietnamese attack on a U.S. destroyer in the Gulf of Tonkin (1964), used by President Johnson to win congressional authority to step up the war, was no Pearl Harbor (and it was later shown to have been misrepresented). Moreover, with so few directly involved in Vietnam, no one I knew felt any sense of a patriotic obligation to "serve." Of course, that probably says a lot about my white middle-class background. I saw the draft as an attack on my freedom. Boot camp and military discipline seemed to me at the time as nothing more than a forced return to gym class and the locker room with the hypermasculine anti-intellectual authoritarianism of PE coaches, going back to the tyranny of the stupid, bullying, thuggish boy culture I had hated and suffered through in junior high and high school. The thought of being lorded over by some hick sergeant who loved guns and tormenting dreamy college boys scared me more than the thought of killing or being killed. I may have been a bit unusual, but no doubt many in my generation (and, admittedly, social class) saw the draft after the summer of 1967 as a personal attack. Later I was briefly classified as 1-A (immediately draft eligible) by my draft board during the summer while not in school. I wrote an angry (and stupid) letter to the board, complaining of their attack on my "rights." Many men my specific age have a story about beating or not beating the draft just like Bill Clinton and George W. Bush.

That summer of 1967 brought much else that signaled a generational break. The Beatles transformed themselves from those loveable moppets who appeared on the Ed Sullivan Show in February 1964 to sing "I Want to Hold Your Hand," into "hippies" with their new album, Sgt. Pepper's Lonely Hearts Club Band, with its druggy allusions to "marmalade skies" and cover of the four Beatles in psychedelic band uniforms. Also appearing that summer was The Graduate, a comedy about a fresh college grad who is advised by his father's friend to get into "plastics" but instead is seduced by Mrs. Robinson, a friend of his parents, even as he falls for and wins her daughter. Generational conflict took a still more threatening form in the summer of 1967 when the media heralded the "Summer of Love" as young people flocked to Haight-Ashbury in San Francisco. Pop singer Scott McKenzie beckoned a "new generation" of "gentle people, from across the nation" to come out to the Bay and "wear some flowers in your hair."[5]

Young people have often rebelled against their upbringing, rejecting the training and culture of their childhoods, but we did so with a

vengeance. We turned on the westerns that defined our idea of manhood when we were boys. Although there were six new westerns on
TV in 1966, there had been twenty-seven prime-time cowboy shows
on TV in 1959 when I was thirteen. Most of the new ones in 1966 were
sentimental or family shows like *Little House on the Prairie* and *The
Waltons* that appealed to older folk, especially women, and children.
I never saw any of them. As an adult, Billy Gray, the one-time child
actor who had played the son Bud Anderson on *Father Knows Best*,
turned on the show. In an interview he apologized for the role that
made him famous: "I think we were all well motivated, but what we
did was a hoax. *Father Knows Best* purported to be a reasonable fac-
simile of life. And the bad thing is that the model is so deceitful. . . . If
I could say anything to make up for all the years I lent myself to that
kind of bullshit, it would be: *You* know best."[6]

A curious cocktail of feelings welled up that summer of 1967: fear
and resentment of elders imposing on us their patriotic memories
of World War II with conscription, but also a profound sense of the
possibilities for change. I recall being positively moved by the Young-
blood song of 1967 (rereleased in 1969): "C'mon people now / Smile
on your brother / Everybody get together / Try and love one another
right now." Although the popular media patronized us by labeling
us childlike and naïve, many of us saw ourselves as intellectually and
morally serious challengers to the "system" that the World War II
generation had created. Ironically, our confidence came in part from
embracing the ideas of some of our elders. Still, we thought we had a
new improved version of male maturity.

Rejecting Our Elders' Politics

This confidence took many forms but none more brash than the
surprising resurgence of the political left in a small but influential
portion of 1960s youth. Unlike their liberal elders, with their New
Deal–like social programs, these radicals mistrusted the "system," not
just corporate America but the government bureaucracy, the military,
the university, and other institutions that seemed to be linked in a
seamless web of controls that undermined democracy and personal
freedom. A leader of the Students for a Democratic Society, Paul Potter, expressed this view in April 1965 to explain the escalation of the
war in Vietnam. Potter argued that government, the military, and big

business were part of a power elite, which had manipulated Americans into accepting a war on the false pretense of defending democracy against a global communist conspiracy. Their "real goal," Potter thought, was the growth and perpetuation of their power and profit.[7]

This analysis came directly from sociologist C. Wright Mills's *Power Elite* (1959). A more subtle influence on this attack on the "system" was derived from Herbert Marcuse's *One-Dimensional Man* (1964), a philosophically sophisticated work by a German émigré with deep intellectual roots in Marxism and Freudianism who came to maturity at the end of World War I. In this and later books, Marcuse argues that Western capitalism had overcome its inherent weaknesses that had historically led to class conflict. Economic growth generated by mass consumption and bureaucratic intervention radically reduced political choice and popular understanding of the true nature of the system. In classical leftist terms, Marcuse explained both the "selling out" of workers (who, through mass consumption were no longer radical) and the need for a new "class" of change agents. Conveniently for us, he found these "revolutionaries" in the blacks and in students who could see the manipulation and phoniness of the "system" in everything from its oversized cars to the absurdity of the nuclear arms race. We were self-righteously outraged by a society that was driven by nothing by "a dumb, malleable urge for enjoyment" without any real goal beyond delivering the goods. At the same time, some of us were attracted to the ideas of Norman O. Brown in *Love's Body* (1966) and *Life Against Death* (1959), where he argued for a revolution in bodily expressiveness against a Western capitalist society that systematically repressed desire and feeling. The assumption was that we could get in touch with our "authentic" feelings while recognizing the managed desires of advanced capitalism.[8]

Such moral disdain for the elder generation is hardly new. But we felt our generational revolt was special, giving us the right to claim that we were "new men." In part, we believed this because our critique seemed so serious, so deeply rooted in moral and philosophical principles, at least at the beginning. "The Port Huron Statement" adopted by the Students for a Democratic Society in 1962 illustrates a brief moment of generational idealism (even though technically its leaders were a bit too old to be boomers). Written largely by University of Michigan journalism student Tom Hayden, the statement in retrospect was surprisingly moderate, more in tune with the humanistic philosophical currents of the 1950s than Marxism or the angry, adult-alienating anarchism that followed 1967. Its opening sentence set the tone: "We are people of this generation bred in at least modest comfort, housed in universities, looking uncomfortably to the world we inherit." The statement identified with the anxieties of youth from the educated white middle class, many of whose fathers went to college on the GI Bill and had made secure and satisfying lives for themselves by working within the system. Rather than embracing their fathers' formula for success, these youths were uncomfortable with affluence and stability and the personal and social price paid for winning it. They were stirred by concerns about nuclear apocalypse and technology that made for "meaningless work and idleness," as well as the moral urgency of "the Southern struggle against racial bigotry." "The Port Huron Statement" boldly called for an end to the "national stalemate" that obscured these pressing problems, and it rejected the false "democratic system apathetic and manipulated rather than 'of, by, and for the people.'" Opposing also the slogans and regimentation of the old left, Port Huron called for "participatory democracy" that would bring the powerless "out of isolation and into community" and displace the "power elite." Although the statement endorsed a string of liberal goals (for example, increased welfare and decreased military spending), its main thrust was broadly humanistic: "men have unrealized potential for self-cultivation, self-direction, self-understanding, and creativity. . . . The goal of man and society should be . . . finding a meaning in life that is personally authentic. . . . We oppose the depersonalization that reduces human beings to the status of things."[9]

This was, as the sociologist Michael Kimmel noted, "an anxious plea for a new definition of manhood," a rejection of the corporate "yes man" and "organization" man as well as a vision of a heroic male fighting for the dispossessed in a spirit of love and social solidarity.[10] The Free Speech Movement (protesting a ban on distributing radical political literature on the University of California–Berkeley campus) echoed these sentiments. In its newsletter of November 1964, one radical demanded that the university not treat students like computer punch cards (used in registration) that students were warned not to "bend, fold, spindle or mutilate."[11]

Much of this feeling was negative (a "Great Refusal," in Marcuse's words), spurning the opportunity to join the system and embrace the tradeoff of soul-sucking work for the empty frivolity of play (in Marcuse's Freudian phrasing, "repressive desublimation," a term that enamored me when I first read it). But this anticorporate mentality would also take the form of enthusiastic and often laborious efforts to establish alternatives to the corporate top-down model: food and housing cooperatives, tenant associations, "free universities," and much more.

Along with this attack on the "system," the white New Left identified with those who were excluded from it, the poor and, especially, blacks. Part of this came from an admiration for the struggles of Southern blacks against segregation. In fact, small groups of young whites from SDS and other groups joined to help Southern blacks win the right to vote and to organize the poor in the urban North. But this identification also emanated from an underlying belief that African Americans were somehow "authentic" while whites (even in the working class) were not. This idea was not new to SDSers. Norman Mailer's militant quest for freedom from boring conventionality in Eisenhower's America led to his essay "The White Negro" (1957), in which he identifies with the gutsy unconventional rebel, the outcast, of which the "Negro" was a part. He longed to be a "White Negro" because "it was cathartic and cleansing and purifying for the individual and, on a more abstract level, it put society closer to the life force, releasing creativity that would counterbalance any destructiveness."[12]

It was a short leap from "The White Negro" to the provocative "Student as Nigger" tract that identified the "oppression" of undergraduates of the 1960s with the plight of African Americans. In 1970, I recall hearing a black anthropology professor (in the 1990s a college president) endorse this view. Similar was Hunter Thompson's fascination with the Hell's Angels in the mid-1960s as well as Ken Kesey's sympathetic take on mental patients in his novel *One Flew Over the Cuckoo's Nest* (1962). These oppressed heroes were not merely economically subordinated groups but people who had been "marginalized" and oppressed culturally and who fought back or found a "truth" in their own worlds. My generation was more willing than its elders to become "Negroes." It was not just an act of self-loathing (we thought) but an expression of courage and daring.[13]

African Americans had, of course, their own story of generational rebellion. Beginning with the sit-in of four black students at a whites-only Woolworth's lunch counter in Greensboro, North Carolina, in February 1960, the civil rights movement became identified with youth. Yet this movement, too, drew on its elders: The civil disobedience began when Rosa Parks in Montgomery, Alabama, refused to yield her bus seat to a white person in 1956 (she had roots in the radical Highland Folk School of the 1930s), and it was expanded by Martin Luther King (born in 1929) and his Southern Christian Leadership Conference. The student drive against the segregation of public facilities led to the creation of the Student Nonviolent Coordinating Committee in 1960. Yet SNCC was brought together by a young, Northern black minister, James Lawson, who showed courage and grit in sit-ins, boycotts, and, later, voter registration drives but still represented a traditional source of black leadership—the church. He called the civil rights movement the "beloved community" that would embrace and activate the poor. At the same time, SNCC, like SDS, was determined not to be a youth branch of the NAACP or SCLC, and though it began with the assertive but nonviolent methods of King and others, SNCC quickly became more political. Like the white left, SNCC embraced the idea of the "maximum feasible participation" by the poor.[14]

I came from a too conservative part of the country to have been affected by SDS or SNCC. But I, like many others, was shaped by another trend of the period—a break of the young from the garrison mentality of the Cold War. I grew up at its height—coming to awareness of the world just as the ICBMs were rumbling through Red Square in Moscow on May Day. As a nine-year-old, I remember how *The Weekly Reader*, assigned to fourth-graders throughout America, told us about the DEW (Defense Early Warning) system that provided a radar arc across Canada, giving America a few minutes preparation for a thermonuclear attack. Not long after, while watching one of the B-52 bombers that flew regularly over my house to and from Fairchild Airforce Base, the Strategic Air Command facility just outside Spokane, my eleven-year old sister, dear soul, wickedly remarked that they "could be" the Russians. I was petrified, worried that our walkout basement, where I had a corner for a bedroom, would not protect me from the nuclear blast of a doomsday attack by the dreaded reds. Brought up during the height of the Cold War and the arms race where air-raid drills were as common as fire drills in school, even my very rational and liberal mother accepted the hysteria. She stocked water and canned goods under the stairs to the basement as far as possible from our basement windows. This spot would be our "fallout shelter." The Cold War may have made World War II vets like John Kennedy feel manly and powerful with their "brinksmanship" with the Soviets,[15] but these games of nuclear "chicken" were oppressive and utterly frightening to me.

By the mid-1960s, however, the logic of anticommunism began to erode. As the Vietnam War heated up in 1965, the SDS leader Paul Potter argued at the first antiwar rally in April that the Vietnam War was not a democratic struggle against global communism but an attack of an imperialist power on a freedom-seeking people. This embrace of anti-anticommunism led to what could be called Third World revolution–cheerleading in the radical press (the weekly *Guardian* out of New York and the pamphlets of the Radical Education Project, for example). For years, these publications defended "anti-imperialist" revolutions throughout the world and promoted the ideas of Mao and other very undemocratic communist leaders. Believing that the American government was bad, "almost by definition [and that] the Vietnamese guerrillas must be right and good," historian David Faber notes, these young radicals turned the bipolar thinking of cold warriors on its head.[16] Carl Oglesby, in his widely read *Containment and Change*, made the point clear: the Vietnam War was not about the "invasion" of a democratic South Vietnam from the communist north. It was a revolution against the U.S. attempt to pick up the pieces of a failed European colonialism in Asia and impose a new kind of empire based on U.S.-dominated puppet regimes that were disguised as free (market) societies.[17] Nothing disturbed our elders more, especially the liberal ones who had fought the fascists in World War II and had struggled to defend the labor, civil rights, and civil liberties movements from the slurs of the anticommunist right than the New Left's seeming embrace of the communists.

By 1968, as young adults some of us were willing to accept the idea that the "enemy" was, if not necessarily America, then definitely not the North Vietnamese. We came to believe that the "communist" cause in Vietnam was really just a nationalist movement for freedom from Western domination. For us, this was daring "revelation," making us feel smarter than our elders who had been deceived by anticommunism for years. Even more, it was also psychologically liberating. I felt like the Munchkins in the Wizard of Oz when they sang, "Ding Dong, the witch is dead!" And, when I, along with others, met a Vietnamese student at the University of Wisconsin in 1973 who had "ties" to the National Liberation Front, I was impressed by his maturity and rational and realistic appreciation of the situation. I felt rather smugly that I had heard a privileged truth.

As we have seen, despite clichés associated with the New Left about never trusting anyone over thirty, the early movement was hardly a break from the past. Kenneth Keniston's study of young radicals in 1967 found that most of them had close ties with liberal or even radical families (and thus were sometimes called red-diaper babies), even though they may have felt that their parents had compromised their progressive values. SDS was founded in 1960 with the support of the League for Industrial Democracy, which was funded by liberal trade unions and Democrats. The language of "The Port Huron Statement" was commonplace in the circles of not only such cultural radicals of the 1950s as Mailer and the Beats but also the liberal establishment—in the popular sociology of Vance Packard and even the human-potential psychology of Abraham Maslow.[18]

Still, despite drawing on the ideas of our elders, we quickly broke from their personal leadership. This was clear with the SDS members, who rejected their elder mentors over their attempts to control the movement and their insistence that SDS hold to an orthodox anti-communist position. As historian W. J. Rorabaugh found, Free Speech Movement activists despaired at a "world created and then frozen into place in 1945." This was the world of their fathers that seemed to promise only "the projection of twenty years of stasis indefinitely into the future" and offered only an "inheritance of a sterile world without any chance to alter it."[19] The students in the Free Speech Movement had sought inspiration from their elders in civil rights movement but criticized the University of California's administration for not living up to the vaunted traditions of the free expression and humanistic values. Mario Savio, its famed leader, was appalled by the claim of university president Clark Kerr that Berkeley was part of the "knowledge industry." Savio concluded that the university administration's goal was to train the young merely to be technocratic cogs in the corporate machine. Though Kerr was a liberal Quaker and Democrat who had opposed a loyalty oath for faculty in the McCarthy era, he was caught between conservative authorities and the student radicals whom he "had neither the wish to stifle nor the will to embrace." To the young radicals, however, he was the generational enemy.[20]

It is worth noting that not all youth calling for a break from the "establishment" were from the left. The Young Americans for Freedom, founded at the estate of conservative publisher William Buckley in September 1964, disavowed the moderate Republicanism of their elders as expressed by Eisenhower and Nixon. These young radicals on the right attacked their fathers' accommodation to New Deal regulation and doctrine of peaceful coexistence with communism, calling instead for liberty against the interventionist state and victory over the reds.[21] Although far less a presence on campus in the 1960s than the New Left, this expression of generational conflict turned out to be more successful than mine, winning control of the Republican Party in Ronald Reagan's election in 1980 (albeit led by a member of the "father's" generation) and subsequently isolating Republican moderates like Gerald Ford.

In any case, despite borrowing from their fathers, these sons ultimately rejected their elders. And as naïve as some of the ideas of the boomers would ultimately seem, they were hardly a retreat into boyhood. Instead, while insisting that the older generation had "lied" or was "duped" and often had "sold out," the radical boomers were certain that they would do a better job. Those youth on the left were convinced that they were about to inherit the world, make affluence (assumed by all to be an unending product of technology) more humane and more fairly distributed, and wrest control from the power-mad. We thought we were "real men," without often using that phrase—telling truth to power and chivalrously defending the oppressed, not being wimpy sell-outs like our "fathers" or caving in to expediency and tolerating evil.

Rejecting Our Fathers' Culture

The politically consciously youth of the 1960s were not the only boomers to rebel against the "Greatest Generation." Some of the young also joined a broader cultural upheaval against the values and life expectations of their parents. In the *Graduate*, the title character, Ben, despite being surrounded by goal-oriented adults with aggressive can-do ethics, has no goals. Many of us boomers understood his lackadaisical attitude about finding a job, as he dreamily floats in his parent's pool all summer after graduating, unwilling to commit to the corporate world. The new youth culture repudiated the "happy slave's" trade-off of repressive and meaningless work for the right to join the consumer society. A 1966 *Newsweek* survey of college seniors found that only 31 percent were seriously considering careers in business and 74 percent felt business was a "dog eat dog" world. A *Fortune* study found that few students embraced making money, and many criticized the conformity and lack of personal fulfillment in business. Though few would have identified themselves as "hippies" or counterculturalists, they had embraced an essential element of the hippie critique of their parents' generation.[22]

A few years later, this countercultural response of college kids seeped into the world of young factory workers, or so it seemed to the many commentators on the productivity lag of the young, as shown especially in the strike at GM's Lordstown, Ohio, plant in 1972, a new factory noted for its fast assembly lines. The traditional pride in work and ability to "take it" (and the willingness to trade off grueling labor for high wages) seemed to have given way to a new definition of manliness, a willingness to stand up to bosses and give priority to pleasure over the drudgery of early family and responsibility.[23]

This seeming rejection of ambition and success (and the comforts that it brought) was hard to understand for our elders, who were brought up during the Depression. In "What Is a Hippie," (1967) Guy Strait tries to explain this apparent refusal to embrace "grown-up" values and culture. The problem is the elders' obsession with financial security. With their Depression mentalities, they hound the young to join the rat race and believe that "competition is holy." The young hippie instead is convinced that "our prosperity is the bringer of misery," meaningless work, and a dehumanizing drive for useless things. "He wants no part of self-defeating goals."[24]

In retrospect, these words sound like those of a boy unwilling to accept the "real world" of adult responsibility and hard work. Yet at the time, the "hippies" believed their elders had been deluded by "self-defeating" goals that deprived them of meaningful relationships and self-awareness. They thought that they had a different understanding of growing up. There is nothing so radical about this rejection of competition for contemplation: such ideas had been at the heart of religious and philosophical movements for ages. And elements in the counterculture embraced alternative models of the "wise man" in, for example, the fascination with Indian gurus such as Maharishi Mahesh Yogi (founder of transcendental meditation).

To be sure, the most obvious sign of the hippie was the seemingly silly rejection of conventional sartorial standards—not only shedding the suit, overcoat, and fedora, for example, but also adopting much more androgynous dress (for example, in more colorful clothing for men). In an informal survey conducted in the late 1970s of 1,005 members of the Woodstock generation, Rex Weiner and Deanne Stillman found that 37 percent admitted that they had stopped using deodorant during the heyday of the 1960s counterculture. I recall a handsome, well-coifed male student I knew in 1969 who nevertheless took pride in the fact that he had abandoned deodorant, saying he wanted "nature's way of smelling."[25] Of course, this was absurd (as I recall thinking, but not saying, at the time), but this quest for a natural life—picking up a theme as old as Rousseau—in contrast to the artificiality of the striving life of corporate America, was not always so puerile.

Even more central to the counterculture was a cynical disdain for conformity and an embrace of tolerance—doing one's own thing and letting others do the same. For many boomers, that disdain for conformity started with the discovery of *Mad Magazine*. *Mad*, originally a parody of comic books ("Superduperman" and Mickey Rodent), was published from 1952 by Bill Gaines (1922–1992), a brash son of a comic book publisher. Gaines, however, was first famous for his outrageous horror "comics," which were the centerpieces of a Senate hearing concerning the effects of violent comic books on children. Wisely, Gaines abandoned horror and the threat of censorship, but he did not give up thumbing his nose at respectable 1950s society. He remained the Greatest Generation rebel and found a new format for *Mad* in 1955: parodies of media celebrities, politicians, movies (mocking the *Sound of Music* as the *Sound of Money*), the Cold War (with the long-running cartoon, "Spy vs. Spy"), and especially advertising. He appealed to our hatred of the endlessly repeated ads on the *Mickey Mouse Club* when it appeared in 1955 (especially the Cheerio's Kid saving the "damsel in distress" after eating the cereal that turned his bicep into a Cheerio "O"). And so we found delight in our weekly trip to the drug store to buy *Mad* ("25 cents Cheap!") to read its mockery of the commercial culture that was fed to us. I started reading it in 1957, when I was eleven. Instead of accepting ads, Gaines made fun of them. My favorite was a full back-cover ad showing a pack of cigarettes floating in a pond surrounded by lush foliage. This suggested a scene, shown over and over in popular "grown-up" magazines of the time, that hyped the presumably cool and gentle taste of Salem, a popular menthol cigarette. *Mad*'s caption, offering typically wicked irony, read: "Sail'em, Don't inhale them." Gaines affirmed our disdain for insulting and manipulative advertising as well as the mores of a bland and conformist culture. As a teenager I read Vance Packard's more serious attacks on advertising in *The Hidden Persuaders* (1957) and on conformity in *The Status Seekers* (1959). Our generation learned not just to question authority but to mock its pretension and hypocrisy.

For younger boomers, *Mad* in the 1960s became an entrée into the world of political dissent, and the magazine reached its peak circulation in 1973 with 2.4 million copies sold weekly. *Mad's* spirit was with me and my pals when we were looking for a place to mount our last poster of a big red fist announcing our student strike in the spring of 1970 at Washington State University.[26] We thought we were very clever when we stapled it to a tree in a daycare playground, thinking somehow that we would "radicalize" the toddlers.[27] Very Bill Gaines and very silly, but we thought we had something to teach the young that was revolutionary, a new way to grow up.

Of course, this rejection of conventionality was often no more than the thrill of provocation. Such was Ken Kesey's romp through drugs and danger in the Bay Area and then on through America with his Merry Pranksters in 1964. The Pranksters traveled in a wildly painted 1939 International Harvester school bus and dressed in superhero capes and goggles that Kesey financed with earnings from *One Flew Over the Cuckoo's Nest*. Recording it all was Tom Wolfe, a so-called new journalist, who told the story in *The Electric Kool-Aid Acid Test*. With the goal of "pranking" everything they encountered (including waving a banner announcing [in obvious mockery] that a vote for Barry Goldwater for president in 1964 "Is a Vote for Fun"). They enjoyed "tootling the multitudes" by "sewing the American flag to the seat of [their] pants."[28] The Merry Pranksters had many imitators. I recall a group of graduate students and faculty from Washington State University in 1970 who roamed the small conservative farm towns of southeastern Washington as a "radical motorcycle gang" in long hair, beards, and leather jackets with "Up Against the Wall Motherfucker" in Swahili written on their backs. This silly replay of *The Wild One* and its profanity was no doubt lost on the conservative townspeople, but the "bikers" found it hilarious. It is hard not to wonder whether the "New Man" wasn't just the boy mocking the old man.

Key to doing one's own thing was expanding one's consciousness with drugs, sex, and rock and roll. And this element of the counterculture is even more difficult to square with the idea of a "New Man," though many tried. Drug use was supposed to free the individual from society's games of role-playing and status and the narrow rules of logical and conventional perception. As drug "philosopher" Robert Hunter claimed of psychomorphic drug experimenters, "What do [they] 'see' while stoned . . . that isn't already apparent to a mind not locked in a conceptual cage. . . . Through their drug experiences they have come to see a reality not split by Aristotelian logic or Christian dualism."[29]

This surge in drug use included the "rediscovery" of marijuana and LSD, a compound invented in 1943 and used experimentally by psychiatrists and scientists. LSD was popularized by renegade Harvard psychologist Timothy Leary in 1962, who passed it on to Allen Ginsberg and his crowd. Drugs emphasized experience, making an ordinary encounter with a tree or a fragment of a conversation extraordinary, if only for a moment. Who from that time doesn't recall how impressed they were about their discovery of some profound "truth" while high on marijuana or LSD only to forget what it was all about the next day? Drugs seemed to give our generation what our parents could not get with alcohol—the appearance of deep meaning and even deeper sensuality. To Leary, writing in 1968, the "LSD trip is a religious pilgrimage."[30] For him, to "turn on" was to turn one's senses into "cameras to put you in touch with the vibrant energies around you." Getting "high" was, of course, not new. Parents used alcohol and tobacco. As the Rolling Stones reminded us, mother had her "little helpers" in the uppers and downers of prescription drugs, but our drugs were "different." Marijuana was a high that broke down barriers—"joints" were passed around a circle, and the drugs did not merely help us cope with stress but opened up "reality." The elders were hypocrites to denounce the new drugs, young countercultural-ists claimed, when they had plenty of theirs, and what's more, the new drugs actually "raised consciousness," taking the young "beyond" the narrow worlds of their elders, promising to shape a new and better way of growing up.

A series of Trips Festivals beginning in January 1966 at the San Francisco Longshoremen's Hall launched the new drug subculture. Luminaries of the acid revolution, including the old Beats (Ginsberg chanting and Neal Cassady dressed as a gorilla bridegroom), appeared along with such relative newcomers as Kesey and his Merry Prank-sters (in clown costumes) and the rock groups the Grateful Dead and Big Brother and the Holding Company. Even the Hell's Angels, the Oakland motor cycle gang, were there. These characters promised somehow to bring a New Age with a strange mix of drugs, Eastern religion, colorful clothes, and outlawry. This "magical moment," as nostalgic old hippies saw it, soon passed, of course, but the drug "rev-olution" seemed to many participants at the time as a liberation from an oppressive past.[31]

The generational break was also about sex, a legacy of the revelations of the Kinsey reports of 1948 and 1953 as well as the 1966 Masters and Johnson study of sexuality. And even if Masters and Johnson provided a fresh understanding of female sexuality (the primacy of the clitoral orgasm, especially), the main proponents of sexual liberation were male (many of whom, of course, learned at the feet of Hugh Hefner). While sexual mores generally changed only in the 1970s, middle-class white college students in the 1960s came to reject conventional views (though even as late as 1969, two-thirds of Americans believed premarital sex was wrong).[32]

Of course, if there was drugs and sex, there was also rock and roll. Typical of the hyperbole of the time were the claims of John Sinclair, working-class anarchist and leader of a Detroit rock band called MC5. He insisted that rock music is one of the most vital revolutionary forces in the West: "It blows people all the way back to their senses and makes them feel good, like they're *alive* again in the middle of this monstrous funeral parlor of western civilization." Rock, Sinclair declared, is a "model of the revolutionary future" as we anticipate the day when useless and antihuman jobs will be "done away with immediately once the people are in power and the machines are freed to do all the work."[33] Over the top and absurd, yes, but this was in tune with the times and the astonishing faith that loud pulsating music was shaping the future.

Rock music may have originated in mid-1950s, but it did not age with the teens that screamed for Elvis. It continued to be the music of youth, constantly changing to meet the demands and earn the spending money of baby-boom youth in the 1960s. Shaped by the independent record companies that sprang up in the 1950s outside the conventional constraints of popular music, rock could cross the color line, blending white country with black rhythm and blues. Mailer's evocative idea of the "White Negro" freed from the boring repressive culture of middle-class affluence was expressed in white attraction to "black" music, even if it was sometimes sold under a white "cover" artist. Elvis borrowed Arthur Crudup's blues, and white-bread rockers like Pat Boone performed sanitized versions of black songs like "Tutti Fruiti." Still, as the journalist Jeff Greenfield recalled in 1973, "Rock and roll was elemental, savage, dripping with sex; it was just as our parents feared."[34] The terror that had gripped white parents, that rock would make their offspring into sex-crazed maniacs, seemed confirmed when singer Janis Joplin said, "My music isn't supposed to make you riot. It's supposed to make you fuck."[35] That must have been a relief to parents! And rock seemed to get a lot more threatening in the late 1960s. The Beatles shifted from such ditties of teen love as "I Want to Hold Your Hand" (1963) to songs influenced by mysticism, drugs, and raw and open sex, such as "Why Don't We Do It in the Road?" (1968). To understand just how "revolutionary" rock was in 1968, we have only to refer to the most popular TV shows of that year, all escapist situation comedies: *The Andy Griffith Show*, *The Lucy Show*, and *Gomer Pyle, USMC*. Another long-running hit was *The Beverly Hillbillies*, which, along with its many imitators, offered a "humorous reconciliation of old virtues and new mores."[36] That certainly wasn't the point of drugs, sex, and rock and roll in the youth counterculture that saw these programs as childish.

The counterculture seemed to create a new community as it invaded and created its own space. As historian David Faber notes, it did this by "taking over a few city blocks or a few acres of countryside and trying to make a world out of it, a place where all the old rules were up for grabs."[37] The hippie quest for "authenticity," associated with the poor and minorities, or even the outlaw, drug user, and causal partaker of mystical religions, became localized in university towns (around Telegraph Avenue in Berkeley or Mifflin Street in Madison, for example) but also in transitional neighborhoods like Haight-Ashbury in San Francisco. When the old beat district of the North Beach became too expensive by 1965, hip clothing stores and coffee shops like the Blue Unicorn moved to "the Haight," an ethnically mixed, working-class and student area east of Golden Gate Park. For a brief time these places became magical blends of individualists doing their thing in defiance of conventional society.[38]

Then there was the Human Be-In of January 1967 in Golden Gate Park, a meeting of Berkeley activists and the "love generation" of Haight-Ashbury. Perhaps 25,000 wandered by to hear music and partake of the free LSD and to soak up the good vibes preached by Timothy Leary, who dressed like a Buddhist holy man. But he talked like a new Moses with a fresh set of commandments, declaring, "Thou shalt not alter the consciousness of thy fellow man," but also, "Thou shalt not prevent thy fellow man from altering his own consciousness."[39] A lot in this counterculture didn't seem that grown-up, but it at least took itself seriously as a revolution in consciousness and community.

As was the case of our political rebellion, the counterculture drew on the past even as it rejected its elders' values. The explanation for this contradiction is simple. Insofar as they embraced free love and the drug culture, counterculturalists were challenging the "Father Knows Best" world of postwar suburbia, but they were also embracing the rebels of their fathers' generation. The hippies were, as many have noted, a "democratic" or mass version of the bohemian tradition of the Beats of the late 1950s, who had protested the models of maturity their own generation inherited. Not only had many of the hippies been exposed to such classical critiques of a conformist middle-class culture as Paul Goodman's *Growing Up Absurd* and J. D. Salinger's *Catcher in the Rye*, but some had even read beat primers like Jack Karouac's *On the Road* and Allen Ginsberg's *Howl*.[40]

In some ways, Charles Reich's countercultural manifesto, *The Greening of America* (1970), amounted to little more than a claim that the Beats' indictment and much of mainstream lifestyle was finally being embraced by American society. To Reich, this was a triumph of "Consciousness III" over the old ethos of rugged individualism and the more recent culture of corporate-consumer conformity. The march of technology and business and bureaucratic consolidation ("Consciousness II") had destroyed the individuality of the frontier and small business and craft ("Consciousness I") not by naked oppression but by enslaving wage earners to meaningless work while satisfying their false wants as consumers. Reich's solution was not to resurrect a frontier individualism (as many, including the Beats, had longed for) but to embrace affluence in a new kind of personal expressiveness (in sex, drugs, and rock and roll), as well as to cultivate a new appreciation for nature and an inner life that had been presumably repressed in the conformist 1950s. This was the New Man, at least, the "hippie" version of it.[41]

Of course, the political and cultural sides of youth dissent were different and even in conflict. The "politicos" (my crowd) were more willing to defer gratification and were even relatively austere and self-consciously rational in contrast to the hippies. I recall, for example, being quite put off by a rock party (where drugs were used), that followed a spring 1970 antiwar demonstration that I helped to organize. I thought the party took away from the seriousness of our cause. I'm sure my "hippie" friends thought that I was a square and didn't appreciate how "liberation" went well beyond politics. There were different versions of the "New Man."

New Men and Feminism

Despite these contrasts, many of us shared a rejection of our fathers' ideals of masculinity. This was no more clearly expressed than in our mockery of the old male heroes: the cardboard cowboy John Wayne, that strong silent man who became for us the unexpressive, authoritarian, and elusive father. We mocked Wayne in *The Green Berets* (1968), which glamorized crack troops in the Vietnam War. But the arch-dysfunctional father was the character Archie in *All in the Family*, whose fury, ignorance, and bigotry was made the butt of the joke in his regular encounters with his graduate student son-in-law, who, despite all of his best efforts, could not bring Archie into the real and modern world (more on this in chapter 4). More profound was the rejection of the military route to male maturity. Since 1940, with the introduction of universal male conscription, the army had become, in theory, an obligation of all American males at eighteen. There were "deferments" for students, assuming that military service might come later and rare exemptions requiring a disability, fatherhood status, religious training, or certifiable pacifism (requiring "alternative service"). Not only was a two-year stint of military training and service a legal obligation, for many it was the price of entry into adult male citizenship, a rite of passage that made a "man" of the boy, teaching him discipline and the ability to take and give orders. We openly broke from this, utterly rejecting the idea that manhood meant military service. Maybe we did this out of self-interest, but we really thought that being a soldier didn't make the boy into a man. We laughed when conservative columnist Stewart Alsop accused us of hiding our cowardice behind our high-flying antiwar rhetoric. "Beating the draft" was a topic of many a Saturday-night party before conscription was finally eliminated in 1973. Like Archie's "meathead" nemesis of a son-in-law, we thought that we could shed a lot of the markers of manhood—obeying and being obeyed, self-repression, and participating in traditional rites of manhood. All of these things, we believed, had nothing to do with "growing up" and instead served as a crutch. We felt we were "together" enough not to require the barracks experience, be it in the Boy Scouts, in the army, or on a hunting trip. Part of our confidence in our maturity was that we felt we didn't need older mentors to show us the way into wisdom and responsibility. Of course, many men of my generation never embraced any of this, but my crowd of radical youth in the late 1960s and early 1970s was hardly aware of them.

Another marker of our "maturity" was the ability of at least some of us to cope with, not "freak out" at, the independence of our "sisters," at least for a time. This wasn't, of course, the case in the earliest phases of the women's movement, in part because that movement was often a reaction to the romance of male heroism that was so deeply involved in both the white and black radical movements of the early 1960s. The September 1968 demonstration against the Miss America pageant in Atlantic City and the crowning of a sheep in mockery of the event, introduced many Americans to women's liberation. This surprising assault by women on what had become the pinnacle expression of female beauty and virtue had its roots in the early civil rights movement and the New Left, where women played significant, if usually subordinate roles. White women activists had been edged out of civil rights organizations by 1967 when African American leaders called for black autonomy. At the same time, these women had become frustrated by their lack of leadership roles in the antiwar movement. An early expression of this disenchantment came in November of 1965, when Casey Hayden and Mary King, who had been volunteers in SNCC, wrote about how treatment of blacks by whites was similar to that of women by men.[42]

The women's movement appeared as part of a broad wave of identity politics that called for building ethnic, racial, gender, or sexual identity around claims of oppressed status and distinct natural or cultural attributes. The movement stressed that participants understand themselves as women who needed to change their relationships with men as lovers, friends, colleagues, and bosses. These personal matters were as political as women's legal and institutional demands for economic, political, and civil equality. An older group of women who in 1966 had revived the early-twentieth-century feminist movement when they formed the National Organization for Women (NOW), were at first hostile to the New Left's call for "personal politics." Betty Friedan, NOW activist and author of *The Feminine Mystique*, mocked New Left feminists for starting a "bedroom war," creating a diversion from traditional political goals, and as divisive, focusing on male attitudes and personal behavior (the male chauvinist pig) rather than attainable and practical political goals. But young white women in college embraced the transformation of what it meant to be female at a personal level. The key institution of new feminist identity politics were women's consciousness-raising meetings, which began in 1968 and excluded men, allowing women to discuss common experiences in dating, child rearing, and other frustrating experiences. For many women, consciousness-raising became a rite of passage into the feminist cause. These radicals not only insisted on making the personal political in consciousness-raising groups but rejected collaboration with the system and instead pushed for women's centers to foster an array of issues from domestic violence and women's health to women's music and spirituality. Among the many manifestations of radical feminism was journalist Gloria Steinem's founding of Ms. in 1971 and the rise of the lesbian movement.[43]

As part of the larger movement of sexual identity politics and a protest against discrimination, the male gay movement emerged in 1969 in response to a "homophobic" riot in New York City at the Stonewall Inn, a gay bar. Like its counterparts in SDS, SNCC, and other black and white radical movements, the gay rights movement had roots among the rebels of the "Greatest Generation" in the 1940s. One source was the International Bachelors Fraternal Order for Peace and Social Dignity (which became in 1950 the Mattachine Society), led by the erstwhile communist Harry Hay. This group became a kind of NAACP for gays. In 1970, Hay adapted to the radicalism of the 1960s by proposing a gay identity that stressed love and reconciliation over violence and competition. He suggested a commonality between the gay and female experience of oppression and expression, eventually referring to his identity as the "third gender." By 1979, "radical faerie" groups inspired by Hay met near Tucson, Arizona, to bond and engage in historical and contemporary forms of gay dress and celebration (including "country dancing" and flamboyant makeup and clothing), making virtue and delight out of the old stereotypes of "silly sissies." This was by no means the only or even dominant movement among gays. Consider the gay clone identity that rejected the "fairy" stereotype for a tough, working-class male look with short hair, bomber jacket, and jeans. But even the gay clone made a caricature of that hypermasculine look and often advocated a profeminist masculinity.[44]

Historians have long noted how the women's movement (and the gay rights movement) broke barriers and challenged the behavior and beliefs of male-dominated liberal (as well as conservative) institutions. It led to confusion among many movement men.[45] Over time, however, it also gave expression to the New Man ideas of boomers. While many men were bewildered by feminism or treated it with patronizing disdain, men of my crowd greeted the women's movement as an opportunity to express *personally* the politics of equality and participation. Over the academic year of 1969–70, I was a "leader" on my old college campus of the antiwar and "liberation" cause. This was the year of the largest demonstrations of the 1960s. During this period, I recall a great change in the roles of women in the movement. The young women who in October 1969 were making coffee and running the ditto machines for the young men who gave the speeches and wrote the leaflets for the Moratorium antiwar marches were, by May 1970, leading the strike committee for a Black Students Center on campus. I and many of my male colleagues not only accepted this change but felt invigorated and even proud of it. Two years later, a Brazilian undergraduate and I provided provisions for women (who included our wives) who had occupied a building at Harvard University in their demand for a Women's Center. During a demonstration in support of the center, we found ourselves in an awkward situation. In the march down Massachusetts Avenue in Cambridge, a corps of women surrounded us, chanting, "Up against the wall, motherfucker! Off the pricks!" Rather than being outraged, we took this seemingly threatening gesture as "just part of the process." Looking back, others would have thought that we were wimps, but we thought we were New Men, strong enough not to need the servility or even civility of women. The New Man was comfortable making and eating quiche. In the late 1970s, he was willing to don a snuggly (an uncomfortable front-loading papoose carrier for newborns) and was eager to go to Lamaze classes to help his partner prepare for natural childbirth. I did all three. And popular culture accommodated a new view of the man in John Travolta's rejection of macho and in an openness to gay culture in the Village People, for example.

Although few joined profeminist male groups (and many of those who did seem to have had personal links with feminist women), the very existence of such groups is instructive about the times. In the early 1970s, while women withdrew into their consciousness-raising sessions, these profeminist men formed their own. They discussed how male prerogatives and traditional macho attitudes were harmful not only to gender relations but to men themselves. Initially, there was little malice between the two groups. In fact, feminist publisher Gloria Steinem wrote an article in the *Washington Post* (June 7, 1970) called " 'Women's Liberation' Aims to Free Men, Too," and later opened *Ms.* to sympathetic male writers. NOW even created a committee led by Warren Farrell to improve intergender cooperation, and women were active in conferences of male feminists that began in 1975. These conferences led eventually to groups like the National Organization for Changing Men in 1985 and its successor, the National Organization for Men Against Sexism in 1990. NOMAS combined support for personal growth outside the traditional bounds of masculine competition and aggression with political support for feminist and gay issues. Inspired by feminist women in their lives, these men rejected traditional masculine roles and saw in feminism an opportunity to express personally the simple and essential justice of gender equality. They embraced, however awkwardly, changes in their language and behavior toward women.[46]

Works such as Warren Farrell's *The Liberated Man* (1974), Joseph Pleck and Jack Sawyer's *Men and Masculinity* (1974), and Jack Nichols's, *Men's Liberation: A New Definition of Masculinity* (1975) linked men's emotional salvation with ending sexism. These works argued that male privilege was a false advantage and even a moral and health danger to men. By abandoning restricted sex roles, men would expand their emotional lives, have deeper relations with women and children, and improve their health and life expectancy. Common was the notion of defining sex roles as "social constructions": The male sex role (defined by competition, aggression, stolidity, etc.) was a cultural imposition (rather than a natural fact) that men could willfully discard. This view was part of the optimism of the era but also reflected the idea that men could "grow up" to be different from their fathers.[47]

As Farrell saw it in 1974, the male sex role "confines men at the same time as it confines women." Obsessing with the rights and duties of the provider limits his time with his spouse and children and deprives him of the delights of domesticity. The male sex role makes him a good talker and thus a bad listener, self-confident but seldom humble, and fixed on sexuality and thus seldom sensual. Growing up male too often means escaping from mother's hold and rejecting all things associated with girls. Masculinity starts with a "fear of femininity," Farrell insisted. He rejected the "myth of the maternal instinct" because it denies the idea that men and women could or should share equally in child rearing and creates a vicious cycle of inattentive fathers begetting sons who become, in turn, hypermale and neglectful of their own sons. Farrell argued for the progressive personal political solution of a rearranged and shorter workweek to make it possible for husbands and wives to balance work and family. Beyond these high-minded social and economic goals (ideas, incidentally, that have animated a lot of my writing over the years), Farrell demanded that men reassess the details of their behavior and feelings in relationships with both men and women. He asked, "Is the wattage of the stereo more important than intimate conversation with one's women? Do I feel particularly concerned about not having some one contradict me in front of another woman?"[48] The "real" grown-up man outgrew these obsessions.

Farrell was hardly alone. Typical was a statement from the Berkeley Men's Center in the early 1970s: "We want to relate to both men and women in more human ways—with warmth, sensitivity, emotion, and honesty. . . . We want to be equal with women and to end destructive competitive relationships with men."[49] The "Statement on the Formation of the National Organization for Changing Men" lamented that men were "taught from childhood to be unemotional, aggressive, un-nurturing, mainly directed toward work and career achievement, unconcerned with the quality of personal relationships, exploitative of women, wary of other men, reflexively competitive, isolated from children, and profoundly afraid of admitting to any interest, hobby, attitude, or other quality that might somehow suggest . . . a homosexual."[50] We saw this not as "self-loathing" but as an accurate assessment of our dilemma as men. We had to change not only for a better world but also to give ourselves a "heroic opportunity" to make a manly break from the old crutches of privilege and emotional constraint.

There were many "creative" ways that we challenged not just conventional manliness but also gender relations. These included abandoning the "traditional" date (such as the rituals of the male inviting and calling on the female and selecting and paying for all activities) as well as a new attentiveness to female sexual satisfaction. One of the notable changes was the wedding ceremony with personally written "vows" eschewing the old dictum from the Book of Common Prayer: "*obey, serve,* love, honor and keep" for the woman, but "love, comfort, honor and keep" for the man. Many would now find these personal vows embarrassing, but at least, the "obey" and "serve" part for women was permanently deleted in many services, replaced by "cherish."

A certainly more lasting and significant change came in the rites of childbearing with the advent of the husband-coached birth and father-newborn bonding. This was not the direct result of the 1960s social movement. It had its origins among physicians who, beginning in the 1930s, opposed the recent advent of the medicalization of childbirth (with the widespread use of anesthetics like "twilight sleep," forceps in birth, and the antiseptic delivery room from which all but medical staff and the birthing mother were excluded). Grantly Dick-Read of England, Fernand Lamaze of France, and Robert Bradley of the United States argued that medicalized birth had made this natural event more painful and traumatic than necessary. Bradley especially encouraged natural birth (modeled after other mammals) to shortened labor and to reduce side effects on mother and baby. Key to natural birth was the preparation of the mother-to-be with detailed instructions in the birthing process and in relaxation and breathing exercises to ease the delivery. These medical reformers were only secondarily (if at all) interested in reintroducing men into the birthing process as a way of emotionally confirming fatherhood roles. Still, in the process of preparing mothers for delivery and facilitating natural birth in the early stages of labor, fathers proved to be practical assets in what Bradley called "Husband-Coached Childbirth" in 1965. Lamaze student Elizabeth Bing popularized childbirth classes in the United States, offering fathers the role of "managers" of the mother's breathing during contractions. This idea took time to spread. Only in 1974 did the American College of Obstetricians and Gynecologists endorse husband (or other) coaching in the delivery room (and then only if the doctor agreed).[51]

By the mid-1980s, however, these classes took off, becoming practically required of fathers-to-be as well as mothers. When my daughter was born in 1985, only the oafish and ignorant man failed to attend these classes in my university town. Men dutifully carried a pillow for their pregnant wives to each meeting and coached the mothers-to-be during labor (reminding her to "puff" during contractions). For many men, the rite included accompanying her into the delivery room, perhaps even "catching" the baby at birth, cutting the umbilical cord, and presenting the baby to the mother for her first breast feeding. This was, in its way, revolutionary. Since the 1920s, medical staff had systematically excluded fathers from the birthing process, reducing their role to preparing the car for the trip to the hospital, building a cradle in anticipating the newborn, conducting a vigil in the waiting room, and passing out cigars after the birth. These new rituals brought men back into the mystery of birth. Even more, these new prebirth and delivery-room practices restored the traditional couvade, those male rituals that drew fathers into a symbolic participation in birth (including simulated birth pains in some non-western cultures). All this was to make fathers "bond" with their newborns, creating an emotional attachment from birth that presumably would make new fathers more engaged with their offspring than had been the case with their own dads.[52] Many of us felt a little silly through much of this, but we also felt innovative and that it did make us better men. Yes, we felt that we had become more "mature" than our fathers had been.

Things Fall Apart

While people like me might find much admirable about the dissidence of our generation (even admitting that this rebellion was often not representative), there was a lot about its challenge to our elders that suggests not so much a New Man as an unhinged boy. Certainly it is hard not to see the history of the New Left, especially after 1967 as the story of lost idealism and ultimately a retreat into childish tantrums. Still, events suggest a complex story that cannot be reduced to adolescent psychology. With the passing of the Civil Rights and Voting Rights Acts of 1964 and 1965 and, even more so, with the Black Power movement of 1967, the white activists' role in the black rights movement sharply declined. The new "crop" of student leaders in SDS had no ties to the old liberal intellectuals and increasingly was influenced by the counterculture. Not many read Mills or Camus as did Tom Hayden and the other founders, and fewer had experience in the very real tough world of organizing Southern blacks to vote. Instead, they had become frustrated with a war and military system that expanded as they protested against them. The activists responded with an escalation of strident antiwar rhetoric and actions, such as blocking troop movements, burning draft cards, taking over buildings at universities, and even firebombing military research centers, as at the University of Wisconsin.[53]

A parallel transformation can be seen in the movement of young African Americans. Despite the enthusiastic participation of Northern white progressives in voter-registration drives in 1963 and 1964, young black leaders became anxious that white Northerners were perpetuating traditional white-black power relations by assuming leadership. By 1965, they were beginning to abandon the integrationist goals of their elders and to call for all-black organizations. SNCC's Stokley Carmichael not only demanded black separation and autonomy from whites in the Black Power movement, but he rejected the religious-inspired tactic of nonviolence of the older generation. This change was not merely an expression of generational conflict; it was a response to white segregationist attacks on black activists, often with police compliance, which led militants to the politically explosive idea of self-defense. Martin Luther King and other older leaders feared that Black Power, with its nationalism and symbols of racial pride (in dress and language), as well as its calls for freedom from white paternalism and even armed self-defense, would only isolate African Americans and provide a justification for white racism.

The Black Panther Party (1966), based in Oakland, California, put the new militancy into practice when this band of young mostly male African Americans ostentatiously armed themselves in urban chapters that quickly formed across the country. They won some community support with their free breakfast program for poor school kids and other self-help projects and offered a culture of male heroic self-sacrifice as an alternative to the self-destructive and antisocial values of black street gangs. As Judith Newton notes, many of the early young male activists in the Black Panther Party had childhood memories of community support networks in the South and embraced Malcolm X's *Autobiography* as a model of heroic masculinity in defense of their neighborhoods. As she notes, "by extending provision for family into service of the black community as a whole and by enlarging personal rebellion into to a militant, collective struggle for structural social change, Black Power would supply new strategies for feeling 'I'm a man.'" Still, the Panthers became notorious in confrontations with police that led to government raids on Panther offices and the deaths of Panther activists like Fred Hampton in Chicago in 1968.[54]

The reasoned philosophical rhetoric of the Port Huron Statement and the respectable demeanor of the nonviolent students of the early sit-ins gave way to slogans and rude defiance against police, whom the new radicals called "pigs." Mark Rudd, strike leader at Columbia in the spring of 1968, borrowing the language of black militant LeRoi Jones, concluded a letter of demands sent to university president Grayson Kirk with these words: "Up against the wall, motherfucker, this is a stick up." As working-class cops billy-clubbed their way into the Columbia University buildings occupied by mostly privileged students, the participants felt as if they were in a war. For the small group radicalized in this and similar confrontations, the police attack on demonstrators at the Democratic Party Convention in August was only a confirmation of their belief that they were fighting not merely the "establishment" but an imperialist monster. These trends may have united student radicals against the authorities, but they didn't create a unified movement. In June 1969, SDS split into factions, divided over which group was the most militant and over arcane ideological issues of which most members had only a brief and cursory understanding. Except for the hard Marxist faction controlled by the Progressive Labor Party, SDS had abandoned all hope of allying with the American working class, who at this point mostly defended the war. Members of the most publicized splinter group, called the Weathermen, declared themselves in armed revolt and went "underground" in the fall of 1969, robbing banks and bombing military and defense targets in the name of supporting Third World revolution. As the historians and former student activists Maurice Isserman and Michael Kazin observed in 2003:

> The standard of political effectiveness used to measure and justify the campus antiwar movement's embrace of ever more militant tactics increasingly became the sense of gratification and commitment such tactics provided to participants. . . . There was a seductive exhilaration of feeling oneself part of a redemptive minority in the United States, allied in some intangible yet deeply felt way to that irresistible majority of peasant revolutionaries abroad who were rising up against the American empire.[55]

The hippie culture similarly lost its world-transforming idealism very quickly. Within months of the 1967 Be-In, the Haight was swarmed by tourist buses offering the curious a glimpse of the freaks. The neighborhood soon succumbed to drug abuse, crime, and the mental and health problems of runaways. "Authentic" hippies fled to less publicized places—rural communes or less conspicuous hip districts of major cities. But the communalism of the counterculture took a back seat to an expressive individualism that ironically led hippies back to the consumerism that they were ostensibly rebelling against. While the counterculture had been individualistic from the beginning, it became even more so over time. As Tom Wolfe noticed, the counterculture was part of a "Happiness Explosion." It led to "new status leagues," formed by Americans seeking "novel ways of . . . enjoying, extending their egos," especially in how and what they bought.[56] This gave rise to a consumer counterculture built around a panoply of stuff: incense, M. Keane posters of wide-eyed children, roach clips, hookahs, beads, beanbag chairs, strobe lights, all expressing rebellion from "conformity" but, in reality, forming just another kind of imitation. Self-expression, "doing your own thing," proved to be elusive. It re-created the quest for distinction that Thorstein Veblen showed was so central in the birth of modern consumer society at the end of the nineteenth century, though the competition was no longer for "class goods" that denoted traditional marks of maturity (like Cadillacs or expensive scotch) but for "cool goods." But this new individualism had nothing to do with challenging the hold of consumerism over American life. Not only that, but the quest for "getting in touch with your feelings" inevitably led to withdrawal from practical and realistic engagement and even cultural change itself. What counted was not conforming to the ways of one's parents.[57]

The hippie's individualism also easily shaded into "revolution for the hell of it" (as Abbie Hoffman defiantly proposed in a book by that name in 1968), an emotionally satisfying but intellectually and morally empty rejection of the status quo because it was the status quo. Hoffman and Jerry Rubin tried to transform the hippie into the politicized "Yippie" based on this dubious political "principle." This small group of counterculturalists abandoned the quietist goals of the hippies for political protest. They had no interest in ideology, program, or organizing. Rather, they sought to radicalize youth by playful defiance of authorities. This went beyond Kesey's Merry Pranksters. The idea was "Energy—excitement—fun—fierceness—exclamation point!" according to Abbie Hoffman in 1966. Provoke the squares even within the antiwar movement. In March 1968, Hoffman, using the media and his own outrageousness, got several thousand youths to a riotous party at Grand Central Station "for no reason." His colleague Jerry Rubin freely admitted, "Yippie is just an excuse to rebel." He encouraged it in all oppressed groups, especially high school students, "the largest oppressed minority in Amerika." He asked impressionable kids, "Why stay in school? To get a degree? *Print your own!*"[58] The idea was to mobilize the energy and emotion of youth by appealing to their visceral resentments of their elders. As Rubin put it: "Our message: Don't grow up. Growing up means giving up your dreams."[59] I could never figure out what were these "dreams" were, but there was certainly pleasure in Yippie "guerrilla theater" when they threw paper dollars from the visitors gallery of the New York Stock Market and watched in delight the as "greedy capitalists" on the trading floor fought for the money. There was sometimes a cultural or political message, but still it is no surprise that Nixon's vice president, Spiro T. Agnew, hit a popular note when he attacked "those who encouraged government by street carnival."[60] I recall that during a "boring" interlude a few days before Nixon's "incursion" into Cambodia in May 1970 our group of antiwarriors bought a junked car, parked it in the center of campus, and invited passersby to help "smash" the "war machine" by hitting the car with a sledge hammer. I never got the point, but the kids who dreamed up this bit of guerrilla theater thought that it let war opponents vent their rage. The Yippies were all about rage and its display. No wonder the pundits and politicians called us babies.

Thinking About My Generation

From the moment that we stepped out of our childhood, my generation (or at least part of it) was controversial. Especially in the late 1960s, our parents' generation raged at us as we raged at them in a battle that still hasn't ended. One of the most extraordinary attacks came from a curious source, the child psychologist Bruno Bettelheim, who had been advising parents on our raising since the early 1950s and who became famous for very thoughtful writings about disturbed children and about fairy tales and their meaning to children. But as a Jewish intellectual and a professor at the University of Chicago, where student radicalism was vocal, Bettelheim took a strong stance against the dissident youth movement in a brief book called *Obsolete Youth* (1969). In what appeared to many of us as an absurd analogy "typical" of the obsessions of his generation, Bettelheim identified student radicals with the Nazis of the 1920s. He found a parallel between these ideological opposites in their youthful rejection of the "system" and abandonment of the culture and reason of their parents. He feared that the universities of the 1960s would capitulate to these loudmouths the way that they did to the anti-Semitism of Nazi youth in the 1920s. More serious was his claim that youth in the 1960s faced a new dilemma that explained their "irrational" behavior. "With no frontiers left for flight or for conquest some try to evade and escape an inner conflict they find unbearable by dropping out" with drugs or confronting their elders "for the sake of confrontation. They are convinced that they are struggling actively for personal autonomy, but they are in fact destroying it as radically as those others who withdraw into solipsistic isolation." The problem, Bettelheim insisted, was that technological society made youth feel obsolete and insignificant as individuals and kept them dependent and in an immature state longer than in the past. The psychologist in Bettelheim found that their longing for "meaning" was the anxious pleading of children for a home or at least a false adulthood in the action of activism. His most lasting critique of the students was really an attack on their parents. In their misreading of Freud's injunction against the excessive repression of needs, boomer parents had overindulged their offspring. These children "do not internalize superego controls over their rages" and, as a result, Bettelheim claimed, often joined the troublemakers. Bettelheim argued from another bit of Freudian thinking that the foul-smelling hippies had hyperclean parents from whom they rebelled. Still, these rebels didn't really run away from father figures. They chant for "strong fathers with strong convictions who powerfully coerce their children to follow their commands," such as Ho Chi Minh or Mao.[61]

Similarly, the political scientist Lewis Feuer reduced the Berkeley student uprising of 1964 through 1966 to Freudian psychology. The students were not making a political or philosophical argument but were engaged in "compulsive gestures" of oedipal revolt against their fathers. Their ideas expressed nothing more than an irrational longing for "the children's world, snug and secure." Using a scholarly history of modern student movements as a backdrop, Feuer argued that the students' demand for "free speech" was a mere ruse, like the ideological claims of earlier youth movements. Their doctrines were merely "carrier movements" that disguised the infantile longings of their adherents.[62] Other old-guard professors piled on, including Harvard sociologist Jesse Pitts, who claimed that the contrameritocracy of the hippies provided losers and dropouts from an achievement society "a haven that neutralizes the pains of failure."[63]

In the heat of the campus unrest, this reaction, by professors trained in Freudian psychology and committed to institutional stability and scholarly protocol, is not surprising. But even after the shouting stopped, these characterizations of the 1960s generation persisted in the writings of conservative representatives of our parent's generation. In 1975, Midge Decter, wife of right-wing Norman Podhoretz and part of the emerging neoconservative intelligentsia, published in *Liberal Parents, Radical Children* a rhetorical "Letter to the Young." There she lectured us thusly: "You have long been in the habit of explaining yourselves by reference to your parents," suggesting an atypical obsession that somehow explains other unusual behavior,

including "dropping out of school, using drugs, sleeping around, creating and defection from a communal way of life." The media and
elite have told you "that the new style of life you were inventing for
yourselves was some kind of great adventure in freedom." This flat-
tery, Decter insisted, only fueled youth irrationality. "Why have you,
the children found it so hard to take your rightful place in the world?"
Her answer was the same as Bettelheim's, the indulgence of liberal,
oh-so-tolerant, parents.[64]

Others followed: Christopher Lasch's famous jeremiad, *The Culture of Narcissism*, found in the 1960s counterculture nothing but the
tragic consequence of fathers' abdicating their authority to mothers,
creating in their offspring narcissistic personalities with "little capacity
for sublimation." Lasch enjoyed revealing how the Yippie Jerry Rubin
gave up his revolutionary posturing for self-indulgence. As Rubin
noted in his autobiography, "In five years, from 1971 to 1975, I directly
experienced Est, gestalt therapy, bioenergetics, rolfing, massage, jog-
ging, health foods, tai chi, Esalen, hypnotism, modern dance, meditation, Silva Mind Control, Arica, acupuncture, sex therapy, Reichian
therapy and More House—a smorgasbord course in New Consciousness." After years of self-discovery, he came to the conclusion that "it's
O.K. to enjoy the rewards of life that money brings." Rubin's transformation perfectly exemplified Tom Wolfe's famous characterization of
the 1970s as the "Me Decade."[65]

These elders all insisted that the ideas and actions of the 1960s
youth movement were essentially irrational, born, in part, of an infantile urge to destroy the father and of bad, that is, permissive parenting. Judging from the ferocity of the argument, however, perhaps
we should reconsider the stress on the oedipal rebellion of the young
against the old. We could equally argue a pathological obsession of the
old against the young, born of an "unconscious" fear of being replaced
and resentment of the personal costs of raising one's replacements.[66]

Still, this Freudian take on generational conflict was not always so
hostile to the boomers. The liberal Yale psychologist Kenneth Keniston, in *The Uncommitted: Alienated Youth in American Society* (1965),
studied a group of disaffected privileged male youth (protohippies,
really). Keniston found that these uncommitted youth had fathers
who were absent at work or war during their critical formative years.
In effect, these alienated young men "won" the oedipal battle with
their fathers for their mothers' attention and thus were not forced to
repress their longing for their mother and identify with their father

(and his achieving world). This is another version of how permissive parents infantilized the boomer generation. Keniston, however, also argued that the resulting pattern of the young being "'stuck' in late adolescence" had wider social causes. Technological society deprived fathers of traditional ways of providing role models for their offspring and also extended the years of youth by requiring longer education and offering opportunities to delay family responsibility. Although this analysis had much in common with Bettelheim and Feuer, it was far less hostile. Youth, experiencing an "enforced alienation" from adult society, tended to idealize childhood and reject maturity as life-less and adulthood as unworthy of commitment. While, apparently, a whole generation of Holden Caulfields had emerged by the 1960s, Keniston did not argue for tougher parenting but for more opportu-nities for creative engagement in society.[67]

Even the radical sociologist Richard Flacks, who had deep person-al ties to the New Left, argued that the boomers grew up "confused," having to endure the contradictory messages of parents who fostered independence but also demanded orderly behavior and cooperation with authorities. But Flacks wanted to do more than psychologize away youth rebellion. The isolated subculture of the 1960s that sep-arated youth from adults and the smooth transition into adulthood was not necessarily a bad thing. The separation fostered the growth of new ideas and music as well as new drugs and sexual values. More important still, it led to the desire to extend youth well into adult life.[68] Based on a study of the lives of former student radicals (published in 1989), Flacks with Jack Whalen concluded that youth subculture was less about a psychological maladjustment than about an experiment with "redefining 'adulthood' in our society." Their group (active in the radical politics at the University of Santa Barbara in 1970) sustained for some years thereafter "the romantic belief that the young could make themselves into new persons, that they need not follow in their parents' footsteps." The radical assumption of these boomers was that the ideal life was not becoming grown-up like their parents. The al-ternative was "a life in which one remained a youth"—not in the sense of emotional dependence or childish fantasy but rather staying in a "time in which one is free to continuously reformulate one's identity." Practically speaking, this meant avoiding the life decisions of their parents in every way imaginable and never settling down or "selling out." Even more, these radical youth shared the "vision that the people should make their own history" in both their everyday lives and in

their impact on public events. While their nonpolitical peers anticipated that their youthful "spree" of fun and frivolity would end with
obligations of family and career, these radicals in 1970 expected to
be "continuously living in history rather than having to face the expected limitations and boredoms of ordinary adult life." Even though
their political collectives and lifestyle communes collapsed and most
drifted into ordinary private lives of work and family, some of the former student radicals tried to combine the personal and the "political"
through careers in social work, education, and the like. But the main
trend was their late and incomplete embrace of "adult" values and behavior—defined by a fixed identity. "The people of the sixties are still
'different' and continue to feel a bond with their age mates."[69]

Looking back, many today are disdainful of the "sixties generation" (even though it extended deep into the 1970s). Harvey Mansfield
of Yale has offered a recent update of this tradition blaming the 1960s
for the collapse of the family by encouraging illegitimacy, single-parent families, and abortion; for destroying a culture of gentility with
a crude taste of rock; and for ultimately promoting a smug relativism.[70] Over and over, conservative ideologues have called my generation "self-absorbed hedonists and Peter Pans who never will grow up
and accept their duty, whose irresponsibility and licentiousness have
poisoned the American well," in the words of Leonard Steinhorn, a
critic of this conservative view. We somehow were responsible for
the rise in the divorce rate (reaching nearly 50 percent by 1973), fatherless families (four in ten families with kids), and the more than
threefold increase in welfare families from 1961 through 1971, even
though these trends predate our maturity. By the mid-1970s, anxiety
about the disappearing family was on the rise, and we were blamed
for our absence from our children or refusal to bear them. As Christopher Lasch and others claimed, we had created a narcissistic culture where women ran families and where the presumed pathology
of the "ghetto black family" had become the norm for even the white
middle class.[71]

Steinhorn's provocative *The Greater Generation* (2006) finds evidence that the boomers were a "generation that fought a great cultural war to expand and advance liberty." By contrast, Steinhorn, in a
reversal of conventional wisdom, argues that the parents of boomers
embraced a shallow religion, climbed the corporate ladder in lock
step, were intolerant of diversity, and were often bigoted about sexual
choice and racial inheritance. That so-called Greatest Generation may

have belonged to more bowling leagues than the boomers, but they often excluded blacks and women. At the same time, Steinhorn cites a mountain of evidence that boomers have been more civic, more tolerant, and less materialistic than their parents' generation and that much of the social conservatism evident in the 1990s and today is due to the longevity of pre-boomers. One-quarter of the electorate was over sixty years of age in 2004, and this group provided about 80 percent of George W. Bush's victory margin that year. While a generation gap remains between boomers and their parents, Steinhorn claims that little conflict exists between the values of boomers and their kids. The sixties generation was "liberally irreverent and irreverently liberal," questioning unearned authority, be it in the madhouse of *Cuckoos's Nest* or in the barracks of *M*A*S*H** (just to mention two popular stories appealing to boomers). But that questioning of the past is also affirmed in evidence of the male boomer's embrace of the self-determination of women and increased acceptance of family responsibilities. Since the 1960s, racial prejudice has been in decline, and, in general, individual freedom to pursue interests, careers, and lifestyles has never been greater and institutions have become more open.[72] The details are debatable, but Steinhorn at least makes an argument that we improved things—and redefined manhood.

I agree more than disagree with this assessment of the boomer generation (even though it certainly oversimplifies that generation and ignores its cultural divisions). But has that generation (even its rebel faction) really done much to modernize what it means to be a mature man? In fact, from the early 1980s the profeminist man, a hallmark of our attempt at transforming our father's definition of manhood, was on the wane and often mocked. Bruce Feirstein's *Real Men Don't Eat Quiche* (1982), a humorous little book that was on the *New York Times* best-seller list for fifty-three weeks, sets up the "real man" of tradition against the "New Man." Feirstein opens with the image of Flex Crush, "a trucker hauling nuclear-waste and eating prime rib, six eggs and a loaf of toast at an all night trucker's pit stop west of Tulsa." He mocks the "Alan Alda" types "who cook and clean and *relate* to their wives, those Phil Donahue clones—who are *warm* and *sensitive* and *vulnerable*." These men have made an America that can't make anything but "electric hair-curlers" or (after the Iran hostage crisis of 1979) defend themselves or their embassies. Feirstein makes fun of both sides, but he reflects a growing nostalgia for an earlier generation of men who were confident and independent: "Back when America

was king—did John Wayne have 'relationships'?" The contrast of generations could hardly be made sharper than when he says: "Instead of
having John Wayne fight Nazis and commies for peace and democracy, we've got Dustin Hoffman fighting Meryl Streep for a four-year
old in *Kramer vs. Kramer*. . . . Thirty years ago, the Duke would have
slapped the broad around and shipped the kid off to military school."
Nevertheless, Fierstein is a comparative moderate. The New Man may
be a wimp, but, in the world of 1980s satire, the "real man" was not
as vicious or vulgar as he is in the books that celebrate the anti-"PC"
man today. Books such as Tucker Max's *I Hope They Serve Beer in Hell*
(2006) or Dan Indante and Karl Mark's *The Complete A**hole's Guide
to Handling Chicks* (2003) show him reveling in sexual exploits and
irresponsibility. By contrast, the real man, according to Feirstein, may
not contribute to PBS or trust the French. Still, he "realizes that, while
birds, flowers, poetry and small children do not add to the quality of
life in quite the same manner as a Super Bowl and six-pack of Bud,
he's learned to appreciate them anyway."[73] Feirstein's real men of the
1980s were not oblivious to or shameful of refinement, but they didn't
make or eat quiche—or embrace feminism.

Looking back, male support for feminism was never strong (especially in its New Left form), and the idea that gender equality and
blending made a man new and better declined quickly. Soon after
Congress passed the Equal Rights Amendment in 1972, conservative reaction set in, preventing ratification in enough states to keep it
from becoming part of the Constitution. Feminism became "a cause
and a symptom of family decline itself."[74]

From the early 1970s, a much more negative men's movement
challenged the optimistic view of the profeminist man and often
clashed with feminism. For example, in 1973 Richard Doyle formed
the Men's Rights Association to defend divorced father's rights. Three
years later, he wrote *The Rape of the Male*, complaining that men were
not oppressors but rather victims of discrimination in divorce courts,
which rewarded former wives large child-support payments but were
lax in enforcing visitation and rarely granted fathers custody, no matter the merits of the case. In the 1980s, about twenty similar groups
sprang up to defend father's rights in divorce. Even Warren Farrell,
a leader of the early 1970s male feminist movement, embraced the
men's rights cause and wrote *Why Men Are the Way They Are* (1987)
to defend it. From Farrell's new perspective the problem was less
male power over women than the attitudes and behaviors of men

that threatened their health and well-being. Farrell now believed that masculine traits (aggression, emotional restraint, and competitiveness, for example) were consequences of their *dependence* on their mothers and wives, not dysfunctional effects of their *dominance* over women. Even more, these negative male traits were sometimes defense mechanisms for coping with their powerlessness vis-à-vis females. Men were the worker bees toiling for the queen bee and often died sooner as a result. Farrell, who once saw women's rights as a "voice of human rights," came to see feminists as an interest group.[75]

As men and women increasingly were pitted in a war of "rights" (and of defining the victim), a group of mostly boomer men dug deeper into the swamp of male dysfunction. A "mythopoetic" strand of the male liberation movement (the word was coined by Shepherd Bliss in 1986) used fantasy stories to explore what they believed were repressed male emotions that needed to be released. Robert Bly's *Iron John* (1990) and Sam Keen's *Fire in the Belly: On Being a Man* (1991) are the best examples of this literature. Rather than calling for liberation from the aggressive masculinity of the past and affirming a more androgynous maturity, Bly argued for a reassertion of the heroic male. The problem, he believed, was that the decline of independence and skill in work had made American men feel powerless. The only way of getting back primordial masculinity was to seek it in the myths of Greco-Roman heroes, Eastern religions, or Jungian archetypes. Inevitably, this also meant an attack on the New Man of the early 1970s, whom Bly mocked as a "nice boy who pleases not only his mother but also the young woman he is living with." He is nice not because he has been won over to gender equality but because he fears being called a sexist and "he doesn't fight back, but just takes it." Such a man, Bly insisted, doesn't really like himself and lacks energy. He is a wimp. He makes his wife into his mother or even refuses to leave his parents' home. He doesn't grow up. In Bly, Wylie's theory of Momism returned. Bly rejected the idea of the culturally constructed male sex role. For him, different sex roles are natural, but this does not mean that the old aggressive masculinity was normal. Rather, real manhood must be nurtured, and if the man doesn't become a heroic "warrior" comfortable with other men, self-aware, and responsible to others, he becomes a batterer of women and children or joins a street gang. Deep masculinity must replace the toxic masculinity resulting from self-loathing and male competition. The "deep" version makes men more cooperative, Bly insisted, more eco-friendly, and better mates for women and children.[76]

The mythopoetic male movement of recent years did not embrace Feirstein's Flex Crush, but it was still was a rejection of the New Man. It abandoned the optimism of the early profeminist men, not only pitting again women against men but focusing on the fathering of sons, not the parenting of children. The mythopoetic male movement looked for liberation from "toxic" masculinity not in gender equality but in replacing the bourgeois man of constraint and competition with the myth of the male war band. But what was this in the modern world but a boy's vision of manhood?

In this, as in so many of our dreams of doing better than our fathers, the long-term results were certainly ambiguous. Far from developing a new, improved form of male maturity, we were tempted by the possibilities of retreating into a world of playful and ultimately childlike myth. The political side of our rebellion died in negative posturing and divisive identity politics. The cultural side succumbed to a quest for the cool in rebellion from the repressive father culture and from the conformity of the "masses." Instead of creating a less consumerist society, we fueled a more dynamic and individualistic one. In doing so, we cut ourselves off from social and political relevance. We prepared the soil for the thrill-seeking culture of our sons even as we created the contradiction of the Bobo, the "mature" bourgeois male at work combined with the bohemian boy-man in play.

We too often reverted back to an elemental impulse in our rebellion against our fathers—a fixation on youth and a refusal to embrace maturity. Stronger than our ideas for a new model of maturity, far stronger, was our infatuation with youth, and so we picked up where the rebels and outcasts of the 1950s left off. We all too often rebuffed the responsibility and sobriety of age and embraced the excitement, hedonism, and even narcissism of youth—and this ultimately trumped the ideal of the New Man.

chapter 4.

My GENERATION Becomes the
PEPSI GENERATION

My generation's obsession with youth and its memories stands out in the history of human vanity. Despite our sometimes-early rejection of commercialism, we found ourselves as we aged trying to buy and make tangible a youth that by its very nature is elusive. In the 1960s, we thought youth was what distinguished us from others rather than seeing it as a phase of life quickly passed through. We even believed that somehow we could be "forever young" as in the popular song of Bob Dylan and Rod Stewart. Thus, for example, as we aged and found we could no longer fit in our old jeans, merchandisers let us keep our youthful informality by offering us "comfort" jeans designed to accommodate our bulging bellies and broader backsides. In our longing for perpetual youth we found that youth was sold back to us, no longer liberating us from the past but enfeebling us by chaining us to our illusion.

The media and merchandisers were only too happy to accommodate us in our self-delusion. Between the late 1960s, when we were entering adulthood, and the early 1980s, when we were becoming nostalgic and anxious about our "lost" youth, the ad makers turned us into the Pepsi Generation. First, they appealed to the pride of youth and its distinction from the "old," and later they helped us evade our aging. Ads directed at men for beer, cars, and other products changed dramatically during this period as merchandisers shifted from appeals to male status, competence, and family responsibilities to a separate youth identity and unrestrained personal desire. We bought into "liberation marketing," (a term coined by Thomas Frank), which told us that we could be free from conformity, authority, and the routine of work by purchasing consumer goods in our leisure time. The hippie side of our youthful rebellion survived, as Joseph Heath and Andrew Potter note, not in a rejection of work and markers of public status but in "consciousness of desire and desire for consciousness" against the presumed repression of conformist consumption. We found freedom in distinguishing ourselves from the duped masses in our quest for our own things: a hip consumerism.[1]

At about the same time, media emphasis shifted from the heroic male in westerns and the parent-bemused "cute" child in sitcoms to far more ambivalent messages. After about 1967, action movies became more violent, anticipating the aestheticized carnage of the 1980s and 1990s, and they largely abandoned the moral and paternal themes of the older westerns. In the wake of humiliation at the hands of OPEC in 1973 and defeat in Vietnam in 1975, as well as fears of falling behind Europe and Japan economically throughout the 1970s, men embraced stories of individual heroism and gung-ho patriotism. This was not, however, a restoration of the ideals of the 1950s. Our stories rejected the maturity of constraint and moral choice for unchained "action," paralleling a loosening of control over desire in general. By the end of the 1960s, TV sitcoms were no longer about the "cute" but about generational and class or ethnic conflict. The media reinforced our boomer longings for youth and repulsed the older twin of the heroic man and the cute child. Over time, we found outlets for our rejection of our father's model of "growing up" in our nostalgia for our youth. In many ways, but especially in our nostalgia for the commercial culture of our youth—in collecting our childhood toys or restoring our teenage cars—we literally bought back our youth. If we think about the late 1960s through the early 1980s as the era of the boomers' maturation, we see those years also as the transformation of "my generation" into the "Pepsi Generation."

Selling Youth to Boomers

Despite the admonitions of our grandfatherly guru, Herbert Marcuse, not to be "co-opted" by the "system," the youth culture of the late 1960s was thoroughly commercialized. From the late 1940s, when marketing experts like Eugene Gilbert began touting the buying power of teens and youth, America's clothing, food, and entertainment industries had adapted to and ultimately shaped youth identity.[2] From the mid-1950s, being a youth meant *buying* rock, not "show tune" records. As the historian Bill Osgerby notes, hippie culture was "disseminated and popularized through the intercession of record companies, magazines, fashion retailers and a growing army of 'Hip capitalists.'" Advertisers and marketers anticipated the themes of youth and individualism in the counterculture. Lee Iaccoca's 1964 Ford Mustang revolutionized the car industry with a sporty but very affordable car that was neither for the family man nor the man of style and success. It was an automobile for young singles who wanted (or so Ford thought) a wide choice of engines, transmissions, seating configurations, colors, roof and window arrangements, and especially "sports packages." Mustang offered "personal expression" through all of these options, and the buyer didn't have to wait until he (or she) had a high-paying job. The point was fun, not utility and responsibility, and having it now. Some 417,000 Mustangs, at that time a record number, were sold in the first year.[3]

It is no surprise, then, that advertising shaped our identity as youth in the 1960s and continued to guide our quest to hold onto youth as we aged. For decades, ads had sold the American dream, including American manhood. This was true since the advent of slick magazine advertisements shortly after 1900, the birth of commercial radio in 1922, and the beginnings of TV in the late 1940s. By the end of the 1950s, TV commercials had abandoned the old radio formulas of jingles and live celebrity testimonials for a more cinematic style, complete with on-location scenes and storylines evoking the "need" to purchase a product. The older, rather genteel custom of the sponsored program featuring, for example, Dinah Shore shilling for Chevrolet or Groucho Marx driving a De Soto convertible in leisurely minute-long messages gave way by 1960 to the thirty-second spot ad. The shots in these later ads were shorter, making the commercials more intense and eye-catching. Often, more time and expense was devoted to the music, photography, writing, and editing of a thirty-second commercial than to a TV show. By 1972, Actor's Guild members were earning more from ads than movies and TV combined. Most important was the increasing role of consumer research, especially in the tracking of social trends and efforts to identify and tap into the emotional lives of targeted consumers, especially the young. By the mid-1960s, commercials were free to associate products with male sexual fantasy. Surely the most famous example was the woman's voice saying "Take it off! Take it all off!" as a man shaves with Noxzema shaving cream.[4]

Of course, this did not mean that the majority of ads directed toward men (or others) necessarily changed dramatically in the mid-1960s. Car commercials still appealed to the techie with details of transmissions and engine displacement. And the old association of the Chevy with "baseball, hotdogs and apple pie" persisted into the 1970s and 1980s (presumably persuading the patriotic buyer not to go foreign). Ad makers still tried to appeal to mass markets, even for products that might seem geared for the young and daring. So an ad for a Honda motorcycle from the mid-1960s featured fathers and sons, an old lady, and a guy and his dogs, assuring would-be middle-class buyers that "you meet the nicest people on a Honda." No longer were motorcycles for scruffy young men in gangs. This attempt to break from the 1950s stereotype succeeded in making Honda a major player in a new age of motorcycling.[5]

Many ads appealed to tradition and to male bonding. A good example comes from beer. Budweiser's long-lasting ad campaign featured workingmen in a wide variety of settings sharing a beer after a long day's work. The familiar slogan was simple: "You make American work and this Bud's for you!"[6] A bottle of Bud was supposed to be a reward for workingmen who rightfully took pride in their accomplishments. Despite notions of "New Men" and feminism, mass-market ads persisted in presenting traditional ideals of masculinity and maturity. Take, for example, a 1983 ad for Old Spice aftershave. It begins with scenes of men playing baseball and a father teaching his son to ride a bike. The ad builds to the sight of a dashing young man wooing a beautiful women who is drawn to the "timeless classical scent" the "unmistakably masculine scent" of Old Spice. The ad closes with this telling message: "It says the right things about you"—that you are a real man, not a girly man. You splashed it on your face not because you wanted to smell as good and attractive as, presumably, a woman, but because it "makes a man feel alive."[7]

Despite attempts of the forever "with it" Hugh Hefner to keep up with the psychedelic revolution and the antiwar and civil rights movements, the *Playboy* magazine of the 1960s remained in many ways a throwback to the 1950s, even a paragon of traditional male maturity. Yes, adult men were to remain playboys, but never simply teen sailors on liberty, much less free-loving "dirty" hippies. *Playboy* featured students dressed in sports jackets and ties in their annual

"Back to Campus" section. In 1967, answering the question: "Who Reads *Playboy*?" Hefner's marketing staff wrote: "A young man [who] knows a beautiful thing when he sees it—and goes after it." And, this meant more than big-breasted women. Not only were *Playboy* ads about cultural aspiration (as much as gratification), but they continued to assume a natural progression in taste and "class" with age. Another ad from 1967 implied that college boys would become men over the course of their four years, as shown in their progressively more sophisticated and formal taste in a lineup of freshmen to seniors. *Playboy* remained a vehicle for young men (mostly from college) to learn the manly codes of status and style through sex advice via the "Playboy Advisor," but also book and record clubs. Being a playboy still meant being a classy consumer as well as a conquering lover.[8]

In the 1960s, however, we begin to see inklings of new directions in ads that appealed not to tradition or the long climb to the pinnacle of achievement but to the vitality of male youth and the right of the consumer to express and satisfy himself now. A well-known story is how Pepsi Cola began in 1961 to address "those who think young" in the company's attempt to pry those born after World War II from the dominance of Coca-Cola. Coke had a "lock" on the older generation who grew up associating soft-drink refreshment with is red and white label and especially on vets, who, while serving as soldiers during the war, had been provided with Coke from scores of bottling plants home and abroad. Pepsi had to look to youth in 1961. Its ads mirrored the post-Eisenhower media mood as Kennedy's youthful optimism reigned: "You can't miss the change that's come across the nation—today people are full of modern ideas, full of vitality, call it thinking young. It's the right life for light, bracing, clean-tasting Pepsi." This campaign was credited with Pepsi's successful challenge of Coke and would be used in a variety of ways for years: "Pepsi: the choice of a new generation," for example, was the tag line in a 1984 commercial.[9]

By the late 1960s, the car industry was following suit with ads calling for a Dodge Rebellion and renaming the venerable, upscale GM Olds the "Youngmobile." The old but poor cousin in the family of soft-drink makers, Dr. Pepper, revived its fortunes with a series of ads from 1971 featuring perky youths dancing and expressing their individuality in a variety of fashion statements, singing "I'm a Pepper. . . . Be a Pepper too."[10] Advertisers naturally tried to reposition goods for the young, shifting, for example, blue jeans from duty as work clothes for farm hands to hip garb for the young of whatever social status. In the 1980s, advertisers tried to make Skittles, a heavily sugared candy, "hot" for teens and young adults. Even chewing tobacco, long a product of rural and working-class men, was marketed with allusions to Indiana Jones, with a cool young guy taking a chew as he uses a whip wrapped around a tree to free himself from quicksand in the jungle.[11]

Advertisers knew that the young boomers of the 1960s and 1970s were a golden market. But the new ads also said that youth was the mark of normality, status, and vitality. As boomers aged, marketers continued to identify them with that vaunted status of "youth" rather than shifting their appeals to "maturity." A Nike ad (1984) featured men in their late thirties trying on their running shoes with the tag line, "not for everyone," suggesting that these guys, at least, were still young at heart. No wonder that as the early boomers aged, ad men appealed to their nostalgic associations with their own youth. This was obviously the point of Lincoln-Mercury car ads (again in 1984) that played 1960s rock music in the background to remind boomers of the "best times of their lives."[12]

Self-expression, but even more, "doing one's own thing," was a common "youth" theme of ads from the early 1960s. A magazine ad hyped the new portable nine-inch Sony TV as an opportunity for a guy to break from the crowd watching baseball at the bar—by viewing hip soccer on his own TV. Another TV commercial featured a single young man who preferred to spend his extra money on "good music"—a stereo and Maxell audiotapes—rather than on the conventional luxuries of furniture or a well-equipped refrigerator. In 1974, in an attempt to cut into McDonald's mass-market share, Burger King flooded the screen with the slogan, "Have it your way" (referring to the chain's special-order sandwiches).[13] No longer was the main appeal to sharing with family and friends or even seeking status. Individualism meant not following the standard path to "maturity."

This appeal to youth was about more than choice or even breaking from the crowd to fulfill personal desire. It was an invitation to enjoy formerly forbidden pleasures, "an abandonment," Thomas Frank notes, "of the values of thrift and the suspicion of leisure that characterized an earlier variety of capitalism."[14] Such pleasures might include a Yamaha motorcycle ("Now do you buy the Yamaha Special for the beauty or the beast of its four stroke power?"). In 1984, Wrangler jeans were linked to the excitement of a jungle scene (again with an Indiana Jones–like character), exhorting men to "live it to the limit." Ads told boomers what they already believed, that they had a right to have it all, in all the intensity and pleasure that they could find, and not to become more sedate or to slow down as they aged.[15]

By the 1970s, advertisers recognized and promoted women's "invasion" of men's old pleasure spaces—showing them driving Toyota trucks and Honda motorcycles or wearing Wrangler or Ditto jeans. This might imply that men would have to cede some of their old prerogatives in this age of feminist consumption, but the ads in fact reassured young men that they had nothing to fear and new pleasures to gain. These ads suggested not economic or social equality but rather that "liberated women" were no longer inhibited in their desires and that their most fervent desires would be fulfilled in exciting the desires of men. A beautiful, hard-bodied woman could beat her man at tennis but still find him "challenging" if he wore English Leather cologne. After all, all her "men wear English Leather, or they wear nothing at all." And, the liberated woman in tight jeans appealed to men's desire, as the ads ceaselessly and shamelessly suggested. Women now could invite a man up for a drink of Harvey's Bristol Cream at 10 P.M. because it was "downright upright." A man should buy Hai Karate Oriental Spice aftershave not because it made him "feel alive," as in the past, but because it drives sexy "liberated" women so wild that men have to be warned: "be careful how you use it." The man might be "objectified" by the female gaze, no longer simply meeting his own needs for comfort and satisfaction, but he had presumably awakened the now liberated libido of hot women.[16]

Advertising and consumer culture more broadly turned youthful rebellion into a commodity that wouldn't change even as boomers aged. Even the "threat" of feminism could be reduced to (male) consumer desire. But there is more here than the cleverness of merchandisers. The transformation of my generation into the Pepsi Generation had much to do with the way that we thought about consumption. Our youthful rejection of our elders' "conformity" seemed to suggest that our lives would somehow be less driven by the need to keep up with or surpass the Joneses. But it didn't happen that way. Of course, for years critics have been saying that we were simply hypocrites,[17] but there was more. The counterculture's celebration of uninhibited self-expression and fulfillment meant that instead of rejecting consumer culture, we moved it to a new level. The counterculture was more a critique of the domesticated consumerism of the 1950s, with its monster finned cars and Weber grills, than an attack on material consumption itself. In fact, the counterculture was about giving vent to previously repressed desires (so easily merchandised in "hippie fashion"). Of course, some of us tried to avoid being "co-opted" by business when we formed cooperative food-buying groups or even stores offering tofu and organic rice to avoid the supermarket's processed products. In Boston in the early 1970s, a group of about a dozen of us pooled time and money to buy lots of plain food from the wholesalers on the North End to distribute among ourselves. I even helped organize a housing cooperative in 1976 from a ten-unit row house in Milwaukee (which, much to my surprise, is still in existence thirty years later). But to be honest, few of these efforts changed much beyond the lives of a handful of dedicated souls. Within a few years, upscale supermarkets accommodated our "hippie" tastes and much more.[18]

Looking back, the counterculture was really part of a broader assault on 1950s consumption, not consumer culture itself. It was an attack on "conformity"—buying the standard package of middle-class goods and seeking status by "moving up" to a Buick. That conformist consumption legitimated male spending if it was a "gift" for spouses and children. As feminists have long argued, much of this form of 1950s consumption was about men justifying going after the "main chance" on the job ostensibly for the wife and kids and establishing their authority and prerogatives at home. In the 1960s, we recognized this immediately and rejected it. But the liberation of the "new generation" from this conformist and patriarchal ethic freed them to spend on themselves as they tried to perpetuate their youth. And the advertising directed to young men from the late 1960s was the first step in this process.

Rejecting Our Fathers' Stories

In modern times, each generation seems to define itself by the stories it embraces and the stories that it rejects. As my generation broke away from our fathers, we, too, wanted new fantasies, and in the process of creating them we rebuffed old models of male maturation. Despite attempts to find alternatives to the 1950s parent, in the long run we failed to create new and abiding understandings of being a grown-up. The *Father Knows Best* duo of progressive parenting and "cute" children growing up gradually declined as a central theme of sitcoms and family TV. Looking back at programs like *The Courtship of Eddie's Father*

(1969–1972), *Family Affair* (1966–1971), or *Webster* (1983–1989), we might think that a 1960s-style revision of the *Father Knows Best* package had taken place. None of these sitcoms had traditional two-parent families with natural children, and, in tune with the avant-garde ideas of "male feminism" of the time, men were role models to children struggling with the difficult choices of maturation. Six-year-old Eddie in *The Courtship of Eddie's Father* was the "best friend" of his single (widowed, not divorced) father. In the endearing opening sequences, where Eddie asks his father apparently naïve, but often deep questions about why flowers have funny names and why Eddie can't have a minibike, we see a loving exchange that permeates the show's modernized and progressive portrayal of males. Eddie's dad, Tom, believes in fun at camp (opposing the authoritarian dad who runs the camp) and proves the virtue of his tolerant approach when the son of a bossy father breaks down emotionally under his dad's pressure. Tom's girlfriends always make a graceful exit to meet the needs of the child and the "best-friends" relationship of father and son. Over and over, Tom and Eddie work out the dilemmas of dealing with the dad's romantic encounters, the responsibilities of friendship, and other serious matters in a way that always leads to deeper understanding and a closer bonding between father and son.[19] In *Family Affair*, "Uncle Bill" and his corpulent English butler, Mr. French, raise two frisky kids, offering still another variant on predecessors like *My Three Sons* and *Bachelor Father*. But *Webster*, a lot like its predecessor, *Diff'rent Strokes* (1978–1983), featured the daring theme of a cute eight-year-old black child adopted by an unlikely white, middle-aged, professional couple who never expected to have children. *Webster* fully exhibited the standard markers of cuteness (especially the delightful combination of naïveté and knowingness beyond the child's years) and the befuddled but loving efforts of the couple to adjust to having Webster in their lives. But the never mentioned fact of the interracial family added a hint of modernity and "social concern," which was important as white America adjusted its racial attitudes in the 1980s.[20] Variations on this family sitcom popped up again and again in the ensuing decades, in, for example, *Growing Pains* (1985–1992); *Good Times* (1974–1979), a family sitcom set in a black housing project; and, of course, *The Cosby Show* (1984–1992). The winning formula was a modernized version of the progressive, understanding, but self-secure dad and the bemused image of the cute child stumbling through growing up and learning gentle lessons on the way.

However, escapism prevailed rather than adjustment to change. In the 1970s, the era of the maturing boomer and increasing divorce, family shows were increasingly set out of their own time. The serial could no longer claim to reflect contemporary reality. Instead, these programs were often nostalgic recollections of the 1950s (*Happy Days*) or earlier (the 1880s for *Little House on the Prairie* and the 1930s for *The Waltons*). Only eight of sixty-nine TV serials in the 1974–75 season featured "traditional" nuclear families.[21] It was as if Americans could not even imagine a family like the Andersons or the Cleavers anymore. Always escapist to a degree, sitcoms in the 1960s and 1970s become particularly fantastic and nostalgic. Remember *I Dream of Jeannie*, one of several shows featuring women with magical powers, or *Beverly Hillbillies* and *Petticoat Junction* (both of which delighted in the clash of rural and sophisticated city folk). TV in the 1960s and 1970s was primarily an escapist medium, especially attractive to older Americans who wanted to have nothing to do with the social and cultural upheavals of the time, much less attacks on the traditional image of the adult man.

Still, there were a few challenges to the "fluff." At the cutting edge was, of course, *All in the Family* (1971–1979), Norman Lear's take on generational conflict. The show pitted Mike Stivic, a liberal and obviously lapsed Christian graduate student, against Archie Bucker, his young wife's bigoted, uneducated father, in whose house the couple lived. Seemingly no topic that divided Americans in the 1970s was left uncovered—from race, religion, and the Vietnam War to the proper roles of adults and children and men and women. Instead of the understanding and unassuming self-confidence of 1950s patriarchs or even the bewildered but good hearted buffoonery of earlier working-class dads, Archie was a blustering fool, ignorant but with opinions about everything, and resistant to change. Curiously, perhaps, Archie was not portrayed as a white Catholic ethnic of the type that supposedly dominated in Queens (where the Bunkers presumably made their home), but instead as a generic white male Protestant, distinguished not by his class or national origin but by his race and especially his generation. This was a break from old takes on the working-class father as an immigrant and a religious minority trying to make it in an America he really didn't understand (in contrast to his WASP, middle-class superior). Instead, Archie was a new type that seemed to emerge in the 1960s—a prototypical "social conservative" who had faith in traditional authority and culture and was hostile to everything the 1960s brought. No doubt he switched parties too: voting for JFK in 1960 but Nixon in 1968 and later becoming a Reagan Democrat. Though Mike and his wife Gloria were liberals, they were made to seem mainstream while Archie was not only retrograde but a fossil whose time had passed (even though Mike did appear self-righteous and a bit of a hypocrite because he sponged off of the Bunkers).

All in the Family, an attention grabber in the media, achieved an unprecedented top ranking in the ratings in its first year on the air and remained on top for four more, watched by close to 50 million people each week. Many of my generation, when viewing *All in the Family*, surely saw our own conflicts with our fathers. At least, we saw what we took to be the bigoted, backward, and essentially insecure reactionaries of our father's generation, bitter old men who wanted nothing more than to send us to Vietnam and cut our hair. But, looking back, *All in the Family* represented more. By mocking Archie's experience, it affirmed our belief in the cultural superiority of youth. It also represented a shift from the narrative of growing up and parenting that had been so important in American culture since the days of Andy Hardy. Lear abandoned the old family-TV formula in a string of successful sitcoms in the 1970s and 1980s, staking a claim to "realism" in the clashes of culture, race, class, and generation of late 1960s and 1970s America. This was the key to the success of *The Jeffersons* (1975–1986), a sitcom about an aspiring middle-class black man and his wife, as well as *Sanford and Son* (a kind of black version of *All in the Family*, 1972–1977).[22] At times these sitcoms introduced progressive and challenging ideas about race and gender equality. Still, they also often reflected the self-assuredness of the boomer generation in its mocking of the values of its elders without really confronting the looming dilemmas of becoming grown-ups.

One of several exceptions to this rule is *Family Ties* (1982–1989), which combined the new stress on generational conflict and topicality with the older themes of the family sitcom. Set in Reagan's America in a family of aging ex-hippie parents and aspiring yuppie children, *Family Ties* was *All in the Family* turned on its head, with dad as the idealistic liberal who worked for PBS and the son as the materialistic conservative looking for the "main chance." The children traded barbs—the self-centered Alex, the clothes-horse sister Mallory, and the driven younger child Jen who was a liberal in reaction to her brother and dreamed of becoming an antitrust lawyer and putting Alex in jail some day. More central were the

stories revolving around the gentle parents' attempts to cope with
offspring so unlike themselves. All this reflected new tensions in
the families of boomers and, even more, the impact of a growing
individualism that boomer parents had fostered. Typical exchanges
include the hypocrisy of the mother not wanting her daughter to
go to school in "pre-ripped" jeans, even though she had worn them
as a girl in the 1960s. Her explanation: back then, torn jeans were a
"political statement." Alex P. Keaton's over-the-top competitiveness
drove the humor of the show, but there was also an undercurrent
of pathos that gave the show a measure of maturity. For example,
in one episode Alex learns to adapt to the success of his girlfriend;
in another, despite his tough exterior, he grieves over the death of
a friend; and in the last show, his mother clung to him as he set out
on his own. All of these themes addressed the problems of parenting and growing up in the 1980s. In the end, the show was a celebration of what was right about the 1960s, even if its offspring were
superficially reacting to its "peace and love" beliefs. After all, Alex
and his sisters loved their parents, and their parents (especially the
dad) knew when to step in and when not to in the serious business
of helping his children grow up. In the end, the family knew how to
resolve what divided them, as evidenced in a line from the theme
song: "I bet we've been together for a million years."[23]

Of course, *Family Ties* was like all sitcoms. Conflicts were happily
resolved by the end of the show, and episodes included a lot of predictable behavior of stereotyped characters. But, like the best of the
old sitcoms from the 1950s, *Family Ties* still addressed the real dilemmas of parenting and growing up and did so for its own time.

In other genres of storytelling, however, the boomers' era produced a much more ambiguous legacy. The transformation of the
western and other male-oriented dramas makes my case. John
Wayne, winner of an Oscar in 1969 for *True Grit*, had for thirty years
represented what his congressional medal of honor called him, "John
Wayne American"—symbolic of strength, manliness, and patriotism
in both war movies and westerns. Still, he never was a cardboard,
comic-book hero as I and many of my generation once thought, but
both tough and compassionate, sometimes showing frailty and loneliness in his roles—never just a body or an action figure, as would
be the case in later manly heroes. In his last movies, he carried a pot
belly and a worn face, as he displayed his gravelly voice and flawed
character in the story.[24]

Our generation rejected Wayne's gung-ho portrayals. We hated him in *The Green Berets*, with its glorification of the U.S. military in Vietnam, and we abandoned our father's and our own childhood fascination with the western. In fact, the movie industry had begun to turn on the traditional western long before Wayne's death in 1979. This was part of a trend toward greater realism and maturity in the western that appeared even at the height of the TV western of the late 1950s. The more corrosive change was the comedic mockeries of the mythology of the west: *Cat Ballou* (1965) with Lee Marvin as a drunken gunfighter and *Buffalo Bill and the Indians* (1976), where director Robert Altman makes Bill Cody into a slow-witted and self-deluding clown. Especially memorable is Mel Brooks's *Blazing Saddles* (1974), which thoroughly spoofed the western. A corrupt railroad operator, trying to destroy a town in his way, gets a black man appointed sheriff to defend the town against his hired thugs with the certain expectation that its bigoted citizens will turn on the black sheriff. Full of not-too-subtle cynical allusions to western stereotypes and white racist reality, *Blazing Saddles* "liberated" a generation of youth brought up on the TV western from its myths. As important were Sergio Leone's trilogy of violent antiheroic westerns that launched Clint Eastwood's career in the mid-1960s (*A Fistful of Dollars*, *For a Few Dollars More*, and *The Good, The Bad and the Ugly*). A number of films reversed stereotypes in this period. *Little Big Man* (1970) turned the cowboy and Indian theme upside down by making the Indian the hero. Billy Jack in the title role in *Half-Breed* (1971) as an Indian war hero who hated the Vietnam War defends the radical and racially integrated Freedom School and the runaway daughter of a vicious deputy sheriff from a southwestern town of bigots and reactionaries. Turning the tables on the classic western where white men defended their families against Indian savages, the Native American Billy is the hero of the young, both a warrior and a pacifist, while the savages are white and old. These westerns were not mere negations of the old stereotypes of manhood but, to a degree, promises of a "new" heroism and new manhood.[25]

The more abiding change, however, was not new models of male maturity but a rejection of the old western myths for presumably greater realism. Over time, this led to an aesthetic of "action"—visually exciting, almost sensual violence—in contrast to the traditional moral tale about making choices and recognizing the consequences of action. Historians see the beginning of this trend with Sam Peckinpah's westerns, including *The Wild Bunch* (1969) and *Bring Me the Head of Alfredo Garcia* (1974). These films featured graphic massacres, with raw meat blown off actors to simulate the impact of bullets, the use of rapid editing to speed up and intensify the pace of the scenes, and slow motion to prolong and aestheticize the most violent shots. For example, the *Wild Bunch* opens with Pike Bishop gang's raid of a Texas town to rob a bank, a raid that ends in the graphic slaughter of innocent bystanders. The film climaxes with the massacre of the gang by Mexican soldiers. The moral bankruptcy of the gunslinger and his inability to adapt to a changing world at the end of the era of the Wild West (set during World War I) is a major theme, but the highly choreographed violence is what drew and repulsed audiences. Censors, following the Motion Picture Production Code of 1934, would not have tolerated Peckinpah's gory choreography, but those rules were replaced with a new rating system in 1968. The new R rating that Peckinpah's films received presumably excluded children and allowed greater freedom to portray "adult" themes. At the same time, according to film critic Stephen Prince, the 1960s cultural shift "away from the chivalric and idealized West of [John] Ford [led the way] toward a more psychopathic and mud-spattered landscape."[26]

Peckinpah represented a typical 1960s reaction against conformity and unrealistic moralistic portrayals of the Old West. By showing violence in all of its graphic realism, he claimed that he was forcing his audience to confront its own aggressive impulses and to face the real consequences of violence "so that viewers would not feel compelled to enact real violence in their homes and on the streets." Peckinpah opposed the Vietnam War and focused on liberal themes of elites destroying the innocent in their way. In many ways this was consistent with the ideas of the 1960s New Man. Peckinpah's films and other violent features (for example, the gangster update *Bonnie and Clyde* and the war feature *The Dirty Dozen*, both from 1967) reflected a rising tide of violence in American society. Just recall the 128 riots in black neighborhoods in 1967 along with the increasingly confrontational antiwar protests. But Peckinpah was also drawn to the sensuality of violence and was fascinated by the fact that he could make audiences want to walk out on his scenes but be unable to do so.[27]

By the early 1970s, graphic and aestheticized violence began to frame a new entertainment genre—the action-hero movie. *The French Connection* (1971) takes the classic police procedural movie in a new direction. As the traditional nonconformist detective, Jimmy

"Popeye" Doyle goes beyond investigating and capturing the criminal (in this case, the leaders of a drug ring). Instead, he subjugates
them in a wild spate of rule-breaking and heart-pounding chases
(as, for example, when Doyle commandeers a car to chase a subway
hijacked by a drug lord).[28] Clint Eastwood's signature role in *Dirty
Harry* (1971) and its sequels take the action film even further. The angry San Francisco cop Harry Callaghan—a loner, defending a community where he doesn't fit in—fights police bureaucracy and the
mayor in his quest to kill the cowardly serial killer Scorpio. Though
midway through the story he captures Scorpio, he breaks the rules,
making the evidence inadmissible in court, to the disgust of Callaghan and no doubt the viewer. Scorpio is set free only to terrorize a
school bus full of kids before the final deadly confrontation. On the
surface this looks like an urban version of the strong but silent western hero who acts rather than preaches. But, as film historian Eric
Lichtenfeld notes, "the organizing principle is its violent conflicts."
The ongoing duel between Harry and Scorpio punctuates the film
in timed "beats" of brutal action. In the series there was no effort
to develop Harry's character or to explain his seething resentments
(besides having to cope with his legalistic superiors). What counted
was his physical and emotional will to prevail over the "bad guys" by
any means necessary.[29]

Dirty Harry certainly opened the way for the Chinese martial
arts movies that were exported to the West after 1970 and starred
Bruce Lee, Jackie Chan, and others, with their flying fists and feet
and display of taut male bodies. By the mid-1970s, we see this shift
toward the sensuality of action and violence, culminating in the
"spectacular" bodies of Sylvester Stallone and Arnold Schwarzenegger. Film historians credit these iconic figures with moving the body-
built male from the "freakish marginality" of tawdry urban gyms and
cheap men's magazines to the mainstream of Hollywood films. Stallone's breakthrough role came in *Rocky* (1976), a throwback, which
Stallone also wrote, to the boxing melodramas of the 1940s. Rocky,
a small-time white ethnic boxer, tenaciously strives for the chance
to fight the champ. What made the film notable was the display Stallone's glistening pecs. Schwarzenegger's *Conan the Barbarian* (1982)
was an update of the old B-movie fantasy adventures of the 1950s.
Schwarzenegger plays a warrior seeking revenge for the murder of his
family by Thulsa Doom and his Snake Cult in a mythological world
of swords and loin-clothed men. The movie is heavy on "action," but

weak on dialogue. Conan speaks only five words to the female love interest Valeria in the whole film![30]

These movies appealed to men, especially the younger men of my generation, who sought a "return" to the heroic male in an era of quiche-eating wimps and the "threat" of strong feminist women and their new independent roles in life and film. As often pointed out, Stallone and Schwarzenegger played to male insecurity. While they downplayed the discredited ideal of male moral and intellectual authority, they also rejected the 1950s tradition of restraint and stoic disdain for the mirror by embracing a narcissistic identification of masculinity with the body.[31]

Western, crime, and adventure movies were transformed from morality tales into spectacles of violence and homages to spectacular white male bodies. At the same time, the black male ideal in the movies was also dramatically altered. The image of the honorable but usually accommodating and asexual African American man—characters played by Sidney Poitier and Harry Belafonte in the 1950s and 1960s, was transformed in the 1970s into a black version of the lawless action man. Gordon Park's role in *Shaft* (1971) opened an era. John Shaft, an African American private eye was hired by a black crime figure to rescue his abducted daughter from a rival white gang. Shaft portrayed an individualist, outside the worlds of both the predominantly white police force and the black gangs, but a "sexually potent hero" in the tradition of James Bond. Yet, as a black Dirty Harry Callaghan, he attracted a young African American audience with his suave, cool demeanor as he used not only his fists but a coat stand, bottles, machine guns, a Molotov cocktail, and even a fire hose to rescue the black girl from the white mobsters.[32]

Melvin Van Peebles's *Sweet Sweetback's Baadasssss Song* (1971) went much further. Opening with the words "Dedicated to all the Brothers and Sisters who had enough of the Man" and the credit "Starring: The Black Community," *Sweet Sweetback* consciously takes up the cause of black militancy and solidarity and, with it, the black male hero fighting the white power structure. Sweet Sweetback, an orphan boy who grew up in a Los Angeles whorehouse where he learned how to please women and display his sexual prowess in the house sex shows, is arrested for murder by police needing a suspect. When, on his way to jail, a Black Panther is arrested and beaten by the police, Sweet Sweetback attacks the officers. He spends the rest of the movie on the run and, after a long chase (reminding us of a slave escape), the injured hero eventually finds freedom across the Rio Grande in Mexico. In between his confrontations with pursuing white cops (and much police brutality), he has a number of sexual encounters, including with a female hanger-on of the all-white Hell's Angels motorcycle gang, who gather around the "couple" and cheer in an act of interracial male sexual solidarity. The film ends with Sweet Sweetback's warning: "Watch out—a baad assss nigger is coming to collect some dues." While showing a gritty portrayal of black urban life and appealing to the liberating black militancy of the era, *Sweet Sweetback* also displayed a violent and oversexed image of the black man (conforming to white bigotry). It certainly seemed to romanticize the lawless rebel. Although *Sweet Sweetback* was clearly political, it set the stage for the commercial and escapist blaxploitation movies in the 1970s and 1980s. The model of the adaptive, though not servile, black male struggling to find dignity in Sidney Poitier's movies gave way to an open celebration of the militant fighter, first against the "man" and then more simply as the fighter for fighting's sake. This new figuration reinforced stereotypes about black sexuality while it made violence not merely an expression of realism but a part of an emerging thrill culture.

The blaxploitation film drew on the language of the heroic man in the civil rights and Black Power movements. Yet it had little to do with the models of manhood exhibited by the brave black youth of the early sit-ins or the Black Panthers. Instead, these films glorified individualism and sometimes the drug culture. In *Superfly*, the hero is the drug dealer who cannot quit to take a "jive job for chump change." Blaxploitation movies may have reflected some parts of reality, as did the violent westerns of the same era. But they promoted, as did the "spectacular body" movies of Schwartzenegger, Stallone, and Bruce Lee, not stories of mature or maturing men but of boy-men living in a fantasy world of the cool. This would be a legacy that my generation would pass down to the next generation in the form of hip-hop and especially gangster rap.[33]

Our Culture of Nostalgia

As my generation aged, many of us bought images of a youth that we were losing but that still defined us. We were sold youth in ads; we embraced generational identity in our comedy; many of us rejected our father's stories and made the infantile fixations of "action" films into mainstream male culture. Inevitably, we also became extraordinarily interested in preserving the memory of our own youth.

Nostalgia is a relatively new phenomenon. It emerged fully only when people found an accelerating rate of change in many things so frustrating and alienating that they tried to capture the fleeting past in their "ephemeral" culture and goods. It may seem strange that we seek "stability" in what lasted only briefly when we were young, but, as we age, our experiences as children and teens seem to be "timeless" even if they were only songs by the Rolling Stones, while the latest thing today seems merely fleeting and confusing. I see evidence of boomer nostalgia in the recent enthusiasm for collecting, preserving, and just glorying in "our" music, cars, toys, model railroads, and even beer cans peculiar to "our" time of growing up. We didn't invent these hobbies. In fact, some date from the 1930s, and those born a decade before the baby boom were some of the greatest innovators in this culture of memory. Nevertheless, we became of part of it as we grew older, especially since the 1980s. I see this nostalgia for the material trappings of youth in old car collectors who gather for hours every Friday night at local fast food parking lots and arrange their vacations to coincide with collector's shows. Others preserve it in nostalgic cultures of old toy collections and model railroading.

The hot-rod culture of my father's youth had been in decline since the late 1960s, but it experienced a surprising renaissance in the late 1970s and early 1980s. Men, long chafing at the downsizing of American cars in the wake of the energy crisis of 1973, welcomed the drop in gas prices in the early 1980s. These males were nostalgic for the 400-cubic-inch V-8 muscle cars of the early 1960s that they felt were the veritable symbols of the American way of life. Some bought GM's guidebook, aptly called *Chevrolet Power*, for modifying engines to get around the emission regulations that neutered their beloved monster cars. Others had nostalgia for the cars of their more distant youth. The point, as sociologist Dale Dannefer notes, was and is less the social interaction of collectors than the shared obsession with the nostalgic object.[34]

Men in their forties and fifties in 1980 who thirty years before had, as youths, rebelled against the conventional car culture by souping up and raking down Model A Fords returned to the obsession of their youth. Too old for the rigors and dangers of drag racing, they collected and rebuilt the hot rods of their teen years, reducing them to "street rods" because they were driven on "cruises" through town and displayed in old car shows. Naturally, a variety of magazines, such as *Rod and Custom* and *Street Rod Action*, books, and aftermarket parts companies appeared to satisfy the demand for restoring pre-1955 rods.[35]

Often as important to these men as restoring and enhancing old cars was reliving the social rituals of youth through these cars, especially during the curious phenomenon of cruise nights. Originally the cruise involved youths trolling along selected streets in central business districts on weekend nights in their personalized and flashy cars, going from one drive-in to another to flirt with the opposite sex or to spar with rival drivers. Cruising along Detroit's Woodward Avenue dates back to 1926.[36] Zoot-suit wearing Chicano youth in their low-riding Chevys cruised "slow and low" down the main streets of southern Californian towns in the late 1940s, a tradition that survives on Santa Clara Street in San Jose today in the (illegal) cruising of Chicano/a youth.[37] In 1964, I recall seeing dozens of teen cars on Friday nights crawling in a circuit down Riverside and up Main Street in downtown Spokane and feeling left out because all I had to drive was a 1956 Ford station wagon (instead of the much favored 1955 or 1956 Chevrolet sedan). By the end of the 1960s, however, authorities were clamping down on kids who congregated in their cars in the parking lots of drive-ins and clogged main streets on Friday nights. By the early 1970s, cruising declined with the coming of expensive gas and fashion changes.[38]

Within a decade, however, the "kids" were back, this time as middle-aged enthusiasts for the cars and culture of their youth. At first, they were mostly men and sometimes their accommodating wives who gathered in old fashioned custard-serving drive-ins to show off their 1931 Model As or 1949 Lincolns. Their owners had appropriately transformed these cars into "personalized" eye catchers with dropped axles, chopped roofs, dual exhausts, and polished engines, proudly displayed to any and all willing to admire their works of art. They gathered, too, in large car shows such as Kustom Cars in Gettysburg or Lead East in the Meadowlands of New Jersey. More common and more intimate were the Friday-night gatherings at a neighborhood restaurant parking lot. As youth, these folks were called greasers. Some never got over Elvis's eclipse by the Beatles in 1964; they might have attended doo-wop concerts to hear the Cadillacs sing "Speedo" and later bought CDs of the "Greatest Hits of 1959." They formed what

was in many ways a distinctly modern crowd, adults gathering to relive their childhoods and to grouse about change. Newspaper writers
recorded their complaints about the lack of style and distinction in
"today's" cars, their longing for the fins and chrome of yore, and their
jibes against contemporary kids who didn't even know what a stick
shift was. But there was more. The collectors met to relive their youth
through very specific and ephemeral commercial goods—a specific
car model that they had lusted after or perhaps been lucky enough
to own when they were sixteen or twenty years old or an Elvis hit of
early 1956 that was "their" song.

Cruisers recalled how radical rock music was when they were
young, how their parent's hated Elvis, and how playing the raw music
of Jerry Lee Lewis made them feel again like innovators. But they also
reminisced about how innocent those times were, when hamburgers
and fries were only a quarter. One of the hit songs the time was "Wake
Up Little Susie" about a couple who had fallen asleep at the drive-in
movie and were worried that their parents would be angry and their
"reputations" would be "shot" among their friends. They were "stuck
in the fifties," as the popular slogan went, and proud of it. Gathering
at a Friday Classic Car Night in a north Milwaukee McDonald's parking lot in the summer of 2003 were the owners of an emerald green
1953 Rambler Country Club, a green 1947 DeSoto Deluxe, a sparkling
white 1965 Buick Electra 225, and a 1971 Plymouth Road Runner, each
with a distinct story to tell. Often the favored car was the most popular used car when cruisers were sixteen years old. For early boomers
that might have been the 1955 through 1957 Chevrolet sedan, and for
a younger group, the 1964 through 1967 Ford Mustang or the 1965
Pontiac GTO.[39] At a car show in July 2007, I met a sixty-two-year-old
man and his wife who were displaying a particularly beautiful 1956
Chevrolet hardtop. He told me that he had one just like it when, as a
seventeen-year-old, he and his wife were dating. I wasn't surprised to
hear how his younger brother wrapped it around a tree and that the
man had been trying to get another like it for years. A nearby farmer
had just the one he wanted in his barn, and the man pleaded with the
owner for twenty years before he was able to buy and restore it.

Other conversations with participants in old car shows confirm
the impression that the old car is often a bridge to the youth of the
owner. At a show in August 2005, I met a couple in their early sixties from the nearby small town of Philipsburg, Pennsylvania, who
displayed a 1957 BMW Isetta, a tiny two-seater (nicknamed "the roll-

ing egg") that they brought to the show on a new flatbed truck. Why would anyone from such a conservative place have such a curious car? It turns out that the husband had briefly owned one when he was in his twenties and had to give it up when he married and had children. He was proud of the fact that his Isetta has appreciated much in value over the past few years, but he certainly had no plans to sell it (or even drive it). The Isetta was a marker of a long-lost youth and an emblem of his (and his indulgent wife's) individuality.

A lot of male old-car owners have understanding wives who help sand rusted car bodies or hand wrenches to their husbands as they reconstruct ancient vehicles. Sometimes the women add their own touches to the men's restoration efforts (like the wife of a fifty-year-old man with a restored pink 1961 Studebaker Hawk who decorated the interior for shows with teddy bears handmade with baby Alpaca wool from her own animals). Another couple, displaying a 1955 Chevrolet sedan (with a bright yellow exterior and a purple engine block with pink hoses), took pride in the fact that they spend two evenings a week on this and other cars they own. It keeps him "out of the bars" and her "away from the malls," they gleefully observed.

The couples who "share" this male nostalgia, however, seem to be older, in their fifties, at least. The younger enthusiasts seldom appear in the shows with women: I asked a thirty-year-old man with a 1948 Chevrolet pickup (including a hand-restored wooden bed) if his wife or girlfriend worked with him on the truck. He replied that he was divorced and happy to devote most of his free time to restoring trucks and other vehicles. After all, "cars don't run away."

The car shows reveal a lot of individuality and complex motives. Men in their twenties told me that they favored 1980s Japanese sports cars because of their fascination with the action film *The Fast and the Furious* (2001), which featured Japanese cars. But most seem to embrace the hobby to get back a long-lost youth. Typical was the forty-three-year-old man I met who, like his high school buddies, was obsessed with late-1960s and early-1970s muscle cars (Camaros and GTOs but also Mustangs). He not only identified muscle cars with the "golden age" of American automobile power when he was a teen but had a visceral disdain for the newly ascendant Japanese cars that so attracted younger men. He had a "rice burners suck" sticker on his engine in reference to Asian sports cars.[40]

The quest for recovering youth took many other forms. Some men, for example, tried to recollect a distinctive memory of the past through toys and other playthings. This craze took off in the 1930s, and with good reason. Men who had been six-year-olds in 1900 had been part of the first generation of American children to experience the world of rapidly changing electric trains, toy trucks, and much else. Memories of these distinct wonders of modern consumption became an obsession thirty years later when these boys had become men. In their thirties and forties, they began collecting toy savings banks; miniature horse-drawn vehicles such as carriages, fire pumps, and circus bandwagons; as well as tiller-steered automobiles, quaint delivery trucks, and especially Lionel electric trains. Comic-strip character toys such as Happy Hooligan and Andy Gump reminded these men of their earliest fantasies, and the naiveté of these playthings served as a contrast with modern toys. From the 1930s on, this was a slowly growing (and probably for many an embarrassing, thus secret) hobby.[41]

Many of the early and most energetic collectors specialized in toy soldiers and ships. Early in the twentieth century, indulgent dads and uncles gave boys sets of toy soldiers made by companies like Mignot (French), Heyde (German), the American Soldier Co., and especially Britains (English). These toy soldiers became collector's items when these boys were old men. Publisher Malcolm Forbes and his son, Robert, legitimated this seemingly childish pastime by displaying their extraordinary toy soldier and boat collections at the National Geographic Society in Washington, D.C., in 1982. Even earlier, in 1971, toy collecting had grown enough to have its own magazine, *Antique Toy World*, which featured stories of rare toys and especially of their hunters. Middle-aged men gleefully wrote their own stories, presenting themselves as fun-loving guys living ordinary, even humdrum lives, who found adventure in trolling the back roads of rural America looking for that special Bing miniature battleship that was for them the fulfillment of a life's dream. The crowning glory came when that special find completed a unique set of rarities (and perhaps promised financial rewards as an object of speculation). Still, what the toy hunter found most important was that the prized plaything brought back a cherished but long-lost memory of a toy that a beloved relative had given him when times were simple.[42]

Each collector invariably focused on a particular type of toy: comic-strip figures and wind-up toys from the 1930s or toy trucks and farm machinery from the 1940s, for example. Whatever the collector's obsession, these toys brought back memories of a particular childhood that took place, say, between 1930 and 1935 or 1945 and 1950 when the collector was five to ten years old. In later years, not only did the older toys (like mechanical savings banks) grow too expensive for average collectors, but new types of toys began to attract the next wave of thirty- to forty-year-old men trying to recapture their boyhoods. Robot toys of the early 1950s became popular collector's items by the end of the 1970s, and TV toys from the late 1950s and early 1960s attracted attention by the early 1980s. Each generation (defined almost by the years that a particular toy line was sold) collected its own childhood memories. A toy expert could practically determine a collector's age by his enthusiasm. Naturally, I am fascinated by (but don't collect) toys like the Fort Apache playset and Davy Crockett coonskin caps of the mid-1950s because they were the rage when I was seven or eight years old. Men, often serious, rich, and powerful, buy back their childhoods with toys that they once loved or longed for but never owned.

Inevitably, this nostalgia also was sold to us. Businesses with names like Toys "Bee" Used and Stuff Mom Threw Out sprang up in the 1980s. Specialized auctions held by such big-name houses as Christie's and Sotheby's presented older, rarer, and more expensive toys. Krause Publications's *Toy Shop* featured not only cast-iron Buddy-L toy tractors from the 1920s and rare Superman windups from the 1930s, but also TV-themed toys from the 1950s and 1960s. Reaching 17,000 subscribers by 1991, *Toy Shop*, with an ad-drenched format, appealed to married men, mostly boomers, from thirty-five to fifty-four years old.[43]

Pittsburgh-area resident Tom Frey, caught the toy bug in 1981 when he bought a Roy Rogers Chuck Wagon for five dollars at a flea market, hoping to give it to his son. Naturally, his boy was totally disinterested in a 1950s toy in those golden days of Star Wars figures. But soon the father was "re-collecting" his own childhood rather than trying to relate to his son's as he filled his own toy box, eventually writing a column in *Antique Toy World* about "classic plastic toys" from the 1950s and 1960s. Frey's story was common in that curious world of collectors and merchants of toy nostalgia. A typical comment: "You see something that you haven't seen since when you were 3 feet tall and maybe those memories have been covered up and forgotten, and all of a sudden you're back in time with the people you were playing with."[44]

Toy nostalgia could take even more elaborate forms—as in the expensive and time-consuming hobby of model railroading. Like toy collecting, the leisure activity of buying and restoring miniature trains, track, stations, and other buildings and scenic effects took off in the 1930s. This was when the children who received the first elec-tric-train layouts in the 1900s had become old and rich enough to return nostalgically to the past in model railroading. For decades, the electric train was a emblem of father-son bonding. From the 1910s, Lionel offered boys tips on how to convince their dads to join them in the fun and fantasy of electric railroading. Nothing had changed in the 1940s when a Lionel ad counseled the boy to "Talk to Dad today. Take him into partnership with you. Make him the senior partner in your railroading company." All this helped to make the electric train the Christmas present of choice for millions of "boys" (both nine-year-old sons and their thirty-five-year-old fathers).[45]

By the 1960s all that changed as a new generation of boys re-jected their dads' gifts of the once-coveted Lionel trains, preferring Mattel's slot cars and, later, action figures and video games. The train station in real life was rapidly disappearing, being replaced by the airport and the passenger plane. The model locomotive simply lost its magic to boys. But something interesting happened by the 1980s. Electric trains, in decline since the 1960s, saw a revival (selling three times more in 1988 than ten years earlier). Large numbers were pur-chased by men forty years old and older, some of whom deluded themselves into believing that they were buying them for their boys, though many openly admitting that they were collecting them for themselves. While many might think that the "golden age" of model railroading was the 1950s, circulation for the *Model Railroader* was twice what it was in the 1950s by the end of the 1980s.[46]

Of course, many of these subscribers were older than the boom-ers, with an enthusiasm that extended back to the 1930s or 1940s. But the hobby took a jump when older boomers stepped on board, being the last generation to share a fascination with the puffing locomotive and the romance of the train and track winding their way through the river and dale of the American countryside. For the older and younger hobbyist alike, model railroading could be and usually was a deeply engaging, almost addictive activity. The range of enthusiasm extended from retrieving the old Lionel set from parents' attics to creating elaborate displays of 1940s railroads winding through min-iature western mining towns, an exhibit that could easily consume most of the family basement.[47] Such hobbyists spent many evenings pouring over articles in model railroad magazines, learning how to cast a skewed arch bridge or to construct a model of the Delaware and Hudson's welded boxcars. Some joined model railroad clubs and met weekly to construct elaborate displays. Some of the biggest were the New York Society of Model Engineers (founded in 1926) and the Baltimore Society of Model Engineers (1932), which offered holiday displays for the public. Many more were small clubs of twenty to forty members who met in private garages or rented spaces for evenings of male bonding in the lore, skill, and competition of model railroading.[48]

A few even tore up their backyards and, with the compliance of very understanding wives, built railroad gardens. A hobby developed by the British in the late nineteenth century, by 1970 it had begun to enchant American men. By 2000, about a hundred clubs were devoted to railroad gardens and were served by a bimonthly magazine called *Garden Railways*. Special oversized trains designed to run on G-gauge track (at a 1:22.5 ratio to the size of a "real train" as compared to the HO-gauge at 1:87). Power was supplied by large transformers, batteries, and, in some cases, even steam engines. To effect the look of an authentic landscape, railroaders used dwarf conifers and shrubs, small-leafed plants pruned to scale, and moss to suggest grass.[49] But behind all this achievement and serious effort was always nostalgia for memories of childhood—the train running around the Christmas tree, the clatter of the wheels over the track, and the smell of the transformer.

Obsessing with the Look and Potency of Youth

While men of my generation tried to recover their childhoods in nostalgia, they also tried to find fountains of youth in clothing, exercise, diet, and pills. Our first act was to reject the sartorial standards of maturity by abandoning at least some of the dress and look of our fathers. This was not altogether new. Back at the end of the nineteenth century, young men abandoned the beards and whiskers and portly paunches of their fathers for the modern "clean cut" look of the shaved face and the quest for the trim body. But another revolution in the appearance of men occurred in the mid-1960s when men began giving up the uniform of maturity in the suit, tie, and fedora for more informal wear. A perusal of men's clothing ads in *Esquire* shows that in the fall of 1965 the hat disappeared as the standard accessory in ads for men's suits.[50] This rejection of the old sartorial marker of manhood preceded the coming of age of boomers by a few years, but we certainly embraced it. By the 1990s, the business suit and even the tie had disappeared from many work settings, even in the professional classes. I stopped wearing jacket and tie to my classroom lectures in 1994; my colleagues in the sciences did so much earlier. Businessmen in sales and finance may still wear the dark suit, but even in commerce and industry the suit and tie has disappeared in many offices. Tom Landry, coach of the Dallas Cowboys football team, was a holdout, noted for appearing in suit and fedora at games from 1960 until his retirement in 1988. He apparently believed that he had a duty to differentiate himself from his young players and to uphold a measure of mature dignity. No one seems to have carried the torch after him.

There are a lot of reasons for this abandonment of "grown-up" clothes (and with them the traditional markers of authority and self-repressed dignity—as in neckties). However, one important trend is what Richard Florida calls "the rise of the creative class." This fashion-setting group of entrepreneurs and technicians in such new industries as computing, information, advertising, and investment abandoned in their work and private life the corporate, authoritarian work culture of their fathers.[51]

Given our rejection of formality and sartorial standards, it is curious that some of us boomers by the mid-1970s were, as Christopher Lasch disdainfully remarked in his *Culture of Narcissism* (1979), joining women in an "enslavement to glamour." As historian Bill Osgerby argues, this was still another form of rebellion from the father: new identities "premised upon youthful hedonism and conspicuous consumerism certainly repudiated and displaced the traditional codes of a bourgeois masculinity rooted in ideals of hard work, thrift and puritanical conservatism."[52]

When the leading edge of the boomers hit fifty in 1996, they began to embrace in earnest a new obsession—aging—and with this came a surge in businesses interested in our evading or denying it. Few of us took the radical steps of Ron Fortner, a Palm Springs, California, radio celebrity who, after a triple-bypass operation to clean his clogged arteries, joined the Life Extension Institute for a regimen of human growth hormone treatments to restore his lost youth. Nor did many join him in supplementing their daily rejuvenation cocktail with melatonin, DHEA, and even testosterone. But many would seek what these drugs promised—an improved sense of well-being, more supple skin and lustrous hair, a leaner upper torso, increased energy, and, of course, enhanced virility. The mid-1990s saw a flood of new products and services to drive the ravages of age from boomer bodies. Enterprising urologists teamed up with smart investors to open impotence clinics, and pharmaceutical companies rushed to market drugs to ward off what some dubbed "viropause" (the male equivalent of menopause). In 1997, three books appeared that addressed the growing consciousness of boomers of their impeding loss of muscle, bone, and height (as well as sperm production) with promises to stave off these physical signs of aging with hormone and other drug treatments. Theresa Crenshaw's *The Alchemy of Love and Lust*, William Regelson's *The Superhormone Promise*, and Ronald Klatz's *The New Anti-Aging Revolution: Stopping the Clock for a Younger, Sexier, Happier You* catalogued the dreary facts of aging to a generation that had seldom thought about it before.[53]

The prospect of some 76 million boomers entering these anxious years of aging naturally excited merchandisers of medical and health products, but the aging boomers seemed to offer a special opportunity beyond their numbers. Marketers, who for decades had been enamored by the wealth and consuming might of those born in the generation after World War II, saw the boomers' transition as unique. Unlike their parents, who entered their fifties acquiescing to their fate and with diminished desire to experiment, the boomers were said to be different (as they always had been). Over and over, the marketing community lectured businesses about the need to change long-established attitudes. No longer did selling to the senior set mean advertising Depends, emergency-communication bracelets, or terminal life insurance. Nor was it correct to think still that the over-fifty crowd simply wasn't worth courting because they had already bought everything they wanted or were stuck in their ways, hopelessly loyal to their brand of beer or toothpaste. "Mature-marketing" consultant Ken Dychtwald lamented the fact that while people over fifty bought 40 percent of consumer goods, they were targets of only 10 percent of ads, and most TV programming was clearly directed to the traditionally prized eighteen-to-thirty-four-year-old group. The graying of the boomers was about to change this. Not only was this group the richest cohort ever to enter their fifties, but unlike their parents, they were far more willing to spend. After all, my generation controlled about 51 percent (at $2.6 trillion) of the wealth in the United States while constituting only 28 percent of the population. As intriguing was the fact that in a 2002 survey, fifty-five-year-old boomers claimed that they felt as if they were in their late thirties or early forties. Marketing consultant John Nielson explained this apparent self-illusion by noting that these aging boomers were "still interested in the same things as they were at that age. But their ambition has subsided, so they can now appreciate the things they really love—whether it's their children or hobbies." They now could spend on themselves as perhaps they had wished they could when they were in their thirties and were obliged to save money. A 2003 Harris poll found that a majority of fifty- to sixty-four-year-olds would prefer to be in their thirties "forever."[54]

This may explain why marketers have offered my generation what one might not expect for an aging population—products to enhance the pleasures of life. Although we, perhaps, were less interested in buying houses and other "real goods," marketing people insisted that we were ready for "feel goods," products that made us feel "better, sexier, more informed, better fed, less stressed." This included health products but also entertainment ranging from restaurants and theme parks to casinos.[55] Spas like the Grooming Lounge in Washington, D.C., discovered that aging male boomers would pay top dollar for facials, pedicures, waxings, and hair coloring, as well as bottled skin toners, moisturizers, and special shaving cream. At these fountains of youth, men bought rejuvenation while they watched ESPN and felt comfortable knowing that they were in a "man's" environment. Most came to spas to find ways to fight hair loss, the most commonly observed sign of male aging, but some men asked also for Botox to erase wrinkles. This 1987 innovation cost from $300 to $1,000 per injection, which lasted perhaps three months before needing renewal. Most users were women, but perhaps 12 percent were men by 2002. Also growing in popularity were new forms of gym exercise, like "hot yoga" designed to optimize flexibility and cardiovascular benefits for men in their fifties, as well as home equipment like treadmills and even light-weight tennis rackets and skis that offered low-impact play. Over half of the 33 million health club members were over forty years old in 2002. Many others joined the $28 billion craze for foods that promise medicinal benefits (nutraceuticals). These include ginkgo biloba and elderberries for improved mental clarity and glucosamine for more limber joints. The market for antiaging products increased fourfold between 1993 and 1997 alone (reaching $1.3 billion). All this, says Michael Weiss in *American Demographics*, would help boomers "timeshift and morph effortlessly, and most importantly, painlessly, into younger versions of their former selves."[56]

One of the most effective ways of reaching the graying young at heart was through direct-to-consumer advertising of prescription drugs. Until the 1990s, organized medicine opposed the advertising of prescription drugs on TV because it threatened the doctor's authority to decide what drugs patients required. Although these ads were required to mention potential side effects and to tell consumers to "ask your doctor" about the wonder drug advertised, this new kind of commercial invited patients to pressure their doctors into prescribing drugs that they otherwise might not. In August 1997, the Food and Drug Administration eased the detailed requirement of listing health hazards on direct-to-consumer commercials. This encouraged the proliferation of these ads (the money spent on them rose from $12 million in 1989 to $595 million in 1995 and an astonishing $4.2 billion in 2005). For a generation of people who are probably more willing to make demands on doctors and to take charge of their medical needs than their parents were, these ads had a special appeal. Without doubt, these commercials exposed the anxieties and hopes of aging boomers. TV has become like a health magazine in the doctor's waiting room, full of ads for every malady and inconvenience of aging imaginable. Boomers are offered Pharmacia's Celebrex to reduce the pain of arthritis, Pfizer's Lipitor to tackle "bad" cholesterol, and Merck's Propecia to reverse hair loss.[57]

Especially frightening to male boomers after fifty was the shock of declining sexual potency. The fact is that the spongelike chambers of the penis fill with connective tissue while the arteries leading these chambers narrow, reducing the capacity for strong and lasting erections. Even though special medical conditions such as heart disease, high blood pressure, and diabetes could lead to hydraulic failure, performance was also a very sensitive manifestation of lost youth. It's no surprise that Viagra, when it went on sale in April 1998, set records for the number of prescriptions written for a new drug. Viagra was first an experimental treatment for angina, but male patients discovered that it facilitated blood flow into the penis. Even if it worked only 70 percent of the time, the idea of taking a pill one hour before sex (rather than having a scrotal implant or doing without) attracted many of the 30 million American men over fifty who, according to Viagra's manufacturer Pfizer, were plagued with "erectile dysfunction." Although Viagra presumably could be obtained only after a medical exam to make sure that the patient had the requisite vascular disorder requiring the drug, sites on the Internet immediately offered Viagra without an embarrassing visit to a urologist (and of course without any guarantee of effectiveness).[58]

For a generation of men openly obsessed with sex since their teens and who had a long history of experimenting with new drugs, it may not be surprising that Viagra found a ready market. Some boomer men replaced marijuana with Viagra to get "good sex." More interesting and amazing, the drug's advertising sparked an open discussion of a topic that had until that time not only never been mentioned on TV or even at "cocktail parties, in trading rooms, or in doctors' offices," as feminist writer Erika Jong noted in 1998. In fact, ads anticipating the sale of Viagra were pulled from the 1998 Superbowl as inappropriate for a family audience. Soon, however, that bit of residual squeamishness disappeared, when former presidential candidate and Senate leader Bob Dole became the spokesman for Viagra. Thereafter, not only Superbowls but also most sport and news programs were regularly sprinkled with ads for Viagra and its many competitors. Sales in 2004 topped $2.33 billion. A similar drug, Levitra, became the official erectile-dysfunction drug of the National Football League; Cialis sponsored golf matches; and Viagra logos were plastered on vehicles at NASCAR races, displaying to the whole world, including children and grandmothers, the triumph of male virility over aging. And how many spam e-mails do each of us receive every morning from vendors of potency pills promising rock-hard erections? It really is amazing.

Viagra brought not only a solution to this age-old problem of aging men but made "erectile dysfunction" a household term. A "problem" that had been previously ignored or treated as a social or psychological issue became medicalized with a simple pill-popping solution. If, as the ads claim, "E.D." is really a common medical problem akin to high blood pressure, then why shouldn't men have the right to pursue "treatment"? More subtly, why shouldn't they expect "erectile function" equal to that of a young man and, by extension, sexual performance from their partners as they had known when both were younger (often to the irritation of wives and girlfriends). As the sociologist Meika Loe notes, Viagra returned men to "normalcy" or, in other words, a perpetual condition of youthful potency. "Normal for males, as defined by Pfizer Pharmaceuticals and its experts, is having a consistently hard and penetrative penis, feeling eighteen again, and never having to worry about occasional problems with erections." And the whole world, including children and grandmothers, has to hear about it every day on TV.[59]

As Michael Weiss wrote in *American Demographics* in 2002, "While previous generations entered middle age without much fuss, many boomers appear to be trying to create a new model of adulthood, a midlife stage focused on renewal. They express no interest in giving up the center stage they've dominated for decades. And thanks to advances in fitness products, sexual performance-enhancing drugs, skin care creams and hair color treatments, they may not have to." We're not called the "Me Generation" for nothing.[60]

chapter 5

New STORIES, New REBELS

Looking back on my own generation and its contribution to the culture of the boy-man, I became less judgmental about my sons' age
group. Still, after watching and thinking about the juvenile antics of
the men on *Saturday Night Live* who later made it in comedy films,
Hugh Grant's boyish roles in light romances, and the cool and meaningless "action" of Arnold Schwarzenegger and many of his younger
followers, it seems clear to me that something has changed. My sons'
generation has gone beyond our rebellion and obsession with youth.
Increasingly, it ignores rather than rejects the past and extends youth
and it culture across a longer age span, ranging from the preteen to
the thirty-something "adult." In its stories, I see a puerile humor often
built on a cynicism toward personal relationships and a cool attraction to displays of aestheticized violence. In the tales embedded in its
advertisements, I observe sometimes appalling appeals to indulgence
and selfishness. Looking back at the men who were born in the late
1960s through mid-1980s and who matured in the 1990s and today,
I am struck by change in the popular culture as compared with what
obtained while I was growing up. The later popular culture helped
shape this younger generation, but, as we shall see later (in chapter 6),
this generation's experiences also help explain the culture.

New Notions of the Funny

In the summer of 1999, film critics took notice of a change. Although
the long-awaited Star Wars prequel, *The Phantom Menace*, was the

predictable hit that all expected (after all, the last Star Wars movie had appeared in 1983, and fans had grown up and old waiting for more), the trend that caught their eye was the amazing success of crude, potty-mouthed comedies. It wasn't the plots (in that they included the usual schmaltzy happy endings) that they noticed, but the astonishing array of jokes and scenes of indisputable bad taste. This included Mike Myers's *Austin Powers: The Spy Who Shagged Me* and Adam Sandler's *Big Daddy* (both of which were among the top-ten grossing movies for 1999) as well as the movie version of Comedy Central's TV hit, *South Park: Bigger, Longer, and Uncut*, and the especially gross teen-sex comedy *American Pie*. Over and over, the bodily fluids usually deposited in the toilet were found in the mouths of the heroes (liquid feces taken for coffee or urine for beer). As creepy is a scene from *There's Something About Mary* where Mary mistakenly uses male sexual discharge as hair gel. The grossly obese Scot, appropriately named Fat Bastard, in *Austin Powers*, has a transmitter put up his backside recording his frequent episodes of passing gas. And in *American Pie*, the theme isn't patriotism. Instead, a teen experiments with what it feels like to get to "third base" sexually with mother's apple pie; after he inserted his finger in the pie like Simple Simon, he can't help but "go all the way." Slightly cleverer is *Austin Powers*, which offers viewers a string of comments about how Dr. Evil's rocket looks like a penis without anyone actually using the word. Even Adam Sandler's relatively serious role in *Big Daddy* has the star teaching his adopted kid to play with his saliva, trip up rollerbladers with sticks thrown in their way, and urinate on some random guy's door.

The summer of 1999 seems to have been the culmination of a trend that accelerated in 1994 when Peter and Bobby Farrelly directed *Dumb and Dumber* and launched the career of Jim Carrey as the king of childish vulgarity. Carrey and his pal Jeff Daniels play goofy morons who aspire to open a "worm" pet store and travel across the country to Aspen in a van that looks like a sheepdog to return a briefcase that a pretty woman left in an airport. The briefcase is full of ransom money to get the woman's husband back. But what drives the film are the amazingly stupid things that the pair do: Daniels relieves himself on Carrey's back; Carrey urinates into beer bottles from which a police patrolman drinks; and Daniels suffers a lengthy bout of diarrhea, clogging up the toilet. The Farrelly brothers followed this hit with *Kingpin* in 1996, where Woody Harrelson, playing an alcoholic, one-handed failed pro bowler, "milks" a bull on an Amish farm and drinks the semen, mistaking it for cow's milk.[1]

While the Farrelly brothers were masters of the bathroom gag, the foolish boyish characters that the summer films of 1999 featured often had their origins on *Saturday Night Live*. The veterans of *SNL* included, Chris Farley, Jim Carrey (as a host), Adam Sandler, and Mike Myers. Created by Lorne Michaels in 1975 for NBC, *Saturday Night Live* was a ninety-minute collection of music and sketches, an "urban comedy for young adults" hosted by celebrities (who ranged from Hugh Hefner to Ralph Nader). Writing in 1981, Tony Schwartz noted how the first three years of SNL were "topical and irreverent, poking fun at hypocrisy, pomposity and ineptitude, its targets ranging from rock star Elton John to kidnapped heiress Patricia Hearst to all three living Presidents" (Gerald Ford, Richard Nixon, and Jimmy Carter). But as "experimentation started giving way to proven formulas, subtlety and complexity to cheap shocks, the show lost much of its satirical sharpness." Over the years, the show became increasingly devoted to juvenile comedy.[2]

Perhaps the biggest force coming out of *SNL* was Mike Myers. After spending six years cultivating his Wayne character on *Saturday Night Live* and in two successful *Wayne's World* comedies for the big screen, Myers produced the movie *Austin Powers: International Man of Mystery* in 1997. Based on a spoof of James Bond movies from the 1960s and the rude comedy of Benny Hill and Monty Python, *Austin Powers* earned $145 million dollars from an $18 million investment. Naturally there were sequels: in 1999, *Austin Powers: The Spy Who Shagged Me* (an interesting lapse in American censorship given the fact that the term "shag" is British slang for sexual intercourse) and in 2002, *Austin Powers in Goldmember* (a spoof on the Bond film Goldfinger and a reference to the penile obsession of young males). Gimmicks included time travel between the 1960s and the 1990s (with Austin and his alter ego Dr. Evil having to cope with changes in sexual mores and inflation). But the core of the Austin Powers films is the amazing immaturity of its key players (most played by Myers himself). Austin is a crude hedonist unaware of his oafishness, outdated 1960s mod clothes, and bad teeth. Dr. Evil is curiously childish and vain, with his pet midget copy of himself, Mini Me, and his efforts to make his estranged and long-lost son into his "evil" successor.[3]

Having to endure these puerile comedies of 1999, film critics noted that sex and violence were no longer the only causes of mother's worry; they had been joined by sheer vulgarity that only a child could find amusing. That humor reminds me of the humor that Ed "Big

Daddy" Roth sold in his Rat Fink crazy cars to the eight-year-old boys of the 1960s. About the same time, these kids were enchanted with the "Blame Its" line of toy figures. The "I Didn't Do It" and "I Didn't Push Him" figures offered images of boys with sheepish looks who obviously did do it. The humor of Carrey's and Myers's movies was hardly more mature, and that was the point. Not-so-young adults flocking to see *South Park: Bigger, Longer, and Uncut* could easily have played with the Garbage Pail Kids "trading cards" of the mid-1970s. Little boys bought these cards to freak out their sisters and mothers with images like that of Valerie Vomit, a girl throwing up into a saucepan that she was stirring on the stove. These comedies of 1999 make arrested male development the joke, but rather than simply mocking it, they also embrace the little boy's sense of humor.[4]

Film critics, looking high and low for explanations of this seemingly bizarre phenomenon, came up with some pretty predicable theories. They offered that these films were nothing more than the latest incarnation of the ribald humor of Chaucer's *Canterbury Tales* and Rabelais's *Gargantua*. They were merely an update of the slapstick comedy of Max Sennett's Keystone Cops and Charlie Chaplin's little tramp roles of the 1910s and 1920s or even the screwball comedies of Katharine Hepburn, when she displays her underwear after tearing her dress in the 1938 *Bringing Up Baby*.

I see the point. The mocking of authority and the pratfalls of the naïve and incompetent have long amused people. Perhaps Carrey and Daniels should be viewed as the contemporary exemplars of the unwitting fools played by Stan Laurel and Ollie Hardy more than half a century ago. But I wonder. The comedic pair who worked together in Hollywood from 1927 to 1951 seem more naïve and gentle than Carrey and Daniels, asexual rather than incompetent at sex. And bodily fluids were for the bathroom; feces were never part of the "fine mess" that Laurel and Hardy got into. Even the very un-PC slapping and eye-gouging of the Three Stooges was strictly lowbrow B-list comedy, not the main feature, as the Carrey, Sandler, and Myers films have become.[5] My generation, as we have seen, certainly had more to do with the films of 1999 than did my father's crowd. Certainly over the top was Mel Brooks's *Blazing Saddles* (1974), with the black sheriff who at one point declared that he was going to "whip it out" (a gun, as it turned out) and its painfully prolonged demonstration of campfire farting. *Flesh Gordon*, the 1973 spoof on Flash Gordon, with a penis-shaped rocket ship, was a precursor of Austin Powers.

John Belushi's *Animal House* (1978) with it frat-boy high jinks, and *Porky's*, the famed 1982 high-school sex comedy, led the way for Jim Carrey. Even more on point is the heritage of Larry Flint's magazine, *Hustler* (appearing first in 1974), with its laddish appeal to sexist images of women and in-your-face vulgarity. Rather more off the main road was John Waters's camp in *Pink Flamingos* (1972), with its scene of drag queen Divine eating dog feces, and his *Polyester* (1981), in "Odorama" with accompanying gross-out scratch-and-sniff cards. They, too, cleared the way for the films of 1999.

A second way to explain the potty comedy of 1999 is to admit that it really is a break from the past—even if the latest in a long list of iconoclastic breaks—the "next taboo" to be flattened. First, there was sex and violence; now there is the toilet. The argument might go as follows. While sexual titillation and graphic violence attracted teens and young adults in the 1980s with an endless array of vengeful cops and Arnold Schwarzenegger, Sly Stallone, and Bruce Willis coolly dispatching "evildoers," these thrills can now be seen by four-year-olds on DVD or cable TV. Presumably, the thrill was gone by the time these kids were teens and young adults. If blood-spurting beheaded torsos won't elicit a shudder of excitement, then the gross-out joke might. Moreover, at the core of potty humor is the thrill of discomfort (your own and others'). What could be more unsettling than to get your mouth caught while performing oral sex on a guy and be forced to call in the rescue squad as happened in *The Sweetest Thing*? The joke was about not sex, but embarrassment. The taboo may have changed, but the point was the emotional rush. The problem was that this, like all thrills, quickly loses its impact, obliging the filmmaker to go one step further, to find still another taboo to shatter. On TV, *South Park* made this point in 2001 when it featured the word "shit" during a half-hour episode. At first this seemed shocking and even funny, but by the time the characters had said it 162 times (duly ticked off on a recorder pictured at a corner of the screen), the surprise and humor were gone. In any case, toilet humor, for all its apparent daring, is a cop out, because it avoids taking on sacred cows in real life (political or religious, for example). Hollywood's seeming outrageousness really is a ruse, but it works because it appeals to the mentality of he who wouldn't know a real taboo if he saw it—the little boy.[6] While, as I shall show, the spectacle of violence was hardly displaced by juvenile humor, potty comedy certainly was the next frontier of the taboo-breaking thrill. But why was it chosen?

The reason should become clear in a third hypothesis to explain the rise of gross humor, that propriety's collapse has brought the bathroom into the living room. The old rules that made it OK to tell a dirty joke in the country club locker room but not at the dinner party have vanished. Adults may have always had a taste for the vulgar and gross, but until recently this behavior was reserved for its "proper" setting. What makes taboo breaking a thrill is that this vulgarity is brought out in the open and even shared in "mixed company." When women were no longer treated as guarantors of gentility, protecting the innocence of the young played this role. The breaking of this taboo seems to signal the "final" collapse of propriety. The gross-out humor of Austin Powers is no longer reserved for the locker room or night club but today is offered in the PG-13-rated movie, which kids as well as young adults flock to.

A bit of background is in order here: With the replacement of the old Motion Picture Production Code of 1930 (enforced in 1934) with the rating system in 1968, the film industry was free to experiment with adult sexual themes and more graphic and realistic violence. The rating system, by separating G and PG from R movies, presumably protected both the innocence of kids and the rights and freedom of adults to see "adult" scenes. But with the rating system came a great increase in violent and sexual film; G films dropped from a third of offerings in 1968 to 4 percent by 2002 (when R films constituted 69 percent). At the same time, kids were attracted to the things that made adult-rated movies taboo because that was what it meant to be "grown up." As PG movies (like Gremlins) became edgier to meet this attraction, the movie industry had to address parental concerns by creating a new category, PG-13, in 1984. This admittedly arbitrary rating did not prohibit kids under thirteen from attending but merely "cautioned" parents about violence and verbal or suggestive sexuality. Jack Valenti, head of the Motion Picture Association of America and designer of the rating system, admitted that there were no psychological or moral principles behind this rating. Still, it served the purpose of filmmakers. Seeking to win the largest possible audience, and recognizing that teens and young adults were their most numerous and thus profitable customers, movie makers realized that a PG-13 rating would bring in both the thirteen-year-old (or younger) and the twenty-five-year-old. Thus the number of PG-13 films rose 50 percent between 1995 and 2001 (while PG movies dropped by 45 percent). In the 1970s and early 1980s, many comedy hits were R-rated, but since 1984, R-rated comedies have been displaced by PG-13 films.[7] While PG-13 movies don't show sexual acts or nudity, for example, they are free to make extremely suggestive scenes of oral sex. The envelope is pushed not only toward knocking down the "next taboo" but by pushing the taboo down the age scale to the thirteen-year-old or lower.

This threat to propriety (and the "proper" exposure of innocent children) is not, of course, really new. We saw it in the 1940s when young-adult fascination with sex, graphic crime, and gruesome horror invaded the child's world of the comic book. Then as now, there was the blending of the fantasies of boys and men. What is different today is the fact that the invasion seems to have also gone the other way—from the potty humor of the six-year-old to the older teen and young adult. The result is another manifestation of the boy-man.

This suggests to me a simple fact—the amazing puerility of the movie-going audience. It isn't just that kids have become exposed to the adult vulgarity, but adults have adopted the bathroom humor of the six-year-old. As Philippe Ariès noted in his famous *Centuries of Childhood* (1962), cultures of the past (in his case the European Middle Ages) were amazingly childlike because they did not rigidly separate the child from the adult. It is only in the seventeenth-century that the church and state made a deliberate effort to isolate the child from the chaos and vulgarity of the street and thus foster his or her self-discipline and refinement. With the "innocent" young separated from older children and adults, the child could be trained to become a less childlike adult. The vehicles of isolation, the "civilizing institutions" of school, church, and youth group (in modern times the scouts and Little League also), became hallmarks of genteel culture. But today these civilizing barriers have been undermined by a popular culture that doesn't separate age groups in large part because it is profitable not to. The result has been a general "return" to a less restrained, more childlike culture.[8]

Not only were the films of 1999 gleefully puerile, but they often revealed a striking and perhaps surprising aggressiveness, the darker side of the boy-man. Like much comedy, these films use physical humor, but they break from the tradition of pratfalls and slapstick where the hero gets as much if not more than he gives. Rather, there is a nastiness about the punch-outs and tricks of these movies. Janet Roach of Columbia University notes that there is less of the "gentle irony" of Steve Martin or the "harsh social commentary" of Richard Pryor in the comedy of 1999. It is cruel, less sensitive to human frailty, less hopeful. I would add more resentful.[9]

Consider Adam Sandler's roles. A stand-up comedian with the tell-tale marks of first fame from *Saturday Night Live*, Sandler became a stock hit maker from 1995 with *Billy Madison, Happy Gilmore, The Wedding Singer, The Waterboy, Big Daddy,* and *Little Nicky.* As film critic Roger Ebert remarked in 2002, "Sandler characters are almost oppressively nice, like needy puppies, and yet they conceal a masked hostility to society, a passive-aggressive need to go against the flow, a gift for offending others while in the very process of being ingratiating."[10]

Sandler characters seldom develop or show much depth. This can be seen in comparing his 2002 remake of Frank Capra's 1936 comedy *Mr. Deeds Goes to Town* with the original starring Gary Cooper. In both versions, Mr. Deeds is a New England rube who, upon inheriting a fortune from an uncle, goes to New York City where he is laughed at and manipulated by Big Apple sophisticates and schemers. The love interest, reporter Babe Bennett, seduces Deeds while making a fool of him in her newspaper but eventually comes around to appreciate his simple folksy ways. In the Sandler redo of Cooper's role, Deeds also plays the populist, but there are some revealing differences. In the 1930s version, we see a classic Capra movie about the virtues of the common man from the small town, but in Sandler's characterization, the ordinary, if sometimes bluntly honest wisdom of Cooper's Mr. Deeds becomes another take on the Sandler doofus. While Cooper punches a literati who makes fun of his career as a writer of humble but moving greeting-card verses, Sandler lashes out repeatedly at anyone who gets in his path. Cooper's Deeds gives away his fortune to farmers on ten-acre lots with all the sensible restrictions one would expect from a New Deal program, but Sandler's Deeds spends his fortune arbitrarily, for example, giving a boy $20,000 for his bike. While Cooper's Deeds asks sensible questions of his company's officers and in the end makes a homely but persuasive defense of himself to a court judging his sanity, Sandler's Deeds has no claim to virtue except his being a regular guy that others have to find and appreciate. Capra's common man of 1936 becomes a mean-spirited simpleton boy of 2002.[11]

The brazen and bold display of puerility in recent movies is perhaps inevitable—after all, it reflects the fact that teens go to the show twice as often as adults, a fact that explains why these were A-list films, not the cheap teen-pics of the 1950s drive-ins. But, there is more to it. This mix of little-boy potty humor and aggressive teen rebellion is now mainstream, reaching not only kids but also adults who don't want to give up their childhoods. It is as if "the whole world wants to be sixteen," says journalist Louise Kennedy. Movies like *Monsters Inc.*, she complains, "have too much winking at adults to make real sense to young kids and too little thematic depth or sophistication to hold lasting meaning for adults."[12]

Of course, not all takes on the boy-man are so negative, a fact that may explain why he is so tolerated and even loved. Hugh Grant offers another version of the boy-man, with his oft-repeated role of the dapper yet youthful sophisticate, made all the more debonair to American ears by his London accent. Hugh Grant may eventually grow into the image of the middle-aged Cary Grant. But in his forties, he is still making a good living as the boyishly befuddled, if sometimes delightfully roguish, and thus ever loveable lead. All this is best seen in the movie *About a Boy* (2002), where Grant plays a man in his thirties who, living off the royalties of his father's sappy Christmas tune, leads a life of total irresponsibility. In the process of the film, of course, Grant's character, Will, grows up—sort of. In his search for a fling, he joins a single parent's club that leads him to meet "another boy" in the form of a twelve-year-old son of a dysfunctional single mom. Grant then rescues the boy from his problems and thereby himself from meaninglessness. But it is not accidental that Will is redeemed by helping the boy become cool and "get" his girl. We are not talking about a classic coming of age story of learning duty and integrity. The boy-man teaches the lad to be smooth, wear the right clothes, and try to fit in.

To be sure, the excesses of the gross-out comedy have more recently been moderated and even some more serious films have been aired to appeal to the achievement-oriented "millennial" teens (even Sandler's *Chuck and Larry* of 2007 teaches tolerance for gay couples), but this is hardly a trend. Consider the appeal of hits like *Borat* and *Idiocracy* (both in 2006).[13] Whether potty-mouthed, self-indulgent, or a loveable Peter Pan, the boy-man permeates popular culture today.

Contrasting the Old and the New: Sitcoms

TV is a relatively tame medium with deeply conservative roots. It was designed for family entertainment in the postwar period. As we have seen, the family-sitcom formula survived for more than thirty years by offering audiences models of maturity and childhood cuteness. So when, in the 1990s, we see on the tube the drift of men to boys and with it an abandonment of the old cross-generational humor, we are witnessing dramatic change. Early sitcoms focused on the gentle guidance of the bemused dad and the whimsical trials of growing up. Despite a number of challenges to these images of growing up and being the grown-up in the 1960s, these themes survived into the 1980s with *Family Ties* (1982–89), *The Cosby Show* (1984–1992), and, perhaps ending the era, *The Wonder Years* (1988–1993). Bill Cosby's Dr. Heathcliff Huxtable was sometimes a cool dad, but, as both a good father and a modern professional, he was always the voice of maturity. The fact that the family was African American probably lent new life to the old themes of father knowing best and cute, confused kids each playing their age and gender role. *Cosby* reached a nostalgic older audience as well as a more hip younger one, leading the TV ratings for four years (1985–1989). *The Wonder Years* followed *Cosby*'s success by situating itself not in a contemporary 1980s setting but in the early 1960s. Seen through the nostalgic eyes of a grown-up Kevin as he looks back on the "wonder years" of his innocent thoughts and dreams, it appealed especially to boomers. The show had to be set in the haze of sugar-coated memory, for it hardly conformed to the real world of families in the late twentieth century.[14]

But nostalgia for the past could hardly sustain the next generation. Sitcoms took a sharp turn away from the bemusement of elders and cute antics of kids by the end of the 1980s, giving way to shows that mocked the old formula. These included *Married with Children* (one of the longest-lasting programs of the 1990s, stretching from 1989 to 1999). The humor was carnivalesque, turning the family sitcom upside-down. The man of the house was Al Bundy, whose life peaked as a high school football player. This sad sack forever reminds us that his life went down hill after that as he got stuck in a dead-end and humiliating job selling women's shoes at the mall and marrying Peggy, who turned out to be a lazy housewife and bad mother. Their two children were equal disasters: Kelly, a sluttish and dim-witted teen daughter, and Bud, girl-crazy and, even if comparatively bright, still inept. Their neighbors are the foil to their incompetence in the upwardly mobile Steve and Marcy Rhoades (though later Marcy marries second husband Jefferson D'Arcy, a free-loading gigolo). This satire on the *Father Knows Best* family is highlighted in one episode where Al Bundy dreams he is has taken the part of George Bailey in *It's a Wonderful Life*. Al gets his wish that he had never been born, and a wisecracking angel takes him to see his family, where everyone is happy, intelligent, and loving without him, just the opposite, of course, of the movie. The never relenting theme is that married men are saps and family life is prison.

The Simpsons, a cartoon reprise of *The Life of Riley* from the 1950s, began as a sketch on the *Tracey Ullman Show* and became a half-hour sitcom in December 1989 (lasting to date more than seventeen years as compared to the fourteen-year-run of *Ozzie and Harriet*). With Homer Simpson playing Chester Riley and Marge Simpson, Riley's wife Peg, *The Simpsons* is a satire on sitcoms featuring the bumbling working-class (or ethnic) father and the long-suffering wife and children that were common before the era of the uplifting family sitcoms. Like Chester, Homer has his pals (in this case at Moe's Tavern) and forever is goofing up. But then the analogy breaks down, for the children include not the cool and competent Junior Riley and his feminine and conventional sister, Babs, but the contrast of Bart Simpson, ten-year-old "underachiever and proud of it," and his protofeminist genius of a sister, Lisa (albeit a perpetual eight-year-old). Bart and Lisa comically reverse gender roles in the siblings featured on many 1950s family sitcoms. More important, they reflect a common 1990s perception—that boys were increasingly locked in a world of the "cool" and lacked ambition (doing less well in school than their sisters, for example), while girls were increasingly having to pick up the slack as they prepared for careers and responsible roles in society. The dysfunctional family became a major genre of the sitcom in the 1990s and 2000s in shows such as *The Family Guy*, *That 70s Show*, and *Two and a Half Men*. Though there are many variations, each of these new family sitcoms has role reversals—where the kids are the adults—or, as is common, where the "family acts as a peer group, rather than a hierarchy" and everyone is obsessed with his or her own desires and foibles.[15]

While the new family sitcoms were increasingly cynical and challenged traditional age and sex roles, a sharper shift in comedy was brewing, in which the shows would no longer be built around families but around peer groups of singles. In contrast to the sitcoms of the past that featured friends and business associates, in these new peer sitcoms, the absurd longings and vanities of boy-men are meant to amuse us. An early, but extreme version was *Get a Life* (1990–1992). It featured a thirty-year-old fool, Chris Peterson (played by the boyish but balding Chris Elliot), who lives in a room over his parent's garage. The absurdity of the situation is accentuated by the fact that he is still a paperboy and rides his bike on his route. Of course, his parents indulge him. His father, a retired cop, grudgingly puts up with him but often betrays his belief that his son is an idiot. His mother still coddles him, only wishing him "to be happy." In the pilot episode, Chris talks his boyhood friend Larry (whose wife is trying to make him into a grown-up) into skipping work one day to go to the amusement park. "Nothing is more important in life than free time," Chris opines as they eat cotton candy, romp in a cage of Nerf balls with toddlers, and revel on kiddie rides. Over and over, Chris messes up like a child. In another episode, he deludes himself into believing that women are attracted to him. When he has a brief affair with Larry's sister-in-law, she soon dumps him, saying, "This is a mindless fling. Anybody would know that." Instead of being hurt, Chris delights in being a "sex object." Though he has the libido of a young man, he behaves like a child. Having never done the grown-up thing of getting a driver's license, he hurriedly decides to take the driver's test and fails (of course). He then "borrows" his dad's car to take out a woman only to be pulled over by the cops and rescued by his dad (promising thereafter to be a good boy).[16]

Perhaps the situations and character of *Get a Life* were just too absurd and unambiguous to offer much variation, so the show only lasted two seasons. But it was followed by more sophisticated sitcoms building on a similar theme—young singles who make a life out of being perpetually without commitments or responsibility. *Seinfeld* (1990–1998) was the template of this genre, built around the interaction of the neurotic personalities of three single men and a woman who were relatively successful in work but hardly mature enough to take on the responsibility of marriage and family. With Jerry (Seinfeld) being finicky and paranoid, Elaine being manic, George, insecure, and Kramer, more or less out of control, the characters amble through life's ordinary events with nothing particular happening. They mirrored, Michael Teuthe notes, the golden demographic of eighteen- to forty-nine-year-old consumers with their "self-centered, cynical, jaded, and opportunistic" behavior, a display of the "dirty secret" of the yuppies to a largely yuppie audience.[17]

This is no doubt a harsh and perhaps even unfair judgment. Yet *Seinfeld* certainly contrasts with earlier sitcoms featuring singles.

Some, like *Mary Tyler Moore* (1970–1977), with its exploration of the working woman, and *M*A*S*H* (1973–1982), with its barracks humor alternating with the pathos of a military hospital, had serious social themes that were missing in *Seinfeld*. There were others, such as *Taxi* (1978–1983), which offered a burlesque of goofy characters; *Three's Company* (1977–1984), the relatively mild sexual innuendo of a man and two women sharing an apartment; and *Cheers* (1882–1993), a more sophisticated collection of dysfunctional but mostly loveable barflies. *Seinfeld* instead has a cynical, knowing edge that separates its characters from the clownish behavior of older peer-group sitcoms; the characters on *Seinfeld* are a group that knows that it is choosing not to grow-up rather than simply not knowing how.[18]

The "classic" expression of this new type of peer-group sitcom that especially attracts my son's (and daughter's) generation is *Friends* (1994–2004), the cast of which consisted of roughly thirty-year-old New Yorkers, three men and three women. Instead of settling down in marriage and family as their parents and grandparents did, they created a symbolic family. These "friends" act like siblings in the old family sitcoms, teasing yet supporting one another through their obsessions and misunderstandings, but they have only distant (and largely irrelevant) parents and few older adult mentors. Instead, they are a circumstantial unit whose members are loyal to one another and jealous of outsiders who occasionally threaten to break up the group. One member may hook up with another member, but until the end of the show, they always return to the group. These friends, far more than the diverse pals in *Cheers*, mirror the peer groups of high school, college, and young-adult singles that have partially replaced the old dating culture. The old rituals of couples "going out," going steady, getting engaged, and marrying survives but has been superseded by the gang of men and women. In many ways, the humor reflects the frustrations and fun of the protracted singledom that prevails among young Americans today. At the same time, the characters, both men and women, manifest not merely obsessions and neuroses (as in *Seinfeld*) but a studied, if usually loveable immaturity, fixating on teenage longings and frustrations that these much older characters once were expected to have outgrown.[19] The new sitcoms both signal and confirm a new culture of extended youth and with it delayed marriage and a new world of young-adult peer groups.

Adventure in the Boy-Man Era

Looking back on my growing up in the 1950s and comparing it to the 1980s childhoods of today's young men, I am struck by an interesting parallel. Both generations had boy and man adventures. My generation had Roy Rogers and his cap gun and holster sets; our dads had *Gunsmoke*. By contrast, my son had *He-Man and the Masters of the Universe* cartoons and Castle Grayskull playsets from that cartoon, and men in the 1980s (fathers or not) had action movies such as *Rambo* and *Terminator*. Across the two periods, male children and adults embraced similar stories, and the adults gave kids toys that reflected their fantasies. So has nothing really changed except the stories? Different ages, different tastes? Aren't the high-tech action fantasies of the 1980s just "updated" westerns? Certainly, one could make that claim regarding the Star Wars movies. The space cowboys in that series brought back memories of childhood matinees to parents and grandparents who took the kids to see the first trilogy between 1978 and 1983. And George Lucas learned from Walt Disney, who always offered something for everyone (often feisty animals for the little kids, love interest for females, conflict and conquest for the older males). Lucas made sure that the cute robots R2-D2 and C-3PO, substituting for Disney's cartoon animals, opened the first movie to welcome children to a sometimes dark and violent story.[20] And even if the action films that emerged in the 1980s, with their gratuitous brutality and profanity, were not exactly for the six-year-old, one could claim that they provided an emotional outlet for older boys' longings for power in their powerless worlds. They even seemed to offer boys moral tales of good guys prevailing over evildoers (in much the way that traditional, dark and violent fairy tales served as vehicles of emotional development for children in the past).[21]

Still, looking again at the westerns of the 1950s and watching often for the first time the 1980s action stories, I am struck by how different they are. I see a shift from the morally complex (if often stereotyped and rigid) world of male courage and decision making to a spectacle of violence, aesthetically appealing and emotionally thrilling but morally obscure. Even more important, I see that the gap between the kid and the adult versions of these fantasies seems to have shrunk between the 1950s and 1980s. While Hopalong Cassidy, from an age that believed not only in protecting children's innocence but in character training, is extremely naïve and moralistic, *Gunsmoke* offers grown-ups tales of moral complexity and choice. By contrast, the action fantasies for kids from the 1980s hardly differed from the action movies rated PG-13 or even R, except for the level of graphic violence (and the profanity). It's as if being a grown-up means nothing except that the hero can call his foe a "dickhead" as he tears up his body with high-caliber automatic-weapon fire. In *He-Man*, the old innocence is gone and replaced by the clash of high-tech enemies with only thirty-second "moral tags" exhorting kids to "be polite, be happy, respect your elders, . . . don't fight," with seemingly no other purpose than to please parents worried about the daily lessons in violence that their boys were seeing on the screen.[22] The kids shows of the 1980s were "older" than the westerns on Saturday morning in the 1950s. The action-hero movies that dads saw on Saturday night were a lot "younger" than was *Gunsmoke*.

I can make my point more clearly by looking at the transition to the new action hero. Sylvester Stallone and Arnold Schwarzenegger were trailblazers of the fantasy life of later boomers and Generation X. In contrast to John Wayne's aging cowboys or Clint Eastwood's Dirty Harry, the lanky cop with a beef against overregulation, Sylvester Stallone and Arnold Schwarzenegger were stolid specimens of male perfection. Their hard-bodied personas were lifted out of the working-class men's muscle magazines (which had long appealed to insecure youth obsessed with their physiques and sexuality) and onto the screen at the suburban multiplex. Even more, their stories were less about tests of honor and courage than about displaying power in a new kind of masculinity that combined "over-the-top stunt sequences and pyrotechnics" with the action hero's "overdeveloped physique, weaponry and combat."[23]

There were differences: Stallone, son of an Italian-born beautician father and a wrestling-promoter mother, won fame in his 1976 starring role in *Rocky*, a nostalgic boxing movie that became the first in a series of five. More important here was Stallone's Rambo trilogy (1982, 1985, and 1988), which relies heavily on his trademark sneer and slurred speech, the result of birth complications, as well as his glistening bared chest, to present a tough but laconic and resentful figure that typecast the action hero.

By contrast, Schwarzenegger, an Austrian-born body builder who became famous for winning the Mr. Universe title five times and Mr. Olympia seven, first appeared in the movies in 1970 in a spoof originally called *Hercules Goes Bananas*. While his movies became much more serious in the 1980s, Schwarzenegger's character generally displayed less of Stallone's gloom and anger. *Pumping Iron*, the 1976 documentary about his drive for another Mr. Olympia title, helped mainstream the image of bodybuilders, who had often been seen as narcissistic homosexuals. Schwarzenegger won stardom with the low-budget "sword-and-sorcery" tales *Conan the Barbarian* (1982) and its sequel, *Conan the Destroyer* (1984). In rapid succession, he followed with the science-fiction spectacle *The Terminator* (1984), the military adventure *Commando* (1985), and other action films, but he broke away from this stereotype in the comedy *Twins* (1988). With a keen eye for business, Schwarzenegger enriched himself with health and real estate properties and became California's governor in a 2003 recall election.[24]

Besides Arnold and Sly, there was Chuck Norris, followed by Steven Seagal and Jean-Claude Van Damme, known less for their physiques than their fists. Norris was an undefeated karate champion, holding the title from 1968 to 1974, when he retired to make movies like *A Force of One* (1978) and *An Eye for an Eye* (1981). He morphed from the protagonist of cheap karate films into a full-blown action-hero gunfighter in, for example, *Invasion USA* (1985). In the 1990s, he was superseded in karate roles by martial-arts expert Seagal and the Belgian Van Damme (a stern, heavily accented character known as the Muscles from Brussels).[25]

It is hard to see these characters as much more than comic-book figures appealing to the teenage boy and the men who haven't given up teen fantasies of displaying superpecs, repressed emotion, and explosive power. These longings aren't new, but they were once confined to B movies and obscure pulp magazines. These stories and characters were mainstreamed in the late 1970s and given blockbuster budgets. Of course, there is more to the story. Let's consider the Rambo series. While Vietnam War movies (such as *Coming Home* in 1978 or *Apocalypse Now* in 1979) explored the pain and brutality of war, the Reagan-era Rambo series focused on the frustration of male heroism in the face of defeat in Vietnam and the presumed dishonoring of the returning soldier. Stallone's character, John Rambo, is a resentful Vietnam veteran, arrested for vagrancy in small town Oregon. Escaping to the woods, he shows his mastery over nature and the incompetence of his pursuers and in a rage of indignation returns to town, destroying much of it. Only his superior officer from Vietnam, Samuel Trautman, can subdue and arrest him. This story of the misunderstood, angry hero and victim of the traumas and failures of Vietnam is only a prelude to the sequel, *Rambo: First Blood Part II* (1985). The critic Pauline Kael summarized it bluntly: "Sylvester Stallone's idea of a movie is a cartoon patriotism that exploits the anger of the Vietnam vets and families of MIAs."[26] Opening with Rambo's early release from jail by the government, which needs him to rescue POWs in Vietnam, we see how the restored American hero can get it right where the brass and politicians had failed. In a tale replete with torture, escape, and betrayal, Rambo takes on the Vietnamese and Russians as a lone guerilla, even playing the part of the Indian "brave" prevailing against impossible odds. In the end, he rescues the POWs but, returning to his base, destroys the bureaucrats' computers in blind anger at the government's betrayal and cowardice. This was a perhaps predictable reaction to the humiliation of the hurried departure of American embassy officials from Saigon in April 1975 as the communists took over. Rambo appealed to a wounded heroic masculinity of boomers and their sons. He vindicated Vietnam veterans who were treated as embarrassments, not hailed as victors as their fathers had been after the Second World War.[27]

This theme of the resentful loner taking on the bad guys despite the incompetence and indecisiveness of the authorities permeates other action movies. Consider the Die Hard trilogy, starring Bruce Willis (1988–1995). Playing the role of an alienated New York cop, Willis defeats a succession of terrorists with daring gunplay and acrobatics. He prevails over bad guys who seized a Los Angeles corporate tower, a Washington, D.C., airport, and billions in bullion from the New York Federal Reserve Bank, despite the interference and stupidity of the FBI, airport security, and the NYPD. These stories reflect a lot about the American of the 1980s and 1990s—right-wing bitterness toward the failure of political and military authorities to "let" American soldiers win in Vietnam, deep hostility to a perceived overregulated society dominated by liberal wimps, and even deeper hatred of foreigners who thumb their noses at America. But beyond the politics is another change: the mainstreaming of the sensibilities of the boy-man—the focus on personal heroism, the comic-strip dualism of good and bad guys, and all those displays of male muscle.[28]

In a lot of ways, the action films of the 1980s were no different from adventure movies of the past: all worked by setting up a moral conflict between antagonists, which was interspersed with comic, romantic, and sentimental relief and culminated in a suspenseful build-up and a final confrontation. The moral theme, of course, changed over time. Defending democracy prevailed between 1938 and about 1950, while defeating mobsters or homegrown communists dominated in the 1950s. The 1980s attack on terrorists or communist regimes abroad gradually faded into post–Cold War clashes set in a dark dystopic future or in outer space.[29]

But the latest format suggests an important change in the formula—the subordination of the moral story to spectacles of violence. Over and over, as Eric Lichtenfeld describes Van Damme's *Bloodsport* (1988), "action pulls free of any narrative context: it is fighting for the sake of fighting." The story wasn't much to begin with: Van Damme as Dux, a martial-arts expert, fights his way through a series of martial-arts competitions with the evil Chong Li. But what makes Chong Li a bad guy? His monsterlike walk and his maniacal grin, certainly, but not, apparently, his evil ideas or deeds. In other action films the story simply gets swallowed up by special-effects wizardry and spirals down into incoherence. How else to explain *Bird on a Wire* as it drifts into a free-for-all in a zoo where the director dazzles the audience with scenes of slithering crocodiles, roaring tigers, and piranhas devouring people.[30]

Perhaps the culmination of this trend is best expressed in John Woo's spectacles of violence (for example, *Face/Off* in 1997) where we are relieved of practically all the comic, sentimental, or romantic relief. "In a Woo film . . . people don't get shot at once or twice but hundreds of times, and all of it is shown in show motion, from as many angles as possible." As the media scholar Thomas Leitch notes, Woo abandons the "ethical end of Aristotle's 'action drama,' " which has been the rationale for scenes of violence in literature for millennia. In its place, Woo introduces spectacle violence. In Woo's "stories," violence seldom is connected with character development, much less the drama of freely chosen, morally consequential acts, as was very much the case in the old westerns. Instead, action has become "the kinesthetic unleashing of fantasies of unchecked violence."[31] The aestheticization of carnage, of course, is not new. In the past the spectacle of violence was dramatized on the bodies of real people in the arena of the Colosseum or in the torture chambers of despots. Woo's displays are mere simulations. But what is new is that the simulations are designed to evoke not horror or even catharsis, but the response, "Cool," uttered by the boy or the boy-man. It isn't too extreme to claim that the point of these films is increasingly less the mythological appeals of the story or identification with the personality, circumstances, longings, and fate of the character but the pure sensual pleasure of experiencing the special effects and the thrill of the sheer intensity and accelerating action. In the end, it makes no difference if buildings are smashed or human bodies tortured. What counts is the excitement.[32]

Schwarzenegger's first urban action film was James Cameron's production of *Terminator* (1984), where he plays a cyborg sent back from the future to kill Sarah Connor before she bears a son who will lead a human resistance against the machines, who in the future have taken over the world. This is the "moral" back story, but what draws in the viewer is the action. *Terminator* shows the continual onslaught of an unrelenting, expressionless man-machine who uses his body as a self-contained arsenal to pursue Sarah. The emotional fury is built on a feeling of pure paranoia, a thrill that will be repeated in a long list of chase films (such as *Runaway Train* and *Speed* as well as the Terminator sequels in 1991 and 2003).[33]

As one would expect in films built on the rush of accelerated action and "kills," the body count rises with the sequels: from 15 to 162 in *Die Hard II* and from 27 to 58 in *Robocop II*, for example, as one- to two-second camera shots of violent scenes became standard, producing a sensory overload that older viewers (like myself) find exhausting. *Die Hard II* was typical of the trend: Willis takes on the gang single-handedly and violently, ramming an icicle into one bad guy's eye and later biting another's hand, spitting out a chunk of flesh, and, for a dramatic finish, while fighting a bad guy on the wing of a plane, pushing him into the jet engine to be graphically ground up as if he were meat in a blender.[34]

Is all this merely the culmination of a thrill-seeking culture where the old mythologies of purpose-driven heroism (like antifascism or anticommunism) no longer have meaning? Is this trend, based as it is on outrage, a consequence of having to become ever more outrageous to attract crowds? Both claims have merit, but something more is in play. Like the boy-man comedies discussed above, action-adventure films reveal the bleeding of the child's taste and fantasy into the "adult," often R-rated film.

Consider how the hero in these movies has changed. His chases, clashes, and conquests remind me less of westerns and traditional epics than of something very new: video games—the toys of boys in the 1980s that have become today the toys of boy-men (as we will see in chapter 6). As with the new comedy, the difference between appeals to adults and children has almost disappeared. Notice how similar the structure of an action movie is to the shoot-'em-up video game. The theater audience may not be able to control the hero as he moves through a maze of enemies and other dangers to reach his "goal," but, as film critic Vincent Canaby wrote presciently in 1983, watching such movies is like

> watching other people play video games. . . . One sits in the dark of the movie theater and squirms helplessly at each successive encounter with the enemy, dodging missiles in 'Star Wars' and dried bones in 'Conan the Barbarian,' reaching for weapons that aren't there, cheering a direct hit on the opposing forces, and feeling exhausted at the end, if not necessarily satisfied. This has always been true of certain kinds of movies, but now that more and more movies look and sound like video games, it seems possible that the new art form might well swallow up the old.[35]

The Indiana Jones films feature, as Leitch notes, the excitement of action series where the hero breaks out of enclosed spaces just as in a video game and then moves to the next level of adventure. Action films extend the physical power of the human body through fantastic technology just as the video game transfers the force of the finger on the control to the illusion of destructive power in a character on the screen.[36] Perhaps as obvious are the ways that movie action heroes not only have made excellent action figures (miniatures for kids' play) but look like and behave as if they were giant action figures on the screen. For many viewers, Rambo was not a right-wing vigilante but simply a powerful man able to impose his will through his muscles and skills onto any foe. In *Invasion USA*, Chuck Norris fights terrorists at a shopping mall with two small machine pistols fired from shoulder harnesses. The weapons become in effect extensions of Norris's body. This was and is all very empowering to a certain kind of psyche. As Susan Faludi observes, it appeals to the frustrated working-class male who, having been made impotent by dead-end and increasingly scarce jobs, is part of the "backlash" against feminism and feels "stiffed" by failed dreams of heroism.[37] But again there is also something childish about the Rambo figure. It serves as a model of power for the powerless boy and as the perfect body to the still developing child. The fighting and posturing of Rambo and other action heroes is surprisingly like that of children's imitative war play. Stallone in the title role of the fighting cop in *Cobra* (1986) and the evil Night Slasher circle "each other like gladiators, the Night Slasher swipes the air with his signature knife, and Cobra wields a chain like a whip." In his final dual with the bad guy in *Invasion USA*, Norris has a shoot-out using rocket launchers—supersoakers in earnest.[38]

The look and dress of the heroes themselves remind me again of action-figure toys. Note how the publicity for Stallone's *Cobra* stressed weaponry: The Night Slasher's "dagger is 12 5/8 inches long, with a blade of 440c stainless steel. The handle is made of 6061T6 aluminum which has been anodized black." Such information is mostly meaningless to readers but still gives them a sense of empowerment—really like the cards on blisterpacks of kids' action figures that detail the same type of pseudo-technological information. Even though the Rambo movies were rated R and presumably off-limits for kids, it is no surprise that Rambo became the lead character in a new cartoon and action figure line introduced in 1986: "Our beloved country (and, indeed, the entire world) has been thrown into peril by international terrorists," trumpeted the publicity launching Rambo action figures. But the Rambo line was hardly political in any real sense. Instead it pitted teams of fighters against each other: The enemy force called S.A.V.A.G.E. (Secret Army of Vengeance and Global Evil) and headed by the "evil GENERAL WARHAWK," fought Rambo and his Forces of Freedom. The point was the thrill of the clash.[39]

Most of the action-figure lines (and their cartoon series) of the 1980s that boys obsessed over were not drawn from the movies. But were the two so different? Mattel Toys introduced the cartoon series *He-Man and the Masters of the Universe* in 1982, and it closely paralleled the Star Wars formula. The youthful, blond, and muscular He-Man and his team of good guys fought the aged, bony, and evil Skeletor and his horde. A major feature of the Mattel's line was Castle Grayskull, shaped like a mountain with a dungeon and a landing platform for a "Fright Fighter" vehicle. Mattel asks, "Who will control its hidden secrets and mystical power?" and invites the kids to decide.[40] The moral tale of the 1950s had become a spectacle of violence.[41] Is this the passing of adult fantasy down to kids, or is it the opposite? I think it is the merging of both, the making of a boy-man culture.

By the end of the 1980s, action movies for men and action figures for boys had grown a bit stale. Sly, Arnold, and Chuck were getting a bit old for their he-man parts, and they drifted into more "serious" or at least nonaction roles. Their successors, designated or not, such as

Van Damme, got less positive press.[42] When Schwarzenegger made an out-and-out spoof on his genre in *The Last Action Hero* (1993), the critics were amused while the public was confused. Many of his regulars did not have the cultural capital to recognize the movie's allusions to Hamlet or even its satire on the especially silly sides of the action film.[43] Action figures also became decadent and eventually declined in popularity. Teenage Mutant Ninja Turtles were a veritable self-parody. The Turtles began their career as a spoof on the martial themes of He-Man and G.I. Joe. According to the comic-book back story, pet-store turtles were doused by a mutagen, grew to human size, and learned ninjitsu from a martial-arts rat. They lived in the sewers of a big city and subsisted on pizza. In 1988, the Turtles themselves became a line of ugly greenish-grey, but mostly smiling action figures. Within three years, 80 million had been shipped to retailers.[44]

The action-figure craze declined by the early 1990s, but it was partially replaced by new video-game platforms, which, of course, featured "action." At the same time, predictions of the decline of action movies also proved premature. Chastised by the failure of *The Last Action Hero*, Schwarzenegger became an action hero once again as a spy in *True Lies* (1994), fighting the Crimson Jihad terrorist group, bigger and better than ever.[45] Van Damme won a new generation of boys and boy-men with derivative but action-packed films like *Timecop* and *Streetfighter*.[46] And action films became relatively cheaper to make with new digital effects replacing sets, pyrotechnics, and even actors; the movies took on even more the look and feel of video games.[47] Despite the ebb and flow of the genre, action thrills have become part of the moral and aesthetic culture of boys that many find hard to give up as men.

Ad Appeals to Boy-Men

There were still other settings for the emergence of today's full-blown boy-man culture. As many know, the Superbowl, America's midwinter Mardi Gras, is watched as much for the ads as for the National Football League championship. Companies from gigantic soft-drink and beer makers to smallish padlock and Internet businesses shell out for ad time. After all, the press comments on which were the best ads the next day and viewers can vote on their favorites over the Internet, adding to their impact. Unlike other "holiday" events, the Superbowl has become an unqualified concession to the aspirations and attitudes of young American males, and the ads reflect this. But it wasn't always this way. In Superbowl I (1967), not only were the ads cheaper and less prominent (merely $85,000 for a full minute compared to $2.6 million per thirty seconds in 2007), but the ads were conventional and the half-time show featured a college marching band. The Superbowl was merely a football game, happily associated by its promoters with more than half a century of tradition in college sports and campus life, not show business. By the 1990s, the shows had become eye-popping displays of the latest and brashest rock and hip-hop groups, culminating in 2004 with Janet Jackson's infamous display of her breast. Given the fact that by 2006 two-thirds of American men watched the game (compared to 45 percent of women), it is hardly surprising that the commercials have become a festive but revealing look at how the advertising industry changed its understanding of their thoroughly researched male target.[48]

A famous ad for Apple Computers in 1984 alluding to George Orwell's novel *1984* set the standard for lavish storytelling and productions that usually said more about the presumed aspirations of men than about the products advertised. It was no longer just that Pepsi tastes good or even creates a "new generation" but that men's desires are practically unquenchable.[49] In a 1988 ad, Michael J. Fox would go to the limit for a can of Pepsi, including fighting off a rabid dog. In 1994, football star Bo Jackson races down a high-rise building to get a can of Lipton Tea dropped from the roof before it hit the ground. He succeeds, of course, and reminds viewers that "It ain't hip to sip" Lipton (anymore) and, as any thirsty man's man would do, he guzzles the can in one gulp. This theme naturally becomes more extreme and comical over the years: by 2002, a young woman calls out to her boyfriend, who is glued to the TV and his snacks. She is on her satin sheets in her teddy and has a Bud Light. Naturally, the man immediately rushes into the bedroom, not for the eager and ready woman but for the Bud Light—and he flies out the window. Another from 2005 shows a man who finds the Ford Mustang convertible so "irresistible" that he is compelled to ride with the top down in the middle of winter; he is found by a cop frozen at a stoplight with a smile on his face. Also placing among the top commercials at the Superbowl in 2007 was a Bud Light ad in which two men reach for the last beer and decide to settle their feud by a game of rock, paper, scissors. One of the men chooses paper while the other man throws a rock at his opponent, knocking him down (and thus getting the beer).[50]

All this may be just a humorous way of making the old pitch, "buy it, you'll like it." But these ads seemed to celebrate lack of restraint as a badge of masculinity. We see this in commercials that feature the man as self-possessed, even a jerk. In 1998, Bud Light offered men the following fantasy. A guy has to tag along with his girlfriend on a shopping trip and is subject to the usual "I won't be long" from her. He stews in a chair waiting and waiting until he hears "Hey, over here in petites!" from a voice under a circular clothes rack. Checking it out, he finds a bunch of likewise imposed-upon guys watching sports on TV and drinking Bud Light. In 2004, ads for Subway sandwich shops featured the theme that if you eat "good" at Subway, it's not OK to be "bad" as sandwich consumers display acts of boorish, even cruel behavior.

But not all men have this "right" of self-indulgence. It seems to be mostly the dominion of the young and the "young at heart." A Pepsi ad from 1994 makes fun of aging baby boomers celebrating a "summer of Love Reunion" at Woodstock as kids, watching bald fat boomers frolic, comment "I hope they don't skinny dip." The tag line says it all: "Wouldn't it be nice if your youth was as easy to hold on to as a Pepsi?" Another even more powerful ad from 1993 shows young male teens sitting on a curb. One asks the other: "Hey, man, what do you want to do?" In response, we hear a long depressing list of likely life events: from marrying, having the in-laws over for a cookout, making middle management, and buying white shoes. The first teen interrupts: "Man, I mean what do you want to do this afternoon?" "Oh, the beach," is the immediate reply. The voiceover makes the point: "Hey, man, before your future gets you, you know what you gotta do" The answer is printed on the screen: "Be young. Have fun. Drink Pepsi." Maturity sucks, we are told. Have fun while you can. This is the same message as in the 1968 film, *The Graduate*, without any of the subtlety of the classic movie. Of course, not all ads, even those presumably directed toward youth and young adults, took this form, but comparatively the trend was clear.[51]

Enveloping these themes is a tone of intensity: the 2003 Superbowl included ads for major action features and off-the-wall comedies, including *Terminator 3*, *Full Throttle*, *Bruce Almighty*, and *Anger Management*, as well as car ads celebrating a frenetic pace and surge of excitement. This was the culmination of a trend stretching back more than a decade. An early signal was a 1990 Superbowl ad that featured the acceleration and speed of the Nissan Turbo Z sports car in dreamlike scenes of the car being chased by motorcycles, other cars, and even a plane. The ad was effective but was pulled because it seemed to glorify speeding. The same year, the Pontiac Sunbird promised to give the owner his "daily requirement of excitement" so that he would never become a "member of the bored." Such ads were certainly not designed to appeal to teens (who could hardly afford sports cars or even new Sunbirds). They appealed to men with responsible jobs, perhaps aspiring to be a member of the board of directors of their company but not willing to give up "excitement" in their free time.[52]

Watching the Superbowl and its ads never ceases to amaze me. It is a festive moment, and a lot of the testosterone-drenched ads certainly are over the top. Perhaps they represent a Mardi Gras moment when viewers break with the hard work of daily life and where men can kick back and fantasize about unrestrained "masculinity" after a long Christmas season of sentimentality and indulging children and wives. But looking at those ads made me wonder if they really were so exceptional and restricted to the Superbowl. Maybe they are closer to the norm and part of a change in the culture of manhood that parallels much of what we have already seen.

Since the beginning of the twentieth century, magazine ads have told stories into which consumers could situate themselves, along with their fears, aspirations, and values.[53] But from the late 1980s, TV commercials did all this with a vengeance, drawing on the talents of Hollywood filmmakers (rather than traditional commercial producers or even TV people) to create emotional messages. Increasingly, they relied on humor, shock, and even the bizarre. Partly explaining this is the advertisers' need to stand out in the midst of the clutter that came with the FCC's deregulating of TV advertising in 1982. It was hard to "break through" in the endless three-minute breaks of thirty-second commercials. Moreover, in order to gain the attention of young people brought up on irreverent TV like *Beavis and Butt-Head* and *America's Funniest Home Videos*, ad makers believed that they, too, had to go to the edge.[54]

During the 1990s, ad makers became especially aware of the need to target Generation X, people born in the generation after 1964 who grew up during the personal-computer revolution and the end of the Cold War. The term was a media invention drawn from Douglas Coupland's novel *Generation X: Tales for an Accelerated Culture*

(1991). Coupland portrayed "Gen Xers" as reacting to the "yuppies" through the antics of three slacker young men who frustrate their baby boomer parents by delaying their departure from home and their first step onto the career ladder. At first, market experts saw Gen Xers as problematic consumers with a presumably jaded view of advertising, more diverse ethnic backgrounds (with 30 percent minority), and a rejection of the slick materialism and hard-working values of the yuppie. Soon, however, Gen Xers became the target of new advertising.[55]

Gen X consumers were apparently attracted to "absurd cartoonish fantasy worlds, postmodern stylizations, and self-reflexive and irreverent themes," as well as "intense emotional appeals," according to media scholar William Leiss and his associates. Ad makers learned to draw "upon audiences' stocked knowledge of popular cultural codes to present visual puns," appealing less to baby boomer nostalgia than a "montage of layered sounds and sights" and engaging in "self mocking forms of humor."[56] Sound like the Superbowl ads?

But I think there was something more afoot than a Gen X style to which ad makers creatively adapted. By looking just a little closer at the contrast between ads directed toward men before the late 1980s and after, we can see that something really did change in the ways that commercial writers appealed to young men and the way that men were becoming boys. This was a long and subtle process, with roots in the 1960s. Consider the evolution of ads for Buick, a car that from the 1920s was marketed to the mature, successful provider. The 1961 Buick was touted on TV as a car that makes a man "feel he can conquer mountains" but also provide comfort and safety for his family with passing power and improved breaks. Likewise, the ad for the 1967 Buick Le Sabre insisted that the car "will be safe on dangerous roads" and "the wife won't have to worry." But the kicker was still, "Wouldn't you really rather have a Buick." The claim in 1964 was simply that "people will think you were promoted before you really were" if you drive a Buick.[57]

But in 1968 we begin to see a shift from these traditional appeals to successful family men as the Buick is touted by a young black sportsman, Dave Bing, and shown on the beach. "The only thing you have to provide," the ad promised, "is the girls." Clearly the Buick marketing staff sensed that the old marker of male maturity was no longer working, but they still were not willing to give up the old pitch. In 1969, a Buick ad offered the dad a station wagon and, in 1970, a

375-horsepower model big enough to "take the mother-in-law home along with all her stuff." At the same time, Buick appealed to the young man with a new model, the Buick Wildcat, which promised "an engine that will be respected . . . even rule." The 1972 Buick Riviera was "not for everybody else" but for the individual, and, in 1973, it was all about "a system of innovation you can actually feel," with deep seats and fuel-injection smoothness, a "sporty car for the family man." The old appeals to comfort, safety, and conformity blended with, even gave way in the boomer era to individuality, power, and sensual indulgence (even for family men). Buick continued for some time to offer two distinct marketing pitches, recognizing the generational divide. While the 1974 Buick Apollo was sold to the "guy who worked twenty years to get where he is," the 1975 Skyhawk (a smaller and sportier Buick) was "dedicated to the free spirit in just about everyone." By 1983, with downsizing (making old standards of luxury hard to sustain), Buick tried to be all things to all people with "five distinct personalities" in five models and even showed women buying this classically male car. The image of the male provider and climber had almost completely vanished by the mid-1980s. In its place we see images of male self-expression, indulgence, and even acceptance of female independence.[58]

A sharper example of this change can be seen in beverage ads. When the communications scholar Neil Postman in 1987 analyzed beer commercials, he unwittingly observed the end of an era in men's ads. The campaign for Budweiser was, as it had long been, built on the theme: "You make America work, and this Bud's for you." This toast to skill, labor, and tradition presumably appealed to the working-class man and to his pleasure in being one of the guys coming together for a beer after a full day on the job. Beer was the reward for adhering to the work ethic, but it was also the occasion for acceptable male emotion and affection—teasing, bragging, and good-hearted sharing. Other beer ads recalled a lost tradition of cowboys and the Wild West and functioned as an appeal to beer as a reward for hard work but also as an expression of a simpler society. As Postman put it, these ads showed "a respect for the most elementary forms of social organization: trust between comrades, protectiveness toward women, children, and the physically weak, rejection of all forms of industrial authority." But the rite was also initiation—as older workers introduced the young male to the world of men and pride. In these ads of 1987, the young honor age, and the sacrifice of father figures and elders initiate young men into the masculine community in a classic affirmation of male maturity.[59]

Yet in 1987 Postman also recorded a very different strain in ads for the new light and premium beers that were pitched to younger drinkers. Bud Light ads showed not mixed-aged or work settings but young, sometimes mixed-gender groups, and Miller Lite ads featured a pseudofight over whether the beer "tastes great" or is "less filling" in a kind of childlike reenacting of schoolyard taunts and competitions. In these ads, the rite of beer drinking is no longer a celebration of the club of men but an erasing of the distinction between men and boys. Another sign of change is the appeal of an ad for the premium Michelob Light, set in a luxurious setting with the tag line: "Who says you can't have it all?" The appeal isn't to status but to rather to unrestrained satisfaction and the right of indulgence.[60]

My generation, as it became a Pepsi Generation of consumers, rejected the old idea that we had to climb the status ladder. Many of us insisted that we could have it now or that we were individuals who knew our own desires and were no longer enslaved, as presumably our fathers had been, by status striving. This certainly came out in the changing portrayal of the Buick in the 1960s and 1970s. By the early 1990s, that transformation was fully revealed for a new generation of consumers in an extraordinary series of ads for an import luxury car, the Infiniti by Nissan. Consisting of a dinner conversation between two businessmen, one about thirty and the other in his fifties, the ad explores the contemporary meaning of luxury. In one version, the older man asks the younger why he is wearing an expensive watch that "says you've done it all." He quizzes his youthful counterpart, "Are you successful in life? Have you done everything you want to do?" to which the confident young man responds coolly "somewhat" and "some things." The older man is persistent: "A man who has lived well, seen everything might wear that watch, but why do you wear that watch?" Out of obvious deference and politeness, the young man says nothing. The viewer knows by the exchange what the older man doesn't understand—that the old meaning of luxury as a sign of status and a marker of a lifetime of accomplishment no longer applies: as the tag line says, "Luxury reconsidered." A young man can enjoy the fine things (like an Infiniti) without jumping through all the hoops. That point is reinforced in a second conversation between the two men in a subsequent ad. This time the older man makes the point in a rhetorical question: Is a luxury "something expensive or something that gives you satisfaction?"[61]

These very subtle appeals to personal satisfaction over status markers of age might work for the up-and-coming young business-man, but it was SUVs, not sleek and classy luxury imports, that many young men bought on six-year loans in the 1990s. And the satisfaction was more visceral and the appeal hardly subtle. A Nissan ad for a sports model from 1996 was more typical: A G.I. Joe figure driving a miniature Nissan through a kids' playroom meets a Barbie in her doll house, leaving a Ken look-alike in his dust as the couple races off to the line "Enjoy the ride."[62] The young man becomes his favorite boyhood action figure and, rather than joining his dad's club and buying a Buick, goes off on his own ride in a child's fantasy. As poet and cultural critic Robert Bly wrote in 1993, "We are always under commercial pressure to slide backward, toward adolescence, toward childhood."[63]

Beginning in the mid-1980s we also see a new stress on the frenetic pace and pulsating light, color, and sound of car ads. Even a commercial for the Chevrolet Cavalier, a small, cheap model, noted especially for its station wagons designed for young families (I had two), tried to attract a young consumer. In a 1985 ad, Cavalier featured an amazing video-game-inspired series of images: a fiery "eye" alternated with pulsating images of flashing fireworks, the car, and its logo with not a word spoken. Its message: intensity. That was the appeal of many ads. In 1978 the average shot in ads was 3.8 seconds long, and the number of camera shots per thirty-second ad was 7.9. By the early 1990s, shot duration dropped to 2.3 seconds and camera shots increased to 13.2. Perhaps this suggests that ads had to adapt to a generation more capable of processing information thanks to the personal computer. But it also may reveal a generational change that required marketers to feature emotional and visual intensity associated with a new youth. They had also to abandon appeals to refinement and maturity. An ad in 1989 compared driving the 90 Quatro sports sedan with the feeling of a little boy in a pedal car. "Remember; your heart pounded. You and your car were one. Ready to feel that way again? You're ready for" the 90 Quatro.[64] The appeal was to the "first thrill," long lost as the "boy" became a jaded man.

Ads went further by encouraging the man to indulge his inner (selfish) child. Best Buy ran a very amusing ad in 1996: when a guy returns to the apartment he shares with his girl friend, he finds her throwing out all of his stuff: TV, stereo, and computer. The voiceover admits, "Maybe he never called when late; maybe he watched too many videos." But the solution was obvious: no one could expect a man to change his natural boyish lack of consideration. Instead, go to Best Buy and get new stuff. Another ad for Calvin Klein jeans makes an even more blatant appeal to indulgence over mature relationships. A young man admits that it is for him "hard to love or be loved" and that he is "jaded emotionally." But no matter: Calvin Klein clothes feel "good all the time." And his girl agrees: "Be a pleasure. Be a pain. Just be Calvin Klein."[65]

Frequently, ads suggest that not only are men jerks—selfish and unable to compromise—but in the end that doesn't matter so long as they get what's theirs and what they want. Sometimes this takes the form of saying that men's needs are insatiable. A 2006 ad for Miller Lite features a young man sent out on a beer run by his buddies, who are gathered around a TV set. Unable either to give up his need for beer or for watching the big game, he strings together an amazing array of extension cords to carry his TV to the shop, pulling the cord out of the outlet just as he arrives at the beer cooler. But his pals save the day by plugging the cord back in just as the play of the day is made. Sometimes the ads encourage men to fantasize they are "just one of the boys," as in the Miller Lite ad in 2005 that shows two busty young women fighting over whether the beer "tastes great" or is "less filling" as two young men (black and white) look on. This was an old gag, but it was upped several notches as the women wrestle in a fountain dressed only in bras and panties. The guys say, "Now that would make a great commercial," while their girlfriends look on in disgust. Men's needs are insatiable, which is OK, though, as ads repeatedly suggest, the guy has to protect his stuff from others. A 1990 commercial for Carlsberg beer shows a man retrieving two bottles from what looks like a refrigerator, but turns out to be a safe. An ad for Remy Champagne's "Men's Club" shows a gorgeous brunette lamenting, "He promised to cherish me, but never promised to share his Club" as she serves him and his buddies, with the kicker line: "At least, not with me."[66]

As if to reinforce the point, by 2001, advertising was increasingly featuring men who had long established reputations for being obnoxious loudmouths. For example, as part of Heineken's effort to break out of its snob image, the brewer signed the tennis bad boy turned TV commentator John McEnroe to a two-year endorsement deal. The comedian David Spade played a repulsive barfly in new commercials for Coors where he hits on women and tries to get free brew from wary bartenders. And in 2005 and 2006 Spade did a long series of commercials for Capital One, playing an agent for an unnamed rival credit card company who never redeems free air travel and torments a nerdy subordinate who can't follow his demand to always say no.[67]

What should we make of these appeals to jerkiness? Obviously, we find humor in them, and they offer men an emotional outlet against political correctness (especially toward women). But these ads also are about men having permission to be selfish and hedonistic. Most of all, these ads are about men's right to act like boys. These commercials remind me of magazine ads in the 1920s that told mothers that it was OK for their eight-year old boys to lust after peanut butter and get their clothes torn. These old ads told adults not only to buy consumer goods for their dears but that children's desires and needs were natural and should not be repressed. That was a lesson perhaps learned too well. Today's commercials directed to men say much the same, but now the mom is the man's "girl" who needs to accommodate her jerk, earning the name by acting like a boy of ten. A very interesting question came up with the appearance in 2003 of those famous "catfight" ads for Miller Lite. Wouldn't these ads offend at least as many people as they attracted? Research suggests that they did: over 50 percent of women disliked them, while only 11 percent of men disliked them. But the point was not to please everyone and rather to attract a young male audience.[68]

Companies, especially those failing to compete in tough markets, have increasingly appealed to the "frat-boy nation," those immature young men who give in to their natural desires and don't give a damn who knows it and whom it affects. In 2002, Coors Lite (a beer from a Colorado company ironically long associated with the conservative politics of its owners) created a hit song that served as a backdrop for the display of bikinied blond-haried twins Diane and Elaine Klimaszewski. They lure a young male to a can of Coors with the suggestion of a threesome.[69]

Hardee's, a fast-food chain that had fared poorly in the late 1990s, embraced the strategy of appealing to the lust and hunger of the eighteen- to thirty-four-year-old man. Hardee's featured color photos of *Sports Illustrated* swimsuit models on its large drinks in 2005 and promoted extra fatty "Thickburgers" that registered between 850 and 1,410 calories. No salads for these guys. Carl's Jr., another chain that was also part of the Hardee's family, featured images of glamour heiress Paris Hilton getting sudsy atop her Bentley. Others hopped on to this bandwagon: Levi's jeans, suffering stagnant sales, in 2004 featured an ad with a former boyfriend who talks his way back into his girlfriend's house with a bouquet of flowers not to make up with her but to get back what he really valued, his Levi's. As one reporter described it, "Advertisers are courting young males by appealing to the jerk that may lurk within. . . . Once fun-loving and wild, these new male commercial characters are manipulative and a little mean."[70] The twin themes of bemused cynicism and emotional intensity permeate today's youth culture. Recent ad campaigns attract young audiences with transgressive themes and appeals to uninhibited and often unrefined male desire. The difference between the 1980s slogan "For all you do, this Bud's for that you do!" and a 2006 Superbowl ad for Bud is striking. By 2006 a beer was no longer a reward for a job well done, shared with friends at the local bar, but had become the object of a personal obsession, so strong, we are told, that a pilot without a parachute would happily jump after a six-pack dropped out of a plane. We've come a long way, baby.

Cable and the New Magazines

Obviously, we should not to take this portrayal of insatiable desire all that seriously. But it is serious that insatiable desire is mostly associated with young men, and this stands in sharp contrast to the way male pleasure, desire, and spending were portrayed as recently as 1990. Since then, advertisers certainly have discovered a "new" demographic, the eighteen- to thirty-four-year-old man. Belatedly, perhaps, marketers recognized that young men had disposable income. After all, they don't marry until about twenty-seven years of age and are no longer obliged to "treat" their wives and girlfriends on dates as in the past. Young men have long had more money to spend on themselves than young women, but they seem to have more now and for a longer time. As important, merchandisers have begun to realize this and exploit it.

More important, though, is that the marketing of consumer goods has become segmented by age, gender, and leisure interests. From the 1980s, especially, ad makers have accelerated a long trend to "separate audiences into different worlds according to distinctions that ad people feel make the audiences feel secure and comfortable," as the communications scholar Joseph Turow notes. The discovery of new lifestyle clusters suggested the need for more focused ads. Magazines pioneered the techniques of targeted ads by linking readers with special interests like antique cars, fashions, or sports to advertisers selling to people with those enthusiasms.[71]

It is no surprise that in 1995 the British magazine *Maxim*, a racy competitor to the comparatively stuffy (or refined) men's magazines *GQ* and *Esquire* was launched. By 2000, this "lad's" magazine was selling 2.4 million copies a month worldwide (compared to only 800,000 for *GQ*) and, with its golden demographic of young men so favored by advertisers, it reeled in $115 million in ads, twice as much as *Esquire* and more than *Playboy* and *Penthouse* combined. Imitators quickly followed in *Maxim*'s wake. For Him Magazine (*FHM*), *Stuff*, and *Gear* try to outdo one another by pushing the envelope of skin and locker-room talk while promoting the idea that young men have a right to fill their lairs with the latest in fashion and fads. The June 2006 issue of *Maxim* was typical, with features like "Could You Become a Living Legend of Sex?" (with brief accounts of the number of "conquests" claimed by celebrities and the odd Italian hotel porter who boasts that he has had sex with "around 8,000 women"). An amusing page challenges readers to identify famous rappers' dental creations by their smiles. A sampling of ads fills in the story: one for a Ford truck shows nothing but tire tracks that have crushed a speed bump; a two-page ad for Trojan condoms features the "winners" in a survey of beach beauties who naturally disclose their favorite variety of Trojans; and an ad for a twenty-four-inch Robosapien V2 (a programmable "consumer robot") is full of technospeak that hardly disguises the fact that the V2 is really no more than a fancy update of a boy's action figure. A four-page ad for Icehouse beer offers guidance in throwing a party: "Coasters aren't to protect furniture. They're weapons for dumb and idiotic comments made during sporting events, movies or video games"; and, "Man hugs may take place only in the event of a game-winning home run, goal, touchdown or slam dunk. And then only briefly." Graphics-heavy with scarcely any prose of more than three sentences, "articles" about sex include a gross but practical advice column by the famous former madame to the stars, Heidi Fleiss, and a global bevy of girls (oddly never nude, but often accomplished). *Maxim* also contains fast-paced factoids about the latest video games, movies, amusement park rides, and male-oriented TV shows, including, in this issue, a salute to chain stores (no critiques of consumer culture here). The reduction of romance to a dirty joke is combined with themes about grooming and clothing that takes Hefner's old formula to a new level. *Maxim* leaves out the pretension of high culture and politics: no interviews with today's Ernest Hemingways or even the pseudointellectualism of a "*Maxim* philosophy."[72] The boy-men who "read" *Maxim* have abandoned the search for refinement and class status of the college men who read *Playboy* in the 1950s and 1960s. And the new spate of lad magazines reinforces this trend by narrowly targeting an age group rather than, as Hefner did, seeking a "mass" audience of men of "all" ages. These new magazines narrowly cultivate a young male peer culture with no obvious aspiration to adulthood.

Something very similar happened on TV. By the end of the 1970s, television, long a bastion of mass audiences, was also beginning to give in to the logic of segmented target markets that magazines had pioneered. One of the many outcomes of this trend was boy-man programming. The coming of cable TV was the critical factor. By adding numerous channels to the existing three networks, cable undermined the logic of *broad*casting. When there were only three competing channels, the networks had an incentive to seek the maximum proportion of a mass market—encompassing men and women across the age spectrum—through programming that appealed to the common denominator. This produced Ed Sullivan's variety show on Sunday nights, for example. With a much greater number of channels on cable, the advantage went to identifying specialized viewers and linking them to advertisers seeking narrow markets. From 1981, MTV targeted teenagers and young adults with popular music videos and age-appropriate ads. As cable entered the vast majority of households and, even more, as TVs became "personal" appliances with the advent of multiple-TV households, everyone, no matter the age, had her own channels. Often each member of the family could watch separately and tune out anything that took him away from his own peer culture. So attractive was "narrowcasting" to cable TV companies that from 1993 to 1997, MTV successfully aired *Beavis and Butt-Head*, a program featuring two obnoxious cartoon characters that greatly annoyed parents while delighting rebellious teenagers. MTV executives wanted the show to drive away unwanted parents and conservatives, assuring a "pure" demographic for advertisers.[73]

It was only a matter of time before enterprising cable network programmers began to design shows to appeal to the same "lads" who read *Maxim*. A gradual pushing back of the old censorship opened the way as "daring" networks like E!, which offered Howard Stern's "all-boy" show, where Howard and his beer-bellied pals "evaluate" would-be Playboy Playmates, and Comedy Central, which presented the animated *South Park*, with its potty-mouthed elementary school kids. Cable became the home of lad TV, where as a 2002 survey noted, "an overwhelming 72 percent [of men aged twenty-one to thirty-four] favor programs on cable or satellite above the broadcast networks."[74]

Sellers of beer, action movies, fast-food, video games, and the latest in electronic gadgetry know the "lads" are their best targets for advertising. It isn't surprising that, when the FX channel was under public pressure to cancel *The Shield*, with its rough-talking cops and crooks, Best Buy, Foster's beer, and software maker Roxio stuck by their male viewers and refused to back out of advertising on the program. Even the recruiters for the U.S. Army admitted that they faced a dilemma: "We want to reach men 18 to 24, our primary target audience, but we want to avoid an extremely offensive content environment. That's the contradiction." So the Army does not hesitate to reach young men by advertising on the raunchiest of cable TV; nor does Pizza Hut, Taco Bell, or KFC.[75]

MTV is a cable company (or conglomerate) that has particularly benefited from the arrival of the young, male demographic. Built up from a once humble cable station known for airing music videos in endless rotation, MTV is now a programming powerhouse, gradually accumulating Comedy Central, Spike, VH1, and many other networks. Its parent company, Viacom, owns CBS, BET, Showtime, Infinity Broadcasting, Paramount Pictures, Blockbuster, and Simon and Schuster, among other media outlets and is an amazingly profitable enterprise.[76] The two cable networks in the MTV orbit that most ardently pursue the lads are Comedy Central and Spike.

Comedy Central, with its nightly lineup of standup comedy and features such as *The Man Show* and *South Park* had a 70 percent male viewership in 2004.[77] But the network most clearly designed to reach the lads was Spike TV. It began in 1983 as The Nashville Network (TNN), appealing to rural viewers and country music lovers. But in 2003, after a short stint as a general-interest channel, Viacom transformed it into a man's channel as Spike TV (launched appropriately at the Playboy Mansion). Surveys found that the shift in programming from TNN to Spike TV resulted in a rise in the household income of viewers from $25,000 to $45,000. Even more striking, the mean age of the viewers dropped from fifty-seven to thirty-seven, and 65 percent of the viewers were male.[78] As MTV had done with *Beavis and Butt-Head* in the 1990s, Spike planned to push the "raw." As Albie Hecht, Spike's first president, noted, "the 18–34 male is OK with the way life really is. They don't have a problem with words like bulls—t." Spike's primetime lineup included an array of violence (reruns of *CSI*), sex (the short-lived cartoon feature *Stripperella*, with Pamela Anderson's voice), and sophomoric physical game shows (like *Most Extreme Elimination Challenge*, taken from Japanese TV and featuring often off-color commentary). When the percentage of female watchers of Spike went up in 2004 (from 32 to 42 percent), network managers became concerned, so important was it to offer advertisers a preponderantly male audience. A new president, Doug Herzog, declared that "in a perfect world, [Spike] will have an 80/20 male/female balance." This is logical only in the world of narrowcast programming. A survey sponsored by the network of 1,300 men led briefly to some practical, job-oriented programs like the career-make-over show *I Hate My Job* and *American Start-Up*, a competition for small-business ideas. Nevertheless, action and sex still predominated: *World Wrestling Entertainment*, *Thursday Night Knock Out*, kung-fu *Films of Fury*, and *Buddy's Garage*, which featured the promise, "He builds 'em, they smash 'em." Spike's *Most Irresistible Women* (shown September 22, 2005) displayed the sexy images of Jessica Simpson and other women (some from *Maxim* magazine). More important, the show offered not only the expert opinions of sports and TV ce-lebrities on the hot women but also the ratings of men of every age and race. "It doesn't matter if you are a fourteen-year old boy or a forty-year old man," the voice-over observed in reference to the fact that a video of Jessica Simpson was made by a young male teenager. "Men" were all alike in a shared lust no matter their age. This was the ultimate expression of the boy-man culture. It starts early and ends late and offers no promise of coming of age.[79]

Hip-hop and the Meaning of It All

Still, it isn't true that all men are alike. Even if age differences have collapsed, boy-man culture takes on many forms, some of them re-flecting America's ethnic and racial divisions. One obvious example of this is hip-hop music and its variations. It emerged in the late 1970s in uptown New York among African American "b-boys" who hated disco but break danced and engaged in "graffiti art." By 1979 some became "DJs" who mixed pop music beats and background for rappers (MCs) who "sang" street-inspired rhyming lyrics about drugs, sex, crime, and poverty. As "post-soul kids" in "post-civil rights era America," hip-hop artists saw many of their fathers return from Vietnam with drug habits. These young men grew up during a time when the divide between middle-class and poor blacks became a gulf. Their often misogynous and violent themes clearly reflected a loss of faith in the promise of integration and uplift that had been so much a part of the civil rights movement of their elders. At the same time, as Nelson George notes, hip-hop was part of the "discovery (and maybe hijacking) of black youths as creators and consumers" by a potpourri of merchandisers and advertisers who have "embraced Hip Hop as a way to reach not just black young people but *all* people."[80] Rap music was hypercommercialized, as, indeed, much African American popular music had been since the early 1970s, when record companies began to hire black producers and musicians to promote African American records to white as well as black audiences. By the late 1980s, rap and hip-hop had spread to Latino youth, among whom it was popularized especially by the New York Dominican group Proyecto Uno.[81]

In some ways the prototypical expression of this culture is Sean Combs and his Bad Boy Entertainment empire. In fact, the name of his company says it all. Going under various aliases (Puffy, Puff Daddy, and, most recently, P. Diddy or simply Diddy), Combs is a walking contradiction. Although born in Harlem in 1969 to a street-hustling father who died when he was three, he was brought up by his mother in suburban Mount Vernon, privately schooled, and briefly trained in business at Howard University. In 1993, after a rapid rise at Uptown Records, he founded Bad Boy and produced recordings for a string of rap and hip-hop artists, including the Notorious B.I.G., Faith Evans, Mariah Carey, and Aretha Franklin. His far-flung enterprises included recording, television and film production, urban clothing lines, and restaurants, and his operation's annual sales approached $300 million by 2005, the year he launched the HBO series *P. Diddy Presents the Bad Boys of Comedy*, a program of raunchy standup humor.[82]

Despite his business success, Combs's image and behavior point to anything but the model bourgeois. Beyond the flashy jewelry, gangster dress, and "Bad Boy" tattoo on his arm, he has engaged in a disturbing pattern of irresponsible and violent behavior. The infamous rivalry between Combs's New York–based rap artists and the West Coast's Death Row Records, along with rumors surrounding the mysterious death of rival rapper, Tupac Shakur, in 1996, may have led to the murder of Combs's friend the Notorious B.I.G. Combs nearly landed in jail himself a few years later on four counts of illegal possession of a gun and one count of bribery, charges stemming from a December 1999 incident at a New York nightclub. Moreover, he refused repeatedly to make court appearances regarding child support even after he named a string of restaurants after his son, Justin.

Combs became a singer in his own right in 1997 by recording hits like "It's All About the Benjamins" (i.e., hundred-dollar bills), and "Bad Boy for Life." These songs, like so many in the tradition, glorified a get-yours-while-you-can philosophy ("We tryin to be rich before we all stop breathin") and a cynical attitude toward moral authority ("Ain't no Scout gonna give this sad nigga a deal"). These hit tunes celebrated an unrestrained materialism ("don't knock me for tryin to bury seven zeros, over in Rio Dijanery"), but they also brooded about death (as in "Is This the End?"). Combs has no evident sense of the father, either in the public heritage of the civil rights movement or in a personal sense of continuity with the past and a responsibility for the future. Combs's bad boy persona is about the here and now. It is the cry, but also the defiance of the boy-man. And it offers an extraordinarily successful commercial message, appealing to both whites and blacks.[83]

This genre has elicited much concern from the white and African American communities for its apparent sabotage of the uplifting culture of the civil rights and other pride movements. Bill Cosby generated a firestorm of debate when he attacked black youth culture (and black parents' toleration of it) for keeping African Americans from rising into the middle class. A variation on this theme appears in a 2007 editorial in the *Washington Post* by Thomas Chatterton Williams:

Hip-hop culture is not black culture, it's black street culture. Despite 40 years of progress since the civil rights movement, in the hip-hop era—from the late 1970s onward—black America, uniquely, began receiving its values, aesthetic sensibility and self-image almost entirely from the street up. This is a major departure for blacks, who traditionally saw cultivation as a key to equality. Think of the days when W. E. B. Du Bois "[sat] with Shakespeare" . . . or when Ralph Ellison waxed universal and spoke of the need "to extend one's humanity and one's knowledge of human life. . . ." This peculiar aspect of the contemporary black experience—the inverted-pyramid hierarchy of values stemming from the glorification of lower-class reality in the hip-hop era— has quietly taken the place of white racism as the most formidable obstacle to success and equality in the black middle classes.

This cocktail of street culture and rebellion against achievement and refinement as phony and hypocritical has long roots. There are obvious links between the rebellion in the hard-boiled crime fiction of the 1940s and the gloomy vision of Snoop Dogg and Tupac Shakur. But in hip-hop, the street-smart goal of "keeping it real" and refusing to "act white" (by doing well in school, for example) may be a particularly destructive form of the boy-man phenomenon. What in the white community coarsens culture and denies maturity, but often coexists with economic success, may, in African American society, undermine achievement (as black high school graduation rates have remained fixed at 70 percent for three decades) and weakened community stability (as births to unwed mothers have doubled since 1960).[84]

Across the scope of modern media, from comedy and adventure in movies and on TV to advertising and music, we see how things have changed. In male-oriented stories, the difference between men and boys has largely collapsed with PG-13 movies, peer-group sitcoms, action-hero films and cartoons, "edgy" ads, and a lot of modern popular music, especially hip-hop and rap. Along with this, the decline of Victorian notions of propriety has allowed the male locker room to be broadcast into the living room (or at least, the boy-man's bedroom), where women and self-proclaimed elders are not welcome.

A very wide and deep group of economic interests obviously benefit from the creation of the boy-man peer culture. This includes movie makers, TV programmers, cable conglomerates, fast-food companies, and a whole generation of popular-culture celebrities. But this boy-man commercial culture could hardly have thrived if it didn't meet a need. Christopher Napolitano, a senior editor at Playboy, sees lad popular culture as a reaction to female empowerment. It is not an expression of hostility but "more of a release—sort of like a steam valve. These shows and products that are geared exclusively to men—they're like a chance to head out to a bar and know that nobody's going to eavesdrop, so guys can get jerky and silly and adolescent and have a big laugh."[85] There is doubtless some truth in this. But this culture also gives men who want to be one of the boys an opportunity to remain a boy. These men avoid growing up and needing to cope with and understand modern women and develop more "refined" standards of thought and behavior. The culture encourages an ultra-individualism built on surfing the endless waves of manic consumerism.

But why do young men "need" or desire to avoid "maturity"? This brings us back once again to the central problem of this book—the declining opportunity to partake in traditional markers of maturity, but also the appeal of rejecting them. Over the course of the 1980s, that decline became manifest (and intensified) in and through the new stories and new heroes of boys and men. The Andy Hardy humor of the bemused if sometimes out-of-date dad and the naïve but striving boy gave way to the comic perpetual adolescent, with no father to aspire to or rebel against, and to a peer culture where (as in *Seinfeld*) nothing really happens. Traditional adventure stories, replete with moral purpose (however crudely defined), have been transformed into displays of aestheticized violence. Ads that associated goods with status and duty have become appeals to self and satisfaction. TV channels, magazines, and popular music that often reached across age and gender have segmented into outlets flattering the frat-boy nation and intensifying the frustrations of the fatherless young black man on the street.

Virtually all aspects of this change point to fatherlessness. Maybe we don't need Judge Hardy or Cliff Huxtable or John Wayne's or Sidney Poitier's characters any more. Maybe we can't have them back. It is difficult when boomer dads try to join their sons on the playground. But without replacements for these father figures, we have a culture that is increasingly fixated on not growing up, often without even realizing it.

chapter 6.

Endless THRILLS

Despite the common image of the couch-potato Gen Xer fixed zombie-like to the ubiquitous screen, my sons' generation is, if anything, more active, more open to innovation than was mine. This means not only a focus on fitness and an adaptability to change but a longing for immersion in the intensity of sensual experience, which has become almost a defining trait of Generation X. This quest for excitement has perhaps always had its appeal to adolescents and youths. Since the late 1970s and especially since the 1990s, however, it has become progressively a longing that extends into manhood. Video games, new and radically more thrilling amusement park rides, and a stress on looks and especially looking young, though these are hardly all-encompassing traits, help to define this pleasure complex. These endless thrills may not consume my sons' generation. Still, they play a large part in making youth into a lifestyle that men do not look back on nostalgically, as in the past, but embrace as a "permanent" way of life. At the end of the chapter, I'll try to explain why this has happened.

Video Games: Toys of a Lifetime

The video game has been the bugbear of cultural watchdogs practically since its first appearance in the 1970s. It seemed to threaten the innocence of children with the excitement of graphic violence and sex, or at the least with shifting their eyes and minds from learning and social development to the exciting screen.[1] But often missed is a more subtle but no less serious issue: how the blending of the video culture of boys and men not only threatens childhood but also arrests the emotional and cultural development of adult males. As with movies, it isn't just that "adult" themes have threatened the innocence of the young but that the childish obsessions of youth permeate the culture of adult men.

Violent video games have long worried parents and pundits. Reaction to the Grand Theft Auto series of seven games first introduced by Rockstar Games in 1998 was typical. Grand Theft Auto: San Andreas (2004), with a "mature" rating and a warning of "blood and gore, violence, strong language, and strong sexual content," appealed mostly to men aged eighteen to twenty-five. It offered gamers the following enchanting scenario: Carl Johnson returns to the tough streets of Los Santos after the death of his mother to restore the power of his old gang. Action begins as Johnson and his friends tear open a car idling nearby, pull out the driver, and steal the car, and, with vintage rap music playing on the radio, they smash sideways into another car, stealing the money and the gun of the driver. Now fully equipped, they lure a trash-talking streetwalker into the car. Following the amusing scene of the car rocking from the activities inside, Johnson and friends dump her on the street, whacking her with the butt of the gun and robbing her of her earnings. And to make the point, they flip the car in reverse over her body before speeding off, leaving black tire tracks across her lifeless back. And on it goes, as the lawless hero engages in an endless string of violent acts in pursuit of the power and honor of his gang across the fictional state of San Andreas.[2]

Grand Theft Auto: San Andreas sold $235 million worth of copies within a week to a variety of consumers, but the audience that particularly caught the public's attention were the teens, especially the emotionally disturbed and those simply lacking the psychological maturity to separate fantasy from reality.[3] After all, Michael Carneal, a fourteen-year-old from Paducah, Kentucky, and a fan of earlier violent video games (like Quake and Doom), had killed three schoolmates in 1997. And the notorious Eric Harris and Dylan Klebold of Littleton, Colorado, were addicted to first-person-shooter games before they indulged themselves in the real thing in the slaughter at Columbine High School in April 1999. Of course, this sort is very rare, but, many asked themselves, where did these middle-class kids pick up their killing ways but in the fantastic and alien world of interactive video? And even if the "normal" teen is merely desensitized to violence, is incapable of sitting through the "slow" pace of school after hundreds of hours of rapid-fire gunplay at the video pad, gets fat from not exercising anything but his trigger finger, or even just avoids dealing with social and academic problems, then video games must be to blame.

A media frenzy over Panty Raider: From Here to Immaturity (2000) pointed to a slightly different concern—the sexual appeals promoted by mainstream publisher Simon and Schuster Interactive to male teenagers. Although rated "M" and clearly designed for adults, the game certainly reached for the psyches of boys going through puberty: Nelson, an innocent lad, is forced by three sex-crazed aliens to get supermodels to strip down to their underwear and then to photograph specific styles and colors of panties to keep the aliens from blowing up Earth. To accomplish this task, the player uses pickup lines supplied by the game, clothes-dissolving goop, and even credit cards and the lure of tiny breath mints that "no self-respecting supermodel can resist" to get them to disrobe. Naturally, groups such as Dads and Daughters complained that this game objectified women, and even seasoned players insisted that only twelve- or fourteen-year-olds could find such a lame concept fun or playable. The subtitle "From Here to Immaturity" said it all.[4]

And that was often the point in the culture of electronic games—the line between the taste of boys and men has long been blurred. Since the mid-1970s and the commercial appearance of Spacewar! and Pong, video games had captured the time and money of both age groups.

But that isn't how the digital game started. The computer scientist William Higinbotham of the Brookhaven National Laboratory in Upton, New York, invented Tennis for Two in 1958, a crude electronic tennis game that was the precursor of Pong. Many students who had previously thought of the computer as a tool for making scientific calculations greeted this game as a revelation that computing could also be fun. In 1961, a MIT lab tech named Steve Russell, aided by fellow geeks from Harvard, taught their new minicomputer (the PDP-1) to play another game, Spacewar!, in which spaceships annihilated one another with blips of light across a black and white TV screen. Unlike Higinbotham, they gave away the computer code to fellow programmers working at corporations, colleges, and governments. Gradually, thousands whiled away their free time playing Spacewar! and writing new games of their own (including Adventure and games meant to emulate Dungeons and Dragons).[5] For another decade, video games remained only a diversion of computer geeks.

In 1972, however, Magnavox appealed to kids with the Odyssey, a console game system that was developed by the TV engineer Ralph Baer. But popular gaming took off only when engineer Nolan Bushnell founded Atari in 1972 to merchandise his arcade version of Spacewar!, and he soon had reinvented Higinbotham's game and renamed it Pong for play in bars and lounges. More important, in 1975, he mass-retailed the Pong game through Sears as a toy, this time for kids. In 1977 he added cartridge software and an ordinary TV screen to a primitive computer, the Atari 2600. The separation of hardware and software led to a proliferation of companies who mass-produced game cartridges for Atari machines. Soon more exciting and fast-paced games appeared with Space Invaders (1978) as well as the Japanese innovations Pac Man (1980) and Donkey Kong (1981). Atari had rivals in ColecoVision and Mattel's Intellivision, which emerged from the toy industry and appealed directly to kids. At first, parents were hardly alarmed, even though video games were first designed for young adults for play in bars. The violence consisted of shooting at crude space ships, not people, and many games were played at home on family-room TV sets or in arcades set in malls. By 1981, five billion dollars in quarters were being spent in video arcades, despite the fact that some health experts and more parents believed that Pac Man and other video games were addictive. Game makers and arcade owners were shocked, when, in 1983, with the market saturated with hundreds of bland look-alike products, the gaming boom went bust. Mattel and Magnavox quickly abandoned the video-game industry, and game makers, including Atari, went bankrupt.[6]

The lesson learned by the industry was that excitement satiates and that the intensity of play and the graphic realism of the screen must be increased to hold young consumers. The Japanese Nintendo Entertainment System (NES) introduced to the United States in 1985, greatly improved the graphics (and Nintendo, unlike Atari, exercised strict quality and financial control over the makers of game cartridges for use on its console). The NES quickly became the most popular toy in the United States, with sales of $3.4 billion by 1990, again crossing the age gap by appealing to boys from six-year-olds to young adults. Still, games remained within the rather gentle, even cute culture of childhood. Nintendo's Super Mario Brothers was hardly a threat to many parents. This Italian carpenter, with the help of the player at the controls, sets out to rescue a damsel in distress while trying to evade barrels and other obstacles thrown at him by a gorilla. Sega's Sonic the Hedgehog was just as cute as he raced through mazes and colorful scenes capturing fruits and avoiding threats. Other game makers, including Electronic Arts (1982), focused on sports games. And, of course, many games were not violent, including car racing, strategy (the Sims series and Ages of Empires, e.g.), puzzles like Tetris, and learning or quiz games based on TV shows or board games.[7] In 1989, Nintendo introduced a much-improved handheld computer game, the Game Boy. It was expensive and diverted children from person-to-person interaction, but it did keep six- to ten-year-olds occupied on long car trips, to the relief of siblings and parents alike.[8]

Subtly, the video game changed as it began to use fast-paced violence to appeal to the older player. In 1991, the Japanese firm Capcom offered a new level of graphic conflict when it introduced the arcade game Street Fighter II to the United States. The player used buttons to simulate the intense combat of kung fu, pitting his fighter against the computer's. The next year, Midway, a Chicago-based company that had long produced pinball machines, entered the video-arcade market with Mortal Kombat, a game that presented players with the opportunity to electronically tear off the head or pull out the heart of a defeated opponent. By 1993, Mortal Kombat migrated from arcades to homes on Nintendo and Sega console versions (though Nintendo at first colored the blood grey to mollify parents).[9]

Two factors seem to have contributed to the escalation of violent themes: First, Sega, as a newcomer in competition with Ninendo, pushed the envelope with more intense and violent games than its rival. Second, and even more important, was the fact that video games were reaching an older and wider age group. Nintendo found that, though it targeted eight- to thirteen-year-olds, 35 percent of its consumers were over eighteen years of age, and 39 percent were between twelve and seventeen years old. Apparently, young men who had learned to play as kids in the Atari days wanted to keep on playing. Of course, this increased the demand for more "mature," or should I say "cool" games. Like the action films and later potty-mouthed comedies, these games featured a potent blend of cynicism, violence, and intensity that attracted teens and young men. Such games also pulled in children as young as seven years of age—a group that many critics believed "should" still be playing Mario or Sonic.[10]

Because the video game does not distinguish between boy and man, it has led to the public's considerable concern about how adult video-game violence and sexuality seep into children's worlds. A U.S. Senate hearing on video games in 1993, led by Senators Herbert Kohl and Joseph Lieberman, focused on this threat to childhood innocence. A Sega official testified that the games had become more graphic because of faster, more powerful computer processors but also admitted that his company had targeted older customers (estimated to be a mean age of twenty-two years old) and marketed violent games to appeal to them. Unlike the earlier Pong and Space Invaders, the new games offered emotionally stimulating images of realistic violence. As had happened so often in the past (with movies and comic books, for example) rather than passing legislation, Congress let the industry establish its own rating system in 1994. The Entertainment Software Rating Board's classifications for each new video game—EC (early childhood), E (everyone), T (teen), and M (mature)—correspond to progressively intense and realistic violence, sexuality, profanity, and other "mature" behaviors in characters. But instead of just informing the consumer and restricting violent video games to adults, something else happened. Just as the movie-rating system encouraged the borderline PG-13 films, so the video-rating system legitimated violent video games. E-rated games earned the disdain of kids who longed for "grown-up" T and M games in the same way that twelve-year-old boys avoided PG movies like the plague.[11] It is hardly surprising to see a moral panic over the threat of this form of "maturity" on the emotional and moral lives of children.

This trend toward violent video games also illustrates the extension of teen cool into adult sensibilities. Let's consider Doom. An offshoot of the popular shareware 3-D "first-person shooter" game Wolfenstein (1992), Doom was first offered free on the Internet by the Texas-based id Software in December 1993, providing players the fantasy of being stuck on Mars fighting an unrelenting onslaught of science-fiction monsters. Gamers hooked by the intense pleasure of blowing up the oncoming hordes bought subsequent "chapters." The sequel, Doom II, drew millions with an even more extreme ride through the hell of kill-or-be-killed as monsters pursue the player's character through mazes and hallways. "Along the way you acquire weapons including shotguns, rocket launchers and chain cannons," noted journalist Colin Covert. "When you use this arsenal against your enemies, they explode in spurting arteries and showering meat."

The words of id's business manager (1994) capture the adolescent glee at defying respectable adulthood so evident in this game: "I wouldn't say 'Doom' is a violent game. It's an extremely violent game! We don't have any suits running around telling us not to do this or that because 5 percent of the population will frown upon it. We all just get together and figure out what's cool, what we want to play. I think that's part of our charm. We don't answer to anybody but ourselves."[12]

What is particularly striking is the language of "sticking it to the man," and, by implication, a youthlike rebellion against respectability and genteel values in general. While children's exposure to this attitude and a game that makes violent and even criminal behavior "cool" is understandably disturbing, rating this game as "M" for mature is bizarre. Not only does teen "cool" bleed into child's play, but it persists deep into adulthood. Thus, chic rebellion against mythical authority (don't the "suits" want to profit from Doom?) has gradually become mainstream. We have seen plenty of evidence of it already in modern advertising, action movies, and sitcoms. Unlike other "toys," even the electric pinball games of the 1930s, video games have not been abandoned as boys become men because the distinction between boys and men has disappeared in their play. Instead, we see men deep in their thirties and even forties who started playing with the Atari in the mid-1970s still playing thirty years later. One of the amazing manifestations of this trend in the last fifteen years is the fact that high school and even college students continue to play the games and enjoy the thrills and pleasures of twelve-year-olds. Part of the process of "growing up" is the shunning of the things of childhood. Or at least that used to be the case.

High school girls now complain that young men, at an age when they once abandoned their enthusiasm for games and sports for an equal passion for the opposite sex, now ignore them at parties as they gather round their PlayStations for some "stupid and boring" game. As one junior told a high school English teacher writing for the *Washington Post* in 2004: "We try to tell them they're wasting their time, but they just keep going. Some guys stay up playing until 3 in the morning on school nights, and then they try to do their homework." Even a senior boy in an AP English class admitted his addiction to video games: "The narrative is so exciting you lose all track of time. . . . Three hours can go by and it seems like 15 minutes. Once I'm into it, it's hard to think of anything else; all my focus is on finishing the story line." Male college students share this enthusiasm. When Halo 2 appeared in 2004, Old Dominion University freshman Nick Pratt reported that his dorm mates skipped classes for three straight days to play. In the midst of the Halo 2 craze, a woman student claimed she heard video games going on in every room as she walked down the hall of a men's floor in her dorm.[13] As with other age groups, the ready access to electronic "temptation" has caused much concern about college-aged men's addiction to online gambling.[14]

Of course, there has been an ongoing debate about the impact of video games on male college students. Doug Lowenstein, president of the Interactive Digital Software Association, argued that the Pew Internet and American Life Project survey of 2003 "shatters the myths that people may have about video games as somehow isolating and anti-social." The survey seemed to show that video play was normal. Two of three male college students still played video games, and the gamers studied no less than the general college population (after all, 69 percent of students study no more than seven hours a week).[15]

Repeatedly, research on video-game violence, however, has shown that time engaged in video play is related to impulsive aggressive behavior and shortened attention spans in adolescents and young adults. What is striking is that students see video games as harmless (as in a 2004 study at the University of Maryland), and the more they play, the less concerned these students are about raunchiness and blood. This may suggest that the more you play video games, the more immured you are to their impact.[16] There is inconclusive evidence that video games by themselves create addiction in more than a small minority of players. This conclusion, drawn from many studies summarized by Mark Griffiths and Mark Davies in 2005, is based on the model of chemical addiction. To qualify as addictive, games must dominate the time and attention of players, require additional stimuli to get desired mood change, and lead to conflict with others and to relapse after painful withdrawal. Still, there is no doubt that many players are hooked on the need for the arousing or calming effects of video games.[17] It is hardly surprising that as early as 1996, universities began to offer students counseling to counter video and online addiction, and some colleges even limited access to computer time (forty hours per week at the University of Maryland, for example). Studies linked dropout rates to late-night time on the Internet.[18]

Certainly, there doesn't seem to be a point when men say that they have had enough and put down the game pad (as so many of my generation put down the roach clip when they reached the age when smoking marijuana made them feel paranoid or old). What really amazes me is that men into their thirties and even forties and fifties regularly play video games. I can understand occasional play, but it isn't hard to find men successful in work and family life, even with exemplary social and recreational lives, who play these games for hours a day. So in 2003 Mark Murawski, a thirty-one-year-old software engineer from suburban Pittsburgh, saw nothing odd about having a PlayStation 2, a Nintendo Game Cube, and Xbox wired up for play in his family room, and also space in his basement dedicated to a dozen more vintage systems, including the Nintendo NES, a Sega Dreamcast, the Atari Lynx, and the Neo Geo. He regularly meets with old college buddies to try out the new games in the way that friends might gather to see the latest movie. "It's not a child's toy you're going to grow out of," declared Murawski, who has been playing ever since the Atari 2600 system came out in 1977 when he was just five years old.[19] In 2001, a fifty-one-year-old insurance man, hooked on video since he was given Mattel's Intellivision's baseball game in 1979, went on to "collect them all," like a child responding to the call of the makers of Pokemon cards.[20]

It certainly isn't surprising that adolescents are attracted to video games. Some have argued that video games, like other play, prepare teens for adulthood, offering a sheltered and consequence-free setting in which to learn necessary survival skills. They certainly offer a modern alternative to the initiation rites that introduced our ancestors to adult roles as hunters and warriors. They give teens who are insecure about their social or academic skills a setting where they can achieve.[21] Why youth play is not hard to understand. The question is, why do adults?

The trend is clear. According to the Entertainment Software Association, which represents the video industry, in 1997 more than half of all video-game players were younger than 18. By 2001, the trade group estimated that 57 percent of players were adults, with an average age of twenty-eight. In 2005, the average age rose to thirty-three years old (with forty being the age of the most frequent purchaser of games) with 25 percent of gamers over 50 and 44 percent from eighteen to forty-nine years old. Thirty percent of games sold are of the "action" variety, 17 percent sports, and 11 percent racing. The typical gamer had been playing for twelve years! Obviously, Generation X players who started as children are still playing (while boomers often too old to start as kids never picked up the habit). Although the ESA takes pains to point out the normalcy of gamers (79 percent claim to exercise twenty hours a month, and 45 percent say that they volunteer for community service an average of 4.5 hours per month), the question still remains: Why do they continue to play children's and teen's games?[22]

Perhaps the simplest answer is a benign one. As a society, we have gradually abandoned the idea that getting older means abandoning "fun," even if it mostly results in getting in touch with our "inner twelve-year-old." As we have seen, there is nothing new about this. The pal dad of the 1950s was supposed to play (especially at home) with his kids and to "rejuvenilate" himself in the process, as Chris Noxon has recently advocated, by holding onto youthful play even past the childrearing stage. Even as children long for M-rated video games, adults drift back into the pleasures of childhood. They collect toys, watch cartoons, and play games. Anyone who has seen the Cartoon Network or the cartoon series on the Comedy Channel (especially *South Park*) has seen that a genre once associated with children has bled into "adulthood."[23]

But this explanation is too general and doesn't explain why a thirty- or forty-year-old would not have changed his definition of play and pleasure as he grew older. A generation of men developed a "taste" for video games when they were introduced as kids to the Atari 2600 in 1977 or the Nintendo console in 1986, and they have stuck with the game pad for twenty or thirty years. This says something extraordinary about the emotional impact of video gaming on these men. Doug Lowenstein, president of the Entertainment Software Association, finds this phenomenon practically self-explanatory: "The games have grown up with the audience, so there's no reason to walk away from them." He goes on to explain, "Many who began playing when they were 15 are still enjoying it because the technology has matured right along with them."[24] In what sense have these games "matured"? Apparently, this means that the graphics have become more realistic and the speed of play has increased as the players have "grown up." Therefore, men stick with chasing bad guys through mazes, collecting weapons, and "wasting" digital enemies. Of course, this isn't entirely fair. Computer role-playing games often take the player into worlds of adventure and surprise and into encounters with interesting and sometimes complex characters, as if the player were acting in an open-ended story. They have increasingly become emotionally engrossing (resulting from what the game designer David Freeman calls "emotioneering").

Still, the basic idea and action of these games has hardly changed, even as their sensual impact and emotional intensity has increased since the days of Pac Man and Duke Nukem. Game makers have learned how to get players more "immersed" in the play and have developed techniques of "optimizing" engagement (neither too difficult nor too easy, neither too shocking nor too familiar, etc). But eliciting emotion and drawing sated players into the game hardly constitutes deeper moral or intellectual engagement (which presumably would come with experience). Will Wright, creator of the Sims series of strategy games, writes that games have broadened their appeal beyond the primitive instincts of "survival and aggression to include the more subtle mechanisms of empathy, nurturing, and creativity." But he admitted that game makers have "a long way to go. . . . Compared to other forms of media (books, films, music), games are still stuck somewhere around the 'small rodent' phase" of animal evolution.[25]

Finally, others argue that a "digital generation" has emerged since the 1980s that rather neatly separates the boomers (who matured with TV) from the Gen Xers and today's youth, who grew up with video games and, more recently, the Internet. According to this view, the digital generation has developed a new ways of communicating, learning, and display of self; new forms of literacy; and even new politics.[26] Gaming is only part of this new generational culture. Henry Jenkins, Jeffrey Goldstein, and others claim that even violent video games are more about new forms of electronic interaction and increased opportunities for choice than about what appears to "outsiders" (especially aging academic boomers like me) to be empty and ultimately childish thrill seeking. It certainly is the case that a lot of the negative psychological effects of playing violent video games have been exaggerated. However, this doesn't change the fact that game "interaction" is hardly moral, intellectual, or even social (though players may cooperate online) and the "choice" is mostly about what weapon to use or what "door" to open in the endless excitement of the fight. Of course, as Jenkins notes, there are "moral" consequences even in Grand Theft Auto III:

> Some of what happens is outrageous and offensive, but this open-ended structure puts the burden on the user to make choices and explore their consequences. If you choose to use force, you are going to attract the police. The more force, the more cops. . . . Every risk you take comes with a price. Early on, players act out,

seeing how much damage and mayhem they can inflict, but more experienced players tell me they often see how long they can go without breaking any laws, viewing this a harder and more interesting challenge. A richer game might offer a broader range of options, including allowing the player to go straight, get a job, and settle into the community.[27]

The problem with this is the obvious fact that no one would play the game to "go straight." How is that "fun" or "challenging"? The point of this and many role-playing and first- person-shooter games is the thrill of conflict and danger. There is nothing wrong with that as a diversion or as a way for youths to "play with power," coping with their temporary state of powerlessness.[28] But are the increasing sophistication of graphics, story lines, and characters in games really a substitute for cultural, emotional, and social maturation?

All this suggests two pretty amazing things: First, modern toys have gradually lost their "expiration dates," the markers that designate the time that children are expected to abandon them after reaching a new developmental stage. Boys once knew that they were too "big" for electric trains when they were old enough for the "real thing," or they abandoned *fantasies* of power and exhilarating action because they were old enough to enter a *real* world of male power and action. But today boys becoming men do not give these games because their manufacturers design them to blur, even deny this historically essential transition from boyhood to manhood. Even when video companies were obliged to rate games for age, these markers hardly designated transitions to maturity. They signaled merely increased violence, sensuality, and vulgarity. Even more troubling is the possibility that many men don't experience that "real thing" of participating in a grown-up world and thus don't put away the toys.[29]

Second, as a result, male players seem to equate personal progress with increased sensual and emotional intensity. This marks a dramatic break from traditional meanings of maturation in personal culture and pleasure. To grow up meant abandoning fantasy and mere thrills for cultivated and complex pleasures. Video games induce otherwise "mature" men to forgo relationships with women and family (as well as more subtle and cultivated forms of leisure) for the highly individualistic and largely isolated encounter with the ephemeral thrill. To be blunt, adult men obsessed with video games are in a state of arrested development because they can't see the difference between a toy and an adult pleasure.

The game makers, whether consciously or not, encourage these trends. They eliminate the markers of childhood (as in the cute images of Pokemon or Mario) and create worlds of "ageless" but still young heroes that seem to appeal to teens and young adults. Video-game makers carefully alternate doses of "payoff" and challenge to draw players, no matter their age, into the flow of the game. Year by year, game designers add new layers of image, sound, and tactile sensitivity, encouraging players to play "for life." So psychologically and even physiologically powerful are these games that they entice players bored with earlier games to keep picking up their game pads. A Stanford University survey found that 70 percent of 40,000 online players have played for at least ten hours at a time and 45 percent admit to being "addicted." Facilitating this inability to stop are psychologists hired by online game companies to identify and eliminate the frustrating and boring parts of games and to smooth out the "flow."[30]

Ever more complex, multilayered games like Everquest (2000) lured ordinary and otherwise quite responsible and rational office managers for up to sixteen hours at a stretch, playing the role of a wood-elf druid who wanders through a digital kingdom of fifty levels of visually rich three-dimensional scenes, acquiring virtual treasures (such as swords). A man on an Everquest newsgroup could admit, "I found dumping the women is about the easiest way to find time to play, I play from 6 p.m. to 12 or 1 a.m. every night. Sacrifices are needed if you want to be high-level."[31]

It is no surprise that treatment centers for Internet and video-game addiction have sprung up, including a thirty-day inpatient program to wean players from their obsession. The key to this passion is the way that the game immerses the player in the fantasy and action so much that he forgets he is playing and for how long. The eminent scholar and elder historian Paul Boyer admitted during research that he found playing Myst, a computer fantasy role-playing game set on a mysterious island, "completely engrossing." Even Lode Runner, based on a character who mines for gold while "zapping mad monks with a ray gun," quickly got his "adrenaline flowing."[32]

What makes video games so absorbing goes beyond the carefully calibrated "payoffs" of emotional "hits." More broadly, it is the sense of engagement and often control in the illusory world of the video game. As the editor of a gaming Web site noted, video and other elec-

tronic devices "give you a sense of entitlement, the idea that everything can revolve around you."[33] The need to interact with anything
but the screen seems to vanish and, as many critics have noted, social
(and political) skills atrophy or don't develop. Instead of learning to
negotiate, nurture, or even cultivate nature in play, most video games
foster a very different set of attitudes and skills. As Boyer found in his
study, the writers of action games are "prophets of fire and chaos, violence and anarchy. Their central, overwhelming vision is of social dis-
integration, paranoid suspicion of government, and raw, unremitting
individualism. . . . Alliances are fleeting and based wholly on expediency."[34] The problem may be less that video games make men violent
(or lead children into acting out violent fantasies) but that these games
reinforce the childish view that the world is full of bogeymen under
the bed and the equally childish response, the cathartic thrill of zapping them. They augment self-absorption in boys and men and divert
them from learning skills of cooperation, persuasion, and teamwork
that are essential in the grown-up world today. These games may not
make men monsters, but they hardly make them gentlemen.

The Thrill of the Ride

Since the days of the Atari, gamers have denied that their control pads
make them violent. Instead, those buttons are merely "fun," relieving
the stresses of daily life. I think there is a lot of truth to this claim, but
that only reinforces my point that the purpose of the game is the intensity of the thrill, which can take innumerable forms. This leads me
to a second theme in the play worlds of today's boy-men, the attraction of roller coasters and other thrill rides in amusement parks. This
phenomenon will serve as representative of a whole range of thrill
activities (extreme sports, paintball combat, and raves).[35]

Since the 1970s, parks like Six Flags and Cedar Point have built
progressively higher, faster, and seemingly more dangerous rides.
They have attracted legions of enthusiasts who sometimes travel from
roller coaster to roller coaster across the country in search of the elusive ecstasy of negative g's. Although these rides appealed to the cool-
seeking teen and "tweens," Gen-X boy-men were also attracted.

In the summer of 2003, long lines formed for the debut of the
latest and greatest attraction at Cedar Point in Sandusky, Ohio, the
Top Thrill Dragster. The state-of-the-art Dragster reaches a height of

420 feet, from which eighteen riders briefly experience zero gravity at the climax of their rapid ascent. Then, in a twisting 270-degree drop, riders feel the fear and rush of "free fall." But this is only the second half of the show. Like a bullet fired from a gun, Top Thrill Dragster riders are thrust in four seconds to the speed of 125 miles per hour along a 900-foot level run, sending the cars up the tower. This is the ultimate in the dragster experience, made possible by an air propulsion system that flattens the flesh on riders' faces, making their heads feel that they weigh four times their real weight. Added to the sensual overload is the anticipation: the roar of the "dragster" engine revving up, the sight of the pulsating green, yellow, and red lights along the track and up the tower, and the pause at the top to see the view of the lake and park, before the dive straight down at seventy miles an hour—and all of this in twenty seconds, often after a wait for hours in line. This ride is a sharp break from the traditional roller coaster, with its gentle pull up an incline by a clanking chain, followed by a drop down a steep incline and a series of dips and curves mostly powered by the momentum of the first drop. By comparison, as journalist Kevin Conley noted in 2004, even the most extreme traditional coaster makes riders feel "like a bird. On Top Thrill Dragster you feel like a veal chop."[36]

So why would anyone want to feel like a veal chop? Maybe because the Dragster distilled the thrill to its purest form: positive acceleration of gravity or g-force in upward acceleration making riders feel much heavier than they are and "negative g's" just before downward acceleration in the sensation of weightlessness and the feeling of floating. Cars banking in curves can produce sideways positive g's. The development in 1975 of a system of three sets of wheels on tubular steel tracks made it possible to go upside down in a corkscrew route. These sensations are capped by the euphoric feeling (similar to the sensation in sex and cocaine use) caused when the brain releases the neurochemical dopamine into the synaptic receptors. This occurs when the brain "thinks" the person is engaging in risk-taking activity and sends distress signals to the heart, lungs, skin, and other vital organs (similar to the bodily reaction to video games). This makes riders feel more aware, more "alive." At the same time, pain-suppressing endorphins are released, producing the equivalent of the "runner's high."[37] The coaster enthusiast has a lot in common with devotees of bungee jumping, skydiving, and other extreme sports that emerged about the same time.[38]

These sensations are precisely what thousands of twelve- to eighteen-year-olds have sought on roller coasters for more than a century. This age group, notoriously easily bored and as yet unrefined in their tastes, seeks thrills.[39] What is more interesting is that adults, some deep in middle age, share a desire for these sensations. But that is part of what appeals to the 8,000-plus members of the American Coaster Enthusiasts, probably the nation's largest club devoted to the thrill ride. The origins of ACE are significant. Its founders, Rory Brashears, Paul Greenwald, and Richard Munch, met during a roller-coaster-riding marathon in 1978 at Kings Dominion, an amusement park in Doswell, Virginia, while the film *Rollercoaster* was being promoted. These men, mostly in their thirties, were a part of a revival in amusement parks that had begun in 1972 when jazz musician Jim Payer went on a nine-day nostalgic tour of old coasters that ended at Comet Coaster in Lincoln Park (Massachusetts). Efforts by nostalgic enthusiasts to save the aging Cyclone at Coney Island from becoming the site of an aquarium trout stream succeeded when it was reopened in 1975. This blend of thrill and boyhood nostalgia won a wide appreciative audience when Robert Cartmell wrote "The Quest for the Ultimate Roller Coaster" in the *New York Times* in June of 1976. Not only did he get about 8,000 letters of interest, but the article led to a movie about Cartmell's quest (*Endless Summer*). Though begun mostly by boomers, the thrill-ride craze was picked up by Gen Xers in earnest and taken much further.[40]

Offered packaged visits to a wide variety of amusement parks, ACE members benefit from the privilege of the highly touted "Exclusive Ride Time" on coasters, and often hundreds of members join in. ACE grew gradually, reaching 1,700 members by 1988 and, with the help of the Internet, to over 8,000 by 2005. Members are drawn from both sexes and across the age span but tend to be white, middle-class males in their thirties and forties. Some are purists and favor "woodies" (which share a laminated wood base to the tracks), while others obsess over the speed, twists, and turns of modern tubular steel coasters. Steve Gzesh, the public relations director for ACE and a training consultant for Cingular Wireless, is typical in his obsession. He has traveled to out-of-the-way parks in the wintertime just to see roller coaster skylines. Some have been married on coasters. Duane Marden, a computer programmer, has devoted much of his spare time to his encyclopedic Roller Coaster Database, a Web site (www.rcdb.com) of roller-coaster statistics and amusement-park listings from around the world.[41]

An abiding purpose of ACE is the preservation and restoration of coaster heritage and history. In the 1980s, for example, ACE helped to rescue seven coasters from demolition, finding new homes for them in viable parks. ACE members regularly visit old and out-of-the-way parks for this nostalgic appeal, and the group awards "ACE Coaster Classic" status to wooden coasters that preserve the traditional experience (allowing riders to sit where they please, slide side-to-side in their seats, and view the upcoming drops and thrills by not installing headrests that restrict this view). ACE and other coaster enthusiasts wax nostalgic about old coasters, but they are especially sentimental about the old thrills, vehemently opposing efforts to make coasters "boringly" safe.[42]

When I read coaster Web sites, magazines, and books and talk to enthusiasts, I entered an esoteric world of special terms and phrases all designed to express and measure the amazing variety and subtlety of the coaster experience. Enthusiasts identify a mind-boggling fifty varieties of rollercoaster loops and turns. They include such colorful examples as the Batwing, Double Heartline Roll, Flying Snake Dive, Helix, Horseshoe, Pretzel, Raven Turn, Wraparound Corkscrew, and Zero-G Roll. Especially important is the sensation of floating in your seat (called airtime) when the car suddenly plunges and the body feels negative acceleration of gravity, often as the traction wheels briefly lift off the rails.[43] The lovingly detailed descriptions of rides on favorite coasters capture both a refined sensuality and a quest for a boyish physical intensity. Scott Rutherford, one of many authors of coaster guides, claims the Magnum of Cedar Point provides an "unforgettable, almost spiritual roller coaster experience." As the first "hypercoaster," it offers the rider the glories of "exposure" as the "ride is perched right on the beach, inches from the lapping waves of Lake Erie." He goes on: "Each succeeding hill offers something unique, whether it's encased in a right tunnel loaded with special light, sound and fog effects, or shaped to produce dramatic (and often abrupt) degrees of sustained airtime." It "is one of those rare ride experiences that remains with you long after you hit the home breaks." The words of ACE president Randy Geisler in 1988 summed up the appeal: "a good coaster combines car racing, bobsledding and sky diving."[44] A thrill in three dimensions.

Then there is Richard Rodriguez. This Chicago-based college instructor in his forties astonished the media by repeatedly breaking his own record for marathon coaster riding, setting fifteen records by 2002. He began this adventure in August 1977 when he rode Coney Island's Cyclone for 103 hours and 55 minutes, under the *Guinness Book of Records*'s "60/5 rule," which allowed him one five-minute break for every sixty minutes. As a child in New York he was afraid of coasters and rode on them only with his parents, braving the Cyclone only at sixteen. Two years later in 1968, when he read about a man who had set a record by riding a roller coaster for about eight hours, Rodriguez found meaning and attention by besting this time and his own records, which rose to 384 hours by 1983. To his dismay, he found himself out-coastered by Norman St. Pierre, a French Canadian fireman who spent 502 hours on a ride at Belmont Park, Montreal. Rodriguez threw in the towel for a decade while in school and working, but in 1994, he got back into competitive form to best his Canadian rival. Working with Geoffrey Thompson, director of Blackpool's Pleasure Beach amusement park in northwest England, he road 549 hours on the famed Big Dipper. In 1998, he went for 600 hours and on a dare did 2,000 for the year 2000, by far besting St. Pierre who quit at 670 hours. Later, he spent 100 days on a coaster at Six Flags in St. Louis and in 2002 rode for 104 days on the Expedition GeForce in Germany. Despite windburn, back ache, and sheer exhaustion, Rodriguez proved he could do it.[45]

This behavior has a lot in common with the practices of the ancient ascetics who for years at a time stood on pillars or carried millstones around their necks to prove their godliness. But why would Rodriquez choose a roller coaster to display his discipline and prowess? After all, the point of the coaster is the anticipation and thrill of a sensual assault on the mind and body that is so compressed that it seldom lasts more than four minutes, not days. But Rodriquez's quest says something about the symbolic power of the coaster today, that a man could bear that kind of thrill over and over. The ascetic's accomplishment of withstanding the pain of physical self-abuse in an act of "denying the flesh" was praised by a culture that saw the material world as a distraction from the spiritual. Rodriquez's feat of enduring the "fun" of the most extreme coasters thousands of times says something about our times. In an era of the thrill, it is an ultimate achievement.

Unlike the carousel, the roller coaster had origins in adult thrill seeking. The first "coaster" appeared in St. Petersburg, Russia, as a wooden seventy-foot high, fifty-degree incline covered in iced snow that seventeenth-century revelers descended on sleds. In the late eighteenth century, a French entrepreneur built a track using closely spaced rollers (hence the name roller coaster). In 1846, the first step to the modern thrill ride was the looping coaster in Paris's Frascati Gardens with a forty-three-foot hill providing the momentum for the rider of a cart to loop through a thirteen-foot wide metal circle. Elsewhere, however, coasters had closer ties to the railroad track. In 1870, an abandoned inclined plane railroad for mines near Mauch Chunk, Pennsylvania, was converted into a novelty ride. The American inventor La Marcus Thompson adapted this device into his invention of a primitive gravity-propelled "switchback" coaster in 1884 (which thrilled riders at six miles per hour). While Thompson's ride required men to push the cars up an incline on both ends of the ride (hence the name "switchback"), steam-powered chain lifts appeared in 1885, and the track became a circuit. Though Thompson added painted scenes along the track to simulate travel to exotic or fantasy places, it was the thrilling sensation of vertigo that made the roller coaster appealing. In 1900, the Flip Flap coaster at Coney Island turned the rider in a complete circle in a ten-second experience that caused neck pains. In 1895, improvements in the loop (by redesigning it to be more oval) made this thrill a minor success. John A. Miller's invention of under-track wheels in 1910 allowed for higher inclines and sharper turns without the cars' jumping off the track. In the 1920s, mammoth wooden coasters were huge successes in amusement parks worldwide (at least 1,500 of them by 1929 in the United States). The most famous was Coney Island's Cyclone, with its sixty-degree plunge from a height of eighty-five feet. Roller coasters became the quintessential packaged pleasure, compressing as much physical arousal as possible in the shortest time possible with minimal cultural content.[46]

Coaster construction ended with the Depression. After the war, amusement parks fell into decline and disrepair, decreasing to perhaps only 200 by 1960. Disneyland (1955) was in many ways designed to be the opposite of the early-twentieth-century amusement park— geared as it was for baby boomer families with small children, parents, and grandparents in tow—where cartoon- and movie-themed attractions on the often genteel principles of the scenic railroad, dark ride, and panorama replaced thrill rides. Disney consciously rejected the "iron rides" of Coney Island—including roller coasters. Thus it is ironic that Disneyland inaugurated a new era of coaster design with the first tubular steel track ride in 1959, which would lead to the modern terror trips of today. Still, Disney's steel track was used on the heavily themed Matterhorn, a ride featuring make-believe bobsleds that took passengers up, through, and around a replica of a Swiss mountain and ended in a "glacier lake." Really only a very mild roller coaster, it has more in common with Coney Island's scenic railroads than it did with a modern thrill ride.[47]

In the 1960s and especially the 1970s, however, there began a revival of the traditional amusement park and a renewed interest in coasters. This only slightly preceded the arrival of the video-game culture, during the childhoods of the earliest Gen Xers. The first of the new parks were Six Flags Over Texas, opened in 1961 in Arlington, Texas, and followed by Six Flags parks in Atlanta (1968) and St Louis (1971). Then came Magic Mountain in Valencia, California (1971), and King's Island in Cincinnati (1972). New coasters like Six Flags' Runaway Mine Train and the Great American Revolution of Magic Mountain featured tubular steel tracks. In 1976, J. Willard Marriott Sr. opened the Great America amusement park on a two-hundred-acre farm in Gurnee, Illinois, north of Chicago. Although heavily themed in the Disney fashion with a simulated Yankee fishing village, Yukon mining camp, and New Orleans French Quarter, what gathered the crowds were its coasters and water flumes. While drawing the same family crowd as did Disneyland and, after 1971, Walt Disney World, these new parks also appealed to the teens and young adults who had flocked to Coney Island in its glory years before 1950. Even old parks were spruced up and brought nostalgic crowds back with new wooden coasters like the Blue Streak at Ohio's Cedar Point (1964) and the Thunderbolt at Pittsburgh's Kennywood Park, (1968).[48] In 1975, the ancient and previously sedate Knott's Berry Farm (dating from 1920 as a folksy restaurant) introduced the steel tubular Corkscrew and its spiral loop.[49] Its southern California competitor, Six Flags Magic Mountain, boosted attendance in 1976 with the vertical-looping Revolution Free Fall (with a fifty-five-mph drop in two seconds) and the Colossus, noted for its height. By 2003, Magic Mountain offered sixteen roller coasters. Ohio's Cedar Point joined the big-time coaster club by also accumulating sixteen thrill machines by 2003, enough to satisfy almost anyone.[50]

Even SeaWorld Orlando, long noted for featuring charming dolphin shows for the family, now offers the Kraken, a floorless roller coaster that reaches the height of a fifteen-story building and turns riders upside-down seven times at sixty-five miles per hour. Seaworld named the coaster for a mythological monster and conjured up this prospect in its publicity: "Riders' feet dangle as they sit on open-air, pedestal-like seats with nothing around them except shoulder restraints. There's no one to hold on to, nothing in front of them and nothing below them—and only sky above."[51] The new steel tubular rides were no longer about nostalgia for boyhood, an appeal that drove the boomers in the 1970s to revive the old "woodie" coasters. Instead, the steel coasters offered at-the-edge exhilaration and the seemingly limitless escalation of excitement for both kids and boy-men.

Another thrill, especially on hot days, is the water park. Its transformation can neatly be summarized by its evolution at Walt Disney World. The first of the Disney water attractions was River Country (1976) located in the rustic setting of Fort Wilderness. With its western appeal (complete with campground and Fort Apache Playground), River Country was an attempt to recover the "ol' swimmin' hole," with rope swings, a barrel bridge, and a water slide all reminiscent of the summer childhoods of past generations. The idea was for dads to introduce their boys to a pleasure that many men had known as kids but that had disappeared in suburban America. In the 1970s, this was the site of boomer and older nostalgia, perfectly in tune with Disney's dream of bringing the generations together in the elders' cinema-coaxed "memory" of their youth. It was like Disney's Main Street USA, that cartoonlike fantasy of small-town 1900 America that led like a funnel into the themed "lands" of Disney's first parks, Disneyland and Magic Kingdom (Orlando). Both Fort Wilderness and Main Street were to let pal dads (and granddads) share with the young a playful setting (much like the electric trains that dads and sons were to share from the 1910s to 1960s). It was a skillful expression of the pal dad/cute kid formula.[52]

Little could be more of a contrast than Typhoon Lagoon, which opened at Disney World in 1989. It was a near perfect reflection of a new age of Gen X thrill culture. With its ninety-five-foot artificial mountain, nine water slides, and especially its wave-making machines that overwhelmed fun seekers with waves up to seven feet high in a gigantic pool, Typhoon Lagoon broke from nostalgia. This was all about the new and especially about exhilaration, the thrill of battling waves and the rush of feeling helpless and brave while sliding down on water in closed tubes of plastic to an "unexpected" splash at the bottom. The third water park, Blizzard Beach (1995), is both more rousing and more novel and fantastic than the other two. Built on a "back story" about a freak snow storm in Florida that led some over-enthusiastic entrepreneurs to construct a ski resort, the park looks like an Alpine resort with the snow "melted" into a tropical lagoon. It features a 120-feet-high Mt. Gushmore with a number of thrilling water slides. The theme is neither the "good old days" nor the exotic setting of the rain forest. Blizzard Beach is ironic and edgy, based on a joke that the makers of the boy-men comedies of the 1990s would certainly have understood.[53]

By the 1990s, most amusement parks featured at least some water rides. In 2000, Knott's Berry Farm introduced a new thirteen-acre water park called Soak City USA and the Perilous Plunge, advertised as the world's tallest, steepest water ride (a 115-foot water shoot at a 75-degree angle).[54] Very much in this tradition is Disco H2o at Wet 'N Wild, the Universal Studios water park in Orlando. Thrill seekers ride on a four-person raft through a dark tunnel and then are shot into an enclosed bowl where, with lights flashing and rock music blasting, they are buffeted about before being fed into a water flume that drops them into a pool where, of course, all get wet.[55]

There were other ways of getting thrills, including simulated rides that took up much less space and in no way were an assault on the body. On the Back to the Future ride at Orlando's Universal Studios fun seekers in an eight-seat vehicle modeled on the DeLorean time machine in the 1985 movie have the sensation that they are roaring through time, sideswiping buildings and rooftops, and diving down into canyons and a dinosaur's mouth. Using a huge concave screen and film-projection system (Omnimax) and seats and climate controls that move in synchronization with the fast paced film, this and later simulated rides trick the eye and body into believing the illusion of flight.[56] The story is more or less immaterial. What counts is the excitement of the unexpected, the illusion of danger that makes riders say coolly, "cool." These rides appeal to a wide age range, both male and female, but they are part of a trend toward the pure adrenaline rush of anticipation, fall, shock, and acceleration, the thrill ride utterly shorn of sentiment, nostalgia, or even beauty, the hallmark of the Gen-X boy-man.

A good indicator of the surge of thrill are the accommodations that the Disney theme parks have made to this culture of the cool. The new amusement parks with their exhilarating coasters, appealing no longer to family groups with young children but to the independent PG-13 crowd, began to threaten the Disney formula of cuteness in the 1970s. Disneyland responded in 1977 with Space Mountain.

Although promoted as an educational ride in a space capsule, Space Mountain was really an indoor roller coaster, a gut-wrenching experience of "twisting and banking" as the rider (according to Disney promoters) "plunges into swirling galaxies, past shooting stars, and meteoric showers." It was a sensation totally divorced from actual manned space travel or the storybook version of it.[57]

From the early 1980s, most of the new rides appealed to the cool rather than the cute in Fantasyland, the nostalgic in Frontierland, the genteel values of progress in Tomorrowland, and didactic exploration in Adventureland. Abandoning the old formulas, Disney reached out to the new by persuading George Lucas to adapt his space fantasies to a theme ride at Disneyland. Since 1955, Tomorrowland had always included futurist and space fantasy, but never was it so devoid of science as in Lucas's Captain Eo (1985). This twelve-minute, three-dimensional film and light-show production featured singer Michael Jackson struggling against alien monsters to save a "music starved planet."[58] The old Disney theme of scientific progress and the adventure of exploring space had almost completely disappeared by the 1990s. In Lucas's 1995 Indiana Jones Adventure, fun seekers experienced a simulation of the most intense action scenes from *Indiana Jones and the Temple of Doom*.[59] Neither the innocent wonder of the small child nor the adult's quest for genteel knowledge and experience remained in these new attractions.

Driving this shift to thrill culture was Disney's competition with MCA's Universal Studio theme parks, especially in Orlando (Universal Studios Florida, built in 1990, and Islands of Adventure, in 1999). Although Universal began its foray into amusement parks with a tram tour of its movie lots in Hollywood in 1965, gradually the company turned to adapting rides and attractions from Universal thrillers (some old, like *King Kong*, and others new, like *Jaws*). The movie-theme attraction survives at the older Universal Studios Florida, but at Universal's Islands of Adventure, the thrill element dominates. Appealing to the teen and young adult, such rides as the Amazing Adventures of Spider-Man combine the characters and stories from movies inspired by Marvel comics characters with the vertigo-induced thrill of a roller coaster. The Incredible Hulk Coaster starts with a "gamma-ray accelerator" that launches riders up a 150-foot incline in two seconds and then on to a state-of-the-art coaster that goes through seven inversions. Beginning with the shock of seemingly being showered by bricks through a simulated drop of forty stories, the

Spider-Man ride offers four and a half minutes of unrelenting terror. Islands of Adventure was designed not to appeal to the six-year-old and her parents, as Disney had been, but to the older child and young adult with "edgier, and with more sophisticated tastes . . . [from] 7 or 8 to 80," or so claimed Cathy Nichols, CEO of Universal Studios Recreation Group in 1999.[60]

Disney hardly ceded the seven- to eighty-year-olds to Universal Studios. Still, behind this absurd claim was the obvious fact that a new aesthetic had emerged, focused on the longings and tastes of post-boomer youth and a post-Disney world of the cool that had replaced the era of 1950s boomer families. Gradually, all of the parks at Walt Disney World found ways of meeting the new demand for "excitement." By collaborating with MGM studios, the Disney organization adopted the same format as Universal, with movie-themed attractions (even beating the competition by opening a year earlier, in 1989). But soon Disney MGM Studios was preparing to accommodate the increasing demand for thrill rides from the youth who did not share the nostalgia for old MGM movies with their parents and grandparents. Disney introduced a relatively tame but imaginative theme ride, the Twilight Zone Tower of Terror in 1994. Appealing to the demands of the new generation of youth, the Disney Company introduced the indoor Rock 'n' Roller Coaster in 1999. Linear synchronous motors catapult riders from zero to fifty-three miles per hour in three seconds, and the coaster winds and twists them through a thrill- packed course with three "multiple complete inversions," while 1950s rock music blares from speakers in each car.[61]

Perhaps the most dramatic examples of this change in Disney World can be seen at the Epcot Center. When it opened in 1982, Epcot forcefully proclaimed its adherence to the genteel tradition of uplift in science and world travel, which had been the legacy of world's fairs since the London Exhibition of 1851. That was the point of the pavilions of Epcot's Future World, which promised to teach the wonders of the imagination, motion, energy, and the land with entertaining stories of the history and future of technology. The World Showcase, a semicircular area across an artificial lake from Future World, was a distant relative of traditional World's Fair villages depicting African, Asian, and European life. But as early as 1989, park planners were already adapting to the challenge of the new generation by breaking with its promise of entertaining education. They opened a simulation ride called Body Wars that featured the sensation of travel through the blood stream in the fun-filled and exciting pursuit of bacteria. Using a format similar to Lucas's sci-fi attraction, this "ride" informed no one about hematology but instead was merely an emotional rush.[62] In 1998, Epcot tore down General Motors's World of Motion, an amusing display of wisecracking mechanical characters who taught viewers the basics of the history of transportation engineering. Replacing it was "an incredibly cool ride" (by Disney's estimation) called Test Track, a thrill experience in a racecar presumably being subjected to endurance tests on a milelong track. Riders learned nothing about automotive engineering, but did enjoy fifty-degree hairpin turns, careening through a series of pylons, and being subject to arctic cold and desert heat before the vehicle is crash tested.[63] Grandpa and grandma still could enjoy the charm of the World Showcase's miniature Eiffel Tower, but even the most sedate Disney park was not off limits to the post-boomer's demand for thrills.

The notion of a "Jurassic Park" full of artificially spawned dinosaurs as a futurist amusement park seemed hardly far-fetched when a movie by that name appeared in 1993. Theme and amusement parks were increasingly becoming sites of simulated danger and evocations of the fear of death.[64] Even without a tyrannosaurus running amok, the unalloyed thrill of confronting physical and psychological stress—so attractive in the young—drove a major portion of the theme park industry. To an astonishing degree, this appeal displaced the amusements of the past. Shorn of nostalgia, the romance of distant places, uplifting visions of the future, and even the inspiration of heroes that had driven Walt Disney's original utopia, the new rides offered a comparatively simple pleasure, the thrill. What was missing were appeals to the older generation—blissful memories of lost childhood, escape from workaday lives, the promise of a better future, and even heartening stories of world-transforming courage. Even more, the old theme park evoked meaning among those who simply had lived life. Of course, children were supposed to learn these things. That was the point of the old Disney as Greatest Generation parents passed on all this to their boomer children in the 1950s and 1960s.

Boomer parents were supposed to do the same. Increasingly, from the late 1970s, however, this did not happen. The young "coolly" rejected of the lessons of the parents, be they the "cute" images of Disney cartoons, nostalgic (but increasingly alien) vistas of Main Street USA, or didactic (if playful) themes of space travel and science. And kids seemed to become "cool" at ever younger ages, foreshortening the time of parental indoctrination.

This was hardly new to my sons' generation. Their grandfathers largely invented the cool, and my generation built on it with a vengeance. And, for the most part, we accepted the demand for the cool in our kids. Boomers tended to give up their "obligation" to pass on the past to the future. We knew that a lot of the "lived lives" that shaped the sensibilities and longings of the past may not be worthy of keeping. Why should a twenty-year old today care about nostalgia for the small-town Main Street of 1900 or the mythic heroics of Davy Crockett? But this shift to the cool was problematic. A youth culture shorn of memory, experience, and even culturally created utopias inherited from its elders is a culture that lacks depth. In part, the cool culture is youth's reaction to their elders' sensibility, but it is more. The cool is fundamentally based on the sensual intensity that comes with youth and on the willingness of parents and other elders to tolerate and even embrace a radically separate culture to youth.

Because of the nature of the thrill, its pleasure inevitably attenuates. The effects of this are evident in the history of the video game and amusement-park ride. Young consumers demanded an acceleration of intensity, more colorful graphics, and faster action on the screen and higher and more frightening roller coasters. But the real thrill is in the anticipation of greater thrills than the past could offer.[65] That is what the makers of video games and amusement-park rides have provided over the past generation. And, although this is by no means a complete or final assessment of the culture of the Gen Xer, the cool is one consequence of youth sensibility becoming divorced from the past and of adults accepting and even embracing it.

Cultivating the Boy-Man Look

This brings me to a final theme—the recent cultivation of the look of youth. This is obvious in comparing the teenage visage of many of today's "leading men" on the screen and in magazines with the "mature" look of only a generation ago (Tom Cruise vs. Paul Newman, for example). Since the 1980s, the appearance of celebrity and fashionable men has become increasingly youthful. Moustaches disappeared, and ads for Calvin Klein and Abercrombie and Fitch increasingly featured the male body as smooth and hairless, muscular but adolescent, even if the model was in his late twenties or older. Euro RSCG Worldwide's survey of twenty-one- to forty-eight-year-old American men in 2003 found a surprising set of attitudes: 89 percent were convinced that good grooming was essential for business success, and almost half saw nothing odd about a man getting a facial or manicure. Three-fourths contended that they would not undo the women's movement, and most were comfortable about gay people. This certainly suggests that these men had accepted a more androgynous world, but it also points to a desire to retain a youthful appearance. Given these views, it may not be surprising that according to *Global Cosmetics Industry Magazine*, men spent nearly $4 billion on grooming products in 2002. Although that number pales in comparison with the $46 billion spent annually on cosmetics by U.S. women, this does represent a major attitude change.[66]

Susan Bordo's *The Male Body* dates this quest for the stylish and boyish body to the 1970s and 1980s: signs of the future were the young Burt Reynolds's nearly nude centerfold in *Cosmopolitan* in 1972 and the favorable image of Tony Manero, the preening, aspiring disco dancer played by John Travolta in *Saturday Night Fever* in 1977. But in 1983, the provocative Times Square giant billboard of lean, bronzed Tom Hintinauss (an Olympian pole vaulter) dressed in sexy Calvin Klein underwear (with discernable penis) heralded a real turning point. Hitherto, men were not publicly displayed as objects, and most men were uncomfortable with the gaze of women (as later exploited in endless episodes of *Sex and the City*). Even more, men were relatively oblivious to their body image. But the success of this ad to men as well as women, to the straight as well as the gay, suggests that men were beginning to identify with a lean, indeed boyish body that paralleled the much older striving of many females for a thin, girlish look. As with ads featuring Barbie-style models, these ads bred, as Bardo notes, "insecurity not identification."[67]

The quest for youth has culminated in the appearance and manner of today's "metrosexuals." This is a term introduced in 1994 by the English journalist Mark Simpson and popularized in 2002 by the media and ad agencies. "Metrosexual" refers to a man (straight and young) who is generally an affluent city dweller, dresses fashionably, grooms himself well (to the point even of getting facials and manicures), and actually enjoys shopping. His hitherto "unmanly" use of skin creams and hair-removal services at spas reflects a change even my generation of dieters, Viagra users, and Hair Care for Men patrons finds astonishing. With the English soccer player David Beck-ham as their model, "metros" think nothing of scheduling salon appointments for highlights. In 2002, Beckham, for example, posed in gay magazines, showed up at parties with frequent changes in his hair styling, appeared naked on the cover of *Esquire*, and even proudly admitted to using eye cream (how else to combat dark circles?) and to donning his wife's thongs on occasion. Contrasted with slovenly dressed and groomed alpha males or the "laddish" British sports-bar man, the metrosexual seemed to signal a shift of men toward their "feminine side," an evolution toward greater sophistication, or even a blending of hetero- and homosexual tastes and styles. The latter point was famously featured in the American reality TV show *Queer Eye for the Straight Guy* (first appearing in 2003), where five gay men "make over" a straight man.[68] But the metrosexual also suggests the boy-man.

Where did the metrosexual come from? Simpson and others argue that he is a creation of modern consumer capitalism, whose marketers have found that the old-fashioned male provider is no longer sufficient to generate sales. "The stoic, self-denying, modest straight male," claims Simpson, "didn't shop enough (his role was to earn money for his wife to spend), and so he had to be replaced by a new kind of man, one less certain of his identity and much more interested in his image—that is to say, one who was much more interested in being looked at." The commercial eroticization of the male body, notes Bordo, may have borrowed many of its themes from gay culture. Still, it was embraced by straight men intent on attracting women not just (or even) with their power and wealth but with their looks and sex appeal.[69]

But the metrosexual cannot be explained merely as a manipulation of merchandisers. The look and manner had to meet the needs of modern twenty- and thirty-somethings. Again, Simpson offers a theory. Young men increasingly feel emasculated by the successful entry of women into formerly male spaces. And so more independent powerful women demand attractive men (just as wealthy men expected attractive women in the past). Moreover, the less men can rely on their wives or girlfriends, the more they have to buy their own underwear and take care of their own appearance. The metrosexual may be the effect, as Simpson suggests, of "the rise of feminism and the fall of the nuclear family, where straight men were increasingly single, uncertain of their identity, and socially emasculated in a world where women were still regents of the private sphere but also competitive in the public world."[70]

But there may be still more. Hidden in the trendy "metrosexual" male is often a longing to preserve a cherished childhood. If we look closer, we see that the image and look of the metrosexual is strikingly boyish. Not only do "metros" try to preserve a youthful appearance by dying their hair and moisturizing their skin, but many go further by removing all body hair (a new razor, Bodygroom, appeared in 2005 for this purpose) and by cultivating a prepubescent look. This stress on appearance has more in common with the insecurity and narcissism of the teenage years than with the elegance of Fred Astaire or the bourgeois dandy of the past. It is no surprise that men stuck in the emotional life of a teenager would try to make themselves more physically boylike. The appeal of looking younger is not merely fashion and style or even avoiding the tell-tale marks of aging in skin, hair, and body. It is about holding onto the look of the young teen, still cute but also cool, a kid who never has to grow up fully.

And that pretty much summarizes the dilemma of the boy-man today. While most men of the World War II generation embraced maturity as it was defined for them when they returned to civilian life, the rebels of that generation "invented" the cool. Boomers made it a badge of their identity by denying age and in nostalgic regression. For the twenty- and thirty-year-olds of today, the cool is less about rebellion or defining their generation. They have gone further. It is a natural world unto itself that knows no other, where increasing emotional intensity and thrills mark progress, where pleasures across generations are shunned, and where the look of the teen becomes the ideal.

What's Going On?

How do we explain the culture of "endless thrills" that has emerged with such force in the last twenty to thirty years? Two distinct (though not contradictory) arguments, rooted in history, help illuminate what I have described in the last two chapters: One explanation focuses on how the thrill culture compensates for "losses" in masculine power and meaning caused by economic and social change. The second explanation stresses how consumer culture itself has created a thrill culture that has perpetuated the boyhood of men. Both had roots that extend beyond the experience of my son's generation.

Today's boy-man is unintelligible without reference to the declining economic and social status of American men. Beginning in the 1970s, real wages stagnated, dual-job marriages proliferated, and other changes reduced the "payoff" of patriarchy and its culture of restraint, refinement, and responsibility. These changes both emasculated men (making "compensation" a psychological necessity) and also reduced male responsibility in work and family, making their lives less "mature." A big decline in male economic power occurred in the 1980s when the median hourly wage for all American men fell 5 percent while the bottom 75 percent of male wage earners saw a reduction of 21 percent. But things have not improved much in recent years. In 2004, the median income of American men in their thirties was still only $35,010, 12 percent less (adjusted for inflation) than that of men of the same age some thirty years earlier. This was not the promise of more and more that generations of sons had come to anticipate. As Amy Best notes, only one in five young men can expect to do better economically than his father. But, at the same time, "as youth encounter an adult world of emptying opportunity, they are also drawn into a culture of hyperconsumption, where desire runs free and the accumulation of endless objects is *the* measure of 'having made it.'"[71] The boy-man culture of consumption and thrills is a substitute for an unattainable world of family but also a positive rejection of that world of responsibility and refinement.

At the core of the change is the decline and delay of the social markers of male maturity. These facts are well know but worth briefly repeating. In sum, marriage is often delayed long after finishing school and getting a job; childbearing may never come; and divorce leads often to a social reversion to "boyhood" again. In a survey comparing high school graduates from 1960 and 1980, the sociologist Marlis Buchmann finds that within four years, only 11 percent of the latter group had finished school, married, and had kids, while 23 percent of the 1960 graduates had already reached these markers of adulthood. This was a trend that continued into the era of Gen X. By 1991, the mean age of men when they first married was 26.3. In 2000, that mean rose to twenty-seven, and 30 percent of men thirty to thirty-four had never married (rising to 32 percent four years later).[72]

As telling are the data offered in Robert Putnam's famous *Bowling Alone* (2000) that detail the changing involvement of young adults in society. While 80 percent of men born in the 1920s (the Greatest Generation) saw military service, only 10 percent of those born in the

1960s did. This comparison of grandparents and their adult grand-children shows an amazing change. Those born in the 1920s were much more likely to trust other people than those born in the 1960s (50 percent vs. 20 percent). The older group voted at nearly twice the rate (80–85 percent vs. 45–50 percent). They were twice as like to attend church regularly (45 percent vs. 25 percent), were much more likely to participate in a community project (35 percent vs. 15–20 percent), and they belonged to 1.9 civic groups per capita as compared to only 1.1 for the younger generation. Putnam attributes half of this change to the impact of generational turnover.[73] Civil engagement has long been a marker of male maturity, and, despite new opportunities (like the reduction of the voting age to eighteen in 1971), few of the men who were born in the 1960s and came to maturity in the 1980s took advantage of them. This evidence does not capture all of Generation X (many of whom were born in the 1970s and early 1980s), but it does suggest a trend toward the boy-man.

There are many reasons for this delay or abandonment of the emblems of the grown-up, but the decreasing role and authority that came with patriarchal providership is certainly a major one. While patriarchy has long historical roots, the power and status that went with the family's total dependency on the father's income is relatively recent and short lived. In 1955, only 18 percent of mothers with preschool children were in the workforce. For the rest of American families, the husbands were virtually exclusive providers. By 2004, 62 percent of mothers with preschoolers were employed (as were 71 percent of mothers with children under eighteen years of age). In a lot of cases, the father remained the major provider but was no longer the exclusive one. And as women enter the workforce and thus often delay marriage and reduce or (less often) reject childbearing, the vaunted male role of providership diminishes further. Boomer women began the trend (17 percent of women born in the 1950s are childless, up from 9 percent of women born in the 1930s). The proportion of households consisting of married couples with kids dropped from 45 percent in 1972 to 24 percent by 2000. Only one in five married couples fulfilled the traditional dyad of male breadwinner and female housewife in 2000.[74]

Not only did this change undermine traditional male notions of self-worth as exclusive providers, but it reduced one of the main ways that men defined their adult identity—as autonomous actors in the public realm and protectors of private life and relationships. With women entering the male-dominated public sphere, men were expected to adopt the traditional trait of female maturity—nurturing private relations in the family. While this has, of course, transformed manhood for many, creating a more symmetrical family, a combination of factors has actually led to movement in the opposite direction. The rate of births outside of marriage has risen from 5 percent to nearly a third between 1960 and 2000 (increasing from a third to two-thirds for black women). This may be a sign of the apparent declining need for fathers, but it is much more a measure of diminishing male acceptance of responsibility for rearing their offspring.[75] It is not merely that men have been "deprived" of their providership roles; many have abandoned them. Despite the advantages of the androgynizing of the public and private spheres, it has contributed to male frustration and confusion over what it means to be a man. The general consequences of the new world of men are clear—a decline in and delay of commitment to marriage and family and a rejection of responsibility to the past and future (including the abandonment of earlier commitment to social causes).[76]

Adding to the decline of these emblems of male maturity, men have been frustrated and confused by the dissonance between male expectations and the reality they encounter. Susan Faludi's *Stiffed: The Betrayal of the American Man* offers an ambitious journalistic account of this phenomenon. Her premise is that men fail to adjust to the modern world not only because they have lost power but because they feel betrayed at the collapse of the heroic model of male maturity that their fathers claimed to exemplify. That pride was based on the myth of the Greatest Generation: "The boys, molded into men [by the war], would return to find wives, form their families, and take their places as adults in the community of a nation taking its place as a grown-up power in the world." Of course, many of the "warriors" of that generation didn't fight but served behind the lines, and most had had to be drafted. Even more, plenty of World War II vets rebelled against this scenario as their generation was forced into accepting corporate subordination and, often, the thanklessness of being the provider. And not a few men of my own boomer generation shared in this rebellion, at least for a time. But Faludi does not focus on the rebels. Rather, she looks to those men who embraced but felt betrayed by their father's ideals, especially those boomers who grew up in the shadow of World War II heroism but had only the tawdry experience of Vietnam to shape their manhood. The Vietnam vet, who thought that a bright future of steady, high-paying jobs upon his return that would earn him love and respect from a grateful family, found instead real wages in decline, delayed marriage, and the bewilderment of having both to be a provider and to change diapers. As Faludi put it: "The boy who had been told he was going to be the master of the universe and all that was in it found himself master of nothing."[77]

So this arguably has led to the compensatory reaction in what Faludi calls the ornamental culture, a commercialism that ultimately is based on reaction to and compensation for the sheer struggle of finding oneself without the guideposts of the past. In the wake of the Vietnam War and the stagflation of the 1970s, which seemed to betray the glorious and secure future of boomer men, these bewildered men were offered a replacement in ornamental culture. According to Faludi, "If the nation would not provide an enemy to fight, he could go to war at home. If there was to be no brotherhood, he would take his stand alone," as is obviously shown in the Rambo series. This pattern continued, of course, with boomer sons: "In the coming media and entertainment age the team of men at work would be replaced by the individual man on display," the action heroes and rock stars who "encouraged young men to see surliness, hostility and violence as expressions of glamour." Thus Faludi finds that "the internal qualities once said to embody manhood—sure-footedness, inner strength, confidence of purpose—are merchandised to men to enhance their manliness." The action hero turns out to be little different from the metrosexual pretty boy. Both are about showcasing the male. "In a culture of ornament, manhood is defined by appearance, by youth and attractiveness . . . , the same traits that have long been designated as the essence of feminine vanity."[78] And like the women of the 1950s, who were deprived of access to the worlds of power and productivity and had to be content with the ornaments of extreme femininity, men have fallen into a similar state and compensated for it with symbols of masculine display. This is what the thrill culture is all about.

But is that all there is to it? Is the thrill culture merely a shallow and illusory replacement for the loss of patriarchy? Is it about finding a substitute for the father's (or grandfather's) band of brothers? Can the thrill culture be reduced to the simple fact that men today can avoid the constraints of responsibility by extending boyhood culture seemingly endlessly into adulthood as men delay or avoid the constraints of family and marriage?

I've argued in this book that consumer culture has had an independent impact, at least, pricking the bud of that urge to remain the boy-man. But I think that there may be more. There are some things about consumer culture that explain the particular character of the stories and thrills that have attracted young men especially, but not exclusively, since the 1980s. Without overly prolonging this chapter, let me suggest points of departure:

As we have seen, businesses have an incentive to expand sales by broadening the age range of their products' consumers. Marketers have created the "tween," appealing across age gaps to "kidsults," "middle youth," and "adultescents."[79] This is obvious in the shrinking cultural distance between G- and R-rated movies that accelerated with the rise of the profitable PG-13 feature. The same is true of the growth of T-rated video games, reaching the psyches of young adults but also teens and even "tweens." This means appealing, for example, both to the potty humor of kids and to the cynicism and aggressive rebellion of teens and young men. It leads to video games that attract ten-year-olds but also thirty-year-old Gen Xers. This trend in marketing popular culture both corrupts the developing psyche of children and retards or denies teens and young adults any recognition of aesthetic markers of maturity. The commercial culture of the cool—dating from the 1930s and 1940s with the appearance of superhero fiction and crime and horror comics—appeals to men long after their years of rebellion from parents and membership in a youth peer culture. One reason for this attraction is that culture has abandoned the theme of growing up and thus enables appeals across age groups to the benefit of sales. The result is a commercialism that reinforces a perpetual adolescence in revolt against an adult authority that no longer exists.

Commercial culture has also promoted male hedonism through advertising, new men's magazines, and the celebrity culture, trumpeting the man's right to his own stuff and the naturalness of his pleasure. This has challenged not only the bourgeois identity of the adult male with self-constraint and even personal austerity but also the expectation that he be a provider. Veblen's notion of men vicariously consuming through wives (and children) has increasingly been replaced with personal male consumption. In their time, *Esquire* and *Playboy* legitimated this hedonism by selling male spending under the cover of its promise of refinement and well-earned status (as well as freedom from domesticity). This consumer culture of the cool is, as I have noted, a descendent of the bohemian world of the 1960s hippie. It has produced, as the conservative cultural critic David Brooks notes, Bobos (bohemian bourgeois) or, to modify his argument slightly, boy-men in consumption who are responsible bourgeois professionals in work.[80]

By the late 1980s, male pleasure was shorn of those promises of cultural maturity and symbolic accomplishment. *Maxim* and *FHM* magazines and much advertising aggressively and defiantly celebrate the frat boy nation. No longer has male hedonism to do with learning how to be well-dressed or cultivate a taste for wine, women, and song. It is about immediate satisfaction of the appetite and pleasures of the youth. Men's media and advertising both identify the man's immediate desires with freedom and with the mien of the teen and young man. Youth and freedom are the same thing. No longer does consumer culture point to the ladder of maturity (even if that meant, as it did a generation ago, the line of cars that led to earned luxury and status in the Cadillac). A teen or twenty-something male should get what he wants now even if that is an SUV bought on a six-year loan.

Instead of a commercial status system based on achievement (or wealth) and refinement, the commercial culture today offers status based on peer culture and fashion or innovation. This status has been for a long time part of the "cool." Peer culture grew with the isolation of youth from adults in the early twentieth century with the decline of apprenticeship and the development of mass enrollment in high school and college. Driving this culture were the waves of fads that had to be "caught" at their height for success in the peer group. Timely embrace of the fad, rather than experience or productive accomplishment, marked status in the peer group, whose members shared a lack of experience and accomplishment. Fads and fashion became the tools for displaying the self in that elusive blend of individual distinction and social participation that so often drives peer culture. The specific brands and products that you buy define you; these tell others how you fit in and stand out.[81] This commercial status system also produced the illusion of exciting innovation as the hot looks of the latest fashion or fresh face of the trendy celebrity were offered consumers only to be replaced soon by a new look and a new star. The flow of the past is forgotten and the future (beyond the immediate) is ignored (even if retro styles are sometimes dusted off and sold as "new" to capture an ephemeral past). And all of this is very profitable.

Finally, the visceral appeal of the "ride" or the sensual impact of the spectacle, producing what Henry Jenkins calls the "wow climax," was an essential product of the mass commercial culture.[82] It certainly wasn't new to the late twentieth century but had permeated the staging of vaudeville at the end of the nineteenth century and was a guiding principle of early-twentieth-century movies, for example. But the wow climax certainly became more central to the pleasures of men from the end of the 1970s with the emergence of action-hero movies, new thrill rides in amusement parks, and video games in the arcades. As we have seen, these pleasures, disassociated from memory or anticipation of the future, become essentially sensual. The problem isn't their sensuality as such but the addictive intensification of pleasure that many identify with progress as in the ever more violent scene, higher and faster roller coaster, or the ever more graphically rich video game. As is shown in theme parks, the thrilling drives out the uplifting and memorable.

In the end, the problem may be a combination of a decline in markers of maturity and the commercialized cool. As the philosopher Bruce Wilshire argues, the disappearance of rituals engaging men (and women) deeply and progressively in nature and social life leads to obsessive needs for episodic hits of the ecstasy so easily provided by commodities. Moreover, if one experiences "satisfactions so great and early [as consumerism offers] that one is fixated on them, [one] fails to achieve the greater satisfactions that might have come from long work and more risk"—thus short-circuiting maturation.[83]

It would be easy to blame all this on the young and complain about their "succumbing" to the temptations of consumer culture or pitifully compensating for their loss of the markers of maturity by embracing a phony world of aggression and display. But this has been a long time coming, and my and my father's generation had a lot to do with the world of endless thrills.

chapter 7.

Life Beyond PLEASURE ISLAND

Carlo Collodi's *Pinocchio* tells the story of a puppet who wants to be a real boy but finds that only after he abandons the temptations of Pleasure Island and embraces responsibility can he transform his wooden self and become capable of growing up. This is a Victorian morality tale that still worked in the 1940s when Disney made it into a feature-length cartoon, and it continued to appeal decades later in rereleases and on TV. It made a case for a genteel notion of maturity based on self-control, responsibility to others, and ultimately on learning from one's life and mistakes. It is a nearly perfect critique of the boy-man culture of today and serves as an introduction to the concluding theme of this book—the problem of finding alternatives to the culture of male immaturity today.

Collodi would certainly agree that there is something seriously wrong in the boy-man as he affects the lives of his partner, his offspring, his community, and himself. Basically, the problem is that the boy-man fixates on adolescent longings for the intensity and variety of experience and escape from his parents and family—just as Pinocchio is lured to Pleasure Island and disobeys his maker-father Geppetto. And Collodi certainly would agree with a Victorian or genteel assessment of the problem: The boy-man stands on the treadmill of endless novelty and passively looks for "hits" of pleasure while the adult man cultivates, savors, and gives back. The boy-man can share in games with his children but offers few guideposts for his offspring's future. He is skeptical of tradition and puffery and is reluctant to join groups, but in his quest for excitement and a personal reality he cuts himself off from deeper and sustained intimacy with friends and community. Finally, the boy-man remains free and open to change, but, because he sloughs off the past and makes the instant and intense the measure of aliveness, he abandons the possibility of accumulating and savoring experience. The error of the boy-man is not that he does not "act his age" but that he does not grow-up. The virtue of the adult is not that he has matured (meaning reached a plateau) but that he has become independent in a lifelong quest for growing and relating.

These are solid tenets of our predecessors, genteel renderings of the adult male life (largely as applicable to women) that transcend the evils of patriarchy. In sentimentalized and imperfect ways, even the heroes in those old movies and TV westerns that I saw as a kid in the 1950s exemplified these ideals. While recently watching episodes of *Father Knows Best* from the mid-1950s, I could not help but think, "What's wrong with this?" and "I wish I could be Jim Anderson and have Bud for a son." But then I realized that there were few Anderson homes even in the 1950s and that we cannot turn back the clock.

Three generations of men have challenged the genteel ideal of manhood. Over time, they have abandoned traditional markers of male maturity and embraced perpetual adolescence, and, because commercial culture reinforces both trends, today the youngest generation has little experience with or taste for alternatives (genteel or otherwise). While personal solutions based on sound advice from psychologists may inspire individual boy-men to reassess their lives, this won't do much to transform the abiding culture of male immaturity. That culture certainly is a large portion of the problem, but it is also a reflection of deep social and economic changes that cannot be wished away. While we may lament the social, cultural, and personal costs of being a boy-man and long for the possibilities and pleasures of being a grown up, one of the key points of this book has been that we must recognize the historical changes that landed us in our current predicament. Can we realistically update Collodi's Victorian advice? Is it possible to be a grown-up today? Is it even desirable?

Clearly, most traditional markers of male maturity have disappeared. Of course, adulthood as exemplified by Judge Hardy was traditional only in a very narrow sense. It was certainly a product of modernity, when life choices expanded, competition increased, and, with these changes, there came the need for knowledge and behavior that marked the adult from the child. Thus "growing up" became an especially urgent task, requiring the separation of the young from the old and their systematic nurture into self-disciplined adults. This is, in part, the point of Philippe Aries's famous *Centuries of Childhood*.[1] One doesn't have to embrace this historical claim to recognize that adulthood has in the past required *social* benchmarks signaling to all its arrival: marriage, childbearing, permanent employment, and the completion of education, for example. In former generations, these social transitions came within a few years of one another (although this too was relatively new, arriving for most American men only in the early twentieth century). These benchmarks gave everyone a clear understanding that the boy had become the man. But as we have seen, all this changed with the coming of the boomers to adulthood in the 1960s and has been much accelerated since the 1980s.

We have become, according to Robert Bly, a "sibling society," insofar as both the young (Gen Xers) and their parents (boomers) have abandoned adulthood, all too often embracing a culture that cynically debunks authority based on experience and escapes into memories of youth. Both generations have abjured their roles as mentors of the young—today's and tomorrow's. "A dignified adult life, with its heights and depths, protected by wisely kept secrets, once attracted children in such a way that they wanted to become adults. . . . Now, they see incoherent emptiness and chaos." There is nothing new in Bly's thoughts on this. In 1970, the anthropologist Margaret Mead claimed we had become a prefigurative society, where adults have been obliged to abandon old ideals in the wake of rapid technological, social, and cultural change and to learn from the young.[2] In the wake of the 1960s explosion of innovation, the liberal Mead could look upon this shift to a youth-oriented culture positively, as did so many others of that era. By the end of the century, however, Bly (hardly a conservative) took a very different tone.[3]

According to *Sibling Society*, this change has been a long process, beginning with the World War II vets who abandoned the city's troubles for the suburbs. Boomers followed, first choosing drugs and self-indulgent rebellion and then greed instead of movements for change over the long haul. Finally, the process culminated in the thrill-seeking cynicism of today's youth. Siblings all, and increasingly like perpetual adolescents, they are slaves of instant gratification and in rebellion against an adulthood that doesn't exist. Echoing Phillip Wylie and others from the 1940s and 1950s, Bly argues that men no longer experience the "oedipal wall" of the past in being forced to compete

with the omnipresent authoritarian father; thus few either hate or respect their dads. With no one to rebel against or to model themselves
after, "there is a tendency to keep everything at a distance, to treat
everything ironically, with no investment in one's investment."[4]

Bly is extreme, of course, but doesn't a lot of his argument ring
true? We've seen it again and again, in the cynical and disengaged culture of TV sitcoms like *Seinfeld*, *Married with Children*, and *Two and
a Half Men*, but also in the 1940s alienation of Holden Caulfield in
The Catcher in the Rye. Moreover, Bly's book reflects a wider view that
parents have abandoned old cultural markers, leaving the young no
aspirational goals. The result is that youth is no longer a stage of life
but a "refuge" from the now tangled and obscured path to maturity.
This leads to a culture of immediacy and makes identity, which requires continuity with the past and future, elusive.[5] All this has led
to confusion for youth, a "generation on hold" as sociologist James
Côté describes the situation, "without sufficient external guidance or
internal resources with which to take stock and mature."[6] The famous
"moratorium" of an extended youth that psychologist Erik Erikson
had hoped might lead to a rich chosen identity in the 1960s has all
too often become a period of uncertainty, producing no resolution.[7]
Without firm ties to the past against which even to rebel, it has become
difficult to imagine a future and create identity-defining goals.

Our age has systematically rejected old models of maturity without embracing new ones. Without the certainty of social indicators
of maturity, adulthood becomes, as Côté notes, "more a psychological process than a social one." This liberates us from convention and
traditional social expectations and taboos. It allows us to experiment
with alternative life courses and to create new models of adulthood in
a self-realizing approach to growing up that Côté calls "developmental individualization." This is a process of "cognitive growth, identity
formation and emotional maturity" that, along with "finding and developing one's special skills, spiritual awareness," should lead to that
wonderful combination of autonomous rationality and emotional re-
latedness. It should also lead to a return to civic engagement that en-
compasses the formula of a "universalizing consciousness with a caring particularism" (a variation of the bumper sticker "Think Globally,
Act Locally" but, more to the point, an expression of much modern
humanistic psychology).[8]

These, however, are very difficult paths for anyone and are bound
to elude the majority of both men and women given their lack of

psychological resources and social connections.[9] Today we not only have lost many of the old social rites of passage into adulthood, but we have precious few cultural guideposts to lead us to psychological maturity. In the end, a still larger problem looms—psychological adulthood in an era of declining social networks is not enough and won't work. Part of the task of forming a secure and meaningful identity is engagement with others not only in personal relationships but also by creating community bonds and responsibilities. But again, the decline of these social ties (as so obviously marked by reduced involvement in political and social movements) has been replaced by the commercial culture of masculinity. It is hardly surprising, then, that adolescence (an age that originally meant "growing up") has become a permanent peer culture of the "cool," a rejection of the grown-up.[10]

Probably such proscriptions for modern maturity are even more difficult for men than women to achieve. Men easily detach themselves from social responsibility (in parenting especially). The breakdown of the social constraints of adulthood over the past thirty years has been manifested in the rise of fatherless children in the United States (23 million children today will be brought up without a man in the house). Male "growing-up rituals," as seen in the action-hero movies that have replaced military experience and in other "male adventures," are still riddled with archaic antisocial appeals (martial heroism especially) that are irrelevant and even hostile to the modern world (especially gender relations). Moreover, ideas about growing up male, even those based on "developmental individualization," have a distinctly bourgeois and genteel cast to them and have been cast aside for that reason. As James Twitchell's *Where Men Hide* shows, modern maleness may not be about "growing up," and, in their cluttered garages, dens, and even pick-up trucks, men not only evade women but resist the genteel implications of the old standards of male maturity, which many men see as an imposition of women.[11]

In any case, even if mature men and women share much, ideas about masculinity inevitability shape male maturity and immaturity. Thus, competing notions about what a modern adult man should be, think, and feel enter into the discussion. Three alternatives to the boy-man are often proposed: First is the benevolent patriarch, restrained and made caring and responsible by religious faith, which shames men into abandoning their wild impulses for the pleasures and duties of bourgeois providership as the head of the household. These ideas run through movements like the Promise Keepers and the Million Man March of the 1990s.[12]

Second is the semisecular but myth-inspired longing of men to recover a lost sense of a caring and sacrificing masculinity, as, for example, at Robert Bly's Iron John retreats. Both of these solutions remain ineffectual and often reinforce some of the most authoritarian and least rational aspects of earlier patriarchal ideals. Bly's retreats are essentially escapist, as the sociologist Michael Kimmel argues, and despite Bly's hostility to the "sibling society," the participants withdraw into a boy's world of fantasy.[13]

Still, a third solution is the nurturing and emotionally expressive role of the androgynous New Man, who abandons his old patriarchal privileges and embraces equality in private and public roles. But how many men (or women) can distinguish this approach from the stereotypical wimp?[14]

In *The Book of Guys*, the American humorist Garrison Keillor expresses a common view from the 1990s that is probably still true: "Years ago, manhood was an opportunity for achievement, and now it is a problem to be overcome." This confusion is reflected the potpourri of male and father groups active today, ranging from the Fathers' Rights Association and the New Warrior Trainers to the National Association of Dads and Kids. The Browsers' Bookmobile of the National Men's Resource Center houses more than 1,000 books, tapes, and videos on sixty different men's issues. Its Web site offers dozens of books and articles on everything from "The Importance of Father Love for Child Well-Being" and "Fathers Juggle Work, Kids, and Stress, Too!" to "Helping Your Teen Decide What to Do After High School."[15] The Fatherhood Project, a traveling exhibit, offers a more sentimental approach, claiming to be "about the love that children need. But it is also about the need that fathers have to love." More assertive of men's rights is the claim of the National Fatherhood Initiative that "fathers make unique and irreplaceable contributions to the lives of children." Wade Horn, a former president of the group and later an official in the Bush administration, noted in 1999 that they reject making "androgyny as a goal." Summarizing the confusion, the journalist James Paterson asks, "Should we master the pony tail and the distribution of pills, fruit roll-ups and consolation . . . or stick to fatherly advice about baseball and shaving? Maybe we just need to grab any territory we can before it all disappears into a video screen."[16] If it is so unclear what it means to be an adult man and father, is it a surprise that many who can't embrace the abstract goal of "developmental individualization" opt for boy-manhood instead?

In any case, popular culture seems to trump all of these alternatives. While men in their twenties have become economically marginalized, these same men without responsibilities and thus with lots of pocket money have become major targets for advertisers, who encourage an infantile longing for instant gratification.[17] This is not to say that the young haven't resisted these blandishments. We did it in the 1960s (or at least we thought we did), and others have followed. But this opposition isn't easy to sustain. Affluence has certainly reduced the necessity of sacrifice and the need to pool resources, perhaps encouraging the culture of narcissism, that "state of restless, perpetually unsatisfied desire" that Christopher Lasch described in 1979.[18] This results in what Côté calls "default individualization," the course followed because it is an easy alternative to developmental individualization.[19]

But this argument doesn't take us far enough. It doesn't explain specifically the regressive character of our culture of narcissism. To do that we need to consider the fact that returning to or never leaving childhood has become far more attractive since the mid-twentieth century. This is in part because being a kid is more fun than ever—in recent years the young have experienced much less subordination to their elders and less need to sacrifice for the comforts of age. As we have seen, men, even after they accept adult responsibilities in work and family, remain nostalgic for the play of their childhood and youth. And today youth are able to extend the pleasures of the cool teen into their twenties and well beyond because that culture of consumption gives them permission to delay and evade the self-denial of family and marriage. In effect, the makers of modern consumer and media culture have learned how to feed on the rejection and collapse of social markers of maturity and the longing to return to or retain youth. No longer is youth a stage quickly and even eagerly passed through but a semipermanent lifestyle. The result is that men and boys see the same PG-13 movies, play with the same T- and M-rated video games, and line up for the same thrill rides at Island of Adventure.

This analysis, however, is still too facile. The problem isn't just the path of least resistance or the reluctance of men to abandon the pleasures of an indulged youth. For Susan Faludi and others, the consumer culture is not really a product of passivity or narcissism. It is also an answer to the betrayal of the promise of masculine power, a substitute for the loss of male dreams of a "band-of-brothers" heroism and the satisfactions of the more bourgeois pleasures of providership. I must admit I never felt betrayal, certainly not by my father or the promises of the "Greatest Generation," but I think that Faludi's argument rings true for many American working-class, minority men, and even men of my class and background.

I would add still one more point. The all-powerful consumer culture is not a product of passivity or merely an expression of narcissistic desire; nor is it just compensation for loss. It is an active force that has packaged and packed pleasure into a thrill culture that displaces refinement and sociotemporal ties. That thrill culture seems to defy all definitions of maturation and makes it very difficult to embrace a more thoughtful and responsible way of being. It has challenged the "reality principle" of the ordered life promoted in Freud's notion of "civilization." Instead, we have a deregulated life where the "pleasure principle dominates with the inevitable trade-off of an exchange of some security of self for immediate happiness." The result has been ever-changing "fluid identities" as described by the Polish philosopher Zygmunt Bauman. We are "seduced by the infinite possibility and constant renewal promoted by the consumer market, of rejoicing in the chance of putting on and taking off identities, of spending one's life in the never ending chase after ever more intense sensations and even more exhilarating experience." There could scarcely be a better description of the boy-man.[20]

In a way, this book has been a story about the broadening in space and time of the peer culture of youth. At the beginning of the century, it was limited to street corners and the occasional visit to the nickelodeon or amusement park. By midcentury it had spread out and become more invasive with the transistor radio, rock music, and the drive-in; today, with Internet social-networking services like MySpace and Facebook, it is far more pervasive, far more accessible—anytime, almost anywhere. And this youth culture, as it dips into younger ages and starts earlier, also lasts much longer. As often noted, peer culture's default status is a result of the disappearance of the elder preparing the young for the future but also of a youth that has embraced a self-defining rejection of the past. The result is a culture of the infinite present, driven not by memory and anticipation but by thrills that have replaced identity-shaping initiation rites. All this leads to an endless quest for that contradictory mix of self-isolating individuality and fleeting belonging that propels and defines the peer culture.

Some Hope?

These trends, rooted deeply in social, economic, and cultural changes, show us the futility of singling out today's youth for blame or even finding the origins of the boy-man culture in the "excesses" of boomers, but these developments also suggest that there are no easy answers. Psychologists may counsel individual therapies to particular problems. They have been doing just that, at least since the publication of the Dan Kiley's *Peter Pan Syndrome* in 1983, which has vivid descriptions of and advice for dealing with the man who is "fun, charming very often successful" but "in relationships . . . frustrating, emotionally immature, and unable to handle love or responsibility."[21] Still, I would argue that the root of male immaturity is ultimately not personal but cultural. We live in a world that glorifies boyhood and fails to offer modern alternatives to rejected models of adulthood.

So does all this suggest a pessimistic conclusion—that men are so deeply mired in a society, economy, and culture that encourage immaturity and obscure the possibility of being a modern grown-up that nothing can be done? Not necessarily. Let me suggest some points of departure for rethinking male maturity.

First, we cannot and should not try to go back to the ideal of maturity as it was portrayed in the 1950s. It didn't work well then, and it won't work now. However, we need to recognize that, while the old markers of maturity are largely gone and today's media and advertising strongly encourage us to join the cynical thrill culture of the boy-man, we can change course and embrace alternatives. We need to think how we might modernize old ideas of male maturity shorn of traditionalism, asceticism, and authoritarianism. Faludi is right to note that this is particularly difficult for modern men because, unlike the feminists of the 1960s and 1970s, they have no external enemy (even "demanding feminists" or affirmative-action advocates won't really serve this purpose). Instead, their enemy is their own internalized expectations of masculinity, and we have to rethink these and discard many of them.

Second, we must learn to celebrate rather than deny generational difference. This means that men of my generation need finally to give up their struggles and obsessions with their fathers and, with this, their fixation on youth. This is a personal matter to be worked out in conversations across the generations or, when this is no longer possible, in thinking about their fathers' time and how that era shaped and limited these men (as I do in this book). My generation needs to recognize more fully that we are the fathers (and, yes, often grandfathers now) and learn to be better mentors. And my sons' generation needs to abandon its fixation on permanent boyhood and embrace the pleasures of maturity.

My generation doesn't or shouldn't need the old markers of patriarchy, and, despite self-doubts, we must recognize that we have experiences to share. This may mean another try at mentoring the young in joint adventures, perhaps in traditional ways (sports and nature exploration) or in less conventional forms (political activism or music). It may also mean "graduating" to new activities that separate the young from the old (not necessarily old men's pleasures like fishing or checkers, but activities that call for skill and experience, even as simple as cultivated conversation).

Third, my own and my sons' generations need to rethink the cynical thrill culture of today's boy-man. This book has tried to show how that culture ultimately is unsatisfying and can lead only to more cynicism and morally empty intensity. Both generations need to think about the possibilities of a culture that embraces accumulated experience, cultivated taste, even "slow" pleasures and finds Hugh Hefner's romping with twenty-year-old blond-haired beauties at his eightieth birthday party the grotesque absurdity that it is.

This will take many forms. We need new stories that explore growing up and being a grown-up. Men may engage in new hobbies that break from the instant and intense appeals of today's video games and offer instead the pleasures of the savored moment and the adventure of prolonged effort. The "slow food" movement is one example. Genteel traditions of gardening, hiking, collecting, and crafts don't have to be imitated, but they can teach us a lot about the value of a less intense, socially and culturally richer aesthetic. This will not be easy given both the satisfactions of the culture of the "cool" and the commercial interests that reinforce it with an endless stream of packed and packaged pleasures. But we need to look for signs that at least some boy-men are dissatisfied with their treadmill lives and frequent failure to establish lasting relationships.

At the same time, we need to recognize that maturity is not about "collecting and piling up experiences and knowledge higher and higher until you are the top dog. It comes from something more humble. . . . It comes from gratitude," as columnist Gary Kamiya reminded us in 2007. It requires the "spirit of regeneration, one that paradoxically springs from an abandonment of illusions. The comedic attitude offers a kind of resignation, a calm surrender to the inevitable. And it's regenerative because it doesn't see change as the enemy. It's an invincible, self-fulfilling belief, one that bubbles up from somewhere unseen."[22] And that is very different from thrill seeking.

Finally, we must recognize that as adults (and, equally, as men) we have responsibilities to our partners, families, and communities beyond our own need for experience and pleasure. This will mean transcending the old, often unsatisfying role of the father-provider and the posturing power plays of the traditional male hero. We can learn from the failures of the "pal dad" of my own and my father's generations and recognize that more successful relationships with partners and children will involve both a commitment of more time to personal life and clearer, less ambiguous roles for husbands and fathers. To be a responsible contributor to his community, the mature modern man doesn't have to join a "band of brothers" (as in World War II) but can share leadership with women and men across the ages of life. As Faludi says, "if husbanding a society is not the exclusive calling of husbands, all the better for men's future. Because as men struggle to free themselves from their crisis, their task is not, in the end, to figure out how to be masculine—rather, their masculinity lies in figuring out how to be human."[23]

This too is no easy task, so disappointing have been our efforts across our three generations. But it is time to stop whining and evading. When I talk to friends my age, we often come to a disheartening point—just how little our generation has contributed positively to history. But this is an unfair self-indictment. We helped to bring greater equality between the races and sexes and, despite our many excesses, a more relaxed, tolerant culture that has much potential still for fostering more open relationships between the generations. We certainly have not lived up to that potential yet. But there still is time, and there are thousands of ways to make a difference. Hopefully this book will be one contribution.

Acknowledgments

This book owes much to friends and colleagues. My agent Steven Wasserman helped me avoid trying to write a book that I shouldn't write and helped me find my voice in writing the book I should. Others who shared ideas include Jim Block, Garry Chick, Tom Engelhardt, Paula Fass, John Gillis, Miriam Forman-Brunell, Caroline Hinkle, Stephen Kline, Nancy Kranich, Steven Mintz, Jorge Schement, and John K. Walton. My editor, Peter Dimock, once again has offered invaluable guidance and support. Michael Haskell's copyediting has truly been peerless. Although they may not know it, the young men in my family—my sons, but also my nephew, Cameron—provided insight and even inspiration for this book.

I especially want to thank Elisa Schement, my student as an undergraduate and now a friend, who has known more than a few boy-men. She provided valuable advice in thinking about this subject, doing interviews, and helping edit the book in its early stages.

Notes

Introduction: Where Have All the Men Gone?

1. Interviews by Elisa Schement, January 2006, in Los Angeles and elsewhere by phone. Her involvement in this project, especially in reading and editing the early stages is much appreciated.

2. Herbert Kline, *A Population History of the United States* (New York: Cambridge University Press, 2004), chap. 8; "Trends," *American Demographics* 25, no. 9 (November 2003): 24–29; Judith Stacey, *Brave New Families: Stories of Domestic Upheaval in Late-Twentieth-Century America* (New York: Basic Books, 1990), 9–15; Ronald Levant, "The Crisis of Connection Between Men and Women," *Journal of Men's Studies* 5 (August 1999): 3–4; "A Good Man Is Hard to Find; They're All in Mom's Basement Playing Video Games," *Pittsburgh Post-Gazette*, 3 November 2003; A. Cavalli, "Prolonging Youth in Italy: 'Being in No Hurry,'" in *Youth in Europe*, ed. A. Cavalli and O. Galland (London: Pinter, 1995), 23–32.

3. U.S. Bureau of the Census, "Estimated Median Age at First Marriage, by Sex: 1890 to Present," Internet release date, 15 September 2004; see http://marriage.about.com/od/statistics/a/medianage.htm (accessed 12 December 2007).

4. "Single Men Responsible for Little but Trouble," *Independent* (London), 9 March 1998; "Marriage 'Unique Effect,'" *Wall Street Journal*, 13 May 2002.

5. Classic expressions of this idea can be found in the literature of evolutionary psychology and anthropology, including Jerome Barkow, Leda Cosmides, and John Tooby, eds., *The Adapted Mind: Evolutionary Psychology and the Generation of Culture* (New York: Oxford University Press, 1992); R. L. Trivers, "Parental Investment and Sexual Selection," in *Sexual Selection*

and the Descent of Man: 1871–1971, ed. B. Campbell (Chicago: Aldine: 1972), 136–79. One of the more recent expressions is David Buss, *The Evolution of Desire: Strategies of Human Mating* (New York: Basic Books, 2003). A popularizing is in Diana Coyle, "Danger: Men at Large," *Independent* (London), 15 March 1998.

6. For a treatment of the economic disadvantages of youth from the 1980s see, James Côté and Anton Allahar, *Generation on Hold: Coming of Age in the Late Twentieth Century* (New York: New York University, 1996), 52–60, and Anya Kamenetz, *Debt Generation: Why Now Is a Terrible Time to Be Young* (New York: Riverhead Books, 2006).

7. Interviews by Elisa Schement, January 2006, in Los Angeles and elsewhere by phone.

8. Howard Stern, quote from a Larry King show, cited in Michiko Kakutani, "Adolescence Rules!" *New York Times,* 11 May 1997.

9. "A Good Man but a Bad Boy," *Newsweek,* 22 March 1982, 37; various obituaries of Chris Farley: *Boston Globe,* 20 December 1997; *Toronto Star,* 21 December 1997; *Variety,* 22 December 1997, 74; *Washington Post,* 19 December 1997.

10. Kakutani, "Adolescence Rules!"

11. Puff Daddy/P. Diddy, www.rockonthenet.com/artists-p/puffdaddy_main.htm, accessed 27 July 2005; Puff Daddy, "It's All About the Benjamins," www.azlyrics.com/lyrics/puffdaddy/itsallaboutthebenaminsremix.html, accessed 23 May 2007.

12. Bob Herbert, "Bush's Echo Chamber," *New York Times,* 19 November 2004.

13. Rich Lowry, "Understanding Bill," *National Review,* 23 June 2004, 12; E. Jane Dickson, "Oh, Do Grow Up: The Generation Gap Has Closed," *Independent* (London), 25 September 1999.

14. Interviews by Elisa Schement, January 2006, in Los Angeles and elsewhere by phone.

15. Interviews by Elisa Schement, January 2006, in Los Angeles and elsewhere by phone.

16. "Hefner," *The Observer,* 15 July 2001, 20; "Tales from the Bunny Farm," *Independent on Sunday* (London), 8 July 2001; 16 December 2002; "Playboy at 50; Hefner's Baby Swings into Middle Age," *Washington Post,* 2 October 2003; "Inside the Playboy Mansion," *Video Business,* 16 December 2002, 38; Scott Allison, " 'What Sort of Man Reads Playboy?' The Self-Reported Influence of Playboy on the Construction of Masculinity," *Journal of Men's Studies* (January 2003): 11, 2, 189–201..

17. Ed Roth, *Confessions of a Rat Fink: The Life and Times of Ed "Big Daddy" Roth* (New York: Pharos Books, 1992). See also his obituary, *New York Times,* 7 April 2001.

18. Barbara Dafoe Whitehead, *Why There Are No Good Men Left: The*

Romantic Plight of the New Single Woman (New York, Broadway Books, 2003). Note also Susan Forward, *Men Who Hate Women and the Women Who Love Them* (New York: Bantam: 1987); "'Bad Boys' Strictly Bad News: Why Do Women Succumb to Their Roguish Charms?" *Toronto Sun*, 1 March 1996.

1. When Fathers Knew Best (or Did They?)

1. Alex McNeil, *Total Television: The Comprehensive Guide to Programming from 1948 to the Present*, 4th ed. (New York: Penguin, 1996), 159.

2. Michael Denning, *Mechanical Accents: Dime Novels and Working-Class Culture in America* (New York: Verso, 1989), 18, 30, 45; Christine Bold, *Selling the Wild West: Popular Western Fiction* (Bloomington: Indiana University Press, 1987), 3–5, 10–15, 33, and chap. 3; Larry Sullivan and Lydia Schuman, *Pioneers, Passionate Ladies, and Private Eyes: Dime Novels, Series Books, and Paperbacks* (New York: Haworth, 1996); Jeffrey Wallmann, *The Western: Parables of the American Dream* (Lubbock: Texas Tech University Press, 1999), 69–71, 95, 125, 128, 137.

3. David Davis, "Ten-Gallon Hero," in *The Western: A Collection of Critical Essays*, ed. James Folsom (New York: Prentice-Hall, 1979), 29; John Tuska "The American Western Cinema: 1903–Present," in *Focus on the Western*, ed. Jack Nachbar (Englewood Cliffs, N.J.: Prentice-Hall, 1974), 25–44. See also, Jim Hitt, *The American West from Fiction (1823–1976) Into Film (1909–1986)* (Jefferson, N.C.: McFarland, 1990); Rita Parks, *The Western Hero in Film and Television Mass Media Mythology* (Ann Arbor, Mich.: UMI Research Press, 1982); Lee Mitchell, *Westerns Making the Man in Fiction and Film* (Chicago: University of Chicago Press, 1994); Andrew Smith, *Shooting Cowboys and Indians: Silent Western Films, American Culture, and the Birth of Hollywood* (Boulder: University Press of Colorado, 2003); Phil Hardy, *The Film Encyclopedia: The Western* (New York: William Morrow, 1983); David Rothel, *Those Great Cowboy Sidekicks* (Metuchen, N.J.: Scarecrow, 1984).

4. John Cawelti, "Savagery, Civilization, and the Western Hero," in *The Western: A Collection of Critical Essays*, ed. James Folsom (New York: Prentice-Hall, 1979), 57–63, shows how cowboys mediated between the inert townies and savage Indians. Peter French stresses the centrality of death in westerns, a very different view from the Christian conquest of death. Peter French, *Cowboy Metaphysics: Ethics and Death in Westerns* (Lanham, Md.: Rowman and Littlefield, 1997), 47; Jane Tompkins, *West of Everything* (New York: Oxford University Press, 1992), 23–45.

5. William Tydeman, "Tom Mix: King of the Hollywood Cowboys," in *Back in the Saddle: Essays on Western Film and Television Actors*, ed. Gary Yoggy (Jefferson, N.C.: McFarland, 1998), 36–37; Peter Stanfield, *Horse*

Opera: The Strange History of the 1930s Singing Cowboy (Urbana: University of Illinois Press, 2002), 72.

6. Stanfield, *Horse Opera*, 11–22; Wallman, *The Western*, 16, 21, 39, 135; Jim Harmon, *Radio Mystery and Adventure* (Jefferson, N.C.: McFarland, 1992), 219–25; David Zinman, *Saturday Afternoon at the Bijou* (New Rochelle, N.Y.: Arlington House, 1973), 153–55; Gary Yoggy, "When Television Wore Six-Guns: Cowboy Heroes on TV," in *Shooting Stars: Heroes and Heroines of Western Films*, ed. Archie McDonald (Bloomington: Indiana University Press, 1987), 123–56.

7. Yoggy, "When Television Wore Six-Guns."

8. *Sky King* episodes: "Disparate Character," 1953, Film and Television Archive, UCLA (hereafter FTA), VA2379T; "Operation Urgent," 1953, FTA, VA2379T; "Two Gun Penny," 1953, FTA, VA2359T.

9. Robert Warshow, "What Is a Western?" in *Focus on the Western*, ed. Jack Nachbar (Englewood Cliffs, N.J.: Prentice-Hall, 1974), 45–56.

10. Michael Tueth, *Laughter in the Living Room: Television Comedy and the American Home Audience* (New York: Peter Lang, 2000), 87.

11. Gunsmoke episodes: "Matt Gets it," 1955, FTA, VA170230; "Gone Straight," 1957, FTA, VA21807; "Baker's Dozen," 1967, FTA, VA11028; "Matt's Love Story," FTA, VA11026; "The Disciple," 1974, FTA, VA104077. Gary Yoggy, "James Arness: Television's Quintessential Western Hero," in *Back in the Saddle: Essays on Western Film and Television Actors*, ed. Gary Yoggy (Jefferson, N.C.: McFarland, 1998), 177–99.

12. *The Life and Legend of Wyatt Earp* episodes: "How Wyatt Earp Became a Marshal," premiere episode, 1955, FTA, VA66511; "Johnny Behan Falls in Love," 1961, FTA, VA 5617T; "Chinese Mary," 1961, FTA, VA18239T; *Have Gun Will Travel*, "Three Bells to Perdido," 1957, FTA, VA104086; *Cheyenne*, "War Party," 1957, FTA, VA101833.

13. *Rawhide* episodes: "The Golden Calf," 1958, FTA, VA170804T; "Incident Below the Brazos," 1959, FTA, VA106167T.

14. *Maverick*, "The War of the Silver Kings," 1957, FTA, VA17039T.

15. *The Rifleman* episodes: "Young Man's Fancy," 1962, FTA, VA7541T; "Assault," 1962, FTA, VA 9786; "I Take This Woman," 1962, FTA, VA14719T; Yoggy, "When Television Wore Six-Guns," 58–60.

16. *Ben Casey*, "But Linda Only Smiled," 1961, FTA, VA2494T; *Dr. Kildare*, "Shining Image," 1961, FTA, VA1491.

17. Chicago Tribune Research, *Men's Clothing Survey* (Chicago: Chicago Tribune, 1958), 3–5, 8, 15.

18. Clothing ads in *Colliers*, 13 April 1912, 7; 12 September 1912, 6; 16 September 1911, 29.

19. Men's clothing features and ads, *Esquire*, October 1949, 42, 48, 54, 75–82; July 1953, 15; October 1956, 19; December 1956, 108; March 1963, 61.

20. Men's clothing features and ads: *Esquire*, March 1963, 61; *Look*, 20 December 1949, 126–27; *Esquire* October 1956, 16–17; March 1956, 108–9.

21. "Madison Avenue Meets Gasoline Alley," Museum of Television and Radio, Beverly Hills, Calif. (hereafter cited as MTR), #116595; *Look*, April 11, 1950, 42; Oldsmobile TV ad, 1953, FTA, VA1781; Ford TV ad, 1958, FTA, VA7719; Ford TV ad 1957, FTA, VA7719; AC oil filter TV ad, 1953, FTA, VA7697.

22. Ajax TV ad, 1965, FTA, VA12868; Mr. Clean TV ad, 1958, FTA, VA7496.

23. Cadillac and Lincoln TV ads, 1954, MTR, #115290; Ford TV ad, 1956, FTA, VA7496; Chevrolet TV ad, 1958, FTA, VA7719; Thunderbird TV ad, 1960, MTR, #115290.

24. Beer TV ads in the 1950s: FTA, VA 5102; beer ad, *Colliers*, 27 November 1948, 77; Corby's whiskey ad, *Look*, 1 October 1954, inside cover; Blatz beer TV ad, 1965? FTA, VA 7496; Aqua Velva TV ad, 1960?, FTA, VA 52239.

25. Frank Fox, *Madison Avenue Goes to War: The Strange Military Career on American Advertising, 1941–45* (Provo, Utah: Brigham Young University Press, 1975), 46, 56, 70–71; Nash ad, *Time*, 20 September 1943, inside front cover; J. Walter Thompson Company, *Fifty Years of Better Ideas: Ford Advertising, 1943–1993* (New York: J. Walter Thompson Company, 1993), np. See also, Cynthia Henthorn, *From Submarines to Suburbs: Selling a Better America, 1939–1959* (Athens: Ohio University Press, 2006).

26. Coke ad, *Time*, 3 December 1945, 31; Plymouth ad, *Time*, 17 December 1945, 1.

27. Hotpoint TV ad, *The Adventures of Ozzie and Harriet*, "David's Engagement," 1955, FTA, VA5777T; Crosley refrigerator TV ad, 1951, FTA, VA7697; Chevrolet TV ad, 1959, FTA, VA28231; insurance ad, *Time*, 7 November 1949, 39; Farmer's Life Insurance TV ad, 1965, MTVR, 12869.

28. Federal Housing Administration, *Home Owner's Guide* (Washington, D.C.: USGPO, 1959), 1.

29. Barbara Ehrenreich, *Hearts of Men* (New York: Doubleday, 1983).

30. Robert Ray, *The Avant-Garde Finds Andy Hardy* (Cambridge, Mass.: Harvard University Press, 1995). Judy Woodside, "Advantages of an Arrested Development: The Onscreen Adolescence of Mickey Rooney" (Ph.D. diss., Pennsylvania State University, 2004).

31. Stephen Frank, *Life with Father: Parenthood and Masculinity in the Nineteenth-Century American North* (Baltimore, Md.: Johns Hopkins University Press, 1998), 122–34, 88–89, 101; David Leverenz, *Paternalism Incorporated: Fables of American Fatherhood, 1865–1940* (Ithaca, N.Y.: Cornell University Press, 2003), 13, 33, 112, 125, 133; John Tosh, *A Man's Place: Masculinity and the Middle-Class Home in Victorian England* (New Haven, Conn.: Yale University Press, 1999), 111–16, 150–60, 163, 173–85; Mark Carnes, "Middle-Class Men and the Solace of Fraternal Ritual," in *Meanings*

for Manhood: Constructions of Masculinity in Victorian America, ed. Mark Carnes and Clyde Griffen (Chicago: University of Chicago Press, 1990), 38–51; Dana Nelson, National Manhood: Capitalist Citizenship and the Imagined Fraternity of White Men (Durham, N.C.: Duke University Press, 1998), 34, 39, 46.

32. Clarence Day, Life with Father, in The Best of Clarence Day (New York: Knopf, 1961), 56, 91, 151, 137.

33. Robert Griswold, Fatherhood in America (New York: Basic Books, 1993), chaps. 2, 5, quotations on p. 97; Ralph LaRossa, The Modernization of Fatherhood (Chicago: University of Chicago Press, 1997), chaps. 1, 5; Frank, Life with Father, 3, chap. 5.

34. Samuel Drury, Fathers and Sons (New York: Richard R. Smith, 1930) 43–44, 47, 49, 57, 61, 145.

35. White House Conference on Child Health and Protection, The Young Child in the Home: A Survey (New York: Appleton-Century, 1936), 226–29.

36. Michael Horn, World Encyclopedia of Cartoons (Detroit: Gale, 1980), 173; George McManus, The Newlyweds and Their Baby (New York: New York World, 1907); Ron Goulard, Encyclopedia of American Comics (New York: Facts on File, 1990), 164–67, 246, 273; David White, The Funnies: An American Idiom (New York: Free Press, 1963), 82; Chic Young, Blondie (New York: David McKay, 1944); "Pop Strikes Back," Collier's Magazine, 22 January 1949, 34; "TV Makes a Fool out of Dad," American Mercury, February 1957, 35–37; Richard Butsch, "Class and Gender in Four Decades of Television Situation Comedy," Critical Studies in Mass Communications 94 (1992): 387–99; Stephanie Coontz, The Way We Never Were: American Families and the Nostalgia Trap (New York: Basic, 1992), 25–29.

37. Victory Appleton, Tom Swift and His War Tank; Or, Doing His Bit for Uncle Sam (New York : Grosset & Dunlap, 1918); Victor Appleton, Tom Swift and His Television Detector (Racine, Wis.: Whitman, 1933); Edward Stratemeyer, The Rover Boys in the Air; Or, From College Campus to the Clouds (New York : Grosset & Dunlap, 1912); Deirdre Johnson, Edward Stratemeyer and the Stratemeyer Syndicate (New York: Twayne, 1993), chaps. 3–4; John Dizer, Tom Swift, the Bobbsey Twins, and Other Heroes of American Juvenile Literature (Lewiston, N.Y. : Edwin Mellon, 1997), 1–10, 52, 324–31; John Dizer, Tom Swift and Company (Jefferson, N.C.: McFarland, 1982); Carol Billman, The Secret of the Stratemeyer Syndicate (New York: Ungar, 1986), chap. 2; Marilyn Greenwald, The Secret of the Hardy Boys: Leslie McFarlane and the Stratemeyer Syndicate (Athens: Ohio University Press, 2004).

38. St. Nicholas, November 1923, 14–15; November 1932, 44–45, and November 1933, 128; R. Gordon Kelly, Children's Periodicals of the United States (Westport, Conn.: Greenwood, 1984), 507–14.

39. Mysto Manufacturing ad, Playthings, January 1911, 99. Good background on Gilbert is in A. C. Gilbert (with Marshall McClintock), The Man

Who Lives in Paradise (New York: Rhinehart, 1953), esp. chaps. 1–3; Bruce Watson, *The Man Who Changed How Boys and Toys Were Made: The Life and Times of A. C. Gilbert* (New York: Penguin, 2003), 38–40, 52–56.

40. Gilbert ad, *Playthings*, January 1921, 201–6, and Gilbert ad, *American Boy*, December 1920, 157.

41. David Marc, *Comic Visions: Television Comedy and American Culture* (Boston: Unwin Hyman, 1989), chap. 1; Tueth, *Laughter in the Living Room*, 19, 22, 35, 53, 68–69; James Baker, *Teaching TV Sit Coms* (London: BFi Education, 2003), 10–18, 22; Jurgen Wolf, *Successful Sitcom Writing* (New York: St. Martin's Press, 1988); Gerald Jones, *Honey, I'm Home. Sitcoms: Selling The American Dream* (New York: Grove Weidenfeld, 1992), 38–77.

42. *Life of Riley* episodes: "Babs' Dream House," 1957, FTA, VA185T; "Nervous Breakdown," 1949, MTR, #108424; "New Den," 1957, FTA, VA185; "After You're Gone, 1958, FTA, VA206T; "Aloha Goodbye," 1957, FTA, VA161T; "All American Brain," 1957, FTA, VA167T.

43. Richard Mitz, *The Great TV Sitcom Book* (New York: Richard Marek, 1980), 39; *Trouble with Father* episodes: "Mr. Lemont Stays Up All Night Long," 1957, FTA, VA1290; "The Pen is Mightier," FTA, VA106259.

44. Tueth, *Laughter in the Living Room*, 68–69; Nina Liebman, *Living Room Lectures: The Fifties Family in Film and Television* (Austin: University of Texas Press, 1995), 7–10, 31.

45. "Father Knows Best," *New York Times*, 25 March 1955.

46. Ella Taylor, *Prime-Time Families: Television Culture in Postwar America* (Berkeley: University of California Press, 1989), 3, 25–26, 39; Marc, *Comic Visions*, 54–56; *Adventures of Ozzie and Harriet*, "Ricky the Drummer," 1957, FTA, VA12843T.

47. *Father Knows Best*, radio episodes: "Bud Quits School," October 1952, #521016 and "Enterprising Kids," November 1950, #501116 (MP3 collection). For additional background see, http://www.museum.tv/archives/etv/F/htmlF/fatherknows/fatherknows.htm, accessed 18 April 2007; Marc, *Comic*, 56–64.

48. *Father Knows Best* TV episodes: "Big Sister," 1958, FTA, VA5815T; "The Big Test," 1955, FTA, VA5815T; "Betty Goes Steady," 1956, FTA, VA729T; "Betty Goes to College," 1956, FTA, VA1705T; "Spirit of Youth," 1958, FTA, VA17057T; "A Crisis About a Kiss," nd, FTA, VA1714T; "The Homing Pigeon," 1956, FTA, VA5811T; "Persistent Guest," 1956, FTA, VA5811; "Spaghetti for Margaret," 1956, FTA, VA706T; Liebman, *Living Room Lectures*, 124; Jones, *Honey, I'm Home*, 98–101.

49. *Donna Reed* episodes: "Do You Trust Your Child?" 1959; "April Fool," 1959, both in FTA, VA718T.

50. *Adventures of Ozzie and Harriet* episodes: "No Noise," 1953, FTA, VA5777T; "Individuality," 1955, FTA, VA14904T; "David's Engagement," 1955, FTA, VA5777T; James Gilbert, *Men in the Middle: Searching for Masculinity*

in the 1950s (Chicago: University of Chicago Press, 2005); Liebman, *Living Room Lectures*, 156; Jones, *Honey, I'm Home*, 94–96.

51. Rick Mitz, *The Great TV Sitcom Book*, expanded ed. (New York, Perigee, 1988), 134–36; 199–220; *My Three Sons* episodes: "Birds and the Bees," 1962, FTA, VA1741T; "Almost the Sound of Music," 1963, FTA, VA214T; "Adjust or Bust," 1960, FTA, VA1752T.

52. *Make Room for Daddy* episodes: "Terry's Crush," 1958, FTA, DVD1372T; "Terry's Girl Friend, " 1958, FTA, DVD1372T; "Danny Roars Again,"1958, FTA, DVD1372T. See also Jones, *Honey, I'm Home*, 105–6.

53. *The Bob Cummings Show* episodes: "Advise to the Lovelorn," 1955, FTA, VA2334T; "Bob and the Ravishing Realtor," 1958, FTA, VA7546M; "Bob Seeks a Wife," 1959, FTA, VA7544T. Marc, *Comic Visions*, 80.

54. I develop this theme in *The Cute and the Cool: Wondrous Innocence and Modern American Children's Culture* (New York: Oxford University Press, 2004), 58–63.

55. *Dennis the Menace* episodes: "Mr. Wilson's Uncle," 1962, FTA, VA19900T; "Dennis and the TV Set," 1959, FTA, VA8850T; "Miss Cathcart's Sunsuit," 1960, FTA, VA15025T.

56. Liebman, *Living Room Lectures*,125; Mitz, *Sitcom Book*, 137–40; Jones, *Honey, I'm Home*, 123–28.

57. "Life Without Father," *Better Homes and Gardens*, June 1944, 12; "When Father Comes Home Again," *Parents' Magazine*, April 1945, 28–29; "Attention New Fathers," *Parents' Magazine*, May 1946, 37, 48; Charlotte Steiner, *Daddy Comes Home* (Garden City: Doubleday, 1944); John Luber, "Family Readjustment of Vets," *Marriage and Family Living* (Spring 1945): 29; William Tuttle, *"Daddy's Gone to War": The Second World War in the Lives of America's Children* (New York: Oxford University Press, 1993), chap. 12; Benjamin Spock, *The Pocket Book of Baby and Child Care* (New York: Pocket Books, 1946), 13.

58. "Why This Schizoid Dad?" *Better Homes and Gardens*, April 1952, 200; Max Lehrer, "Vanishing American Father," *McCall's*, May 1965, 95; Philip Wylie, *A Generation of Vipers* (New York: Holt, 1942), 198–200; "Decline and Fall of the American Father," *Cosmopolitan*, April 1955, 21–25; "American Men are Lousy Fathers," *American Weekly*, 27 November 1955, 99; "Decline of the Male Sex," *McCall's*, October 1961, 81; Robert Griswold, *Fatherhood in America: A History* (New York: Basic, 1993), 8, 143–60, 32, 167–73.

59. Griswold, *Fatherhood*, 14–15, 25, 33, 197, 190, and 142 for quotation. Note also Elaine Tyler May, *Homeward Bound: American Families in the Cold War* (New York: Basic, 1988), chap. 7; George Lundberg et al., *Leisure: A Suburban Study* (New York: Columbia University Press, 1934), 183–85; Robert Lynd and Helen Lynd, *Middletown* (New York: Harcourt, 1929), 80–87.

60. Robert Griswold, "If Not Ward Cleaver, Then Who?" *Journal of Women's History* (Fall 2001): 160; Jane Levey, "Imagining the Family in Post-

war Popular Culture," *Journal of Women's History* (Fall 2001): 125–49; Frank Gilbreth and Ernestine Gilbreth Carey, *Cheaper by the Dozen* (New York: Thomas Crowell, 1948), 2, 122–23, 169, 191.

61. "For Fathers Only," *Parents' Magazine*, October 1945, 140–41; "A New Role for Fathers," *Hygeia*, January 1950, 68; "A Man's Place Is in the Home," *McCall's*, May 1954, 28–34.

62. "Pals Forever," *Parents' Magazine*, November 1950, 23; "Grow with Your Child," *Parents' Magazine*, May 1950, 31; Marion Faegre, *Children Are Our Teachers* (Washington: U.S. Department of HEW, Childrens' Bureau, 1953).

63. "What Is the Father's Part in Discipline," *Parents' Magazine*, November 1952, 44–45; "Job of Being a Father," *Hygeia*, November 1949, 754; S. Gruenberg, *Our Children Today* (New York: Viking, 1952), 15; Faegre, *Children Are Our Teachers*, 2–3, 8–11.

64. "A Man's Place is in the Home," 28–30

65. "It's Hard to Be Your Age," *Collier's*, 17 April 1948, 32; "What Is Maturity," *Harper's Monthly*, May 1951, 70–78; "You Are Grown up When," *Rotarian*, June 1956, 29; "Man of All Seasons," *McCall's*, December 1962, 149."

66. O. Spurgeon English, "How Bad Is It to Spank your Kids?" *Better Homes and Gardens*, June 1950, 197; "Are We Too Good to Our Children," *Better Homes and Gardens*, March 1950, 110; "Decline and Fall of the American Father," 22; "Should Mothers Have Outside Jobs?" *Better Homes and Gardens*, January 1952, 34–35, 105; W. W. Bauer, *Stop Annoying Your Children* (Indianapolis: Bobbs-Merrill, 1948), 83–85, 94, 248.

67. Benjamin Spock, "How My Ideas Have Changed," *Redbook*, October 1963, 51; Benjamin Spock and Mary Morgan, *Spock on Spock: A Memoir of Growing Up with the Century* (New York: Pantheon Books, 1989); Margaret Mead, "A New Kind of Discipline," *Parents' Magazine*, September 1959, 50, 84; Katherine Misher, "Why I Deprive My Children," *Saturday Evening Post*, 24 February 1962, 10.

68. Hilda Graef, "Cult of Immaturity," *Catholic World*, June 1960, 158–60; "Maturity, Man's New Horizon," *National Parent-Teacher*, September 1967, 16; "American Man Symposium," *Look Magazine*, 1 January 1967, 13–16; "Pointers for Playful Fathers," *Life*, 28 December 1959, 125.

69. "Rights of the Man Around the House," *New York Times Magazine*, 22 October 1955, 48; O. S. English made a similar point in *Fathers Are Parents Too* (New York: Putnam, 1951).

70. O. Spurgeon English, "How to Be a Good Father," *Parents' Magazine*, June 1950, 32, 85–87; "Are American Dads Big Shots in the Office and Spineless Meal Tickets at Home?" *Better Homes and Gardens*, April 1952, 200; Gruenberg, *Our Children Today*, 176–78; Bruno Bettelheim, , "Fathers Shouldn't Try to Be Mothers," *Parents' Magazine*, October 1956, 36–37, 125–29; T. Berry Brazelton, "What Makes a Good Father," *Redbook*, June 1970,

270

1. when fathers knew best (or did they?)

70, 121; Benjamin Spock, "What a Child Needs from a Father," *Redbook*, September 1974, 24.

71. "Paternal Instinct," *Good Housekeeping*, November 1946, 43–43; "Daddy, the Fix-it Man," *Parents' Magazine*, September 1945, 36; "Trips They Can Take with Dad," *Parents' Magazine*, August 1950, 40; "What's Daddy to Do?" *Parents' Magazine*, November 1950, 29; "Build-Up for Dad," *Parents' Magazine*, June 1948, 19; "It's a Man's Job Too!" *Parents' Magazine*, September 1951, 164–65; "Life with Father, 1955 Model," *New York Times Magazine*, 23 January 1955, 15; "How Fathers Changed?" *New York Times Magazine*, 9 May 1954, 12.

2. Living Fast, (Sometimes) Dying Young

1. Film noir begins with *The Maltese Falcon* (1941) and ends with *Touch of Evil* (1958), mostly concentrated in the period 1946 through 1950. Raymond Borde and Etienne Chaumeton, *A Panorama of American Film Noir, 1941–1953* (San Francisco: City Lights Books, 2002), 15, 19; Mike Chopra-Gant, *Hollywood Genres and Postwar America: Masculinity, Family, and Nation in Popular Movies and Film Noir* (London: I. B. Tauris, 2006), 83–84, 89.

2. John Leland, *Hip: The History* (New York: HarperCollins, 2004), 90–91.

3. Michael Walker, "Film Noir," in *The Book of Film Noir*, ed. Ian Cameron (New York: Continuum: 1993), 8–17; Florence Jacobowitz, "The Man's Melodrama," in *The Book of Film Noir*, ed. Ian Cameron (New York: Continuum: 1993), 152–53; William Hare, *Early Film Noir* (Jefferson, N.C.: McFarland, 2003), 4.

4. William Grimes, "The Nitty-Gritty Flip Side to 'Father Knows Best,'" *St. Petersburg Times* (Florida), 7 August 1994.

5. Chopra-Gant, *Hollywood Genres*, 4–13, 18.

6. There has been a long history of this crisis of masculinity from the 1890s when men, fearing emasculation in office work, sought to prove their virility in hunting, sports, and war (Peter Filene, *Him/Her/Self: Sex Roles in Modern America* [New York: Harcourt Brace Jovanovich,1975]). Others attempted to redefine the male as a personality free from family duties in magazines like *Colliers* and *Esquire*. (Tom Pendergast, *Creating the Modern Man: American Magazines and Consumer Culture, 1900–1950* [Columbia: University of Missouri Press, 2000]). A more negative view of brutalized masculinity is in Roger Horrocks, *Masculinity in Crisis: Myths, Fantasies, and Realities* (New York: St. Martin's, 1994). Men have long sought community apart from the family. Mark Carnes (*Secret Ritual and Manhood in Victorian America* [New Haven, Conn.: Yale University Press, 1989]) shows

how mid-nineteenth-century men found community in clubs but eventually dropped them when leisure and work provided alternatives. James Gilbert, *Men in the Middle: Search for Masculinity in the 1950s* (Chicago: University of Chicago Press, 2005), 3, 31, rejects the manhood-crisis theory of Barbara Ehrenreich and Elaine May, finding much more variety in masculine models in the 1950s and insisting that stress on violence and heroism in the media is merely fantasy.

7. "Crime Wave Coming," *Time*, 3 April 1944, 6; Chopra-Gant, *Hollywood Genres*, 122, 256; Edward Strecker, *Their Mother's Sons: The Psychiatrist Examines an American Problem* (New York: Lippincott, 1946), 117–18.

8. Philip Wylie, *Generation of Vipers* (1942; New York: Rinehard, 1955), 188, 197, 198, 205–6.

9. Philip Wylie, "The Abdication of the Male: And How the Gray Flannel Mind Exploits Him Through his Women," *Playboy*, November 1956, and "Womanization of America," *Playboy*, September 1958. John Keats offered a Freudian take on the madness of the suburban matriarchy and its impact of emasculating sons in *The Crack in the Picture Window* (New York: Ballantine, 1956), 57.

10. Defining works include: Allen Ginsberg, *Howl and Other Poems* (San Francisco: City Light Books, 1956); Jack Kerouac, *On the Road* (New York: Buccanneer Books, 1957); William Burroughs, *The Naked Lunch* (New York: Grove Press, 1956). Note also Leland, *Hip*, 137; Steven Watson, *The Birth of the Beat Generation* (New York: Pantheon, 1995), 206–7.

11. James Campbell, *This Is the Beat Generation: New York–San Francisco–Paris* (Berkeley: University of California Press, 2001), 141, 157; Leland, *Hip*, 137.

12. Cited in Edward Foster, *Understanding the Beats* (Columbia: University of South Carolina Press, 1992), 22. Quotation in Leland, *Hip*, 87.

13. Foster, *Understanding the Beats*, 8.

14. Campbell, *Beat Generation*, 27.

15. Watson, *Birth of the Beat*, 28–30, 49, 56, 69, 152–54; Jack Kerouac, *On the Road*, in *Portable Beat Reader*, ed. Ann Charters (New York: Penguin, 1992), 11, 3–85, 68, 134.

16. Ginsberg, *Howl*, 1–3.

17. Leland, *Hip*, 115; David Sterrit, *Mad to Be Saved: The Beats, the '50s, and Film* (Carbondale: Southern Illinois University Press, 1998), 5.

18. Paul Goodman, *Growing up Absurd* (New York: Vintage, 1956), 181.

19. Campbell, *Beat Generation*, 247–49; Watson, *Birth of the Beat*, 258–62.

20. *Time*, 6 February 1959, cited in Leland, *Hip*, 15, also 154–55; William Manchester, *The Glory and the Dream* (New York: Bantam, 1975), 592; Campbell, *Beat Generation*, 247–49.

21. Watson, *Birth of the Beat*, 133, 253, 255.

22. Bill Osgerby, *Playboys in Paradise: Masculinity, Youth, and Leisure—Style in Modern America* (Oxford: Berg, 2001), 64–69, 77; Sloan Wilson, *Man in the Gray Flannel Suit* (New York: Simon and Schuster, 1955); William Whyte, *The Organization Man* (New York: Simon and Schuster, 1956); David Riesman, *The Lonely Crowd* (New Haven, Conn.: Yale University Press, 1950); John J. Palen, *The Suburbs* (New York: McGraw Hill, 1995), 56–67; Ferdinand Lundberg and Marynia F. Farnham, *Modern Woman: The Lost Sex* (New York: Harper, 1947), 370–71.

23. Norman Mailer, "The White Negro," (1957), in *The Portable Beat Reader*, ed. Ann Charters (New York: Viking,), 588; Goodman, *Growing up Absurd*, 14; Sterritt, *Mad to be Saved*, 23–30.

24. *Saturday Evening Post* cover September 1958. See also Ogersby, *Playboys in Paradise*, 69–71.

25. Russell Miller, *Bunny: The Real Story of* Playboy (New York: Holt, Rinehart and Winston, 1984), 17, 27, 31, 44, 135.

26. Miller, *Bunny*, 109, 75–82, 71, 111.

27. Auguste Comte Spectorsky, *The Exurbanites* (New York: Lipincott, 1955), 77–83; Ogersby, *Playboys in Paradise*, 45; Miller, *Bunny*, 111–12; Hugh Hefner, *The Playboy Philosophy* (Chicago: HMH, 1962–65), 3, 5, 7, 11–13, 17, 41.

28. Hefner, *The Playboy Philosophy*, 44; Pierre Bourdieu, *Distinction: A Social Critique of a Judgment of Taste* (Cambridge, Mass.: Harvard University Press, 1984), 367.

29. Ogersby, *Playboys in Paradise*, 132–42; Miller, *Bunny*, 46.

30. Ogersby, *Playboys in Paradise*, 29; Barbara Ehrenreich, *Hearts of Men: American Dreams and the Flight from Commitment* (Garden City, N.Y.: Doubleday, 1983).

31. Ogersby, *Playboys in Paradise*, 151–62.

32. Miller, *Bunny*, 170–211.

33. Ogersby, *Playboys in Paradise*, 132; Miller, *Bunny*, 2–7; Izabella St. James, *Bunny Tales: Behind Closed Doors at the Playboy Mansion* (Philadelphia: Running Press, 2006), 128.

34. Miller, *Bunny*, 145, 148, 155, 166.

35. Miller, *Bunny*, 49–52; P. F. Brady, *Hefner* (London: Weidenfeld and Nicolson, 1975); and T. Weyr, *Reaching for Paradise: The Playboy Vision of America* (New York: Times, 1978).

36. Ed Hulse, "Inside the Playboy Mansion," *Video Business*, 21 January 2002, 1; Peter Carlson "Playboy at Fifty; Hefner's Baby Swings into Middle Age," *Washington Post*, 2 October 2003; Scott Allison, " 'What Sort of Man Reads Playboy'? The Self-Reported Influence of Playboy on the Construction of Masculinity," *Journal of Men's Studies* (January 2003): 189–220.

37. Edward Radlauer, *Drag Racing: Quarter Mile Thunder* (New York: Abelard-Schuman, 1966) 28; H. F. Moorehouse, *Driving Ambitions: An Anal-*

ysis of the American Hot Rod Enthusiasm (Manchester: Manchester University Press, 1991), 42–44; Michael K. Witzel and Kent Bash, Cruisin': Car Culture in America (Osceola, Wis.: MBI, 1997), 72–89.

38. Drag-racing articles: Colliers, 26 July 1941, 14, 56; Time, 26 September 1949, cited in Moorehouse, Driving Ambitions, 33, also 5, 81; W. Smitter, "Souped up Speed," Colliers, 5 April 1947, 34.

39. Bill Hayes, The Original Wild Ones: Tales of the Boozefighters Motorcycle Club (Osceola, Wis.: Motorbooks, 2005).

40. Moorehouse, Driving Ambitions, 50, 36–38, 45, 63, 78; Wally Parks (president of the National Hot Rod Association), Drag Racing: Yesterday and Today (New York: Trident Press, 1966), 26–27, 2–3, 14, 22.

41. Moorehouse, Driving Ambitions, chap. 7, 106, 119, 145, 151, 6–8, 156, 201; see also Robert Post, High Performance: The Culture and Technology of Drag Racing, 1950–2000 (Baltimore, Md.: Johns Hopkins University Press, 2001).

42. Tom Wolfe, "Kandy-Kolored Tangerine-Flake Streamline Baby," on Hot Rods and Custom Classics: Cruisin' Songs and Highway Hits, sound recording (New Rhino Entertainment, 1999); essay also in Tom Wolfe, "Kandy-Kolored Tangerine-Flake Streamline Baby," in The Kandy-Kolored Tangerine-Flake Streamline Baby (New York: Noonday, 1963), 87–98.

43. Obituaries for Ed Roth: Baltimore City Paper, 12 December 2001; Los Angeles Times, 6 April 2001; The Washington Post, 7 April 2001; New York Times, 7 April 2001.

44. Ed Roth, Confessions of a Rat Fink: The Life and Times of Ed "Big Daddy" Roth (New York: Pharos Books, 1992), 84–85, 49, 17, 45, 159.

45. Ehrenreich, Hearts of Men, chap. 3.

46. Jessica Weiss, "Drop-In Catering Job: Middle-Class Women and Fatherhood, 1950–90," Journal of Family History 24, no. 3 (1999): 374–90; Ruth Tasch, "Role of the Father in the Family," Journal of Experimental Education (June 1952): 319–61; Robert Griswold, Fatherhood in America (Basic Books, 1993), 203–4.

47. Lionel Trains ad cited in James Twitchell, Where Men Hide (New York: Columbia University Press, 2006), 73. See also Lionel Trains ad, Parents' Magazine, December 1946, 164.

48. Caroline Hinkle McCamant, "From Mother's Enforcer to Boy's Pal: The Changing Ideals of Fatherhood in the American Middle Class, 1900–1929," paper presented at the AHA Meeting 2005; Frank Cheley, Dad, Whose Boy Is Yours? (Boston: W. A. Wilde, 1926), 9–10 and The Job of Being a Dad (Boston: W. A. Wilde, 1923), 181, 183, 187, 254; Wallace Vincent, Say Dad: Chummy Talks Between Father and Son (New York: Fleming H. Revell, 1926), 16, 23, 41–42, 112.

49. Boy Scouts of America, Fundamentals of the Boy Scout Movement (New York: BSA, 1945); August Kietzman, Why I Became a Scoutmaster:

Forty-Eight Years of Youth Work (New York: Comet, 1958); Boy Scouts of America, *The Father and Son Idea and Scouting* (New York: BSA, 1928); Frank Mathews, *Boy Scouts Book of Hobbies for Fathers and Sons* (New York: Appleton-Century, 1942).

50. Gary Fine, *With the Boys: Little League Baseball and Preadolescent Culture* (Chicago: University of Chicago Press, 1987), 5, 17, 21, 27, 32; Carl Stotz, *A Promise Kept: The Story of the Founding of Little League Baseball* (Jersey Shore, Penn.: Zebrowski Historical Services, 1992), 1.

51. Stotz, *A Promise Kept*, 2–4, 12, 26, 49, 82, 105, 142; Harvey Frommer, *Growing Up at Bat: Fifty Years of Little League Baseball* (New York: Pharos, 1989); Lance Van Auken and Robin Van Auken, *Play Ball! The Story of Little League Baseball* (University Park: Pennsylvania State University Press, 1997); Carl Stotz, *At Bat with the Little League* (Philadelphia: Smith, 1952); David Voigt, *Little League Journal* (Bowling Green, Ohio: Bowling Green University Popular Press, 1974); Lewis Lablonsky and Jonathan Brower, *Little League Game: How Kids, Coaches, and Parents Really Play It* (New York: New York Times Books, 1979).

52. Garret Mathews, *Swing Batta!* (East Lansing: Michigan State University, 2001); Jeff Burroughs, *Little League Instructional Guide* (Chicago: Bonus Books, 1994), vii–x, 122–35; Ned McIntosh, *Managing Little League Baseball* (Chicago: Contemporary Books, 1985), xvii, 5, 9, 12, 16, 25, 37, 45, 87, 121; Lablonsky and Brower, *Little League Game*, 12, 23.

53. Articles on adult behavior at Little League games: *San Francisco Chronicle*, 4 June 2004; *Seattle Times*, 20 May 2003; *Boston Globe*, 17 May 2003; *Tampa Tribune* (Florida), 18 October 2001; *Milwaukee Journal Sentinel*, 18 October 2001; *Pittsburgh Post-Gazette*, 16 July 2000; *USA Today*, 5 April 2000.

54. Daniel Herman, *Hunting and the American Imagination* (Washington, D.C.: Smithsonian Institution Press, 2001), 1–7, 92–95, 134.

55. "Take Your Boy Hunting," *Parents' Magazine*, October 1942, 24, 112; William Tapply, *Sportman's Legacy* (New York: Lyons and Burford, 1993), 2–4, 11, 25, 29; "Start Your Boy Right," *Outdoor Life*, December 1957, 68–69; Borden Deal, "The Christmas Hunt" (from the *Saturday Evening Post*, 1959), in *A Boy and His Dad*, ed. Albert Tibbets (Boston: Little, Brown, 1964), 75–96; "Ross and His Rifle," *Outdoor Life*, February 1963, 36–39, 115. Other articles on raising boys to be hunters are in *Field and Stream*, November 1953, 12; December 1953, 14–18; November 1961, 36; and October 1965, 22–24.

56. Agnes Benedict, *The Happy Home: A Guide to Family Living* (New York: Appleton-Century, 1948), 48, 219–24.

57. Various articles and books about hobbying: *American Modeler*, April 1958, 17; *Profitable Hobbies*, February 1950, 20–21; Bruce Greenberg, *Greenberg's Guide to Early American Toy Trains* (Sykesville, Md.: Greenberg,

1993) 163; Albert Kalmbach, *How to Run a Model Railroad* (Milwaukee, Wis.: Kalmbach, 1944), 9, 21; William Winter, *Radio Control for Model Builders* (New York: JF Rider, 1960); Lionel Corp., *Model Railroading* (New York: Bantam, 1951), 120, 321; Ernest Carter, *Boys Book of Model Railways* (New York: Roy, 1959), 1–8; *Popular Science*, August 1958, 23; *American Modeler*, April 1958, 39; February 1951, 57; Pierce Carlson, *Toy Trains: A History* (New York: Harper and Row: 1986).

58. Twitchell, *Where Men Hide*, develops this theme.

59. Articles about crafts for men: *Popular Science*, October 1958, 162; May 1956, 210, 211; December 1956, 16; 120–21, 127; October 1956, 177–79; *Workbench*, March–April 1957 and May–June 1957.

60. Stephen Ducat, *The Wimp Factor: Gender Gaps, Holy Wars, and the Politics of Anxious Masculinity* (Boston: Beacon Press, 2004), 27, 31, 33, 47, 49, 53, 57 (quotation, 1). Variations on this thesis are found in Lundberg and Farnham, *Modern Women*, 67, 126, 159, 317; Marie-Louise Von Franz, *The Problem of the Puer Aeternus* (1970; Toronto: Inner City Books, 2000). It is presented from a feminist perspective in Nancy Chodorow, *The Reproduction of Mothering: Psychoanalysis and the Sociology of Gender* (Berkeley: University of California Press, 1978), 17, 79–81.

61. Ducat, *Wimp Factor*, 64, 79; Anthony Rotundo, *American Manhood: Transformations in Masculinity from the Revolution to the Modern Era* (New York: Basic, 1993), 11.

62. Gail Bederman, *Manliness and Civilization: A Cultural History of Gender and Race in the United States, 1880–1917* (Chicago: University of Chicago Press, 1995), 12, 77–120.

63. J. D. Salinger, *The Catcher in the Rye* (Boston: Little Brown, 1947), 2, 7, 13, 15, 117–20, 131, 198.

64. Susan Bordo, *The Male Body: A New Look at Men in Public and in Private* (New York: Farrar, Straus and Giroux, 1999), 132–33.

65. Kenneth Keniston, *The Uncommitted: Alienated Youth in American Society* (New York: Dell, 1965), 3, 39.

66. Randolph Bourne, *Youth and Life* (New York: B. Franklin, 1971).

67. Howard Chudacoff, *The Age of the Bachelor: Creating an American Subculture* (Princeton, N.J.: Princeton University Press, 1999), 51–67, 106–45.

68. Pendergast, *Creating the American Man*, 21, 136–41, 206–22; Osgerby, *Playboys in Paradise*, 206–22, 31–33.

69. "The Editor Speaking," *True*, March 1948, 8–9, cited in Pendergast, *Creating Modern Man*, 234 and 232–33; Kevin White, *The First Sexual Revolution* (New York: New York University Press, 1993), esp. 188–89.

70. Osgerby, *Playboys in Paradise*, 5, 31–33, 4–58. See also K. Breazeale, "In Spite of Women: *Esquire* Magazine and the Construction of the Male Consumer," *Signs* 20, no. 1 (Autumn 1994): 1–22.

71. Osgerby, *Playboys in Paradise*, 90–91; James Gilbert, *Cycles of Out-rage* (New York: Oxford University Press, 1986), 214; Thomas Doherty, *Teen-agers and Teenpics: The Juvenilization of American Movies in the 1950s* (London: Unwin & Hyman, 1988).

72. Dwight Macdonald worried about a manipulated caste of youth: "A Caste, a Culture, a Market," *New Yorker*, 29 November 1958; Osgerby, *Playboys in Paradise*, 95–96.

73. David Leverenz, *Paternalism Incorporated: Fables of American Fatherhood, 1865–1940* (Ithaca, N.Y.: Cornell University Press, 2003), 35.

74. Gillian Avery, *Behold the Child: American Children and their Books, 1621-1922* (London: Bodley Head, 1994), chap. 5; Jackie Wullschläger, *Inventing Wonderland: The Lives and Fantasies of Lewis Carroll, Edward Lear, J. M. Barrie, Kenneth Grahame, and A. A. Milne* (New York: Free Press, 1995), 109–12.

75. David Kirby, *Boyishness in American Culture: The Charms and Dangers of Social Immaturity* (Lewiston, N.Y.: Edwin Mellen Press, 1991), 45.

76. Jacqueline Rose, *The Impossibility of Children's Fiction* (London: Macmillan, 1984), 1–9. Others emphasize the construction of innocence around adult sexual and power desires. See also Kenneth Kidd, *Making American Boys: Boyology and the Feral Tale* (Minneapolis: University of Minnesota Press, 2004).

77. Edward Tilyou, "Human Nature with the Brakes Off—or: Why the Schoolma'am Walked into the Sea," *American Magazine* 94 (July 1922): 19, 92; Woody Register, *Kid of Coney Island: Fred Thompson and the Rise of American Amusements* (New York: Oxford University Press, 2001), 12.

78. David Zinman, *Saturday Afternoon at the Bijou* (New Rochelle, N.Y.: Arlington House, 1973), 288–300; Jim Harmon, *Great Movie Serials: Their Sound and Fury* (Garden City, N.Y.: Doubleday, 1972), 2–5; Kalton Lahue, *Continued Next Week: A History of the Moving Picture Serial* (Norman: University of Oklahoma Press, 1964), 5–6, chaps. 4–10.

79. Jim Harmon, *Radio Mystery and Adventure* (Jefferson, N.C.: McFarland, 1992), 18–19, 24, 30–32, 102–3; Marilyn Boemer, *The Children's Hour: Radio Programs for Children, 1929–1956* (Metuchen, N.J.: Scarecrow Press, 1989), 7–16; Ray Barfield, *Listening to Radio, 1920–1950* (Westport, Conn.: Praeger, 1996), 109, 115, 121; Rafael Vela, "With the Parents' Consent: Film Serials, Consumerism and the Creation of a Youth Audience, 1913–1938," (Ph. D. diss., University of Wisconsin–Madison, 2000), part 2.

80. Roy Kinnard, *Science Fiction Serials* (Jefferson, N.C.: McFarland, 1998), 67–76; Harmon, *Movie Serials*, 27–33, 40–41; Matthew Pustz, *Comic Book Culture: Fanboys and True Believers* (Jackson: University of Mississippi Press, 1999), 30–32, 40.

81. Ron Goulart, *Comic Book Culture: An Illustrated History* (Portland, Ore.: Collectors' Press, 2000), 27, 43–47; Kinnard, *Science Fiction Serials*,

63–67, 77, 102–3, 78, 156–57;Harmon, *Mystery and Adventure*, 43–45, 197; Pustz, *Comic Book Culture*, 27–28; and Bradford Wright: *Comic Book: The Transformation of Youth Culture in America* (Baltimore, Md.: Johns Hopkins University Press, 2001), 8–21.

82. Goulart, *Comic Book Culture*, 5–43.

83. Pustz, *Comic Book Culture*, 234.

84. Wright, *Comic Book Nation*, 201–25.

85. Daniel Harris, *Cute, Quaint, Hungry, and Romantic: Aesthetics of Consumerism* (New York: Basic, 2000), 52–74.

3. Talking About My Generation

1. David Farber, *The Age of Great Dreams: America in the 1960s* (New York: Hill and Wang, 1994), 57.

2. Terry Anderson, *The Movement and the Sixties* (New York: Oxford University Press, 1995), v–vi.

3. Lawrence Baskir and William Strauss, *Chance and Circumstance: The Draft, the War, and the Vietnam Generation* (New York: Knopf, 1978), cited in John McWilliams, *The 1960s Cultural Revolution* (Westport, Conn.: Greenwood Press, 2000), 13.

4. Mark Lytle, *American's Uncivil Wars: The Sixties Era from Elvis to the Fall of Richard Nixon* (New York: Oxford University Press, 2006), 217.

5. Lytle, *America's Uncivil Wars*, 218–26.

6. Gary Yoggy, "When Television Wore Six-Guns: Cowboy Heroes on TV," in *Shooting Stars: Heroes and Heroines of Western Films*, ed. Archie McDonald (Bloomington: Indiana University Press, 1987), 218–54, and Billy Gray, quoted in "Billy Gray," NNDB, 2006, http://www.nndb.com/people/523/000092247, accessed 30 August 2006. See also Gerald Jones, *Honey, I'm Home. Sitcoms: Selling The American Dream* (New York: Grove Weidenfeld, 1992), 101.

7. Paul Potter, "The Incredible War," in *Takin' It to the Streets: A Sixties Reader*, ed. Alexander Bloom and Wini Breines (New York: Oxford University Press, 1995), 214–19.

8. Howard Brick, *Age of Contradiction: American Thought and Culture in the 1960s* (New York: Twayne, 1998), 73; Herbert Marcuse, *One Dimensional Man: Studies in the Ideology of Advanced Industrial Society* (Boston: Beacon Press, 1964); Herbert Marcuse, *An Essay on Liberation* (Boston: Beacon Press, 1969); C. Wright Mills, *The Power Elite* (Oxford: Oxford University Press, 1959); Norman O. Brown, *Love's Body* (New York: Random House, 1966); Norman O. Brown, *Life Against Death: The Psychoanalytical Meaning of History* (Middletown, Conn.: Wesleyan University Press, 1959).

9. "The Port Huron Statement," in *Takin' It to the Streets: A Sixties Reader*, ed. Alexander Bloom and Wini Breines (New York: Oxford University Press, 1995), 61–74.

10. Michael Kimmel, *Manhood in America: A Culture History* (New York: Free Press, 1996), 267, and Judith Newton, *From Panthers to Promise Keepers* (Lanham, Md.: Rowman & Littlefield, 2005), 107–9.

11. Free Speech Movement Newsletter, Fall 1964, "Do Not Fold, Bend, Mutilate or Spindle, " in *Takin' It to the Streets: A Sixties Reader*, ed. Alexander Bloom and Wini Breines (New York: Oxford University Press, 1995), 117.

12. SDS borrowed also from the community-organizing ideas of Jane Jacobs and Saul Alinsky created the Economic Research and Action Project in the summer of 1963 to "mobilize" the urban poor in the North. Lytle, *America's Uncivil Wars*, 77–87; Norman Mailer, "The White Negro: Superficial Reflections on the Hipster" (1957) in *Advertisements for Myself* (New York: Putnam, 1959), 339.

13. Peter Whitmer, *Aquarius Revisited: Seven Who Created the Sixties Counterculture that Changed America* (New York: Macmillan, 1987), 61–62.

14. Lytle, *America's Uncivil Wars*, 77–87; Brick, *Age of Contradiction*, Wini Breines, "'Of this Generation': The New Left and the Student Movement," in *Long Time Gone: Sixties America Then and Now*, ed. Alexander Bloom (New York: Oxford University Press, 2001), 25–35.

15. Tom Engelhardt, *The End of Victory Culture: Cold War America and the Disillusioning of a Generation* (New York: BasicBooks, 1995).

16. Faber, *Age of Great Dreams*, 139–41.

17. Carl Oglesby and Richard Shaull, *Containment and Change: Two Dissenting Views of American Foreign Policy* (New York: Macmillan, 1967), 26, 32; and Carol Oglesby, "Trapped in a System" (1965), in *Takin' It to the Streets: A Sixties Reader*, ed Alexander Bloom and Wini Breines (New York: Oxford University Press, 1995), 220–25.

18. Tom Hayden, *Reunion* (New York: Random House, 1988), 78–102.

19. Faber, *Age of Great Dreams*, 198; W. J. Rorabaugh, *Berkeley at War: The 1960s* (New York: Oxford University Press, 1988), 178.

20. David Burner, *Making Peace with the 60s* (Princeton, N.J.: Princeton University Press, 1996), 137.

21. Lytle, *America's Uncivil Wars*, 88–95.

22. Gordon Fish, "Students in Business: What Do They Think About It: Why?" *Vital Issues*, March 1969, 1; "The Private World of the Class of '66," *Fortune*, February 1966, 130.

23. Stanley Aronowitz, *False Promises: The Shaping of American Working-Class Consciousness* (New York: McGraw Hill, 1973), 21–50; Daniel Yankelovich, *New Morality: A Profile of American Youth in the 1970s* (New York: McGraw Hill, 1974), 3–5; "The Great Male Cop Out from the Work Ethic,"

Business Week, 14 November 1977, 156; Natasha Zaretsky, *No Direction Home: The American Family and the Fear of National Decline, 1968–1980* (Chapel Hill: University of North Carolina Press, 2007), 105–20.

24. Guy Strait, "What Is a Hippie?" in *Takin' It to the Streets: A Sixties Reader*, ed. Alexander Bloom and Wini Breines (New York: Oxford University Press, 1995), 310–12.

25. Rex Weiner and Deanne Stillman, *Woodstock Census: The Nationwide Survey of the Sixties Generation* (New York: Viking, 1979), 40, 42, 47.

26. I had graduated from college in 1968 but had an internship on campus in 1969–70.

27. "About Mad Magazine," *Washington Post*, 6 April 1997; "Mad: 50 Years of Stupidity," *The Atlanta Journal-Constitution*, 25 October 25, 2002; Maria Reidelbach, *Completely Mad: A History of the Comic Book and Magazine* (New York: Little, Brown, 1991).

28. Whitmer, *Aquarius Revisited*, chaps. 10–11; Tom Wolfe, *The Electric Kool-Aid Acid Test* (New York: Farrar, Straus and Giroux, 1968).

29. Robert Hunter, *The Storming of the Mind* (New York: Doubleday, 1971), 88.

30. Timothy Leary, *The Politics of Ecstasy* (Putnam, 1968), in Irwin Unger and Debi Unger, *The Times were a Changin': The Sixties Reader* (New York: Three Rivers, 1998), 177.

31. Jane Stern and Michael Stern, *Sixties People* (New York: Knopf, 1990), 152–56.

32. Faber, *Age of Great Dreams*, 183; Beth Bailey, *Sex in the Heartland* (Cambridge, Mass.: Harvard University Press, 1999).

33. John Sinclair, "Rock and Roll Is a Weapon of Cultural Revolution" (1968), in *Takin' It to the Streets: A Sixties Reader*, ed. Alexander Bloom and Wini Breines (New York: Oxford University Press, 1995), 301–3.

34. Farber, *Age of Great Dreams*, 57–61; Jeff Greenfield, *No Peace, No Place: Excavations Along the Generational Fault* (Garden City, N.Y.: Doubleday, 1973), 29, quoted in Glenn Altschuler, *All Shook Up: How Rock 'N' Roll Changed America* (New York: Oxford University Press, 2003), 8. Altschuler explores the connections between race, rock, and generational conflict.

35. Quoted in Godfrey Hodgson, *America in Our Time* (New York: Random House, 1976), 341.

36. McWilliams, *1960s Cultural Revolution*, 20; Farber, *Age of Great Dreams*, 52.

37. Farber, *Age of Great Dreams*, 169.

38. Barney Hoskyns, *Beneath the Diamond Sky: Haight-Ashbury, 1965–1970* (New York: Simon and Schuster, 1997), cited in William McConnell, *The Counterculture Movement of the 1960s* (San Diego: Greenhaven Press, 2004), 84–88; Lytle, *America's Uncivil Wars*, 96–206.

39. Stern and Stern, *Sixties People*, 152–56.

40. Note Michael Harrington's view of hippies as a democratization of bohemia made into banality: "We Few, We Happy Few, We Bohemians," *Esquire*, August 1972, 164; and Leonard Wolf, *Voices from the Love Generation* (Boston: Little Brown, 1968), xxi.

41. Charles Reich, *The Greening of America* (New York: Random House, 1970), 192, 194, 196, 222, and 152–53; and Theodore Roszak, *The Making of a Counter Culture* (Garden City, N.Y.: Doubleday, 1969), 9, 49, and 65.

42. Casey Hayden and Mary King, "A Kind of Memo," available at http://www.cwluherstory.org/classic-feminist-writings/a-kind-of-memo-2.html, accessed 30 May 2007.

43. Sarah Evans, "Beyond Declension: Feminist Radicalism in the 1970s and 1980s," in *The World the Sixties Made*, ed. Van Gosse and Richard Moser (Philadelphia: Temple University Press, 2003), 52–60; Newton, *From Panthers to Promise Keepers*, 110–15; Ruth Rosen, *The World Split Open: How the Modern Women's Movement Changed America* (New York: Viking 2001), 113–24.

44. John D'Emilio, *Sexual Politics, Sexual Communities: The Making of a Homosexual Minority in the United States, 1940–1970* (Chicago: University of Chicago Press, 1983), 35–41; Newton, *From Panthers to Promise Keepers*, 84–97; Daniel Harris, *The Rise and Fall of Gay Culture* (New York: Hyperion, 1997).

45. This point is stressed, for example, in Newton, *Panthers to Promise Keepers*, 110–15.

46. Amanda Goldrick-Jones, *Men Who Believe in Feminism* (Westport, Conn.: Praeger, 2002), 3, 4, 33, 34. Note also Tom Digby, ed., *Men Doing Feminism* (New York: Routledge, 1998); Clyde Franklin, *The Changing Definition of Masculinity* (New York: Plenum Press, 1984), 103; and Newton, *Panthers to Promise Keepers*, 116, 122–26.

47. Deborah David and Robert Brannon, eds., *The Forty-Nine Percent Majority: The Male Sex Role* (Reading, Mass.: Addison-Wesley, 1974).

48. Warren Farrell, *The Liberated Man, Beyond Masculinity: Freeing Men and Their Relationships with Women* (New York: Random House, 1974), 9, 17, 35, 39, 121, 132, 145, 226.

49. Joseph Pleck and Jack Sawyer, eds., *Men and Masculinity* (Englewood Cliffs, N.J.: Prentice-Hall, 1974), 173–74; and Jack Nichols, *Men's Liberation: A New Definition of Masculinity* (New York: Penguin, 1975).

50. "Press Conference Statement of March 12, 1983," *Brother* 1, no. 2 (1983), cited in Michael Kimmel and Thomas Mosmiller, *Against the Tide: Pro-Feminist Men in the United States, 1776–1990* (Boston: Beacon, 1992), 430.

51. Richard Reed, *Birthing Fathers: The Transformation of Men in American Rites of Birth* (New Brunswick: Rutgers University Press, 2005), 63, 92, 93, 99; Robert Bradley, *Husband-Coached Childbirth* (New York: Harper and Row, 1965), 59.

52. Reed, *Birthing Fathers*, 104–34, 139, 143, 154; Celeste Phillips and Joseph Anzalone, *Fathering: Participation in Labor and Birth* (Saint Louis: C. V. Mosby, 1978), 11; and Ingrid Mitchell, *Giving Birth Together* (New York: Seabury, 1975).

53. Brick, *Age of Contradictions*, 158–65; Lytle, *America's Uncivil Wars*, 227–39.

54. Newton, *From Panthers to Promise Keepers*, 54–57; David Hilliard and Lewis Cole, *The Autobiography of David Hilliard and the Story of the Black Panthers* (New York: Little Brown, 1993), 115–20.

55. Maurice Isserman and Michael Kazin, *America Divided: The Civil War of the 1960s* (New York: Oxford University Press, 2004), 190; Faber, *Age of Great Dreams*, 196–98.

56. Reich, *The Greening of America*, 231; and Tom Wolfe, *The Kandy-Kolored Tangerine-Flake Streamline Baby* (New York: Farrar, Straus and Giroux, 1965).

57. Farber, *Age of Great Dreams*, 64–65; Abbie Hoffman, *Revolution for the Hell of It* (New York: Dial Press, 1968). Although I do not agree with a number of their presumptions, Joseph Heath and Andrew Potter make these points in *Nation of Rebels: Why Counterculture Became Consumer Culture* (New York: HarperBusiness, 2004), 103, 129, 185, 191–96.

58. Abbie Hoffman, *The Best of Abbie Hoffman* (New York: Four Walls Eight Windows, 1989), cited in William McConnell, *The Counterculture Movement of the 1960s* (San Diego: Greenhaven Press, 2004), 75–81; and Jerry Rubin, *Do It: Scenarios of a Revolution* (New York: Simon and Schuster, 1970).

59. Rubin, *Do It.*

60. Spiro Afnew, speech delivered in Harrisburg, Pennsylvania, October 1969, in Agnew Papers, III-7-2, Pennsylvania Fundraiser, Harrisburg, Pennsylvania; speech transcript cited in Lane Williams, "The Robespierre of the Great Silent Majority: Spiro Agnew's Des Moines Speech on Network Commentators," http://emp.byui.edu/WILLIAMSL/agnew.html, accessed 26 December 2007.

61. Bruno Bettelheim, *Obsolete Youth: Toward a Psychograph of Adolescent Rebellion* (San Francisco: San Francisco Press, 1969), 5, 21.

62. Lewis Feuer, *The Conflict of Generations: The Character and Significance of Student Movements* (New York: Basic, 1969), 389, 437, 445, 447, 469.

63. Jesse Pitts, "The Hippies as Contrameritocracy," *Dissent* 14 (July–August 1969): 326–37, reprinted in William McConnell, *The Counterculture Movement of the 1960s* (San Diego: Greenhaven Press, 2004), 66–74.

64. Midge Decter, *Liberal Parents, Radical Children* (New York: Coward, McCann and Geoghegan, 1975), 17, 21, 26, 32.

65. Christopher Lasch, *The Culture of Narcissism: American Life in An*

Age of Diminishing Expectations (New York: Norton, 1978), 85; Jerry Rubin, *Growing (Up) at Thirty-Seven* (New York: M. Evans), 1976, 20–21, and 116; Tom Wolfe, "The 'Me' Decade and the Third Great Awakening," *New York Magazine*, 23 August 1976, 36; Zaretsky, *No Direction Home*, 195–210.

66. Leon Shaskolsky Sheleff, *Generations Apart: Adult Hostility to Youth* (New York: McGraw-Hill, 1981), 4–5, 8, 248, 277.

67. Kenneth Keniston, *The Uncommitted: Alienated Youth in American Society* (New York Harcourt, Brace and World, 1965), 30, 251, 293, 298, 302–3, 305. 394. Similar views appear in James Coleman, *Adolescent Society* (Glencoe, Ill.: Free Press, 1961), and Herbert Hendin, *The Age of Sensation* (New York: Norton, 1975).

68. Richard Flacks, *Youth and Social Change* (Chicago: Markham, 1971), 26, 29, 32, 51–57.

69. Jack Whalen and Richard Flacks, *Beyond the Barricades: The Sixties Generation Grows Up* (Philadelphia: Temple University Press, 1989), 2, 9, 72, 74, 156–59, 275.

70. Harvey Mansfield, "The Legacy of the Late Sixties," in *Reassessing the Sixties: Debating the Political and Cultural Legacy*, ed. Stephen Macedo (New York: Norton, 1997), 31, 37; Leonard Steinhorn, *The Greater Generation: In Defense of the Baby Boom Legacy* (New York: St. Martin, 2006), xiii.

71. Lasch, *Culture of Narcissism*, 67–68. A good explanation of this concern with family decline (linked with national decline) is Zaretsky, *No Direction Home*, 10–13, 19, 51, 145.

72. Steinhorn, *Greater Generation*, xv, 20, 21, 25, 28, 36, 65, 68, 72–77, 90, 138, 141, 99.

73. Bruce Feirstein, *Real Men Don't Eat Quiche* (Simon and Schuster, 1982), 1–4, 9–11, 15–16, 39.

74. Zaretsky, *No Direction Home*, 17.

75. In 1977, small groups devoted to overcoming what they saw as the oppression of men formed a loose Coalition of Free Men that published the journal *Transitions* in 1980. The Coalition joined with Men's Rights Inc. in 1980 to become the National Congress for Men, which promoted father's legal rights. Bob Connell, *Masculinities* (Berkeley: University of California Press, 1995), 77–78; Amanda Goldrick-Jones, *Men Who Believe in Feminism* (New York: Praeger, 2002), 34–35, 55; Kenneth Clatterbaugh, *Contemporary Perspectives on Masculinity* (Boulder, Colo.: Westview Press, 1990), 62–74; Herb Goldberg, *The Hazards of Being Male: Surviving the Myth of Masculine Privilege* (New York: Signet, 1976), 4–6.

76. Robert Bly, *Iron John: A Book About Men* (New York: Addison-Wesley: 1990), 1–28; Michael Schwalbe, *Unlocking the Iron Cage: The Men's Movement, Gender, Politics, and American Culture* (New York: Oxford, 1996), 198–207; Newton, *Panthers to Promise Keepers*, 138–44.

4. *My Generation Becomes the Pepsi Generation*

1. Thomas Frank, *The Conquest of Cool: Business Culture, Counterculture, and the Rise of Hip Consumerism* (Chicago: University of Chicago
Press, 1997), chap. 1; Joseph Heath and Andrew Potter, *Nation of Rebels:
Why Counterculture Became Consumer Culture* (New York: HarperBusiness,
2004), 6–7.

2. Eugene Gilbert, *Advertising and Marketing to Young People* (New
York: Printers' Ink Books, 1957), and James Gilbert, *Cycles of Outrage* (New
York: Oxford University Press, 1988), ch. 12.

3. Frank, *The Conquest of Cool*, chap. 1; Bill Osgerby, *Playboys in Paradise* (Oxford: Berg, 2001), 115–16, 181.

4. Erik Barnouw, *The Sponsor* (New York: Oxford University Press,
1978), 79, 119; Jonathan Price, *The Best Thing in TV Commercials* (New York:
Viking, 1978), 1–8, 38–40, 57; Lawrence Samuel, *Brought to You By: Postwar
Television Advertising and the American Dream* (Austin: University of Texas
Press, 2001), 117, 119, 171; and William Leiss et. al., *Social Communication in
Advertising*, 3rd ed. (New York, Routledge, 2005), 266–70.

5. VW ad, 1980, Museum of Television and Radio in Beverly Hills (hereafter MTR), #115370; Ford Granada ad, 1977, MTR, #120961; "Best Commercials of 1986," MTR, #115299; Yasutoshi Ikuta, *The 60s America Portrayed
Through Advertisements (Automobile)* (San Francisco: Chronicle Books, nd),
54–55.

6. Stroh's beer ad, 1978, MTR, #120961; Schlitz beer ad, 1978, MTR
#14016; Budweiser ad, 1985, MTR, #115379.

7. Old Spice ad, 1983, MTR, #115406 and Old Spice ad 1979, UCLA Film
and Television Archive (hereafter FTA), VA5109.

8. Various ads, *Playboy*, June 1967, 179, 212, 116; January 1967, 26, 181,
85; September 1967, 91, 15; October 1967, 217, 113; February 1973, 1–2, 50, 69;
September 1973, 4, 17, 27.

9. Pepsi ad, *Life Magazine*, April 1962, reprinted in Ikuta, *The 60s America Portrayed*, 23; Samuel, *Brought to You By*, 153–56; Pepsi ad, 1984, FTA, VA
3508; Richard Tedlow, *New and Improved: The Story of Mass Marketing in
America* (New York: Basic, 1990), 101–2.

10. Frank, *Conquest of Cool*, 136, 31; Dr. Pepper ad, "Fifty Years of Thirty
Seconds," FTA, VA10186.

11. Mary Cross, *A Century of American Icons* (Westport, Conn.: Greenwood Press, 2001), 123; Skittles ad, 1984, and Silver Creek Chewing Tobacco
ad, 1984, MTR, #15807.

12. Nike ad, 1984, FTA, VA3508; Lincoln-Mercury ad, 1984, MTR,
#115301.

13. Ikuta, *The 60s America Portrayed*, 98–101; Maxell ad, 1978, MTR,
#115370; Cross, *A Century of American Icons*, 159.

14. Frank, *Conquest of Cool*, 11–20. See also Todd Gitlin, *The Sixties: Years of Hope, Days of Rage* (New York: Bantam, 1987), chap. 1, and Warren Susman, *Culture as History: The Transformation of American Society in the Twentieth Century* (New York: Pantheon, 1984), xxviii, xx.

15. Toyota truck ad, 1984, MTR #15806; Honda ad, 1984, MTR, #15806; Diet Coke ad, 1984, MTR, #15807; Wrangler Jeans ad, 1981, FTA, VA5109; Ditto Jeans ad, 1980, FTA, VA5239; Wrangler Jeans ad, 1984, FTA, VA15807.

16. English Leather ad, 1978, FTA, VA5243; Harvey's Bristol Cream ad, 1978, FTA, VA5109; Hai Karate ad, 1970s? FTA, VA5243.

17. Note, for example, David Brook, *Bobos in Paradise: The New Upper Class and How They Got There* (New York: Simon and Schuster, 2000).

18. "On the Cutting Edge," *Progressive Grocer*, July 1995, 52; Carl Frankel, "Green Marketing," *American Demographics* (April 1992): 34; "Rethinking the Supermarket Business," *Supermarket Business Magazine*, May 1987, 45; Warren Belasco, *Appetite for Change: How the Counterculture Took on the Food Industry* (Ithaca, N.Y.: Cornell University Press, 1993).

19. *Courtship of Eddie's Father*, 1969, 1970, 1972 episodes, FTA, VA1972.

20. *Family Affair*, 1968, 1970 episodes, FTA, VA14917; *Webster*, pilot episode, 1973, FTA, VA5327.

21. Rose Goldsen, *The Show and Tell Machine* (New York: Delta, 1977), 29–33.

22. A good treatment is in David Marc, *Comic Visions: Television Comedy and American Culture* (Boston: Unwin Hyman, 1989), 178–84. See also Gerard Jones, *Honey, I'm Home! Sitcoms: Selling the American Dream* (New York: Grove Weidenfeld, 1992), 204–10.

23. *Family Ties*, 1982 premier, and 1984, 1987, 1989 episodes, FTA, VA11095T, 18186, 3208, 6152.

24. Neil Sinyard, "Decline of the Western Hero," in *Movies of the Seventies*, ed. Ann Lloyd (London: Orbis, 1984), 97–98; Graham Fuller, "John Wayne," in *Movies of the Seventies*, ed. Ann Lloyd (London: Orbis, 1984), 52–55.

25. David Lusted, *The Western* (London: Longman, 2003), 177–78; Sinyard, "Decline," 98–99; Eric Lichtenfeld, *Action Speaks Louder: Violence, Spectacle, and the American Action Movie* (Westport, Conn.: Praeger, 2004), 5–12.

26. Laurent Bouzereau, *Ultraviolent Movies: From Sam Peckinpah to Quentin Tarantino* (Secaucus, N.J.: Citadel Press, 1996), 14–18. Stephen Prince, *Savage Cinema, Sam Peckinpah and the Rise of Ultraviolent Movies* (Austin: University of Texas Press, 1998), xvii, 5–17, 38, 40, 48,49, 51, 115; 188 for quotation. Of course, there were precedents for these new violent features of the 1960s in B movies that had been produced by Monogram and American International especially for the drive-in theaters. With the growth of drive-ins (from 2,200 to about 5,000 between 1950 and 1956), many of

these films had hot rod themes (*Hot Rod Guy, Hot Rod Girl*, and *Hot Rod Rumble*) and played on generational conflict. Horror films also proliferated in the B movie, culminating perhaps with the *Texas Chainsaw Massacre* (1974). See Randall Clark, *At a Theater or Drive-in Near You* (New York: Garland, 1995).

27. Bernard Dukore, *Sam Peckinpah's Feature Films* (Urbana: University of Illinois Press, 1999), chap. 3; National Commission on the Causes and Prevention of Violence, *Report of the National Commission on the Causes and Prevention of Violence: To Establish Justice, to Assure Domestic Tranquility*, (Washington: USGPO, 1968), 51.

28. Lichtenfeld, *Action Speaks Louder*, 17.

29. Lichtenfeld, *Action Speaks Louder*, 22–25, and John Taylor, "Dirty Harry," in *Movies of the Seventies*, ed. Ann Lloyd (London: Orbis, 1984), 172–73.

30. Derek Elley, "Martial Arts Films," in *Movies of the Seventies*, ed. Ann Lloyd (London: Orbis, 1984), 190–91; Yvonne Tasker, *Spectacular Bodies: Gender, Genre, and the Action Cinema* (New York: Routledge, 1993), 2–3, 79, 80.

31. Susan Jeffords, *Hard Bodies: Hollywood Masculinity in the Reagan Era* (New Brunswick, N.J.: Rutgers University Press, 1994); Ashton Trice and Samuel Holland, *Heroes, Antiheroes, and Dolts: Portrayals of Masculinity in American Popular Films, 1921–1999* (Jefferson, N.C.: McFarland, 2001), 193–95.

32. Thomas Cripps, *Black Film as Genre* (Bloomington: Indiana University Press, 1978), 50; Lichtenfeld, *Action Speaks Louder*, 5–12; Mike Phillips, "Chic and Beyond," *Sight and Sound* (August 1990): 25.

33. Keith Harris, *Boys, Boyz, Bois: An Ethics of Black Masculinity in Film and Popular Media* (New York: Routledge, 2006); M. J. Koven, *The Pocket Essential Blaxploitation Films* (New York: Harpenden Pocket Essentials, 2001); Judith Newton, *From Panthers to Promise Keepers* (Latham, Md.: Rowman and Littlefield, 2006), 70–71; Barbara Ransby and Tracye Matthews, "Black Popular Culture and the Transcendence of Patriarchal Illusions," in *Words of Fire: An Anthology of African-American Feminist Thought*, ed. Beverly Guy Sheftall (New York: New Press, 1995), 528–31; Nelson George, *Hip Hop America* (New York: Viking, 1998), 103–5.

34. Dale Dannefer, "Neither Socialization nor Recruitment: The Avocational Careers of Old-Car Enthusiasts," *Social Forces* 60, no. 3 (December 1981): 395–413; Dale Dannefer, "Rationality and Passion in Private Experience: Modern Consciousness and the Social World of Old Car Collectors," *Social Problems* 17, no. 4 (April 1980): 392–412.

35. "The Muscle Car," *New York Times*, 31 January 1982; "The Little Deuce Coupe Lives," *Boston Globe*, 20 June 1993; "Hot Rodders Losing Rebel Image as Hobby Matures," *Toronto Star*, 27 September 1997; "The Kids Are All

Right: The New Generation of Hot-Rodders," *AutoWeek*, 9 November 1998, 31; "Kids These Days . . . ," *AutoWeek*, 17 April 2000, 8.

36. For an account of cruising in Detroit see, http://info.detnews.com/ history/story/index.cfm?id=216&category=life.

37. Amy Best, *Fast Cars, Cool Rides: The Accelerating World of Youth and Their Cars* (New York: New York University Press, 2006), 31–55, and Michael K. Witzel and Kent Bash, *Cruisin: Car Culture in America* (Osceola, Wis.: MBI, 1997).

38. Witzel and Bash, *Cruisin*, 56–67.

39. "Lost in the Fifties," *Boston Globe*, 14 August 1999; "Classic Crusin'," *Milwaukee Journal Sentinel*, 28 July 2003; "Cruisin' Together on a Friday Night," *Baltimore Sun*, 17 August 2005.

40. Largely from notes taken at a visit to a old car show in State College, Penn., 13 August 2005. For insight into the racist implications of the term "rice burners," see Best, *Fast Cars*, 103–6.

41. See Gary Cross, *Kids' Stuff: Toys and the Changing World of American Childhood* (Cambridge, Mass.: Harvard University Press, 1997), chaps. 2 and 3; "Toys and the Man," *Washington Post*, 6 August 1989.

42. "Toys and the Man."

43. "Toys Not Just for Tots," *Plain Dealer*, 20 May 1994.

44. "The Enduring Charm of Playthings from the Past," *Washington Post*, 25 April 1985; "More Than Fun and Games," *American Demographics* (August 1991): 44; "Boomers in Toyland," *St. Louis Post-Dispatch*, 26 March 1992; "Antique Detective," *Chicago Sun-Times*, 19 December 1993; "Toy Palace," *Pittsburgh Post-Gazette*, 15 November 1996.

45. "Railroads That Carry Grown Men Away," *New York Times*, 22 December 1988.

46. "Railroads That Carry Men Away"; "Toys for Adults," *Playthings*, 1 September 2002, 30.

47. "Back on Track: Toy Trains Take Off," *Washington Post*, 26 December 1994.

48. "Train Fans' Love for Locomotives Keeps Chugging Full Steam Ahead," *St. Louis Post-Dispatch*, 11 December 2003; "Super Models: For Members of the Train Set," *Denver Rocky Mountain News*, 29 September 2000; "On Track for Another Century, Kids in a High-tech Era Refuel a Classic Joy Ride," *USA Today*, 15 December 15, 2000; "Railroad Hobbyists Creating Tiny World: Gaithersburg Society Building," *Washington Post*, 28 September 2000.

49. "Model Railroading, Romantics' Hobby," *New York Times*, 17 July 1986; "Making Tracks: Railroad Gardening," *Star Tribune* (Minneapolis), 8 August 2002; Hobbies Plus, "Scale and Gauge," http://www.hobbiesplus .com.au/scaleandgauge.htm, accessed 31 October 2006

50. Men's formal wear ads, *Esquire*, March 1962, March 1963, Novem-

ber 1964, October 1965, and November 1965. Bob Hope still was wearing a fedora in an ad for American Tourister in September 1965, 23, but the hat disappears from suit ads, though a sporty hat is worn advertising a Dan River topcoat in August 1965, 48. Ads for collegiate men's blazers showed no hats by March 1965, 108–9.

51. Richard Florida, *The Rise of the Creative Class* (New York: Basic, 2002), 189–90.

52. Osgerby, *Playboys in Paradise*, 203–4.

53. Combined book review, *Newsweek*, September 16, 1996, 68

54. "Senior Savvy?" *Brandmarketing*, October 1999, 12; Michael Weiss, "Chasing Youth," *American Demographics* (October 2002): 9; Leo Bogart, *Over the Edge* (Chicago: Ivan Dee, 2005), 60.

55. "The Entertainment Economy: How Mega-Media Forces Are Transforming Our Lives," *Brandweek*, 20 December 1999, 5.

56. Weiss, "Chasing Youth"; "Significant Obsession," *Progressive Grocer*, 1 July 1998, 1. See also Lynne Luciano, *Looking Good: Male Body Image in Modern America* (New York: Hill and Wang, 2001).

57. Manuel Vallee, "Swaying the Physicians: The Role of Advertising in the Prescription Process" Society and Consumption Conference, University of California at Berkeley, 8 March 2005; Weiss, "Chasing Youth"; Francis Palumbo and C. Daniel Mullins, "The Development of Direct-to-Consumer Prescription Drug Advertising Regulation," *Food and Drug Law Journal* 57 (February 2002): 423, 431; "The Direct-to-Consumer Advertising Genie," *The Lancet*, January 7, 2007, 1; Meika Loe, *The Rise of Viagra* (New York: New York University, 2004), 14–15, 41–61.

58. "Chasing Youth"; "Botox Boom," *Newsweek*, May 13, 2002, 50; "When They're Sixty-four," *Brandweek*, October 7, 2002, 5.

59. "Take a Pill and Call Me Tonight," *Newsweek*, 4 May 1998, 48; "The New Era of Lifestyle Drugs," *Business Week*, 11 May 1998, 92; Erica Jong, "It's Hard to Please Everyone," *Guardian*, 2 May 1998; "Viagra Heats Up Market for Sexual Supplements," *Health Foods Business* (December 1998): 36; "Warning: Super Bowl Ads May Cause Blushing," *Star Tribune*, 6 February 2005; Susan Bordo, *The Male Body: A New Look at Men in Public and in Private* (New York: Farrar, Straus and Giroux), 60–62; Loe, *The Rise of Viagra*, 19–20.

60. Weiss, "Chasing Youth."

5. New Stories, New Rebels

1. For an analysis and critique of this trend toward "edgy" movies, see Leo Bogart, *Over the Edge: How the Pursuit of Youth by Marketers and the Media Has Changed American Culture* (Chicago: Ivan Dee, 2005).

2. Tony Schwartz, "Whatever Happened to TV's 'Saturday Night Live'?" *New York Times*, 11 January 11, 1981; Tom Shales and James Andrew Miller, *Live from New York: An Uncensored History of "Saturday Night Live,"* (Boston: Little, Brown, 2002).

3. Film Reviews: *Columbus Dispatch* (Ohio), 11 June 1999; *USA Today*, 30 June 1999; *Maclean's*, 14 June 1999, 54.

4. Bill Bruegman, *Toys of the Sixties* (Akron, Ohio: Cap'n Penny Productions, 1992), 89–97, and Hawk Model ad, *Playthings Magazine*, March 1963, 206–8.

5. Film Reviews: *Washington Post*, August 8, 1999; *Washington Post*, August 8, 1999; "Gross Obsession: It's Been Said Comedy Isn't Pretty—but Has It Ever Been Quite So Ugly?," *USA Today*, June 30, 1999.

6. "Gross 'Em Out to Pull 'Em In: Toilet Humour Is the Latest Hollywood Cash Cow," *The Guardian* (London), 30 July 1999; John Seabrook, *Nobrow: The Culture of Marketing, the Marketing of Culture* (New York: Vintage, 2001), 100–101.

7. "Do You Know Where Your Children Are? Most Likely, They're Watching PG-13 Movies," *Washington Post*, 16 November 2003; film review: *Chicago Sun-Times*, 7 June 1998; Bogart, *Over the Edge*, chap. 6, esp. 160–61.

8. Philippe Ariès, *Centuries of Childhood: A Social History of Family Life* (New York: Vintage, 1962). For a more recent development of this analysis, see Neil Postman, *The Disappearance of the Child* (New York: Dell, 1982), 28, 46, 89–90.

9. Film review: *Washington Post*, August 8, 1999.

10. Film review: *Chicago Sun-Times*, 18 October 2002; Roger Ebert, "The Sandler Example," *Buffalo News*, July 2, 1999.

11. Film reviews: *Houston Chronicle*, June 28, 2002; *Toronto Sun*, June 28, 2002

12. Louise Kennedy, "Movies," Boston Globe, 13 January 2002.

13. William Strauss, "Teens Shun Gross-out Movie Genre," *Los Angeles Times*, 15 July 2001. See also Neil Howe and William Strauss, *Millennials Rising: America's Next Great Generation* (New York: Vintage, 2000).

14. Alex McNeil, *Total Television*, 4th ed. (New York: Penguin, 1996), 181–82; John Fiske, *Television Culture* (New York: Routledge, 1987); Vincent Terrace, *Television Sitcoms* (Jefferson, N.C.: McFarland, 2000), 145–48.

15. James Baker, *Teaching TV Sitcom* (London: British Film Institute, 2003), 48–49.

16. *Get a Life*, 1990, UCLA Film and Television Archives, (hereafter, FTA), VA9825; Vincent Terrace, Television Sitcom Factbook (Jefferson, N.C.: McFarland, 2002), 97–98.

17. Michael Tuethe, *Laughter in the Living Room: Television Comedy and the American Home Audience* (New York: Peter Lang, 2005), 192.

18. David Marc, *Comic Visions: Television Comedy and American Cul-*

ture (Boston, Unwin Hyman, 1989), 100–18, 166–74; Gerald Jones, *Honey, I'm Home. Sitcoms: Selling the American Dream* (New York: Grove Weidenfeld, 1992), 193–202, 235–236; Thomas Hibbs, *Shows About Nothing: Nihilism in Popular Culture from the* Exorcist *to* Seinfeld (Dallas: Spence Pub. 1999), chap. 6.

19. Baker, *Teaching TV Sitcom*, 49; For analysis of the changing culture of courtship and young sexuality, see Beth Bailey, *Sex in the Heartland* (Cambridge: Cambridge University Press, 1999), and *From Front Porch to Back Seat: Courtship in Twentieth-Century America* (Baltimore, Md.: Johns Hopkins University Press, 1988).

20. Lucas, like Disney, made the Star Wars series to appeal both to kids and the to regressive longings of adults for their childhood fantasies and memories and even "to indulge in infantile fantasies of omnipotence and Oedipal strife." *The Phantom Menace* grossed $920 million worldwide and $430 million in the United States, twice as much as *The Matrix* in 1999. Kids who watched the first trilogy in 1978 through 1983 brought their own children to the 1997 theater reprise. Peter Kraemer, " 'It's Aimed at Kids—the Kid in Everybody': George Lucas, Star Wars, and Children's Entertainment," in *Action and Adventure Cinema*, ed. Yvonne Tasker (New York: Routledge, 2004).

21. To be sure, because boys are both conditioned against the display of all emotions other than anger, violent movies are one of the few outlets for their channeled emotions. Action-adventure films, with their Manichean message of good vs. evil and their happy endings, are like fairy tales that "serve to guide children and adolescents toward adult ways." Fairy tales let the child confront his fears, displace his aggression toward the powerful, play the hero, and make moral choices, and perhaps action movies do the same. See Bruno Bettelheim, *Uses of Enchantment* (Vintage 1989), 8–11; Theresa Webb and Nick Browne, "The Big Impossible: Action Adventure's Appeal to Adolescent Boys," in *New Hollywood Violence*, ed. Steven Schneider (Manchester: Manchester University Press, 2004), 80–99.

22. "Is the Toy Business Taking over Kids' TV?," *TV Guide*, 12 June 1987, 5–7; "TMA Meeting," *Toy and Hobby World*, February 1985, 49; see also Donald. Kunkel and D. Roberts, "Young Minds and Marketplace Values: Issues in Children's Television Advertising," *Journal of Social Issues* 47, no. 1 (1991): 57–72.

23. Eric Lichtenfeld, *Action Speaks Louder: Violence, Spectacle, and the American Action Movie* (Westport, Conn.: Praeger, 2004), 59, 145. See also Tasker, ed., *Action and Adventure Cinema*.

24. "Calendar Desk," *Los Angeles Times*, Sept. 3, 1989.

25. Lichtenfeld, *Action Speaks Louder*, 104.

26. Film Reviews: *New Yorker*, 17 June 1985, 117; *New Republic*, 1 July 1985, 16; *Business Week*, 26 August 1985, 109.

27. On this theme, see Elliot Gruner, *Prisoners of Culture: Representing the Vietnam POW* (New Brunswick, N.J.: Rutgers University Press, 1993); Susan Jeffords, *The Remasculinization of America: Gender and the Vietnam War* (Bloomington: Indiana University Press, 1989).

28. Lichtenfeld, *Action Speaks Louder*, 164.

29. John Muir, *Encyclopedia of Superheroes on Film and Television* (Jefferson, N.C.: McFarland, 2003), 11–24.

30. Lichtenfeld, *Action Speaks Louder*, 114–15; film reviews: San Francisco Chronicle, 7 April 1989; *St. Louis Post-Dispatch*, 18 May 1990.

31. Larent Bouzereau, *Ultra-Violent Movies* (Secaucus, N.J.: Carol Publishing, 1996), 91; Thomas Leitch, "Aristotle vs. the Action Film," in *New Hollywood Violence*, ed. Steven Schneider (Manchester: Manchester University Press, 2004), 116–17.

32. Rikke Schubart, "Passion and Acceleration: Generic Change in Action Film," in *Violence and American Cinema*, ed. J. David Slocum (New York: Routledge, 2001), 192.

33. Lichtenfeld, *Action Speaks Louder*, 78–79, 91.

34. "Body Count II," *Newsweek*, July 30, 1990, 6; Lichtenfeld, *Action Speaks Louder*, 186–87; "'Die 2': Runway Bloody Runway," *Washington Post*, 6 July 1990.

35. Vincent Canaby, "Review," *New York Times*, 15 May 1983

36. Leitch, "Aristotle vs. The Action Film," 116.

37. Susan Faludi, *Stiffed: The Betrayal of the American Man* (New York: Perennial, 2000) and *Backlash: The Undeclared War Against American Women* (New York: Anchor, 1992).

38. Lichtenfeld, *Action Speaks Louder*, 77.

39. James Korkan, "Toy Counterterrorists vs. Toy Counter Terrorists," *Advertising Age*, 5 May 1986, 43–45; Coleco Press Kit, June 1986, Toy Fair Collection, Please Touch Museum, Box 5/2; Lichtenfeld, *Action Speaks Louder*, 71, 85.

40. Mattel catalogue, "Mattel Delivers" (Hawthorn, Calif.: 1983), 102–3, and Mattel catalogue, "Mattel Sets the Pace" (Hawthorne, Calif.: 1986), 166–89, both in Toy Fair Collection, Please Touch Museum, FC, Box 3/6b.

41. Tom Engelhardt, *The End of Victory Culture: Cold War America and the Disillusioning of a Generation* (New York: Basic Books, 1995), 81–86, 300.

42. Movie review: *The Independent* (London), December 8, 1996.

43. "Arnold's Big Action Flop," *The Oregonian* (Portland, Oregon), July 6, 1993.

44. Playmates Press Kits, February 1987, February 1989, Toy Fair Collection, Please Touch Museum, Box 6/1 and Box 9; "Heroes in a Half Shell," *Forbes*, 28 October 1991, 49–55.

45. "Arnold's Back," *Pittsburgh Post-Gazette*, 15 July 1994.

46. "Van Damme," *Chicago Sun-Times*, 2 October 1994.

47. "Action Films," *Economist*, 24 December 1994, 25, and 6 January 1995, 12.

48. "Superbowl Ads," *Atlanta Journal-Constitution*, 5 February 2006.

49. "Warning: Super Bowl Ads May Cause Blushing," *Star Tribune* (Minneapolis), 6 February 2005.

50. For an array of 2007 Superbowl ads, see http://www.ifilm.com/superbowl, accessed 28 May 2007.

51. In the 1980s, for example, ads still stressed a variety of themes: Amana refrigerators as "energy savers," Radar ranges as lifesavers for husband and wife because "both work" (1985 ads, FTA, VA7802), as well as Pepsi Free ads that appealed to those seeking sugarless refreshment, not as a calorie saver but "because life is stimulating enough" (ads November 1985, Museum of TV and Radio, Beverly Hills [hereafter MTR], #115240).

52. "Superbowl Showcase of Commercials," MTR, #115367; Superbowl ads http://www.ifilm.com/superbowl, IFilm Web site, 2002–2006, accessed 2 February 2006.

53. As Asa Berger says: "It is best to think of commercials as short plays, as manufactured dreams, as micronarratives that are meant to persuade viewers to purchase a given product or service. . . . We analyze these narratives the way we analyze any narrative, in terms of plot, characterization, and dialogue" (Berger, *Manufacturing Desire: Media, Popular Culture, and Everyday Life* [New Brunswick, N.J.: Transaction Publishers, 1996], 41).

54. D.B. Holt, "How to Build an Iconic Brand," *Market Leader* (Summer 2003), cited in William Leiss et al., *Social Communications in Advertising*, 3rd ed. (New York: Routledge, 2005), 430, 437.

55. Leiss et al., *Social Communication in Advertising*, 469–77, chap. 13. See also S. A. Macmanus and P. A. Turner, *Young v Old: Generational Combat in the Twenty-first Century* (Boulder, Colo.: Westview, 1995); David Rushkoff, *The Gen X Reader* (New York: Ballantine, 1994).

56. Leiss et al., *Social Communication in Advertising*, 479, 483, 488–507.

57. Buick ads, 1961–1967, MTR, #115633.

58. Buick ads, 1968–90, MTR, #115633.

59. Neil Postman et al., *Myths, Men, and Beer: An Analysis of Beer Commercials on Broadcast Television* (Falls Church, Vir. : AAA Foundation for Traffic Safety, 1987), 16–17, 36–37, 39, 43.

60. Postman et al., *Myths*, 17–20, 23–24, 27.

61. Infiniti TV ads, 1990?, FTA, VA12131.

62. Nissan ad, 1996, MTR, #117828.

63. John Bemrose, "A Generation That Refuses to Grow Up; Robert Bly, *The Sibling Society*," *Maclean's*, 22 July 1996, 61.

64. Ads for Cavalier and 90 Quatro, MTR, #115379, #12356; J. MacLachlan and M. Logan, "Camera Shot Length in TV Commercials and their

Memorability and Persuasiveness," *Journal of Advertising Research* 33, no. 2 (1993): 57–63.

65. Best Buy and Calvin Klein ads, 1996, MTR, #117828.

66. Carlsberg beer and "Men's Club" ads, 1990, FTA, VA4074

67. "Money," *USA Today*, 24 July 2001.

68. "Money," *USA Today*, 17 February 2003.

69. "Frat Boy Nation," *Sacramento Bee*, 8 August 2002.

70. Ad articles: *Baltimore Sun*, 31 July 2005; *St. Louis Post-Dispatch*, 31 October 2004; *Denver Post*, 11 April 2004.

71. Joseph Turow, *Breaking Up America* (Chicago: University of Chicago Press, 1997), 2, 6, and 65–67; John Tebbel, *The American Magazine* (New York: Hawthorne, 1969), 234.

72. "What Do Men Really Want?" *Gazette* (Montreal), 3 November 2001.

73. Turow, *Breaking Up America*, 4, 106, and 111; *Christian Science Monitor*, 28 February 1995.

74. "Where the Boys Are," *Mediaweek*, 27 October 2003, 57.

75. Matthew Grimm, "When the Sh*t Hits the Fan," *American Demographics*, 1 December 2003, 10.

76. "Behind the Music," *CFO: The Magazine for Senior Financial Executives*, September 2003, 26.

77. "Where the Boys Are."

78. "Where the Boys Are"; "Spike TV," *Television Week*, 1 September 2003, 1.

79. "Spike TV;" "Spike TV's Self-Evident Rationale for Its Existence," *Cable World*, 16 June 2003, 24; "Spike TV's Feminine Side?" *BusinessWeek*, 21 February 2005, 16; "Spike Puts Roadies' Role on Reality Tour," *Multichannel News*, 5 July 2004, 24; "Spike TV Offers up Male-Focused Research," *Mediaweek*, 26 August 2004, 3; "Cable TV," *Mediaweek*, 18 October 2004, 4.

80. Nelson George, *Hip Hop America* (New York: Viking, 1998), ix, 56–96; Eithne Quinn, *Nuthin' but a "G" Thang: The Culture and Commerce of Gangsta Rap* (New York: Columbia University Press, 2005).

81. Michelle Habell-Pallán, *Latino/a Popular Culture* (New York: New York University Press, 2002).

82. "Puff Daddy/P.Diddy/Diddy," www.rockonthenet.com/artists-p/puffdaddy_main.htm, accessed 27 July 2005.

83. George, *Hip Hop America*, 120–128; Puff Daddy, lyrics, "It's All About the Benjamins," www.azlyrics.com/lyrics/puffdaddy/itsallaboutthe-benjaminsremix.html, accessed May 13, 2007; Puff Daddy lyrics, "Bad Boy for Life," wwww.lyricsfreak.com/ accessed 27 July 2005; "Girl I'm a Bad Boy," www.sing365.com/lyrics.nsf accessed 27 July 2005. Articles on Combs: *Essence*, November 1997, 111; *Ebony*, April 1998, 54; *Washington Post*, 26 March 1997; *New York Daily News*, 9 January 2000; 30 December 1999; *Guardian*, 29 December 1999; *Washington Post*, 8 December 1999.

84. Thomas Chatterton Williams, "Black Culture Beyond Hip-Hop," *Washington Post*, 28 May 2007. See also John McWhorter, *Losing the Race: Self-Sabotage in Black America* (New York: Free Press, 2000). For a brief debate on the social consequences and meanings of hip-hop, see John Woodward, ed., *Popular Culture: Opposing Viewpoints* (Farmington Hills, Mich.: Greenhaven Press, 2005), 47–60. Note especially the debate generated by actor Bill Cosby in his critique of black youth culture, for example, in Hamil R. Harris and Paul Farhi, "Debate Continues as Cosby Again Criticizes Black Youths," *Washington Post*, 3 July 2004.

85. "Frat Boy Nation."

6. Endless Thrills

1. An excellent source for the literature concerning the impact of video games, especially on youth is Kwan Min Lee and Wi Peng, "What Do We Know About Social and Psychological Effects of Computer Games? A Comprehensive Review of the Current Literature," in *Playing Video Games: Motives, Response, and Consequences*, ed. Peter Vorderer and Jennings Bryant (Mahwah, N.J.: Lawrence Erlbaum, 2006), 327–45. I discuss this further in *The Cute and the Cool: Wondrous Innocence and Modern American Children's Culture* (New York: Oxford University Press, 2004), 159–60, 177–79.

2. J.C. Herz, *Joystick Nation* (Boston: Little Brown, 1997), 191; "What Are Video Games Turning Us Into?" *Boston Globe Magazine*, 20 February 2005, 18; "Games Violence Bloody Alluring," *Toronto Sun*, 31 October 2002; Rock Star Games, "Grand Theft Auto San Andreas," http://www.rockstargames.com/sanandreas, accessed 4 August 2006; "Grand Theft Auto (series)," http://en.wikipedia.org/wiki/Grand_Theft_Auto_(series), accessed 4 August 2006. A balanced survey of the range and impact of violence and sexuality in games is Stacy Smith, "Perps, Pimps, and Provocative Clothing: Examining Negative Patterns in Video Games," in *Playing Video Games: Motives, Responses, and Consequences*, ed. Peter Vorderer and Jennings Bryant (Mahwah, N.J.: Lawrence Erlbaum, 2006), 57–75.

3. "What Are Video Games Turning Us Into," 18.

4. "New Game Is Modeling Bad Behavior," *San Diego Union-Tribune*, 6 May 2000; Lakshmi Chaudhry, "Parents Fuming Over Panty Raider," http://www.wired.com/news/culture/0,1284,36144,00.html, accessed 4 August 2006; "Games Draw a Range of Protests," *New York Times*, 18 May 2000.

5. F. F. Schwarz, "The Patriarch of Pong," *American Heritage of Invention and Technology* 6, no. 2 (1990): 64; Barry Atkins, *More Than a Game: The Computer Game as Fictional Form* (Manchester: Manchester University Press: 2003), chap. 1; Henry Lowood, "A Brief Biography of Computer Games," in *Playing Video Games: Motives, Responses, and Consequences*, ed.

Peter Vorderer and Jennings Bryant (Mahwah, N.J.: Lawrence Erlbaum, 2006), 28–32; Stephen Kline, Nick Dyer-Witheford, and Grieg De Peuter, *Digital Play: The Interaction of Technology, Culture, and Marketing* (Montreal: McGill-Queen's University Press, 2003), 84–108.

6. Lowood, "A Brief Biography," 35–36; "Computer Games," *Boston Globe Magazine*, December 10, 2000, 16. For the rise and fall of the "Atari generation" of games, see David Sheff, *Game Over: How Nintendo Conquered the World* (Wilton, Conn.: Gamepress, 1999), 150–57; Herman Leonard, *Phoenix: The Fall and Rise of Videogames* (Springfield, N.J.: Rolenta Press, 2001), 89–99; Steven Malliet and Gust de Meyer, "The History of the Video Game," in *Handbook of Computer Games Studies*, ed. Joost Raessens and Jeffrey Goldstein (Cambridge, Mass.: MIT Press, 2005), 26–28.

7. Good reviews of the range and type of video games and the motivation of players are in Barry Smith, "The (Computer) Games People Play: An Overview of Popular Game Content," in *Playing Video Games: Motives, Responses, and Consequences*, ed. Peter Vorderer and Jennings Bryant (Mahwah, N.J.: Lawrence Erlbaum, 2006), 43–56; and G. Christopher Klug and Jesse Schell, "Why People Play Games: An Industry Perspective," in *Playing Video Games: Motives, Responses, and Consequences*, ed. Peter Vorderer and Jennings Bryant (Mahwah, N.J.: Lawrence Erlbaum, 2006), 91–100.

8. Herz, *Joystick Nation*, 14–22, 33–37, 55; Geoffrey Loftus, *Mind at Play: The Psychology of Video Games* (New York: Basic, 1983), 100–101, 9; and Eugene Provenzo, *Video Kids: Making Sense of Nintendo* (Cambridge, Mass.: Harvard University Press, 1991), 8–9, 31–35.

9. Kline, *Digital Play*, 128–50.

10. Provenzo, *Video Kids*, 34–35; Marsha Kinder, *Playing with Power in Movies, Television, and Video Games* (Berkeley: University of California Press, 1991), 105, 118; and House Subcommittee on Telecommunications and Finance, *Violence in Video Games*, 103rd Congress (Washington, D.C.: USGPO, 3 June 1994), 1–3; Diane Ravitch, ed., *Kid Stuff: Marketing Sex and Violence to America's Children* (Baltimore, Md.: Johns Hopkins University Press, 2003); Roman Espejo, *Video Games* (Boston: Greenhaven Press, 2003).

11. Senate Joint Hearing of the Judiciary Committee, *Rating Video Games: A Parent's Guide to Games*, 103rd Cong. (Washington D.C.: USGPO, 19 December 1993, and 4 March and 29 July 1994), 2, 35, 36, 41–41; House Subcommittee, *Violence in Video Games*, 4, 14; Herz, *Joystick Nation*, 191; http://www.answers.com/topic/entertainment-software-association, accessed 2 August 2006; House Committee on Energy and Commerce, Subcommittee on Commerce, Trade, and Consumer Protection, *Violent and Explicit Video Games: Informing Parents and Protecting Children*, 109th Cong., 2nd sess., 14 June 2006.

12. David Kushner, *Masters of DOOM: How Two Guys Created an Empire*

and Transformed Pop Culture (New York: Random House, 2003); Colin Covert, "The Doom Boom," *Star Tribune* (Minneapolis), 21 November 1994.

13. Patrick Welsh, "It's No Contest; Boys Will Be Men, and They'll Still Choose Video Games," *Washington Post*, 5 December 2004; Brenda Brathwaite, *Sex in Video Games* (Boston: Charles River Media, 2007).

14. "Ante Up at Dear Old Princeton: Online Poker as a College Major," *New York Times*, 14 March 2005; "Old Game, New Players," *Boston Globe Magazine*, 21 February 1999, 14.

15. "Video Games Enhance College Social Life," *USA Today*, 7 July 2003. For other positive takes, see John Beck, *The Kids Are Alright: How the Gamer Generation Is Changing the Workplace* (Cambridge, Mass.: Harvard Business School Press, 2006), and Steve Johnson, *Everything Bad Is Good for You: How Today's Popular Culture Is Actually Making Us Smarter* (New York: Riverhead Books, 2005).

16. "Students See Video Games as Harmless, Study Finds," *Washington Post*, 6 February 2005. More sophisticated studies include J. B. Funk and D. D. Buchmann, "Video Game Controversies," *Pediatric Annals* 24 (1995): 219–28; K. E. Dill and J. C. Dill, "Video Game Violence: A Review of the Empirical Literature," *Aggression and Violent Behavior* 3 (1998): 407–28; R. A. Salguero, T. Moran, and R. M. Bersabe, "Measuring Problem Video Game Playing in Adolescents," *Addiction* 97, no. 12 (December 2002): 1601; Craig Anderson, *Violent Video Game Effects on Children and Adolescents: Theory, Research, and Public Policy* (New York: Oxford University Press, 2007); and Lee and Peng, "Review of Computer Game Studies."

17. Mark Griffiths and Mark Davies, "Does Video Game Addiction Exist?" in *Handbook of Computer Games Studies*, ed. Joost Raessens and Jeffrey Goldstein (Cambridge, Mass.: MIT Press, 2005), 359–69.

18. "Hooked On-Line, and Sinking," *Washington Post*, 22 May 1996.

19. Mark Murawski's wife, as is common with men who stick with their childhood games, has adapted to his passion (perhaps as many as 43 percent of gamers are women), though she prefers the tamer and more intellectual games like the Sims series to her husband's action games, such as Tomb Raider. "Adults at Play," *Pittsburgh Post-Gazette*, 9 September 2003.

20. "Adults Driving Video-Game Market," *Columbus Dispatch* (Ohio), 24 December 2001; "What Are Video Games Turning Us Into?" 18.

21. Jon Goldstein, "Immortal Kombat: War Toys and Violent Video Games" in *Why We Watch: The Attractions of Violent Entertainment*, ed. Jon Goldstein (New York: Oxford University Press, 1996), 53–68; Brian Sutton-Smith, *Toys as Culture* (New York: Gardener Press: 1986), 64; Arthur Raney et al., "Adolescents and the Appeal of Video Games," in *Playing Video Games: Motives, Response, and Consequences*, ed. Peter Vorderer and Jennings Bryant (Mahwah, N.J.: Lawrence Erlbaum, 2006), 16; Herz, *Joystick Nation*, 47; T. L. Garner, "The Sociocultural Context of the Video Game

Experience" (Ph.D. diss., University of Illinois at Urbana-Champaign, 1991); David Buckingham and Rebekah Willett, eds., *Digital Generations: Children, Young People, and New Media* (Mahwah, N.J.: Lawrence Erlbaum, 2006).

22. Dmitri Williams, "A Brief Social History of Game Play," in *Playing Video Games: Motives, Responses, and Consequences*, ed. Peter Vorderer and Jennings Bryant (Mahwah, N.J.: Lawrence Erlbaum, 2006), 205; D. Williams, "The Video Game Lightning Rod," *Information, Communication, and Society* 6, no. 4 (2003): 523–50; "Adults Driving Video-Game Market," *Boston Globe Magazine*, 10 December 2000, 16; Entertainment Software Association, http://www.theesa.com/archives/files/Essential%20Facts%202006.pdf, accessed 2 August 2006.

23. "What Are Video Games Turning Us Into," 18; Christopher Noxon, *Rejuvenile: Kickball, Cartoons, Cupcakes, and the Reinvention of the American Grown-Up* (New York: Crown, 2006).

24. "Adults at Play"; "Adults Driving Video-Game Market."

25. Will Wright, foreword to David Freeman, *Creating Emotion in Games* (Indianapolis: New Riders, 2004), xxxii. Freeman sums up his idea of improving games: "The goal of Emotioneering [in game design] is to move the player through an interlocking sequence of emotional experiences" (36).

26. Don Tapscott, *Growing Up Digital: The Rise of the Net Generation* (New York: McGraw Hill, 1998).

27. Henry Jenkins, "The War Between Effects and Meaning: Rethinking the Video Game Violence Debate," in *Digital Generations: Children, Young People, and New Media*, ed. David Buckingham and Rebekah Willett (Mahwah, N.J.: Lawrence Erlbaum, 2006), 28; Jeffrey Goldstein, "Violent Video Games," in *Handbook of Computer Games Studies*, ed. Joost Raessens and Jeffrey Goldstein (Cambridge, Mass.: MIT Press, 2005), 341–57.

28. Kinder, *Playing with Power*, 105, 118.

29. This is the point of Susan Faludi's idea of the ornamental culture described in *Stiffed: The Betrayal of the American Man* (New York: William Morrow, 1999), chap. 7.

30. "Lost in an Online Fantasy World; as Virtual Universes Grow, So Do Ranks of the Game-Obsessed," *Washington Post*, 18 August 2006.

31. "Joy Sick; Games Can Be an Addiction," *Chicago Sun-Times*, 9 January 2000; Jennings Bryant and John Davies, "Selective Exposure to Video Games," in *Playing Video Games: Motives, Responses, and Consequences*, ed. Peter Vorderer and Jennings Bryant (Mahwah, N.J.: Lawrence Erlbaum, 2006), 181–94.

32. "Three Quarters Away from Being a Video Junkie," *Chicago Sun-Times*, 10 October 1999and Paul Boyer, "Apocalypse Now," *Washington Post*, 25 May 1997.

33. "Computer Games," *Boston Globe Magazine*, 20 February 2005, 18; "What are Video Games Turning Us Into?"

34. "Apocalypse Now."

35. On extreme sport, see, Garrett Soden, *Falling: How Our Greatest Fear Became Our Greatest Thrill: A History* (New York: Norton, 2003). On paintball combat, Robert Rinehart, "Sport as Postmodern Construction: A Case Study of Paintball," in *Players All: Performances in Contemporary Sport* (Bloomington: Indiana University Press, 1998), 84–96. On raves, parties involving avant-garde techno music, all-night dancing, and drug use, see D. Martin, "Power Play and Party Politics: The Significance of Raving," *Journal of Popular Culture* 33 (1999): 77–99.

36. "Cedar Point," *Lighting Dimensions*, 1 November 2003, 11; "Thrills at Cedar Point," *U.S. News and World Report*, 4 July 2005, 76; "The Thrill Isn't Gone," *New Yorker*, 30 August 2004.

37. "Supercoasters: Facts," http://channel.nationalgeographic.com/channel/supercoasters/facts.html, accessed 7 August 2006; Todd Trogmorton, *Roller Coasters* (Jefferson, N.C.: McFarland, 1993), 35; Robert Coker, *Roller Coasters* (New York: MetroBooks, 2002), 8–11.

38. Soden, *Falling*, 1–18.

39. Marvin Zuckerman, *Sensation Seeking: Beyond the Optimal Level of Arousal* (New York: L. Erlbaum Associates, 1979); and Marvin Zuckerman, *Sensation Seeking and Risky Behavior* (Washington, D.C.: American Psychological Association, 2007), find that those prone to boredom and with low tolerance for routine jobs seek the sensual intensity of thrill rides.

40. "Along for the (Wild) Ride," *Milwaukee Journal Sentinel*, 10 July 2005; Robert Cartmell, *Incredible Scream Machine* (Bowling Green, Ohio: Bowling Green State University Popular Press, 1987), 187–88, 191.

41. "Those Roller-Coaster Thrills," *Newsweek*, 29 August 1988, 74; ACEOnline, http://www.aceonline.org, accessed 7 August 2006; Scott Rutherford, *The American Roller Coaster* (Osceola, Wis.: MBI, 2000), 120.

42. "Those Roller-Coaster Thrills."

43. Roller Coaster Data Base, http://www.rcdb.com/g.htm, accessed 7 August 2006; "The Thrill Isn't Gone," 76; Rutherford, *The American Roller Coaster*, 82.

44. "Those Roller-Coaster Thrills"; Rutherford, *The American Roller Coaster*, 141.

45. "Cedar Point"; "Thrills at Cedar Point"; "'Roller Coaster King' Breaks His Record," BBC News, 3 September 2002, http://news.bbc.co.uk/2/hi/europe/2234589.stm, accessed 7 August 2006; and especially Andrew Martin, "The Rollercoaster Champion of the World," *Granta* 79 (2005), http://www.granta.com/extracts/1855, accessed 7 August 2006.

46. William Mangels, *The Outdoor Amusement Industry from Earliest Times to the Present* (New York: Vantage, 1952), 37–50, 137, 163; Todd Throgmorton, *Roller Coasters in America* (Oscelola, Wis.: Motor Books, 1994), 26–27; Todd Throgmorton, *Roller Coasters: United States and Canada*

(Jefferson, N.C.: McFarlane, 2000), 1–18. See *Scientific American* pieces: "Looping the Double Loop," 93, 8 July 1905, 493; "Leap-Frog Railway," 93, 8 July 1905, 29–30; and especially "Mechanical Joys of Coney Island," 99, 15 August 1908, 101; "Mechanical Side of Coney Island," 103, 6 August 1911, 104–5, 112–113. "Supercoasters: Facts"; "How High Can You Go," *New Yorker*, 30 August 2004, 48.

47. Throgmorton, *Roller Coasters of America*, 26; Cartmell, *Scream Machine*, 182; "Sequence of Opening Pay Attractions at Disneyland, Aug. 29, 1974," Disneyland 1955 file (Anaheim Public Library); "New Disneyland Attractions," *News from Disneyland*, 13 May 1956; "Matterhorn," *News from Disneyland*, 12 Dec 1959.

48. Throgmorton, *Roller Coasters*, 32–33; Rutherford, *American Roller Coaster*, 102–3; "America's Theme Parks," *Newsweek*, 4 August 1980, 56; "Roller-coasters. Hold on to Your Hat," *Economist*, 24 February 1996, 87.

49. "The Year of the Roller Coaster Has Enthusiasts in a Free Fall," *Insight on the News*, 22 July 1996, 42; "Knott's Berry Farm Upgrades with New Thrills and Themes," *Architectural Record* 187, no. 11 (November 1999): 50.

50. "Roller Coasters: A Steep Upswing," *BusinessWeek*, 21 June 1999, 8; "The Year of the Roller Coaster."

51. Hershey Park, a landmark on central Pennsylvanian farmland since 1907, followed in 2003 with the Rocket Coaster, bragging that it reaches seventy-three miles per hour in two seconds, drops vertically 180 feet, and takes riders through a 135-foot cobra loop and two and a half barrel rolls. Added to the attraction was "air time" for enthusiasts of off-the-seat thrills: "Hersheypark Adding 10th Coaster," *Amusement Business*, 4 August 4, 2003; http://seaworldorlando.com/SWF/ar_kraken_ride.aspx,accessed 13 November 2006.

52. "River Country," *Walt Disney World News*, July 1977, 2.

53. "Theme Parks," *Disney News*, Summer 1987, 4; "Water Works," *Disney Magazine*, Spring 1999, 44–47.

54. ""Knott's Berry Farm Upgrades," 50.

55. "They're Wet and Really Wild," *BusinessWeek*, 6 June 2005, 120.

56. "Riding the Movies," *Maclean's*, 11 March 11, 1991, 48; "America's Theme Parks Ride High," *U.S. News and World Report*, 26 June 1995, 49.

57. "New Thrill Ride," *Los Angeles Times*, 21 August 1978.

58. "Captain Eo," *Disneyland Gazetteer*, October 1985, 4; "Captain Eo," *Disney News* (Fall 1986): 7–10.

59. "Uncovering the Indiana Jones Adventure," *Disney Magazine* (Spring 1995): 18–21.

60. "Riding the Movies"; "Mousetrap," *U.S. News and World Report*, 10 May 1999, 62.

61. "New Attractions in Honor of Mickey," *USA Today*, June 1, 1988;

"Rock 'n' Roller Coaster," *Eyes and Ears* (WDW in-house newsletter), 23 April 1998, 1, 3.

62. "Body Wars," *Disney News* (Spring 1989): 36.

63. "General Motors Corp.: Plans for Overhaul of Ride at Epcot will be Unveiled," *Wall Street Journal*, 13 February 1996; "On Track," *Disney Magazine* (Fall 1998): 44–47.

64. "Booming Amusement Parks," *Newsweek*, 30 March 1998, 12.

65. "Burned Out and Bored," *Newsweek*, 15 December 1997, 18.

66. "'Metrosexual' Guys Embrace Cooking, Fashion, Feelings, Study Says," *Knight Ridder Tribune Business News*, 1 July 2003, 1; "It's a Guy Thing," *Star Tribune* (Minneapolis), 25 November 2002; "Adonis Complex? Men Joining Impossible Chase for the Body Beautiful," *Pittsburgh Post-Gazette*, 31 August 1999.

67. Susan Bordo, *The Male Body: A New Look at Men in Public and in Private* (New York: Farrar, Straus and Giroux), 17–18, 32, 181; See also Lynne Luciano, *Looking Good: Male Body Image in Modern America* (New York: Hill and Wang, 2001).

68. Mark Simpson, "Meet the Metrosexual," Salon.com, 22 July 2002, http://dir.salon.com/story/ent/feature/2002/07/22/metrosexual/index.html; Mark Simpson, "MetroDaddy v. UberMummy," *3AM Magazine* (December 2005), http://www.marksimpson.com/pages/journalism/MetroDaddy_v_UberMummy.html; "Metrosexuals: The Future of Men?" *Euro RSCG*, 22 June 2003, http://www.eurorscg.com/press/press_204.htm, all accessed 4 August 2004. For other articles on metrosexuals, see *International Herald Tribune*, 18 Jan. 18, 2005; *Village Voice*, 29 July 2003, 48; *Christian Science Monitor*, 7 April 2004, 12; *New York Times*, 28 March 2004.

69. Simpson, "Meet the Metrosexual"; Bardo, *Male Body*, 171–225.

70. Simpson, "Meet the Metrosexual"; Mark Simpson, "Here Come the Mirror Men," *Independent*, 15 November 1994, 3.

71. Kathleen Gerson, *No Man's Land: Men's Changing Commitments to Family and Work* (New York: BasicBooks, 1993), 8–9; Amy Best, *Fast Cars, Cool Rides: The Accelerating World of Youth and Their Cars* (New York: New York University Press, 2006), 10, 156–57. See also Mike Males, *Framing Youth: Ten Myths About the Next Generation* (Monroe, Maine: Common Courage Press, 1999); D. Kellner, "Beavis and Butthead: No Future for Postmodern Youth," in *Kinder Culture: The Corporate Construction of Childhood*, ed. S. R. Steinberg and J. L. Kincheloe (Boulder, Colo.: Westview Press, 1997); Gilles Lipovestsky, *The Empire of Fashion: Dressing Modern Democracy* (Princeton, N.J.: Princeton University Press, 1994), 155.

72. A good summary of this analysis is in Marlis Buchmann, *The Script of Life in Modern Society: Entry Into Adulthood in a Changing World* (Chicago: University of Chicago Press, 1989), 17, 81–87, 181; Cheryl Merser, *"Grown-Ups"*:

A Generation in Search of Adulthood (New York: New American Library, 1987), 214–15; "Timing of Marriage," http://www.pobronson.com/factbook/pages/25.html#1705; "Percentage Never Married," http://www.infoplease.com/ipa/A0763219.html, accessed 7 January 2008.

73. Robert Putnam, *Bowling Alone: The Collapse and Revival of American Community* (New York: Simon and Schuster, 2000), 248, 254, 283.

74. "Mothers in the Labor Force," http://www.infoplease.com/ipa/A0104670.html, accessed 2 August 2007.

75. Tom Smith, "The Emerging 21th-Century American Family," National Opinion Research Center, 2002, cited in Leo Bogart, *Over the Edge* (Chicago: Ivan Dee, 2005), 29; Herbert Kline, *A Population History of the United States* (New York: Cambridge University Press, 2004), chap. 8.

76. James Côté, *Arrested Adulthood: The Changing Nature of Maturity and Identity* (New York: New York University Press, 2000) 21–24, 110–111. Carol Tavris, *The Mismeasure of Women: Why Women are Not the Better Sex, the Inferior Sex, or the Opposite Sex* (New York: Touchstone, 1992), 296.

77. Faludi, *Stiffed*, 3–35; and Susan Faludi "The Betrayal of the American Man," *Newsweek*, 13 September 13, 1999, 48.

78. Faludi, *Stiffed*, 35–40. Simon Kuper, in "American Masculinity Takes a Prolonged Time-out," *Financial Times*, 29 January 2005, makes an interesting argument that American masculinity, based a generation ago on action (hunting, soldiering, etc.) has been replaced with a spectator and surrogate hypermasculinity in the Superbowl and violent video games.

79. Rebekah Willett, "Construction the Digital Tween," in *Seven Going on Seventeen*, ed. C. Mitchell and J. Reid Walsh (Oxford: Peter Lang, 2005), 278–93; David Buckingham, "Is There a Digital Generation?" in *Digital Generations: Children, Young People, and New Media*, ed. David Buckingham and Rebekah Willett (Mahwah, N.J.: Lawrence Erlbaum, 2006), 4–5.

80. David Brooks, *Bobos in Paradise: The New Upper Class and How They Got There* (New York: Simon and Schuster, 2000).

81. Alissa Quart, *Branded: The Buying and Selling of Teenagers* (New York: Basic, 2004).

82. Henry Jenkins, *The Wow Climax: Tracing the Emotional Impact of Popular Culture* (New York: New York University Press, 2007), 4–10.

83. Bruce Wilshire, *Wild Hunger: The Primal Roots of Modern Addiction* (Lanham, Md.: Rowman and Littlefield, 1998), 106.

7. Life Beyond Pleasure Island

1. This argument is also summarized in Cheryl Merser, *"Grown-Ups": A Generation in Search of Adulthood* (New York: New American Library, 1987), 52–56.

2. Margaret Mead, *Culture and Commitment: A Study of the Generation Gap* (New York: Doubleday, 1970), 1.

3. Robert Bly, *The Sibling Society* (Reading, Mass.: Addison Wesley, 1996), 132.

4. Bly, *Sibling Society*, 48–51, 67, 80. See also reviews in *USA Today*, 28 June 1996, and *Observer*, 19 May 1996, 11.

5. Merser, "*Grown-Ups*," 93.

6. James Côté, *Arrested Adulthood: The Changing Nature of Maturity and Identity* (New York: New York University Press, 2000), 38–39; J. E. Côté and A. L. Allahar, *Generation on Hold: Coming of Age in the Late Twentieth Century* (New York: New York University Press, 1996).

7. Erik Erikson, *Childhood and Society* (New York: Norton, 1963), Erikson, *Identity: Youth and Crisis* (New York, Norton, 1968).

8. Côté, *Arrested Adulthood*, 112, 212. Bruce Wilshire seems to say something similar in *Wild Hunger: The Primal Roots of Modern Addiction* (Lanham, Md.: Rowman and Littlefield, 1998), 108, 122, 150.

9. Robert Kegan, *In Over Our Heads: The Mental Demands of Modern Life* (Cambridge, Mass.: Harvard University Press, 1994); Côté, *Arrested Adulthood*, 37, 43.

10. Côté, *Arrested Adulthood*, 4, 15.

11. James Twitchell, *Where Men Hide* (New York: Columbia University Press, 2006), esp. 93–96, 133, 137.

12. John Bartkowski, *The Promise Keepers: Servants, Soldiers, and Godly Men* (New Brunswick, N.J.: Rutgers University Press, 2004); Rhys Williams, *Promise Keepers and the New Masculinity: Private Lives and Public Morality* (Lanham, Md.: Lexington Books: 2001); Frank Kelleter, *Con/tradition: Louis Farrakhan's Nation of Islam, the Million Man March, and American Civil Religion* (Heidelberg: Winter, 2000); Judith Newton, *From Panthers to Promise Keepers: Rethinking the Men's Movement* (Lanham, Md.: Rowman and Littlefield, 2005), 213–40.

13. Michael Kimmel, "Born to Run: Fantasies of Male Escape from Rip Van Winkle to Robert Bly," in *The History of Men: Essays in the History American and British Masculinities*, ed. Michael Kimmel (Albany: State University of New York Press, 2005), 19–36; Michael Kimmel, ed., *The Politics of Manhood: Profeminist Men Respond to the Mythopoetic Men's Movement (and the Mythopoetic Leaders Answer)* (Philadelphia: Temple University Press, 1995), especially 32–44; Newton, *From Panthers to Promise Keepers*, 137–56.

14. Among the many sources on this vast subject, consider Steven Schacht and Doris Ewig, eds., *Feminism and Men: Reconstructing Gender Relations* (New York: New York University Press, 1998); Tom Digby, ed. *Men Doing Feminism* (New York: Routledge, 1998); Harry Christian, *The Making of Anti-Sexist Men* (London: Routledge, 1994).

15. National Men's Resource Center, Men's Stuff, http://www.menstuff .org/frameindex.html, accessed May 21, 2007; Newton, *From Panthers*, 164–179.

16. Garrison Keillor, *The Book of Guys* (New York, Viking, 1993), 3; James Paterson, "Unlimited Horizons for New Fathers," *Washington Post*, 15 June 1999; Brian Johnson, "The Male Myth," *Maclean's*, 31 January 1994, 38.

17. For a treatment of the economic disadvantages of youth from the 1980s see Côté and Allahar, *Generation on Hold*, 52–60, and Anya Kamenetz, *Debt Generation: Why Now Is a Terrible Time to Be Young* (New York: Riverhead Books, 2006).

18. Christopher Lasch, *The Culture of Narcissism: American Life in an Age of Diminishing Expectations* (New York: Warner, 1979), 23; Côté, *Arrested Adulthood*, 93.

19. Côté, *Arrested Adulthood*, 25.

20. Zygmut Bauman, *Postmodernity and Its Discontents* (Cambridge: Polity, 1997), 2–3, 14; Bauman, *Liquid Life* (Cambridge: Polity, 2005); Ulrich Beck, *Risk Society: Towards a New Modernity* (London: Sage, 1992) 3, 13.

21. Dan Kiley, *The Peter Pan Syndrome: Men Who Have Never Grown Up* (New York: Avon, 1983), back cover.

22. Gary Kamiya, "I'm Younger Than That Now," *Salon.com*, 5 June 2007, http://www.salon.com/opinion/kamiya/2007/06/05/aging/index1.html, accessed 5 June 2007.

23. Susan Faludi, *Stiffed: The Betrayal of the American Man* (New York: Morrow, 1999), 607.